LT. CHARLES GATEWOOD

& His Apache Wars Memoir

CHARLES B. GATEWOOD

Edited and with additional text by
LOUIS KRAFT

University of Nebraska Press
Lincoln & London

Library of Congress
Cataloging-in-Publication Data

Gatewood, Charles B.
Lt. Charles Gatewood & his
Apache wars memoir /
Charles B. Gatewood; edited and with
additional text by Louis Kraft.
p. cm.
Includes bibliographical references and index.
ISBN-13: 978-0-8032-2772-9 (cloth: alk. paper)
ISBN-10: 0-8032-2772-8 (cloth: alk. paper)
ISBN-13: 978-0-8032-1884-0 (paper: alk.paper)
1. Apache Indians—Wars, 1882–1886.
2. Gatewood, Charles B.—Diaries.
3. Geronimo, c.1823–1909.
4. United States. Army. Cavalry, 6th.
I. Title: Lieutenant Charles Gatewood &
his Apache wars memoir.
II. Kraft, Louis, 1947–
III. Title.
E99.A6G27   2005
973.8'4—dc22
2005005556

For my sister and her husband, Linda and Greg Morgon,
who have always been there for me

Contents

Illustrations

Figures

Map

Acknowledgments

In the acknowledgments to *Gatewood & Geronimo* (2000), I wrote that a conversation I had with Ruth Kantor Cohen and Aaron Cohen (Guidon Books, Scottsdale, Arizona) in 1995 "initiated a search that continues to this day (and most likely will never end)." As it turns out, they were prophetic words.

This project probably began subconsciously during the creation of *Gatewood & Geronimo*. As that volume moved toward publication, I became more and more aware of just how much of Gatewood's days among the Apaches would not be told because of the page limitations that the publisher imposed. Then it hit me: Charles Gatewood had drafted a number of chapters in the hope of writing a book. Unfortunately he never completed the project, and his words have since remained in obscurity.

The Arizona Historical Society, Tucson, houses the Gatewood papers, so I called them to find out about their availability and to express my desire to compile the lieutenant's words into a readable manuscript. The project became reality when Bruce Dingus, director of publications, and Riva Dean, former archives director, of the Arizona Historical Society in Tucson graciously allowed me to gather Gatewood's writing and assemble it into a readable document. As the project moved toward completion, archives director Deborah Shelton and photographer Heather Dominick have played key roles. Bruce has also been very supportive of my Gatewood and Apache research and has done everything possible to help me, including supporting my efforts to speak on the subject.

Staff members at the Arizona Historical Society in Tucson have always been very helpful, assisting with queries via mail, phone, or in person. My association with them began in May 1995 and continues to this day. Special thanks go to librarian Debbie Newman and former photo librarian Susan Sheehan.

Gayle Piotrowski, a researcher from Tucson, found information about Gatewood's children and a number of the people involved in the lieutenant's civil difficulties. Her efforts have played a large role in my continued understanding of Gatewood's life. John R. Johnson, a genealogist in Los Angeles, performed invaluable research on Charles and Georgia Gatewood's families. The institutions that have provided information are numerous. Without the treasures that their archives store, along with their staff, who make these materials available, I would not be able to explore Gatewood and the Apaches. Jessica J. Hurley, former archives assistant, Arizona Department of Library, Archives, and Public Records, Archives Division, Phoenix, located the indictments against Gatewood for the false arrests. Bill Doty, archivist, National Archives, Laguna Niguel, gave invaluable assistance in locating the transcript of the Zuck, Kay, and Jones trial. Nan Card of the Rutherford B. Hayes Memorial Library, Fremont, Ohio, supplied the George Crook Collection. Michael Pilgrim, of the National Archives, Washington DC, helped locate other documents that have been cited. John Lovett, assistant curator, Western History Collections, University of Oklahoma Libraries, Norman, again made photos available to me. Kim Walters, director, Braun Research Library, Autry National Center, Southwest Museum of the American Indian, Los Angeles, has made me feel at home at this marvelous institution. The El Segundo Public Library, El Segundo, California, continues to fill my orders of interlibrary loan requests and keeps me up and running on their "new" and very cool microfilm machine. Also, the Los Angeles Family History Center played an instrumental role in securing hard-to-find biographical information on the Apaches stored at the Church of Jesus Christ of Latter-day Saints in Salt Lake City and allowed me to view it on their microfilm machines.

Many people have played major roles in my exploration of Gatewood, the Apaches, and race relations. Going way beyond supplying information, they have supported my efforts, giving me the strength to push forward into areas that perhaps historians should not explore. They are always there for me. We met professionally in one way or another, but over the course of time we have become friends. They have played a big part in the shaping of this effort as well as my other work. Aaron Cohen, owner of Guidon Books in Scottsdale, Arizona, and his daughter and son-in-law, Shelly and Gordon Dudley, have done everything possible to help me advance my words on Gatewood and the Apaches. Greg Lalire, editor of *Wild West*, has constantly made me feel a welcome member of the small group of people who write about the West. Over the years he has printed and promoted my work and become a friend. Writer-historian

Eric Niderost, whose own writing has dared to step beyond the borders of racial intolerance, is always there for me. He is very supportive—be it in the written word, the vocal word, or in spirit. Since editing *Gatewood & Geronimo*, Durwood Ball, who is also a historian, has moved on to become a professor at the University of New Mexico, Albuquerque, and editor in chief of the *New Mexico Historical Review*. But that has not diminished the friendship and kindness he displayed during our working relationship, which continues to this day. Ed Sweeney is perhaps the premier Apache historian of his time. He is also a kind and giving person. Ed has helped to ensure the integrity of the manuscript by reading it and offering technical suggestions. Like Durwood, he is always available to help and advise. Leo Oliva and his wonderful wife, Bonita, have played a major part in my development as a writer-historian, and more—they have given my first love, creative interpretation, new life. Although our collaborations have dealt with Indian agent Edward W. Wynkoop and the Southern Cheyennes, they coincide with my Gatewood exploration, and although the research does not interlink, the creative juices do intertwine. Leo and Bonita, thank you for giving me the chance to visit your glorious state of Kansas and explore race relations. Writer, director, actor, and private eye Tom Eubanks is a good friend. I should mention that he is so talented that whenever I am around him, his energy jumps at me, giving me the drive to press onward. He has certainly helped me with my word selection over the years, and more recently he brought my two-act one-man historical drama about Ned Wynkoop to life in Kansas, California, and Colorado. Two people at the Palace of the Governors, Museum of New Mexico, Santa Fe, have helped me develop as a writer and historian: Tomas Jaehn, Fray Angélico Chávez History Library, and Wm. Charles Bennett Jr., historian and former assistant director, Museum of New Mexico. Always encouraging me in my quest to explore our Indian wars, they have done everything possible not only to promote my understanding of race relations on the frontier but also to give it life in New Mexico. Tomas played the key role in the Chávez History Library housing my papers and writing, an honor I'll never forget. All of you—Aaron, Shelly, Gordon, Greg, Eric, Durwood, Ed, Leo, Bonita, Tom, Tomas, and Charles—have played a huge part in my life during the creation of this manuscript. Besides being my friends, you constantly offer suggestions, raise questions, and link me to others who might help my writing, speaking, and theatrical projects. Thank you.

As always, writer George Carmichael read the first draft and sent me his comments, questions, and edits. George's efforts play a large part in making the manuscript readable. It is shocking when I glance back at our meeting at a writing class at UCLA a lifetime ago and realize that although we always had opposing views about the American West, we have remained good friends. George, it has been my great, great pleasure knowing you all these years.

During the creation of the manuscript, which coincidentally also saw the deterioration of my health, Joanie Kraft has steadily stood by and offered tremendous suggestions on healthier living that I am certain are the basis of my good health today. Life is wonderful. Thanks, Joanie.

My sister, Linda Kraft-Morgon, whom I love with all my heart, and her husband, Greg Morgon, have always been there for me, cheering me on and giving me the strength to press forward, no matter how dark the clouds on the health or publishing horizon looked. Their confidence and enthusiasm for my words, nay, my life, have been a blessing. God bless you.

Cynthia Tengan played a major role in the creation of this manuscript. She is forever ready, willing, and available to assist in every way imaginable, from the tracking of information to the polishing of text. The time we spent together during the development of this project has been some of the best in my life . . . and some of the worst as my health fell apart. Her participation and involvement in this manuscript, as well as in my recovery, cannot be understated, for without Cyn there would be no writing and perhaps no life by Kraft. There will always be a special place in my heart for her.

Marissa Kraft will forever be my little girl, even though she is now a young lady. It pleases me greatly when she tells me that she again stood up to a teacher when something inaccurate was said about our history during the nineteenth century. For instance, when a teacher said something that was untrue about Kit Carson, Marissa immediately said, "No, that's not right," and proceeded to enlighten the class. Over time I have seen her mastery of words and creativity in art and design explode, but best of all, I am seeing her develop into a person with no racial prejudice.

Diane Moon is bright, funny, caring, and extremely supportive. She has given my life new direction, new hope. Diane has my heart, she is my lady, and I love her.

I would be remiss if I did not mention the University of Nebraska Press. Elizabeth Demers, the history acquisitions editor, had immediate and continuing enthusiasm for the project, and she became the driving force behind the acceptance of the manuscript. Beth Ina, managing editor, and Jeremy Hall, acquisitions assistant, answered all my questions and saw to it that I knew exactly what I needed to supply the press. Copy editor Elaine Durham Otto kept the text focused and improved my prose. Gary Dunham, director, graciously accepted some of my input. Carolyn Einspahr, production coordinator, and Tish Fobben, direct response manager, shared production progress, kept me informed, and welcomed my comments. Finally, Ann Baker, assistant project editor, capably took charge of the production process and brought *Lt. Charles Gatewood & His Apache Wars Memoir* to successful completion. Thank you.

Charles Bare Gatewood was born in Woodstock, Virginia, on April 6, 1853.[1] His father, John Gatewood of Shenandoah County, Virginia, married Emily A. Bare, also of Shenandoah, on March 22, 1841. Over the next three decades his parents would raise six children. Charles's sisters (Mary Frances, Julia McKay, and Cornelia Susan) were born during the 1840s, and his brothers (Samuel Deyerle and DeWitt Clinton) were born in the late 1850s. His father earned his living first as a printer for the *Shenandoah Herald* in 1845 and later as editor of the *Zenith Legins*. By 1860 he owned fifteen hundred dollars of real estate.[2]

As a boy Gatewood saw his father march off to fight for the South when war erupted in 1861, and then lived through the horror of the Civil War and its aftermath. Whatever prejudices were inbred in him during his early years only increased as the nightmare of Reconstruction intensified hatreds in a time of extreme racial conflict. In 1868 he moved with his family to Harrisonburg, Virginia. Gatewood's father opened a printing shop and edited the *Commonwealth*. Gatewood finished his education in Harrisonburg and then briefly taught school. During this time he applied for admission to West Point. Receiving his appointment to the military academy in 1873 through the Honorable John T. Harris, M.C., of Harrisonburg, he never dreamed what awaited him when he graduated twenty-third in a class of seventy-six in 1877.[3]

Shortly after graduation, the five-foot-eleven-inch Virginian was commissioned a second lieutenant in the Sixth U.S. Cavalry. Although he accepted the assignment in June 1877, he remained on graduating leave until January 1, 1878. The young lieutenant arrived at Fort Wingate, New Mexico, on the first day of 1878 and served there until January 29, when he left to report for duty with his regiment at Camp Apache, Arizona Territory, on February 5.[4] Camp Apache did not become Fort Apache until 1879.[5] A year after his introduction to the Southwest, he became commander of Apache scouts. From March 31, 1879, until June 30, 1880, and then from November 12, 1881, until October 1885, he commanded Indian scouts.[6] This assignment placed him in intimate contact with a people totally foreign to his upbringing. While at West Point, he probably studied recent Indian campaigns, particularly the actions against the Sioux and Cheyennes on the plains. However, it is unlikely that he ever thought that his coworkers would speak one of the Athapaskan languages. It must have been a great cultural shock.

But here is where Gatewood excelled. He immersed himself in his task, knowing that his success, even his life, depended upon two key factors: understanding the Apaches and gaining their acceptance. Even though he knew that he could never hope to obtain their mastery of the Southwest environment, he realized that he had to learn all he could.[7] Suppressing whatever feelings of racial superiority he harbored, he began consulting the scouts daily.[8] By being open to their views and not talking down to them in matters in which they were his superiors, he earned their respect and loyalty. At the same time he learned their ways and, more important, he learned that Indians were no less human than whites.[9] This did not mean that Gatewood did not have his reservations about the Apaches. After he had been removed from command from Apache scouts and assigned to commanding Navajos in New Mexico (1886), he was certain that he would never again command Apache scouts for the simple reason that "they no longer have any liking for me."[10] But later that same year Gatewood would hear Geronimo say to him: "You can come to our camp anywhere. . . . Never fear harm."[11] These are momentous words coming from the warrior who constantly felt that the whites' only goal was to kill him and his people. Geronimo must have felt that Gatewood was an exceptional white man and worthy of his trust.

Actually, Gatewood's personality suited him for this assignment. Although popular with his fellow officers in the Sixth, he remained stand-offish.[12] There were, of course, exceptions. Matthias Day, a classmate at West Point, would remain a close friend.[13] For the most part Gatewood walked his own trail and kept his own council. This trait of keeping to himself, along with doggedly staying with a task until completing it, made him an excellent choice to command Indian scouts—Apaches were impressed by actions rather than words. He spent many long, lonely hours tracking a foe whose trail was all but invisible except to the native scouts who were his only companions.

The young lieutenant's first contact with the Apaches happened when he arrived at Fort Wingate in January 1878 and was with Victorio's people—the Warm Spring Apaches (also known as the Ojo Caliente), who had merged with the Mimbreno (or Membreños) Apaches.[14] They have since become known as the Chihenne (cíhénè, Chi-hen-ne, Chi-hinne), which means Red Paint People. This tribe of Apaches included the Mogollones and Coppermines.[15] Originally they ranged from southwestern New Mexico through southeastern Arizona territories, but in 1877 they had been moved to the wasteland at the San Carlos Indian Reservation in Arizona.[16] Victorio and the Chihennes ended up at Camp Goodwin, some six miles west of Fort Thomas on the Gila River. This part of San Carlos has been described as "malarial, barren, unattractive, with no good hunting ground nearby."[17] The removal did not last long. On September 2, Victorio and Loco stole horses from the White Mountain Apaches who lived on the reservation to the north of them and broke out.[18] However, by the end of October most had surrendered.

Some Apaches came into the area near Fort Wingate while Gatewood was there, giving him his first contact with natives.[19] The Chihenne, who wanted nothing more than to return to their homeland at Ojo Caliente, New Mexico, spent roughly a year in limbo while the U.S. government argued about what to do with them. Some would return to Ojo Caliente, some moved to the Mescalero Apache Reservation in New Mexico, and others struggled to survive as they remained in hiding.[20] At the beginning of his career, Gatewood found himself assigned to watch the Chihennes at Wingate. Eventually he escorted some of them back to Ojo Caliente, where he supposedly turned them over to Lt. Charles W. Merritt (Ninth U.S. Cavalry).[21]

The first year and a half of active duty set the stage for the entire tenure of Gatewood's service in the Southwest. He spent an enormous amount of time in the company of native scouts in pursuit of warring Chihennes and, as he put it, their "recruits from renegade Comanches, Navajos, and Mescaleros."[22] He clocked many miles over a harsh, unforgiving land and saw more than his share of violent death. He lived and he learned how to survive. But it was his strength of character that pulled him through, for his body often failed him. As the years passed, the time his body required to recuperate would grow longer.

The peace did not last long. In August 1879, when Victorio mistakenly thought the government intended to move him to San Carlos, he revolted for the last time. Gatewood believed that "restlessness, caused by robbery and mismanagement by their agents," along with an "innate desire to slay, pillage, steal and create havoc generally, summed up in the word 'revenge,'" caused the hostilities.[23] Even though Victorio was their foremost chieftain at this time, he felt that Nana, Tomas, and Torivio were the driving force behind the outbreak.[24]

Victorio's outbreak spread fear across the Southwest like wildfire. By September 1879, Gatewood and one of his West Point classmates, Lt. Augustus P. Blocksom (Sixth U.S. Cavalry), who also commanded Indian scouts, had moved into New Mexico Territory and reported to Maj. Albert P. Morrow (Ninth U.S. Cavalry) with their scout companies at Fort Bayard.[25] Morrow was a veteran who had served during the Civil War first as an enlistee, then as a non-com, and finally as an officer.[26] Alchesay, a White Mountain Apache, served as one of Gatewood's sergeants in Company A, beginning a relationship that would eventually become a friendship.[27]

Morrow went on the offensive upon hearing of a fight with Victorio on Animas Creek (September 18, 1879) in which Gatewood's friend, Day, against orders of Capt. Charles Beyer (Ninth U.S. Cavalry) and under heavy fire, carried one of his wounded men to safety while the soldiers retreated.[28] On September 22, Morrow moved east from Fort Bayard with his command, which consisted of 6 officers, 191 enlisted men, and 36 scouts.[29] Although Gatewood and Blocksom were mounted, their scouts walked, as did 73 soldiers. This was not unusual for scouts, as they often walked. Their objective: pick up the natives' trail. Thus began weeks of endless marches under harsh weather conditions that ended with either the pursuers finding the enemy gone or firefights so hot that on a number of occasions Gatewood thought he would die.

After the first night's camp, Morrow sent Blocksom and Gatewood, their scouts, pack mules, and a detachment of cavalry to blaze a trail directly through the Miembres Mountains to the Beyer-Victorio battle site, while Morrow and the rest of his command, including a wagon train, were forced to travel over a road by way of Fort Cummings.[30] As Gatewood remembered, "It took us several days to toil across the Miembres, because most of the way we had no trail and the mountain was rough and precipitous."[31] The plan was to hit the raiders from two sides at one time. But when they reached the site of the recent fight, northwest of Animas Cañon, Victorio had gone.

Blocksom and Gatewood decided not to wait for Morrow and set out after the Chihennes. As Gatewood remembered, "[We cut] loose from our pack trains, leaving behind all animals, in fact, with the scouts and a dismounted detachment of cavalry, we followed that trail for three nights in succession, each man carrying his rations and equipments."[32] The striking force hid during daylight hours and traveled at night. Rain pounded the ground continuously, and for fear that fire would expose their presence, everyone remained constantly soaked. Gatewood wrote, "The only part of the little we had to eat not spoiled by the rain was the bacon. Bread and tobacco fell into a pulpy mixture that could neither be eaten nor smoked." The situation soon reversed; the rains stopped and the sun came out, and within a few days they had to search for water.

By the twenty-eighth, they were on the eastern side of the Black Range. [33] That day they found a campsite and surrounded it, only to find it deserted. By this time Morrow's command closed on them, and the next day, even though they had found yet another camp in a deep cañon, they halted and waited for the soldiers in the vicinity of Cuchillo Negro Creek.[34] Morrow arrived at 5:00 p.m. and immediately decided to attack. Morrow reported: "The Indian scouts under Blocksom and Gatewood rushed immediately to the assault and got possession of the hostile camp. The troops followed under fire from the surrounding hills. The firing was kept up until after ten o'clock when I ordered the command to go into camp."[35]

Morrow stated the Chihennes lost three dead, but Gatewood was a little more specific—two men and one woman. Morrow also stated that they captured fifteen saddled horses and some stock. Again Gatewood differed from Morrow, stating, "They managed to drive their stock away with them, and as they carry very little plunder while on the warpath, their camp was not worth much after we got it."[36]

The fight was far from over.

Due to a shortage of water, Gatewood, Blocksom, and the scouts camped about one mile from Morrow in a cañon eight hundred feet deep. The next morning at breakfast Victorio attacked Morrow. Gatewood not only paints a good word description of the battle but also pokes fun at his own heroic image:

> A single shot rang out down the cañon, then a volley, suddenly increasing into more shots and more volleys, with shouts of command, all doubled and trebled in reverberations up the valley, until it was one roar of pandemonium that was enough to set a nervous man wild, . . .

. . . Blocksom sent me with twenty men on foot to report to Colonel Morrow as soon as possible, and away we went. More noise and more excitement, until I didn't believe there was a sane man in the country, except the Corporal, who cool[l]y informed me after awhile that I was sitting on the wrong side of a rock to be safe from a cross-fire. Up to that time, it seemed to me, we would all be killed, for every man had lost his head, and was yelling with all his might and shooting in the air. But once anchored on the right side of the rock, I was astonished to see how cool they were, and how steady was their aim.[37]

Two black soldiers died that day.

Pursuit of the Chihennes in the cañon proved to be fruitless; Morrow's command never saw their foe, except when one would jump from hiding to jeer and laugh at them. By 3:00 p.m. Morrow, fed up with the situation, abandoned the battle site. As he retreated back toward Cuchillo Negro, Victorio and his warriors harried the fleeing soldiers and Indian scouts until he tired of the harassment and vanished.

A day later, Morrow's force picked up a woman who had gotten separated from the fleeing Indians. She claimed that Victorio headed for the Mogollons, a range of mountains just east of the Arizona–New Mexico boundary and east of the San Francisco River.[38] A scouting party found the Indian campsite, but by the time Morrow could get to it and strike, the Apaches were gone. The trail now led east-northeast beyond the Black Range and into the San Mateo Mountains.[39] During this time, Morrow's command grew and shrunk as men joined it or departed from it. The latter included Blocksom, who returned to Arizona to muster out his scouts.

Then Gatewood's scouts found a hot trail moving south on the eastern side of the Black Range and headed for Mexico. By the eighteenth, the lieutenant was at Fort Cummings, where he again joined up with Morrow. The trail continued southward. Gatewood followed it to the Florida Mountains, and then the international boundary between the United States and Mexico. On the twenty-second, Morrow ordered him to cross the border, even though the major did not have permission to do so.[40]

During a grueling march through the desert north of the Guzman Mountains in Mexico, men and livestock suffered terribly from the sun and lack of water. By the end of October Gatewood and Morrow caught up with Victorio's Apaches near Lake Guzman. By this time the command was in serious need of water that had not been contaminated by the Apaches. According to Day, Gatewood "led the scouts & Capt. [Charles] Campbell's Troop A over the rock wall which cut us Americans [off] from the only water in the desert." [41] In the heated engagement, a fight in which both sides were alarmingly low on ammunition and rations, Gatewood thought he would "buy it." During this fight, the Chihennes captured some of his mounts, including a horse that belonged to him, his favorite mount, Bob. Other horses died, and saddles were burned to prevent them from falling into enemy hands. With water a major problem, Day claimed that he and Gatewood "walked together, had been [together] for the three days & nights." Afterwards, the Apaches scattered and Gatewood hurried to Fort Bayard, where he was ordered to return to Fort Apache to muster out his scouts, whose term of enlistment was about to expire. Gatewood would later put in for reimbursement for the loss of Bob. The government refused to pay him—a sore point with the lieutenant for the rest of his life. From that time forward, Gatewood rode army-issued mules. [42]

Early the next year, on March 8, 1880, Gatewood led a patrol from Camp Thomas, Arizona Territory. It included Second Lt. Thomas Cruse, a West Point graduate who had joined the Sixth the previous October, Dr. Dorsey McPherson, twenty-one Indian scouts from Company A, thirty soldiers from the Sixth Cavalry, and six civilians. [43] Gatewood's mission: hunt the Chihennes and the Mescaleros, some of whom had also left the reservation. Before month's end, Gatewood had reached the Río Grande in New Mexico. One day, according to Cruse, while Gatewood, Cruse, and McPherson rode near the river, Gatewood

expatiat[ed] on the good fight old Vic was putting up, the damage he had done &c., and giving most intimate personal descriptions and experiences with old Vic, Nana[,] and all the others of that famous outfit; whereupon both McPherson and myself expressed the opinion that he was "stringing" us and probably had never seen any one of the outfit. Then he waxed indignant and said[,] "You darned chumps, I had charge of that band at Apache for six months and got permission to take them back home to Ojo Caliente in 1878, and ate, traveled, slept and played with them daily."

. . . Taking those Apaches back was a joyous trip for Gatewood and his first detailed service on his own, and he always
spoke of Victorio as "quite some man" and regretted that he
could not have remained with them.[44]

Writing for publication in 1894, Gatewood described Victorio as "a
palsied, aged and decrepit chief, [who] was barely able to accompany
the squaws and children in their forays."[45] This has garnered negative
comment, mainly from historian Dan L. Thrapp. Without listing any
specifics, Thrapp wrote: "This description [Gatewood's] should not be
taken too seriously in the light of unqualified assertions by agents, army
officers, and others who dealt directly with him that he was vigorous,
able, and the true chief of the Mimbres."[46] Thrapp concluded that Gatewood "may have confused Victorio with Nana, already an old man,
though still vigorous." Perhaps. However, First Lt. Joseph Alton Sladen
(Fourteenth U.S. Infantry), who, as aide-de-camp, accompanied Brig.
Gen. Oliver O. Howard into the Dragoon Mountains, Arizona Territory,
to negotiate peace with Cochise in 1872, wrote in his journal: "Victorio,
even then [in 1872], appeared like an old man. Hardship and exposure,
disease and lack of food makes wild Indians grow rapidly old in appearance. He was, then, a leader among his people, and his treachery,
cunning, and cruelty seemed stamped upon his face."[47] Sladen's words
describe Victorio six years before Gatewood reported for duty in the
Southwest.

Early in April, Gatewood and his patrol reached the barren San An-
dreas Mountains, which are between the Tularosa Valley and the Jor-
nada del Muerto—the journey of death—in New Mexico.[48] About 8:00
a.m. on the seventh, he discovered a Chihenne camp. Careful not to
announce his arrival, he moved into position, attacking at 9:30 a.m.
The fight lasted five and a half hours. Although heated, none of Gatewood's men were hit and only two Chihennes died. Gatewood kept on
the move. By the twelfth he reached the Mescalero Apache agency, and
just after midnight four days later, Gatewood left his pack train and
moved out, taking Cruse, McPherson, the scouts, and a detachment of
soldiers. Cruse remembered the orders as a herding operation to force
the Mescaleros back onto the reservation: "Our instructions were to go
about six miles from the Agency, then at daylight return, sweeping the

cañon as skirmishers and firing upon whatever Indians we might see. We were to pursue slowly if they rushed towards the Agency."[49]

It was still dark when Gatewood halted. He "instructed soldiers and Scouts not to kill any of the campers, especially the women and children, nor any of the bucks unless, with gun in hand, it was evident they intended resistance." He gave directions for everyone to make as much noise as possible and shoot into the air when they began the sweep back toward the reservation. When the sun rose over the plains, Gatewood signaled the attack, and everyone yelled as they rushed into the valley. Cruse continues, "It was magically filled with running Indians and their ponies, all trying to reach the Agency in the shortest possible time. Each probably thought that the ones behind them were being killed by our gunfire. . . . We neither killed nor hurt anyone."

There has been a lot of confusion surrounding this action. Although Gatewood's scouts did not suffer a loss during the skirmish, they may have captured two animal herds, which is very strange, as Gatewood supposedly was only forcing the natives who were off the reservation back onto it. Also, the zero native casualties that Cruse reported may have been as high as five dead, a number that has grown in the telling over the years.[50] By the end of the month the lieutenant had reached Cañada Alomosa, New Mexico.

After the patrol ended, Gatewood returned to Fort Apache and recruited a new company of Apache scouts. He then moved to Ash Creek to watch for any of Victorio's people who might try to return to the reservation. This duty was cut short when he became ill with inflammatory rheumatism and reported to Fort Thomas to recover.[51] His condition continued to worsen until Gen. Orlando B. Willcox, commander of the Department of Arizona, granted Gatewood a one-month leave of absence on November 24, 1880, "with permission to apply to the proper authority for an extension of five months."[52] Gatewood was unable to begin the leave until January 8, 1881, at which point he left Fort Apache—presumably for Woodstock, Virginia, as this was the forwarding address he left with the military. His rheumatism had not calmed down sufficiently by February to allow him to resume his military duties, and on the second, he applied for the five-month extension that had been originally specified.[53]

Another month passed, and still Gatewood saw no improvement in

Lt. Charles Gatewood and Company A, Apache scouts, during the Victorio campaign. The photograph was probably taken on October 30, 1880,
two days before the scouts' discharge. The photograph includes Gatewood
(center), First Sergeant Alchesay (on Gatewood's right), Dutchy (second
left of Gatewood in second row, in dark hat); Sam Bowman, interpreter
(behind Gatewood); Lt. Thomas Cruse (extreme left in back row); and Dr.
McPherson (right of Cruse). Courtesy: Arizona Historical Society/Tucson,
AHS #19763.

his health. At the beginning of April, he went to Dr. Basil Norris. After a month's treatment, Norris gave him a signed certificate on May 5:

> I hereby certify that I have been treating this officer one month for rheumatism of knee, ankle, hip and shoulder joints. This articular rheumatism is the effect of much exposure on duty with Company "A" Indian Scouts, in the Department of Arizona. This officer will be obliged to continue medical treatment during the time of his leave, & therefore respectfully recommend that it be charged to sick leave in order that he may have the benefit of his full pay, as necessary to enable him to incur the expense of bathing at the Hot Springs or for such other treatment as may seem best in his case.[54]

Gatewood forwarded the doctor's statement, along with a written request for sick leave.[55] The time off, with pay, from that date until July 7, was granted.[56] He traveled to Virginia but did not remain there long. By June he was in Frostburg, Maryland, where his sweetheart, Georgia McCulloh, lived. Georgia, who at times has been called Georgie and Georgiana, was born on October 6, 1855.[57] A native of Frostburg, Georgia was the third of eight children born to the Honorable Thomas G. McCulloh and Sarah Ellen Huddleson, who were married about 1850.[58] A man of property, McCulloh owned five thousand dollars of real estate in 1860; this grew to thirty-five thousand dollars of real estate by 1870. By 1880 McCulloh employed two servants: Ann Hurst of England and Sarah Griffith of Wales, who may have been Hurst's daughter, as she was only eight or nine at this time. The McCullohs' first child, Sarah Virginia (born 1851), was followed by Mary E. (1853), Georgia, Hetty, Nannie (1860), May (1864), Ernest (1866), and Bessie (1871).

Gatewood married Georgia on June 23 in Cumberland, Maryland.[59] After the wedding, he took his new bride to Woodstock, Virginia. It is unclear what happened next—there are no records showing that Gatewood requested an extension of his leave. Anyway, July 7 arrived and passed—and the lieutenant did not return to Fort Apache.

During Gatewood's absence, tension began to mount in the vicinity of Fort Apache. A Cibecue medicine man named Nock-ay-det-klinne talked of the dead returning after the White Eyes—the Apache name for white men—left Indian land.[60] Frightened of an uprising by the Western Apache tribes, which included the White Mountains, Willcox ordered Colonel Eugene Carr to arrest the instigator. [61] The Western Apaches include the Cibecue, Tonto, and San Carlos, as well as the White Mountains. In Arizona, the White Mountains ranged from the Gila River in the south to above the White River in the north. The Cibecue were to the west and northwest of them, while the Tontos were even farther to the north and west, and the San Carlos were to the south of them between the Gila and San Pedro rivers. Both the White Mountains and San Carlos had been on good terms with the Bedonkohe, Chihenne, Chokonen, and Nednhi Apaches until the 1870s when their warriors served as scouts for the military. From that time forth, relations between these groups were strained at best. [62]

Carr moved out from Fort Apache on August 29 with five officers, seventy-nine soldiers (Troops D and E, Sixth U.S. Cavalry), and twenty-three native scouts from Company A under Cruse's command. Carr's arrival at Nock-ay-det-klinne's village on Cibecue Creek and his subsequent arrest of him a day later ignited a firefight that resulted in a revolt by native scouts (White Mountain and Cibecue Apaches), the medicine man's death, and a war with the White Mountain Apaches. [63]

The adjutant general's office realized Gatewood's sick leave officially ended in July. It was now September, and he still had not reported for duty. On the seventh they wrote him in care of the Woodstock, Virginia, address: "You are therefore viewed as absent without leave commencing with July 8, 1881, and the General of the Army demands that you forward to this office through the regular channels, an explanation of your failure to rejoin your station at the expiration of your leave." [64]

Gatewood hurried back to Arizona. He must have had an acceptable explanation, for on September 17 Willcox ordered him and his scouts (currently Mojaves and Yumas) to join Carr's command. [65] The general planned a four-pronged movement against the Cibecue and White Mountain Apaches, whom reports placed on the Cibecue and the Black River. [66] Carr, leading one of the four prongs of the attacking force, planned to gather those who wanted peace and kill those who wanted war. Carr's command, which now consisted of 12 officers and 182 soldiers (Sixth U.S. Cavalry Troops B, C, D, E, F, and G), 20 civilians, and Gatewood with 54 scouts, moved from Fort Apache on the eighteenth. On the nineteenth they passed through Sanchez's cornfields near the Carrizo River. [67] As Sanchez was blamed for taking part in the attack on the soldiers at Cibecue, his fields were destroyed. Before the march con-

tinued, Gatewood's scouts took some of Sanchez's livestock. Reaching
the battle site on the twentieth, all they found were the white dead that
Carr had hastily buried under the cover of darkness before his original
retreat from the site. They had been dug up and mutilated.[68]

Over the next few days, scouting parties found nothing but a few
old women. On the twenty-third, Carr sent Capt. Tullius Tupper (Sixth
U.S. Cavalry) with Troops C and G (65 soldiers), along with Gatewood
and his scouts (50 natives), 6 packers, and *Chicago Times* correspondent
John F. Finerty, down the east side of the Cibecue until they reached the
Black River, there to move toward the Carrizo.[69] Finerty reported that
the command moved

> straight down the canyon, past a small Indian village, entirely
> deserted, until we came to a deep ravine, in which we struck a
> large Indian trail, apparently ten days old, which led out of the
> canyon in the direction of Carrizo Creek. The major [Tupper's
> brevet rank] halted his column and sent the scouts down the
> Cibicue to find out whether there was an outlet to Black River
> by that route. They followed it a couple of miles and then found
> that it was utterly impracticable for animals, forming what is
> known as a "box canyon"—a ravine with precipitous walls, out
> of which it would be difficult to extricate even a command on
> foot.[70]

After passing a very cold night, they continued their search. They
crossed the trail of another column in the field, then reached what Finerty called "one of the most damnable hills, or mountains, that I have
ever breasted, over a lovely mesa, all studded with beautiful trees." Soon
Tupper and Gatewood reached the "devil's own country." Finerty continues:

> We were very soon in the bowels of a most formidable canyon,
> down one side of which we slid and stumbled, leading our
> horses, to an astonishing distance. The sun beat upon us terri-
> bly. The chaparral tore our clothes, and the whole proceeding
> was thoroughly uncomfortable. . . . After scrambling down the
> wild mountainside for some time we suddenly came in sight of
> water, and then we knew we had struck an almost unknown
> portion of Carrizo Creek Canyon, over which white troops on

horseback had never, to all appearance, marched before. There was a pretty well-defined Indian trail, which we knew was the best guide to follow.

By this time, even Gatewood's scouts were worn out. That night's camp was an uneasy one, as the position they held was not defensible against an attack. Nothing happened, and the next day the hunt continued. They did not find any Apaches. After climbing some steep mountains and descending Cedar Creek, they spotted Carr's command, which had come down Cedar Creek.

A major war never developed. By October 3, forty-seven White Mountains had been arrested, forty surrendering on their own. Although the war slowly wound down on its own, the Western Apache uprising alarmed the Chiricahuas (Bedonkohes, Chokonens, and Nednhis), and seventy-four warriors and their families left the reservation. By the middle of the month some of the scouts who had revolted at Cibecue were in custody. On October 18, Alchesay—Gatewood's former sergeant who had not been at Cibecue—was arrested, along with a number of White Mountains when troops swept through the villages on the northern edge of the reservation. On October 25, Gatewood accompanied Lt. Edward Dravo's (Sixth U.S Cavalry) Troop D with his scout company on a patrol.[71] During the scout, Gatewood's scouts killed two Indians near Cañon Creek, then killed two more while capturing a woman and child north of the Black River. That November, the Indian scouts who had mutinied at Cibecue were tried, and three were sentenced to death. Sanchez surrendered; in captivity he would be vocal about the unfair treatment of his people—they should be tried and punished if guilty or set free, but not held indefinitely.[72]

As the war drifted aimlessly, the Bedonkohe, Chokonen, and Nednhi Apaches who had recently left the reservation roamed free in Mexico.[73] The grouping of tribes that has come to be known as the Chiricahuas consists of four tribes (or three, depending upon the source). Besides the Chihenne, there was the Chokonen (cókánén, Cho-kon-en), the Nednhi (Netdahe, Nednai, Nedni), and the Bedonkohe Apaches (Be-don-ko-he, Bedonkohes, ᴺdéʼì ᴺdà í).[74] When Gillett Griswold, the director of the U.S. Army Field Artillery and Fort Sill Museum in Oklahoma, compiled background information on the Apaches living at Fort Sill, he wrote: "However, in as much as the Bedonkohe and Nednai [Nednhi]

Apaches had merged with the Chiricahuas [Chokonens] prior to their surrender in 1886, and the Mimbre[ñ]o Apaches had merged with the Warm Springs prior to the same period, for the purpose of contemporary classification the Bedonkohes and Nednais [Nednhis] are regarded as Chiricahuas and the Mimbre[ñ]os as Warm Springs."[75] The Chokonen, the first band to have the name "Chiricahua" applied to them, lived in southwestern New Mexico and southeastern Arizona. Naiche, son of Cochise and the last hereditary Chiricahua chieftain, had Chokonen and Chihenne blood.[76] The Nednhi, which translates to "enemy people," lived in the Sierra Madres of northern Mexico. The Bedonkohe originally lived in the Mogollon Mountains of New Mexico but now also called the northern Mexican states of Chihuahua and Sonora home. Geronimo,[77] a Bedonkohe war leader and mystic who led a small band of Bedonkohes but who was never a chieftain, came to the fore at this time. Born in a cañon on the middle fork of the Gila River, some two hundred miles north of present-day Clifton, Arizona, he was born between 1823 and 1829. His mother was Juaña, and his father was Taklishim, whose father was Mahko, perhaps the last chief of the Bedonkohes. Daklugie, who was Ishton (Geronimo's sister, also known as Ish-keh) and Juh's son, got to know Geronimo intimately when they were prisoners of war. In fact, when Geronimo told his story to S. M. Barrett (1905–6), Daklugie translated his words. Daklugie later told Eve Ball, "Though my uncle Geronimo exercised the prerogatives of a chief, he was never elected to that position. In later days, when Naiche was chief of the [tribe that has since been grouped together as the] Chiricahua Apaches, Geronimo continued to direct the fighting but scrupulously required the warriors to render to Naiche the respect due a chief. He acted as leader of war parties, but acted rather in the relationship of general to commander in chief."[78]

Later, while a prisoner of war, Geronimo would say: "Still the four tribes (Bedonkohe, Chokonen, Chihenne, and Nednhi), who were fast friends in the days of freedom, cling together as they decrease in number. Only the destruction of all our people would dissolve our bonds of friendship."[79] While care has been taken to distinguish between the Bedonkohe, Chokonen, Chihenne, and Nednhi Apaches, at times this is impossible. Also, it should be noted that both military and civilian personnel, writing during the 1880s, commonly combined the four tribes and referred to them as Chiricahua Apaches.

Naiche (Chokonen and Chihenne Apache) became the last hereditary chieftain of the Chiricahua Apaches when his brother, Taza, died in 1876. Courtesy: Arizona Historical Society/Tucson, AHS #19798.

Cliché and error paint Geronimo as one of the bloodiest villains of the Indian wars. This is not so. His rampage—if one could call it such—began when his wife Gee-esh-kizn, mother, Juaña, and three children were murdered at what has since become known as the Massacre of Kas-ki-yah, near Janos, Mexico, in 1858.[80] He would lose more wives and children as the years passed. Geronimo had nine wives. As mentioned, Gee-esh-kizn died in 1858. His other wives included Chee-hash-kish. A Bedonkohe Apache, she and Geronimo had two children: Chappo (the warrior-son with him during the last breakout) and Lulu. Geronimo married her after Gee-esh-kizn's death. His third wife, Nana-tha-thtith (?–1861), was also a Bedonkohe Apache. Geronimo married her shortly after he married Chee-hash-kish. According to Griswold, they had one child. In 1861, Geronimo raided Chihuahua, Mexico (near Casas Grandes). Mexican troops trailed his war party back to Arizona Territory. When Geronimo and most of the warriors were away from their camp, the Mexicans attacked and killed most of the women and children including Nana-tha-thtith and their child. Chee-hash-kish was captured during the Mexican treachery at Casas Grandes, Chihuahua, Mexico, in 1882, and Geronimo never saw her again. Geronimo's fourth wife, She-gha (probably a Nednhi and Chokonen), was the warrior Yahnosha's sister. On August 7, 1885, Wirt Davis's scouts attacked Geronimo's camp near Casas Grandes, Chihuahua, Mexico. She-gha and their three-year-old daughter were captured during the attack. A month and a half later, on September 22, 1885, Geronimo raided the White Mountain Indian Reservation, Arizona Territory, and rescued She-gha and their daughter. She-gha surrendered with Geronimo in 1886, but has since disappeared from history. Shtsha-he (birth and death dates unknown), a Bedonkohe Apache, became Geronimo's fifth wife when he married while on the reservation (somewhere between 1872 and 1875). She joined the 1878 outbreak with Geronimo but then (supposedly) died sometime after he rejoined the Nednhis in Mexico, and she did not leave him any children. She died before Geronimo took his sixth wife. Zi-yeh (1869–1904), a Nednhi, whose name is pronounced "Zy-yay." Zi-yeh and Geronimo had two children: Fenton (born in 1882) and Eva (born in 1889). Both Fenton and Zi-yeh were with Geronimo during the 1885 outbreak. Wirt Davis's Apache scouts captured them on August 7, 1885, when they raided Geronimo's camp. Geronimo took his seventh wife, Ih-tedda (1851–?), a Mescalero Apache, whom he captured during the September 1885 raid

A rarely seen portrait of Geronimo drawn by Seward in 1913. The drawing, created four years after Geronimo's death, shows the warrior–medicine man's determination. Courtesy: Western History Collections, University of Oklahoma Libraries, Campbell Collection, no. 2044.

into Arizona and New Mexico. He had met her earlier on the San Carlos Reservation (1877–78), but they did not have a relationship until 1885. Geronimo's eighth wife has not been remembered by history. His ninth wife was Azul (1850–1934), a Chokonen who had been captured by Mexicans early in her life. After learning to speak Spanish, she escaped and returned to her people. She didn't marry Geronimo until the Apache prisoners of war moved to Fort Sill, Oklahoma Territory (probably 1907). She remained with him until his death in 1909, and she never remarried.[81]

When you add that Geronimo fought to keep his land, his religion, his culture—not to mention his loved ones—who can fault him? The tragic deaths in 1850 set him off on a campaign of vengeance against Mexicans. The vengeance would grow through the years as the enemies of his people—which eventually included the Americans—decimated everything he held dear. Although Geronimo and Gatewood would have very little contact until 1886, fate decreed that they were on a collision course that would ultimately affect the rest of their lives.

War had almost been a constant in the Southwest since Willcox's arrival. It had to stop. In July 1882, General Orders no. 78 assigned Brig. Gen. George Crook to command the Department of Arizona and Willcox to command the Department of the Platte.[82] When Willcox questioned negative comments in the press regarding his tenure in Arizona, Commander of the Army William Tecumseh Sherman, who wanted results, did not join the bandwagon of criticizing him. Instead, he wrote, "These Apaches know Genl. Crook, and fear him."[83] And indeed the Apaches did fear him. Crook had commanded the department once before (1871–75). At that time he had led the devastating Tonto Basin campaign against the Apaches. Although the top brass considered him one of their top Indian fighters, a number of officers considered him little more than a fool who did not know his business. Crook championed three modus operandi that brought him success: use Indians to fight Indians, use mules to haul supplies, and treat the foe in a humane manner.[84]

By the time Crook assumed command of the Department of Arizona in 1882, Gatewood had become one of the army's premier "Apache" men. He had ridden the war trail with native scouts almost constantly since his arrival in the Southwest; his only respite came when his body failed him, forcing him to go on medical leave. Crook recognized this and appointed him military commandant of the White Mountain Indian Reservation, headquartered at Fort Apache. The general could not have made a better choice, not because of his belief that Gatewood knew the Apache character, which he did, but for the reason that Gatewood believed staunchly in justice. Gatewood's assignment placed him in close contact with White Mountain Apaches, people he already knew from both campaigning with them and fighting against them. Over the course of the next two years, they would play important roles in his life— and he in theirs. In 1884 Gatewood would put his career on the line and demonstrate his true character when he realized that white men cheated his Indian wards. His actions would result in the deterioration of his working relationship with Crook and his banishment from the last Apache war, and it would certainly affect his career. But this is his story to tell.

Gatewood's Manuscript

It is unclear exactly when Gatewood began thinking about writing about his experiences with the Apaches. However, on August 26, 1886, the day the warring Apaches agreed to return to the United States with him, a sick and worn-out Gatewood began writing a letter to his wife Georgia, which read in part: "I must begin work on a memoir. My life has been more full of incident & adventure than that of any other l[ieutenan]t in the Army. I realize that more every day, . . . scenes and incidents . . . come back to my memory, . . . & soon I must begin to jot them down in a book, . . . when we are all together again."[85]

Soon after the campaign he began writing drafts of chapters he hoped would eventually become a book. As the Apache people played a major role in his career, he rightfully assumed that his close association with them would play a leading role in his writing.

Gatewood took a proactive approach to performing his duty and quickly accumulated a vast understanding of the Apache lifeway. His knowledge of the Apaches—especially the White Mountain Apaches— was unique. His very life depended upon those under his command accepting and obeying him at all times. Like most of us, he befriended some of his coworkers—his native coworkers. Predating the handful of Apache ethnologists of the twentieth century, such as Grenville Good-win, Morris Edward Opler, and Eve Ball—who through years of hard work of befriending Apaches and then interviewing them have docu-mented both a cultural and historical oral tradition that could have been lost, Gatewood literally walked in their footsteps before they did. It is this "everyday" knowledge that he attained during his time (1878–85) with the Apaches that makes his views and observations so valuable.

By the time Gatewood decided to write a book, his firsthand knowledge was extensive. But as he had not anticipated a book and had no training in ethnology, his research, if we can call it that, did not follow any rules. He did not take copious notes and had not made a systematic study. He had simply lived the life of a "nantan" among his wards.[86]

After Gatewood realized the uniqueness of his specialized knowledge, he made a concerted effort to put down on paper what he knew. The first occurrence of his writing probably took place in 1885 shortly after Geronimo and the Apaches broke out from the reservation for the last time. Almost another two years would pass before he had enough free time and/or desire to pick up the pen again. Then, sometime in 1887, Gatewood began drafting chapters for what he hoped would become a book dealing with his Apache duty. Gatewood did not write in a linear fashion, did not move in chronological order from chapter to chapter. Instead, he made each chapter self-contained much like magazine articles. Because of this, his chapters overlap. For example, his chapter dealing with his civil problems begins in 1884 and concludes at the time of Crook's meeting with Geronimo at Cañon de los Embudos in March 1886. No effort has been made to break up his organizational structure and move his contents to other chapters. However, some overlapped information has been edited out.

Unfortunately, fate decreed that Gatewood would live a short life, and he never finished his book. Nevertheless, he has succeeded: he left us a number of rough drafts of various chapters that are both observant and fresh, and he was not restrained by rules that limited what he could or could not say. More important, he was not influenced by other written material of questionable accuracy that dealt with the subject of the Apaches. What he wrote came from what he heard, saw, and felt. Because of this, some of what he says might be in complete variance from everything that has been written since his death.

Some might argue that his untrained skills at recording living history allowed him to misinterpret the Apache lifeway. This does not follow, for when one combines the accuracy of his reports and recordkeeping with his firm stance against anything that was wrong and untruthful, one has to conclude that his reporting did not deviate from what he heard or saw, at least not by intent.[87]

Although he based his writing on his experiences or from what the Apaches told him, most of his writing took place during the last nine years of his life, when he had no contact with the Apaches. Although it is obvious that he consulted reports, notes, or news clippings, he can be vague, and he often got his dates wrong. This stems from the practiced convention that many used during the Victorian Age, that of not naming names. Regardless of some of the failings just listed, he has not only recorded Apache oral history before it became known as "oral history," but he has documented arguably the most singularly spectacular feat of the Indian wars—meeting Naiche and Geronimo in Sonora, Mexico, in 1886, and talking them into returning to the United States to surrender. His memories of the Apaches are special.

Editorial Approach

What follows is intended to help the reader understand the approach I took when preparing Gatewood's manuscript for publication.

I used headers both to separate Gatewood's text and to allow for a text lead-in to the next section. I hope that the text lead-ins offer information that is helpful in understanding Gatewood's text that follows. Types of information that are presented include identification of participants, including short biographical sketches (although unfortunately at times this is not always possible), identification and description of locations, dating of events, and background information to give the reader a more complete picture of what leads up to and what is happening in Gatewood's text.

During the course of transcribing Gatewood's words, a few things in the text that were commonplace during his day but that may grate on the modern reader have been altered for an easier read. Additional paragraph breaks have been inserted to break up text that at times rambles from subject to subject. Also, spelling has been adjusted. We all at times misspell words; Gatewood was no different. For example, he misspells "pursuit" as "persuit." This has been corrected, as have other misspellings. Although not misspelled, Gatewood often makes two words out of what now is one word. These words have been combined to become one word; for example: "any body" is now "anybody," "some times" is now "sometimes," "any thing" is now "anything," and "near by" is now "nearby."

I have made every effort not to vary Gatewood's sentence structure. However, when he becomes passive and rambling, I have, with as little editing as possible, shortened his sentences and made them more active and readable. He wrote as many as three drafts describing the same event, sometimes having three sentences that were similar yet different. The best selection of text from his drafts has been merged to create the best possible combination of his words. When words are missing from his text or when added words would clarify his meaning, additional words have been added. When this happens, the added text appears in [brackets].

I have not used "[sic]" after misspelled words unless it follows a word Gatewood has created and the use of brackets would destroy his meaning. This does not happen often, as I do not like the usage of "[sic]."

Finally, the following is not a biography of Charles Gatewood, a history of the last Apache war, or an ethnological study of the Apache Indians and should not be construed as such. My lone goal has always been to gather Bay-chen-daysen's attempt to document his service in the Southwest during the 1880s and present his words in one volume. Additional text and notations have been added whenever it was deemed appropriate to give the lieutenant's words further explanation and clarity.

Lt. Charles Gatewood & His Apache Wars Memoir

Prologue

The Adventure Begins

What follows is a typescript entitled "My Experiences among the Apaches"[1] by Lt. Charles B. Gatewood, Sixth U.S. Cavalry. It appears that Gatewood had plans to enlarge the scope of his project.

Gatewood mentions two classmates from West Point whose careers soon carried them in different directions and out of his life. Cunliffe Hall Murray, of New York, graduated twenty-fifth in their class. He joined the Fourth U.S. Cavalry, which was then stationed in the Southwest, but quickly dropped from sight. Richard Hulbert Wilson (June 10, 1853– Mar. 21, 1937) graduated twenty-sixth in their class. Although Wilson initially reported for duty at Fort Wingate, Arizona, with Gatewood, before reporting to Camp Apache on February 5, 1878, he did not join the Sixth U.S. Cavalry with Gatewood. Instead, Wilson had been assigned to the Eighth U.S. Infantry. On July 20, 1878, he left for Camp Gaston, California. Wilson remained on duty in California until 1889, missing the last Apache wars.[2]

Upon graduation in June, the U.S. Military Academy Class of 1877, of which I was a member, were all given leaves of six months before reporting for their new duties as officers of the Army. The majority of available vacancies were in organizations serving in the far West, so we knew that most of us would be sent to distant frontier stations, but just which of us, or to which posts, we would not know until December when our orders came out.

I spent most of my leave with my widowed mother [Emily], a sister, and a brother at our home in [Harrisonburg], Virginia, for no one could tell how long it might be until I saw them again. As it turned out, I saw my sister again many years later, but [returned home] too late to see the others.

Murray, a classmate [at West Point] and close chum, came with me as our guest for a few weeks. Before he left, we had a bit of fun together, and we all saw to it that he was at least entertained. I remember we rode out one morning a few miles in the country to call upon two young ladies I had known since childhood. For Murray, who was very short in

Charles Gatewood graduated twenty-third in a class of seventy-six at the
U.S. Military Academy in 1877. Courtesy: Arizona Historical Society/Tucson,
AHS #19556.

stature, I had the livery stable send up the largest horse they could find, and they succeeded in finding a Percheron weighing a ton or more; for me, who was tall and slender, there was a plump little pony with legs so short that I could almost mount him without taking my feet off the ground.[3] Murray's feet stuck out on each side of his vast steed like fancy trimmings on the edges of his saddle. As we rode along, I had to look upward and shout, as to someone on a rooftop, in order to talk to him, while he had to lean far over the side of his horse to see me below. I was careful to route our expedition through the main street of town so that [everyone] could see us and marvel, which they did.

My orders [arrived] on December 8th, and said to report for duty at Camp Apache, Arizona [Territory].[4] It wasn't difficult to find out exactly where Arizona was, but the best Atlas in town utterly failed to show any trace of Camp Apache. It was not until after reaching Santa Fe, [New Mexico Territory], that I found out where it was. The orders were very liberal in point of time, so I spent a few more pleasant days in Virginia. At last [I] tore myself away and hit the iron trail for Chicago, where several of us had made a tentative agreement to meet and have a few more days of holiday together before dispersing to our remote stations. There was no especial hurry, and we would get enough of our posts and frontier service before ever again we saw the civilization of the East and our home.

But at Chicago, I found they had all been there and gone, having received their orders several days earlier than I had—all except Murray. [He] had missed his train the day before by taking too long trying to climb a ten-foot iron gate with spikes on the top, instead of opening it and walking through, which he could readily have done if, in his haste, he had seen and lifted the latch on the gate instead of trying to open it by shoving. We were both late, so we only [stayed] that day in Chicago, and [leaving] that wonder city unexplored, [we] journeyed on to St. Louis together.

At Emporia, Kansas, I overtook Wilson, another classmate, bound also for Camp Apache, and we banded together for mutual protection and support. We remained at Pueblo, Colorado, a day, partly to admire Pike's Peak at a distance of fifty miles, but principally to await the next train on the narrow gauge railroad to El Moro. At this latter place, and at Trinidad, we learned that smallpox was "cleaning out" the Mexican sections, probably in lieu of any cleaning that might otherwise have been done with the use of soap [&] water [or] disinfectants.[5]

[The] stage ride from Trinidad to Santa Fe [was] two hundred and sixteen miles; a sort of preliminary breaking in for the longer and rougher and more daring ride from there to Camp Apache. There were nine of us passengers, and the stage, about the size of a small dry-goods box, would allow four to squeeze inside and one up alongside the driver. How to get all nine in was a knotty problem solved only by taking up a collection of a dollar apiece for the agent who thereupon granted us the use of a larger coach. So we set out and made the trip in less than thirty-eight hours, stopping only for meals and change of horses. Our unusually swift progress was mainly due to the doses of "cheer" with which our driver continually plied himself from a good-sized demijohn kept handy under his seat. Being thus continually in a cheerful and expansive state of mind, he did not at all seem to care if the coach frequently ran on only two wheels, with considerable danger to our bones.

At Santa Fe we had a rest of a week, and after that journey we needed it. When I first saw the towns' squat little one-story adobe houses it seemed as though Pike's Peak, in some playful mood, must have sat on them and driven them into the ground. And then the burros! They interested me, and I studied them in order to send home an adequate description: nice little brutes, no bigger than a yearling calf, heads no larger than their bodies, ears no longer than their heads, and legs shorter than their ears. Even at work they seem to be in deep medi-tation, possibly on the subject of emancipation from slavery, for their owners do maltreat them shamefully; in lieu of a rein to guide them, [they give them] a blow on the side of the head to make them change direction.

Chapter One

Mismanagement and the Last Outbreak

This chapter is probably the earliest of Gatewood's attempts at recording his Indian experience.[1] Actually, he does not speak of his experiences here; instead, he delivers a discourse on Apache treatment by the U.S. government. Undoubtedly his disgust and frustration at yet another Apache outbreak—an outbreak he felt should not have occurred—prompted him to vent his feelings on the mismanagement and mistreatment of the Apache people.

It is easy to date this draft, as Gatewood gives two references that cannot be mistaken: he refers to Crook's 1883 invasion of Mexico as "since my return from Mexico with the hostile Apaches two years ago," and the Chiricahua outbreak of 1885 as "the present outbreak." Immediately following Geronimo and Naiche's break for freedom on May 17, 1885, Gatewood spent the next month and a half either in the field or recruiting Indian scouts. It is reasonable to assume that the frenzied activity at the beginning of what would become the last Apache war demanded all his waking hours, making it safe to state that Gatewood did not start to write until sometime after July 1, 1885.

As the summer of 1885 wore on, two things became very obvious in Gatewood's life: both his relationship with the White Mountain Apaches and his relationship with Gen. George Crook were nearing an end. He had been military commandant of the White Mountain Indian Reservation since the fall of 1882, and he had reported directly to Crook and worked closely with his wards since his appointment. By this time, Gatewood had become an expert on the subject of Apaches and their management. He had played a major role in their lives, seen all the ills heaped upon them by the white man, and not only known of their discontent but also sympathized with it. The problems he discusses at the beginning of this chapter he saw firsthand as military agent on the reservation. He immersed himself in what follows during his tenure at White Mountain. The Indians saw this and knew that in Gatewood they had a real friend—someone who would risk everything for them. This is not a small feat. Nor is it one that can be ignored, for it is the key to Gatewood's relationship with Geronimo. They did not have much contact prior to their historic meeting in Mexico in 1886, and yet the old warrior knew that he could trust Gatewood. Why? Because he had heard from the White Mountains and the Chiricahuas, who were lucky enough to come under his control, that here was a man who did not lie. When Gatewood's two native scouts announced that he wanted to meet to discuss ending the war, Geronimo knew that when Gatewood said something, he meant it.

Although Gatewood probably did not intend to write a book about his experiences at the time he drafted these words, his words present a good introduction to one.

The control of the Indians and the management of their affairs are fields so fruitful of discussion, that it may be thought little new can be advanced in regard to the subjects. It would seem, however, that the theories presented are more pronounced, the further their authors are removed from their application and from acquaintance with the character of their subjects. Of those who are in proximity to Indian reservations, some who are moved by apprehensions of danger from their depredations, and most who are influenced by greed for what is invaluable of their possessions are convinced that confinement to the most remote and barren localities, with capital punishment for every discontent, is the only means of safety, while that far distant theorist presents a prompt and happy solution in acts of Congress and the donation of a one hundred and sixty acre farm. From some considerable experience with them, I am convinced that Indians are no different from other persons in that they are governed, actuated, and influenced by self-interest—self-interest as *they* see it, not as their covetous neighbor or their far distant adviser may see it for them, but as it presents itself to the instincts, tastes, and habits with which they are endowed.

It should be remembered that these people discontinued labor at the building of the tower of Babel, and they still maintain most of their aboriginal customs and loyalty to their nomadic habits. Nothing can be more mistaken than to endeavor to crowd upon them in quick succession the customs of civilization and coerce them to their observance. It is as unreasonable to expect them to realize all at once the benefits of law and order and industrial pursuits, as to be satisfied with the absorption by an alien of whatever is valuable of their bands, and the best fruits of such industries as they may be induced to engage in.

None other than the slowest, most patient, fair, and open processes can succeed in creating them desirable citizens. As promoting to this result some incentives other than legislation and advice are necessary. Grist mills where they can procure flour & the grain they raise themselves in place of its purchase from the sole trader permitted upon the reservation, whose prices are limited only by his conscience; the licensing of more traders, that competition may secure them better prices for their products and less prices for their purchases; the exclusion of intruders from their lands and no special permits to speculators of any description; supplies furnished them to be in quantities as agreed upon and of wholesome quality; the employers furnished to be qualified for their employment and required to engage for the interest of the Indians and not for themselves; schools with intelligent and competent teachers; agents of character who will reside with their constituency and interest themselves faithfully in their welfare. No people more fully understand what belongs to them than Indians, and being equally prompt to resent trespass, trifling matters often lead to most important results. Suspicious, secretive, and averse to experiments, they form conclusions from their own standpoint in every regard to motives and results of varying regulations affecting them, and are quick to retaliate, equally against what is objectionable to them and what they do not comprehend.

The present outbreak [1885] of a small party of Chiricahuas illustrates their aversion to changed methods of administration.[2] By an act of Congress approved the 3rd of March last, the jurisdiction of certain crimes committed by Indians upon their reservations was transferred to the civil courts. Heretofore among these Apaches, this jurisdiction had been exercised by the Indians themselves according to their tribal customs. About the latter part of March or first of April—before it was known to me or to anyone at my headquarters that such an act had passed—I was informed in a private letter from their reservation that the Chiricahuas had learned and were discussing it, and that it was likely to occasion trouble. On April 18th the officer in charge of the police control of the reservation wrote me, inquiring the scope of the act and how it applied to his charge. A newspaper copy had just been received and from it he was informed April 30th—his letter having been delayed by the mail—that the law was operative according to its tenor, from date of approval, and that the Indians should be "thoroughly advised of the law, its operation and its consequences, and that it would be complied with to the letter: that they should be carefully instructed what offences subjected them to arrest and delivery to civil authority for trial, and that for all offences not specified in the law, they would be subject to trial and punishment as heretofore."[3] These instructions were mailed to the officer on the day of their date, and were communicated to the Indians as directed, and on May 17th, Geronimo and his band left the reservation. There is [no] doubt in my mind that this act of Congress was the moving cause of their doing so. Simplicity of administration is quite as important as uniformity and fairness. The authority to administer at once upon any matter which may arise, and their confidence in the power and the justice of the one exercising that authority, are the prime elements of their control, and it is the conflicts of authority, delays of redress and the accumulation of small things, undetermined and unsatisfactory, which leads to outbreaks and ultimate disaster. They cannot understand the transfer of their matters from one tribunal to another, the distribution of their affairs into various departments of government, or their reference to higher authority than that charged with their immediate direction. To still further extend this by giving their criminal jurisdiction to the local authorities cannot but occasion such vague ideas of where and to whom they are responsible and how many agencies have a hand in their management. [This] lead[s] to restlessness and disturbance. With them, as with all other people, the possession of property is a potent restraint against disorder; not so much the possession of land, in which they do not as yet realize proprietorship, but movable property, something tangible, stock and goods for comfort and convenience, and everything which will encourage them in its acquirement and afford them opportunity to accumulate, is more than anything else in the direction of their civilization.

Since my return from Mexico with the hostile Apaches two years ago, every effort has been made to procure the erection of mills upon their reservation, to dispossess old intruders [from the reservation] and to exclude new ones, to have more traders licensed among them and discontinue the monopoly by one, to see that healthy and suitable stock was furnished, and to give them a ready cash market for all their surplus produce.[4] Except in the last respect, which was immediately within my own control, my efforts have not been attended with [a desired] success.

It may be claimed with confidence, as showing the effect of even one adjunct to the accumulation of property, that the encouragement of having a ready market for their products restrained those who had planted from engaging in the recent outbreak, and that a chief so noted among them as Geronimo was able to muster less than fifty men to leave their occupations and engage in their native employment of marauding and pillage.[5] Should the other facilities to their self-support be furnished them and they be permitted to manage their internal affairs their own way, under proper restrictions as to the rights of others, I am satisfied that the Apaches in this territory will be in the future as peaceable and progressive as any other Indians in the country.

Chapter Two

The Apache Indians

Beginning with his arrival in the Southwest in 1878 until the end of the last Apache war in 1886, Gatewood worked very closely with the Apache Indians. When he became military commandant of the White Mountain Indian Reservation in 1882, he did not remain aloof from his wards. Instead, he made himself as involved in their needs and problems as he possibly could. He easily bridged the racial chasm that was so foreboding to many because of his previous experience as commander of Apache scouts. Gatewood often spent days, weeks, and sometimes even months in the field with native scouts. He knew that to survive, he not only had to trust the men he worked with but they had to trust and respect him. Although he preferred to retain his own culture and never "went Indian," as many who harbored racially inclined prejudices labeled whites who dared to embrace a native lifeway, he did befriend many warriors and their wives.

During his time among the natives of the Southwest, Gatewood made no attempt to inhibit his curiosity—he wanted to know about them. His study was not scientific, nor was it something that he pursued with any particular forethought. He simply wanted to know about the people who now played a major part of his life, especially the Apaches. Gatewood asked questions—questions that were answered because of the trust and friendship that increased as time passed. While some of the information Gatewood gathered is refreshing, some may be considered heresy by modern-day anthropologists and historians. His informants were not elders telling their stories thirty, forty, fifty, or more years after they happened. Gatewood walked and rode across the harsh terrain with the people he wrote about. He tramped down long, rocky, thorny trails after an enemy that only his guides could track. He ate with Apaches, slept with them, and risked his life with them. He knew them, and because of this, his view of their life and history is important.

Gatewood's efficiency reports state: "Has given attention and study to the history and character of Indians, especially the Apaches."[1] Yes, he did interview and gather information, but at the same time Gatewood made no effort to compare what he heard with what was then known about the Apaches. Using modern terms, it might be said that his position as military commandant of the reservation included "on-the-job training." Unfortunately, he did not take the next step and confirm what he heard.

At the beginning of the twentieth century, ethnologist Frederick Webb Hodge wrote: "The Apache are divided into a number of tribal groups which have been so differently named and defined that it is sometimes difficult to determine to which branch writers refer."[2] His words are still true today. It is a shame at this late date that anthropologists, historians, and Apaches cannot work together to come up with an accepted determination on just which Apaches belong to which group.

The Apaches are of Athapaskan descent—that is, their descendents migrated from the old world of Asia. As Hodge wrote: "The Southern division held sway over a vast area in the S. W., including most of Arizona and New Mexico, the s. portion of Utah and Colorado, the w. borders of Kansas and Texas, and the no. part of Mexico to lat. 25°. Their principal neighbors were the members of the Shoshonean family and the various Pueblo tribes in the region."[3] All the Southern Athapaskan people, the family group to which the Apaches belong, originally hunted buffalo on the plains as they slowly migrated from the north. The drift southward neared culmination when they reached the Rio Grande Valley shortly after the Spanish began their invasion of the Southwest. In 1541 the conquistador Francisco Vásquez Coronado encountered native-hunters living in a ranchería, and wrote: "These natives are called Querechos. They do not cultivate the land, but eat raw meat and drink the blood of the cattle they kill."[4] Archeologists C. L. Riley and Curtis Schaafsma, among others, confirm that these natives were "Apachean." Sixty years later fray Francisco de Velasco encountered natives on the Canadian River: "Occasionally we found rancherías inhabited by people of the Apache nation, who are masters of the plains."[5] Soon these "masters of the plains" would migrate westward, where they would split into two well defined divisions. Perhaps this is the split that Gatewood refers to when he mentions the horrendous war that split the "people" apart. Certainly this severing of ties and moving in different directions is key to the history of the

Apache people, for it marks the defining line between Southwestern and Plains Apaches.

Indeed, the Spaniards initially called the Apaches "Apaches de Nabaju," which may be based upon the Zuñi word for the Navajos—"pachu," which means "enemy." In contrast, the Western Apache word for non-Apaches is "inda," which also means "enemy." Over the years, the Apaches have called themselves "N'de" or "nde," "Tinde," "Inde," and "Dinë," which mean "people" or "man."[6]

Often Apache tribal names are based upon the location where they live, and the Western Apache tribal groups are a prime example (White Mountains, Cibecue, San Carlos, etc.). They, along with the Chiricahuas (that is, Bedonkohes, Chokonens, Nednhis, and Chihennes), Mescaleros, Jicarillas, Lipans, and Navajos, all speak an Athapaskan language, which is linked to the Alaskan language Eyak. Each tribe has its own particular dialect, including a spattering of regional words, and much as English is the same language for Americans living in Boston, Atlanta, and Los Angeles even though they have different and distinct accents, it is still a language that can be understood by all. It is this linguistic link that ties these tribes together as one.[7]

When Gatewood began writing his manuscript, he had a firm idea of what he wanted to write about. Logically it should follow that he began writing this chapter in 1886, shortly after the Apaches surrendered for the last time in September; however, other events named in this chapter date the writing as mid-1887 at the earliest. To further date this chapter, Gatewood mentions that Apache prisoners of war had been moved from Florida to Alabama, which now gives a more specific date for this writing or rewriting. The first batch of Apache prisoners arrived at the Mount Vernon Barracks in Alabama in April 1887, whereas Naiche and Geronimo and those still with them did not arrive at their new home until May 13, 1888.

In the course of his writing, Gatewood sometimes wrote more than one version, and that is the case here. Gatewood wrote one complete draft of this chapter and then began a rewrite, which he never completed.[8] Since both drafts cover the same topic and are very close in content, they have been merged into one chapter with the rewrite as the base draft for this publication. When the text differs between drafts and does not lend itself to merging, but does warrant inclusion, the alternate version has been placed in a footnote. This does not happen often. The best choices of words are taken from both drafts, with no notation. Once in a while, stand-alone sentences from the first draft are incorporated into the flow.

In the eastern part of Arizona there is a tract of country about seventy-five miles square, set apart by the United States Government for the use & benefit of some five thousand Indians, commonly called "Apaches." The reserved land is the "White Mountain," or "San Carlos" Reservation.[9] The valleys of the Gila & San Carlos Rivers in the southern part of it, & those of the Black & White Rivers, with their tributaries, in the northern, embrace thousands of acres of rich arable lands, & many square miles of fine pasture & forest. The garden spot of Arizona, in fact, is the northern third of this reservation—plenty of wood, fine water, grass, trout, & until of late years, turkey, deer, bear, & elk. In the White River Valley, at the confluence of its two main branches, is situated the military post of Fort Apache, & in the Gila Valley to the south of Apache & just thirty-five miles east of the San Carlos Agency, Fort Thomas.

According to their traditions, these aborigines are descended from a people that emigrated from the northwest ages ago, & overran what is now Colorado, northern New Mexico, & western Texas where they settled in their peculiar fashion.[10] The date of their arrival cannot be fixed even approximately, for they have kept no records themselves, except such as are set forth in the dim traditions of old medicine men who handed them down from generation to generation.[11] These medicine men, as in other tribes, are the historians, or repositories of their traditions, & belonging to a race of men endowed with most lively imaginations, it is impossible to separate truth from fiction. They have not tried to keep account of the number of these fine old romancers that lived & passed away, but they say that there were "a great many of them" from first to last. Indeed, so careless are they as to the flight of time, that few of the adults of today can give an idea of their own ages.

At the time of their migration, or soon thereafter, they called themselves "Noo-tah-hah." But just what the word means—the wisest do not seem to know.[12] That many generations ago they appropriated as much of this vast Southwestern territory as their nomadic habits required, there can be no doubt, as their own traditions & those of other tribes, as well as the general history of "The Land of the Cactus" from the time of Cortez & the missionary priests, to the present day, amply prove. The sparse population that was first encountered almost suffered extermination, the small remnant that was left, flying southward. Their descendants are the Yaquis, who have of late years given so much trouble to the Mexican government.[13] Whether this is absolutely true or not, I do not know, but that is what the Apaches say. The ruins of the cliff dwellers, & those in the valleys as well, were then, just as they are now—"a marvel & a mystery." The Indians have often asked me if the white men knew anything of the race that once inhabited those old ruins.

The Pueblo Indians, or those who lived in towns, made their debut by sufferance of the "Noo-tah-hah," & held their possessions by establishing villages, or pueblos, & building their habitations of mud & stone with a view to defense.[14] Until within a few generations, they paid tribute to their nomad superiors, & probably would yet be contributing to the support of their conquerors, except that the recipients of their bounty had so much of their time taken up in paying respects to their numerous other visitors who gradually drifted into that region as the years rolled by, that they could not attend to mere collection [of] taxes. On the other hand, it seems, the Pueblos, Pimas, Papagos, Yumas, Mojaves, & other tribes claim priority of residence over the "Noo-tah-hah," & say their places for defense were built on account of the coming of the latter. However this may be, one thing is certain, the race we speak of came & its descendants are there yet in the shape of Apaches. Which came first & the dates of such events are not sought to be settled in this narrative; but it is apparent that the much-mixed American race will in time record the date of the disappearance of them all.

Another fact seems to be well established in the history of these people, & that is, when they did appear, they proceeded to make their presence known in an exceedingly disagreeable manner. Contact with others meant war, for war, pillage, & the chase are the chief occupations on which they relied for sustenance & amusement.[15] No matter whom [they] met, a fight was sure to follow.[16] Hostilities were not begun by sending out into the land a herald with banners & trumpets, proclaiming that the conquering hero was coming & that all must bow down before him, or suffer pains & penalties for disobeying his mandate. They proceeded by different methods, their cardinal principle in warfare being to do the greatest damage to the enemy with the least possible risk of injury to themselves. It was, & is today, no disgrace in a warrior to turn his back upon an enemy & fly "fast & far," if by so doing he can avoid harm to himself. No sentiment of fair play ever entered his head; & he never fought hand to hand where he could run away. "Kill your enemy & save yourself" rules all his actions, & he will patiently await a favorable opportunity to carry out his purposes.

When a raid was determined upon, the priests performed the mysterious rites of their order to determine the success, or failure, of the projected foray, the meaning of which were supplications to the good spirits, or influences, to aid them in their enterprise, & to the evil spirits, or influences, to refrain from exerting their powers to cause failure. If the supernatural beings this supplicated announced through the medicine men that success would attend the expedition, there was great rejoicing throughout the tribe, & preparations immediately began. If failure was predicted, there was satisfaction in knowing that a great calamity was avoided. When success was announced, a great dance took place, attended with feasting, & the deeds of their forefathers were chanted in wild, weird tones. All this was intended to raise the courage of the war party & incite them to acts of "high emprise."

Then the "command" would quietly steal away in small parties, to assemble at some appointed place near an unsuspecting, or unprotected, settlement, or lay in ambush for a traveling party. The party as it advanced, would be surrounded by a cordon of watchful vedettes to prevent surprise & gain knowledge of the enemies' movements. These wily guerillas always took good care to have accurate information as to the numbers of their victims & their means for defending themselves, so that whenever they attacked, success was pretty well assured.

Then at the most propitious moment—generally at the break of day, a surprise—a rapid & furious attack, accompanied by the most demonical yells. The surprised party, paralyzed with fear [&] unable to make a concerted defense, massacred. Women & children, old & young, butchered, & such as they fancied carried into captivity—slavery—& the dead left horribly mutilated & unburied.[17]

All property, of course, belonged to the victors, generally to the individuals of the party who seized the particular article, but sometimes distributed equally among the members of the party.

After a successful foray, there was always great rejoicing on the return of the warriors; especially so, if all came back. Dancing, feasting, & general hilarity prevailed. But defeat or any considerable loss set all the squaws to howling all night & moaning all day, for weeks at a time. At sundown, the widows of those who do not return, along with all the female relatives of the dead, betake themselves to the nearest mountainside & there pour forth their mournful wailing till the first streak of dawn. Their cries, uttered as loudly as possible, are not exactly screams, but more like prolonged howls of the coyote, tinged with ineffable sadness & ferocity. To an unaccustomed ear, they are the saddest &, at the same time, the most bloodcurdling sounds that are produced by human beings. The writer, on several occasions, has moved his camp three or four miles to get some sleep & escape positive torture. One squaw can keep a whole valley awake. Then imagine the effect of twenty.[18]

Stories of the most horrible torture & cruelties practiced by North American Indians on their captives are not exaggerations when applied to these. The reader is familiar with such & his imagination may supply the place of a description of acts so repulsive. So skillfully were their plans laid & carried out, coming & going like the whirlwind, that they terrorized a country that was afterwards populated by numbers many times greater than their own, & continued to do so until our friend Geronimo made his celebrated journey to the Atlantic seaboard in 1886 & finally pitched his tent in Alabama.[19] (By the way, Alabama means "here we rest," which is rather suggestive.)

In these long continued hostile demonstrations, caused by an almost implacable enmity to the rest of mankind, they frequently met with losses & reverses, which sensibly lessened the natural proportion of men & women. Although the female child [is] treated as an article of merchandise to be bought & sold, "all same as a horse," the male child [is] well cared for & also trained in games of chance & skill in the use of the weapons designed for war & the chase. Polygamy naturally resulted from the number of women exceeding that of men, & is practiced among them at the present time.[20]

Birth of the Name "Apache"

Although anthropologists have placed the Apaches' and the Navajos' arrival in the Southwest via the Bering Strait somewhere between 1000 and 1500 AD, they are still in disagreement over the route they followed southward or which tribe arrived first. The Navajos are usually credited with the earlier arrival, which in turn makes them a distinct tribe from the Apaches. Grenville Goodwin addressed the "who arrived first" theory:

> that the Apache in general probably arrived in the Southwest later than the Navaho and that somehow or other they were all congregated on the plains in northeastern New Mexico in one heterogeneous mass, which then pushed its head southward and westward until the thrust culminated in the extreme westward position of the Western Apache. The only apparent reason for allotting the Navaho an earlier arrival in the Southwest is that they have absorbed Pueblo culture to a greater degree; the only reason for insisting that the Apache thrust came from the plains to the east is because the Coronado expedition mentions great numbers of people on the plains of eastern New Mexico who probably were Southern Athapaskans of some sort.[21]

Nevertheless, they have closely related dialects of a single language (Athapaskan), and at times the tribes have been referred to as cousins. Most likely the Apache people were still "a single group or a number of very closely related groups" as late as 1300.[22] Although their arrival in the Southwest may have been as early as 1000, others place the date of arrival between 1400 and 1525, while others think they arrived during the thirteenth or fourteenth century.

Unfortunately, very little is known of the Apaches' prehistory. Although Keith Basso refers to the Western Apaches in the following quotation, his words can be expanded to include the Navajos, Chiricahuas (that is, Chokonen, Bedonkohe, Nednhi, and Chihenne Apaches), Mescaleros, Jicarillas, and Lipans, as their dialects all stem from a single language (Athapaskan): "Owing to the almost complete absence of excavated Western Apache archeological sites and to an equally small number of early Spanish documents concerning these people, the reconstruction of Western Apache prehistory is made extremely difficult. However, this has not prevented anthropologists and historians from speculating on the matter."[23]

Regarding the ethnic background, Hodge said it was "the most widely distributed of all the Indian linguistic families of North America, formerly extending over parts of the continent from the Arctic coast far into N. Mexico from the Rio Colorado to the mouth of the Rio Grande at the S—a territory extending for more than 40° of latitude and 75° of longitude."[24]

Gatewood probably did not know any of the above, and that is both good and bad. It freed him to listen to what the Apaches told him with an unbiased outlook, and it does not appear that he ever questioned what he heard. Although he does make it perfectly clear that he does not know if anything the Apaches told him is true, he believes it is. Looking back, it is a shame that he did not make an attempt to confirm anything he heard. Still, if there is any truth in the story he tells below, then the above might warrant a reevaluation.

Here Gatewood mentions the White Mountain Apaches for the first time. They are one of the five Western Apache tribes: White Mountain, Cibecue, San Carlos, Northern Tonto, and Southern Tonto. These tribes (or groups) are further divided: White Mountain (Western White Mountain and Eastern White Mountain), Cibecue (Canyon Creek, Carrizo, and Cibecue), San Carlos (San Carlos, Arivaipa, Pinal, and Apache Peaks), Northern Tonto (Fossil Creek, Mormon Lake, Oak Creek, and Bald Mountain), and Southern Tonto (Mazatzal, which was further divided into six "simibands"). Many of these names are specific to the area in which the band lived (for example, the White Mountain group lived near the White Mountains and the Cibecue group called the Carrizo lived near the Carrizo River). Also, "San Carlos" was originally used as a reservation designation and did not become applied to a tribe or group until Dr. P. E. Goddard used it as such in 1931.[25]

After the Apaches permanently settled in New Mexico [&] western Texas there were quarrels brought about by certain chiefs & their adherents, over the division of spoils accumulated in their various forays— captives, horses, & plunder generally. In fact, every raid bred more [or] less discontent on this account, until finally the return of a war party who had paid an unfriendly visit to the Comanches in Texas & Indian Territory, bringing back an unusually large amount of booty, caused the nation to be divided into two great factions. To share, or not to share, that was the question.[26]

Some demanded that these things should be divided among the warriors who composed the raiding party, as nearly equal as possible, while others insisted on the right of each individual's having & holding what he had actually taken into his own personal possession.[27] The quarrels waxed hotter & hotter, the friends of each side joined the discussions, & friends' friends took part also until the whole nation was embroiled in a political excitement greater than one of our presidential elections, which divided it into two great factions. As neither side would give in to the other, the "knock-down-&-drag-out" argument was soon introduced, & once started, a bloody battle followed. Even women & children took sides with their husbands, brothers, & sires, so that every soul that could draw a bow, wield a club, or sling a stone was engaged in the combat. It is said to have lasted for days, & the slaughter was something terrible. Party lines were drawn close, & as the fight was for the mastery, even suckling babes were not spared. If the combatants had been equally divided in numbers, there probably would not have been the usual one man left to tell the tale. Unfortunately, shall we say, this was not so. The minority of course got the worst of it, & succeeded in withdrawing from the scene of the fight, taking with them their families & what property they could carry, leaving their dead & wounded behind. They [did not] halt until far beyond the reach of their pursuers. The latter, however, did not follow far, on account of exhaustion caused by hunger & exertion, for you must know that neither side stopped for refreshment during the fight. Fear supplied the losers with the strength that lack of nourishment & the hard labor undergone had taken away, & this enabled them to outstrip their competitors in the race.

Out of reach of the victors, they tarried a short time to consider what should be done. The chiefs & "medicine men" could not agree among themselves on any measure for the weal of all, because each wanted to exercise supreme control in his own sphere, & another general engagement was averted by the tribes seeking each its own future home for itself. One resolution, however, received unanimous approval of the convention, & that was that the name of "Noo-tah-hah" should be forever discarded, & the new appellation "Apache" be adopted. This word means The Man, in capital letters, the superior of all men; & they have striven ever since to demonstrate that the adoption of this name was no idle boast.

The victors in this celebrated battle are now the "Navajos" (probably a corruption of "Noo-tah-hah") living in northeastern Arizona.[28] The proceedings of this convention were somewhat hastened by the fear that the Navajos might recuperate & follow them & thus embarrass the situation. So it was adjourned in short order & the separation of the tribes accomplished. From that time there was hatred that bred bitter feuds among them. The Jicarillos sought refuge in the rugged mountains of northwestern New Mexico; the Tontos stayed not upon the order of their going till they reached the fertile valleys of what is now Tonto Basin in central Arizona. The White Mountains, or more properly Coyoteros, settled east of the Tontos, & gave name to the range of mountains on the northern edge of the present reservation. The San Carlos, or Arivaipas, went further south & occupied the valleys of the San Carlos [&] San Pedro rivers, & part of that of the Gila, into which these other streams flow. [29] The Chiricahuas, from whom Geronimo is descended, "took up," or "took in," Sulphur Spring Valley with its adjacent mountains. [30] East of them in New Mexico, the Warm Springs, & east again the Mescaleros, & still further east, the Lipans. The last carried on their operations from the mountains near the upper Río Grande in Texas.

It is not intended to enter into a history of the numerous wars they carried on, for that would be an endless task since their traditions speak of little else than war. Suffice it to say that there was "trouble" from Southern California to Texas [to the south] of them (for there were numerous settlements along this line by this time), misunderstandings to the north [of them] with the Utes, Pueblos, & Navajos—all this varied & enlivened with feuds among themselves. These bitter internecine struggles, as well as those with their neighbors, rendered the practice of polygamy still more popular, among a people who taught their youth that the chief end of "The Men" was to gamble & to fight, & that by nature's laws they were the great hunters & mankind was their game. Thus for thousands of miles, & continued through hundreds of years, did they commit their depredations till the cry "Apache!" created terror & dismay throughout the length & breadth of a territory equal in extent to six hundred thousand square miles or one-fifth the area of the United States. Their very name became the synonym of all that is cruel, heartless, relentless, & treacherous. There are abundant evidences of their visits into Mexico hundreds of miles below the international line— ruins pointed out by the natives, which mark the spots where these wild guerillas did their deadly work so long ago that the records of them have become only traditions.

Apache Character

Gatewood has a very revealing comment when he compares fighting Apaches and working with them:

> For some years past, army officers have been detailed as agents, or for the purpose of helping them in their farming & other peaceful pursuits, or protecting them in their rights entailing considerable labor & hardship, all for their benefit, yet that duty is more dangerous than following them on the war path.

His comment is revealing not by what he says but by how little he expands upon it. During his entire tenure with the Apaches, he walked a tightrope. He commanded them, he ruled them, yet he had to find a way not to be their oppressor, not to be their conqueror. Rather, he had to win their respect. To do this, he had to know and understand the people known as Apache. Gatewood took this task seriously, and that makes his views valuable today.

Gatewood was aide-de-camp to Gen. Nelson Miles on June 1, 1887, when the Apache Kid (Has-kay-bay-nay-ntayl) and several other Apache scouts, after being AWOL and on a drunken spree that resulted in murder, returned to San Carlos to surrender.[31] When Capt. Francis E. Pierce (First U.S. Infantry), the current military agent at the agency, ordered them to dismount and surrender their weapons, other Apaches opened fire before they could be arrested.[32] German-born chief of scouts Al Sieber, who had a long career in the Southwest, was crippled in the foot by the fusillade.[33] The Kid and his companions fled. Miles considered the outbreak serious, and he and Gatewood traveled from Los Angeles to San Carlos to investigate. Gatewood knew the Kid personally, as he had spent two tours of duty with Company A, Apache scouts, from June 23 to December 22, 1882, and from August 1, 1883, to July 31, 1884.[34]

What has been written so far is, in substance, what these people say of themselves, & from the writer's eight years' experience among them, he is prepared to believe whatever they choose to allege against themselves, & more too, & yet to give them credit for all their good qualities, some of which may be developed as we go along. A catalogue of good & bad might be given here & so end the chapter, but that would be more tiresome than what has gone before. However, for fear it may be forgotten,

it is just as well to mention now that gratitude, as Webster defines it, can scarcely be regarded as a prominent feature in the general make-up of the Apache character. An obligation [on the other hand] is duly recognized & also duly discharged, which discharge puts the parties on the same footing as before the obligation. A favor, or an injury, receives its proper return, whether fancied or real.

For some years past, army officers have been detailed as agents, or for the purpose of helping [the Apaches] in their farming & other peaceful pursuits, or protecting them in their rights entailing considerable labor & hardship, all for their benefit, & yet that duty is more dangerous than following them on the war path. Several [officers] have lost their lives & many have made narrow escapes. In June 1887, [the Apache] Kid & his followers tried to kill an officer who was their agent at the time, & who did everything in his power for their welfare, even to the extent of buying them merchandise & groceries with his own money. That officer was Captain F. E. Pierce of the First [U.S.] Infantry. At that time, they succeeded in wounding Al Sieber, an old government scout who has been their friend for well nigh twenty years. They knew perfectly well that these two men always dealt fairly & justly by them, & yet they did their best to murder them.

As an example of the recognition of an obligation: In 1878, near Fort Apache, lived a petty White Mountain chief named Petone.[35] He was a pretty "hard citizen," & had a bad reputation among his people, & our people too for that matter. Threatened with a severe attack of pneumonia, he lost all faith in the "medicine men" of his band, & came to the post to be treated by the army surgeon. He was placed in the hospital, & in the course of time was cured. In bidding good-bye to the surgeon, he said, "I have no money, no horse, no gun, in fact, nothing to pay you with. I want to discharge my debt to you, in some way, so if you have an enemy around this post that you want to get rid of, lend me your gun & I'll do the job for you." The surgeon declined his amiable offer, with an expression of horror on his face. Whether Petone ever paid him for his services, I do not know.[36]

Apache Scouts

Oftentimes the question is raised: Why would someone serve in the army of their enemy? Gatewood was in a position to know.

The hatred, which each tribe bears to all the others, & which was engendered at their separation after the great battle referred to, has not to this day been materially lessened.[37] This bitter hatred thus engendered has been the trump card in the hands of the white man.[38] After the Civil War, the old policy of enlisting allies from the enemies of those who took to the war path, which was a powerful factor in the subjugation of the aborigines in the Atlantic states in the olden time & in the West afterward, was revived by the military in their operations against the Apaches, & with considerable success. When the San Carlos tribe "broke out" some years ago, the White Mountains aided the troops in effectually subduing them. And so with the others.

The Chiricahuas under the leadership of Cochise, & the Warm Springs under Mangas Coloradas, did, some forty years ago, form an alliance, which made them virtually one tribe after the deaths of these two chiefs.[39] At the time this coalition was formed, they could muster over a thousand warriors, & at no time in their history, probably, had their depredations been carried on with more energy & persistence. At the present time Naiche & Mangus, sons of the above-named chiefs, respectively, can scarcely count one hundred capable of bearing arms, & they are in captivity in far-off Alabama.[40] Such figures need no comment.

The others of late years have increased in numbers though not very rapidly.

They seemed to take turn about in annual eruptions, it seldom happening that more than one tribe raided the white settlements at one time. And if they did, each went out independent of the other.[41] It therefore happened that the scouts of one year would be turning the Territory topsy-turvy the next, & the officer commanding a company would be pursuing a party of ex-scouts with an assortment of ex-hostiles. They could be relied on provided due care was taken to make enlistments from those who had old scores to settle with the renegades. These could generally be found by anyone who had some idea of the many feuds that exist among them. These feuds, by the way, extend to bands of the same tribe & even exist among families of the same band. It should be explained that each tribe is divided into a number of what are called "bands" (a collection of two or more families) under a nominal chief.

In addition to giving individuals a chance for revenge, there were the further inducements of pay, rations, & clothing, furnished by the

Company A of Apache Scouts (White Mountains). Gatewood commanded
Company A from 1878 until his release from Indian duty in 1885. Courtesy:
Arizona Historical Society/Tucson, AHS #19761.

government the same as received by the enlisted men in the U.S. Regular Army; & further again, in case of defeat, they had these same regulars to fall back on.[42] However much this policy may be criticized, & mistakes of enlistments in several instances dilated upon, in the main, it rendered the task of the troops easier, & God knows it was bad enough at best. For several years preceding the surrender of Geronimo's band, however, the service of the scouts was not so efficient generally. This arose from many causes, among which may be mentioned: the danger to the scout himself from ranchers who could not distinguish him from a hostile, for the country had become comparatively thickly settled by whites & Mexicans who couldn't tell a scout from a hostile, thus rendering it necessary that at least one white man should accompany a reconnoitering party if it went far from the column or camp of the troops, to prevent the scouts from being fired at.[43] [This] interfered with their usefulness in finding trails off some distance in rough mountains from the line of march.

No white man [who] was ever in the service, or employment, of the United States, except the few who had been practically trained & educated by the Indians from their youth, can keep pace with an Apache on foot when he is in a hurry, especially in a mountainous country. Even a "govern-mule," a class of animals so celebrated in the annals of our army, had to be put on his mettle, when the marches were long & continued for weeks & even months, as they often were. "Played out" government mules were very common in the Southwest in those days, but "played out" Apaches were very few. Again, even the best & most energetic among the men had acquired many of the wants of the white man, such as coffee, sugar, flour, clothing, &c, which have now become almost necessities. The sequel will show the amount of farming & stock raising they did in order to purchase them. If this class enlisted, it was for pay, & an opportunity to rest from labor, though the most industrious would scarcely kill themselves with working. Then there were "professional scouts," about on par with "professional jurors" among us—they were called "coffee-coolers." In fact, they were losing their old-time independent martial spirit, except the White Mountains who as a rule were the most efficient trailers & the bravest fighters. It was scarcely possible for an enemy on land to cause more than delay by attempts to cover his tracks. If he jumped from rock to rock barefooted so as to leave no particle of the sole of his moccasin behind him, he was sure to knock off the heads of dry blades of grass, disturb the branches of trees or brush, turn the rock the least bit, or leave behind him some other sign which his pursuers' keen eyes would detect. The old "dodge" of proceeding up or down a creek would cause little trouble. They could soon discover which direction was taken, & while assuring themselves there had been no "doubling" on the tracks & no hiding along the banks, it was only necessary to watch where the footprints came out of the water.

It often happened that a trail almost the size of a wagon road would gradually lessen to two or three tracks, & they take different directions so that there was only one left that was going in the general direction indicated by the large trail. Many an old campaigner has been surprised to find fifteen or twenty broken down horses or even more, & then "nothing more."

Where did they go? Up in the air apparently. No, some fifteen miles back on the "wagon road," perhaps, they began, one by one, leaving the main body, & going to some place of rendezvous agreed upon, which may be to any point of the compass from the place where the last disappears; or they may intend to break up into small parties & act separately; or—who could tell what a body of Chiricahuas would be likely to do? Several times when the writer commanded the scouts (not White Mountains) of a column that found itself on such a "vanishing point," & before he learned to be on the lookout for a decrease in the number of footprints, he was "hauled over the coals" for knowing nothing about such work, & for having such a lot of good-for-nothing tramps with him. "Ask your Indians where the hostiles are?" When asked, the answer was, "No sabe," with shrugs of the shoulder. "Well, where do you think they are?" "I can't say, Sir." Then mortification set in all around, for we had obliterated the main trail with our horses & pack mules. There was nothing to do, however, but to march back & follow the greatest number of hostiles which could be found to go in any one general direction, which we did, the while engaging in deep reflection.

Now, this never happened, so far as I know, with White Mountains in advance. On several occasions, they gave dire notice that this trick was being played, & while the column either halted or marched slowly ahead, they followed the several tracks nearest, & from signs & indications & their own judgment, soon announced the direction the main body would take. In every instance they were right. But when they became sulky, they would cross a [well-traveled] turnpike, if such a thing were in the country, & swear they didn't see it. So, it is easy to see that they had to be humored somewhat.

Reservation Corruption and Discontent

The problems on the reservation were real. After becoming military commandant of the White Mountain Indian Reservation in 1882, Gatewood found himself in a position to observe the problems his wards faced. By the time of his appointment he had been working closely with Apache scouts for almost three years. He understood them, respected them, trusted them, and was sympathetic to their plight.

Although Gatewood moves quickly through his knowledge of the Indian situation, he does take the time to point out the corruption that he believes undermines the reservation system. His views are strong and hit the mark. He refuses to ignore the "Indian Ring," a subject most treated with "kid gloves" in the nineteenth century.[44] An article in the October 24, 1882, *Arizona Star* had this to say:

> Fraud, peculation, conspiracy, larceny, plots, and counterplots seem to be the rule of action on this reservation [San Carlos]. The grand jury little thought when they began this investigation [on Indian agent J. C. Tiffany's tenure] that they were about to open a Pandora's box of iniquities seldom surpassed in the annals of crime.
>
> With the immense power wielded by the Indian agent, almost any crime is possible. There seems to be no check upon his conduct. In collusion with the storekeeper and chief clerk, rations can be issued *ad libitum* for which the government must pay, while the proceeds pass into the capacious pocket of the agent. . . .
>
> Government contractors, in collusion with Agent Tiffany, get receipts for large amounts of supplies never furnished, and the profit is divided mutually and a general spoliation of the United States Treasury is thus effected. While six hundred Indians are off on passes, their rations are counted and turned in to the mutual aid association consisting of Tiffany and his *confreres*.[45]

Hitherto, it may strike the reader that this record contains little to the credit of the red man & as little to the discredit of the white. It may

not therefore be uninteresting, or out of place, to insert a few pages of the experiences of the followers of Geronimo & of others of the same nation, by way of variation.

Soon after the formation of the alliance between Cochise & Mangas Coloradas, already referred to, they inaugurated predatory warfare on a larger scale than had ever been attempted before, thus increasing, if possible, the terror & alarm of the settlers who were exposed to their visitations. This lasted for some years, until the Mexican government gave them a reservation & induced them to agree to remain on it for a while. The new departure, however, was not a success, for the Mexicans did not deal out rations & supplies, generally, with a liberal hand. The land on which they were induced to settle produced plenty of cactus & some water, but required tilling & imagination to add to the above products. Now, this condition of things did not suit the wards of our neighboring republic, for they did not know how to labor & at that time did not propose to learn. Consequently, for want of occupation & the wherewithal to live upon cactus & water as a steady diet, the old wandering, fighting life was resumed without regard to the imaginary line between the two republics, and with the usual result to the people on both sides. The boundary line was rather an assistance, for they were aware of the fact that the troops of neither nation dared to follow them into the territory of the other without giving offence or running the risk of bringing about international complications. It was not till 1882 that by treaty, both sides were allowed to pursue them into the other's country.[46]

About 1870, if I am not mistaken, our government tried its hand at granting reservations, & after much "powwowing" & smoking of the pipe of peace, the Chiricahuas agreed to settle in Sulphur Spring Valley, Arizona Territory, & the Warm Springs at Ojo Caliente, New Mexico.[47] These places were claimed by each as their old homes, & great satisfaction was expressed by all parties concerned. To carry out its promises, the government established agencies, erected the necessary buildings— quarters for agents & employees, corrals, shops, storehouses, &c—and shipped immense quantities of provisions, farming implements—in fact, all things necessary for the prosperity of the people, including missionaries, a goodly store of [religious] tracts, Bibles, & school books, &c. It did seem that there would be an end at last to Apache atrocities, for [they had] all they could need & more too (there were threshing

& sewing machines, & other things they could not use, which were appropriated to the use & benefit of the whites). Why should they not live up to their promises of good behavior?

They did so for several years, until supplies began to diminish perceptibly. Like an engineer who cuts a canal through a dry desert of sand, & does not allow for seepage & evaporation in regulating his supply of water, the government failed to appreciate leakage & evaporation & likewise "stickage" [sic] in the formation of its channel of supply. Uncle Sam was exceedingly liberal in his donations to these people, but his servants had an awful capacity for absorption. In other words, Uncle Sam had to satisfy the rapacity of the celebrated Indian Ring, [as well as] individual officials, before the beneficiary was allowed to receive anything. It would have required the surplus & the sinking fund of the treasury combined to have sated the Ring & its adherents for even a short time. When the Indian received his share, he found it to be not worth having. Ranchers, teamsters, employees, miners, cowboys, & others wore the Indians' clothes, slept in his blankets, & ate his rations, & the Indians knew it as well as they.

Ranches were stocked with cattle that were intended to be issued as beef at the agencies. White farmers near the reservations tilled the soil, chopped & hauled their wood, cooked their food, & so on, largely at the expense of the Indians. All this was done openly, so that the latter knew it well. What wonder then that when they got hungry, they considered it but just & right to appropriate a stray steer which they had good reason to believe belonged to themselves? Of course, the cry of "outrages by the red fiends" was set up by the white innocents, & trouble began again, & the old story was repeated. The blame was all laid on the Apaches, & no one thought of finding fault with the administration of Apache affairs; or if thought of at all, there were too many men profiting by it for any protest to be made, until after the Indian Ring was broken.

In the meantime, the other tribes had been gathered together on the San Carlos [Indian] Reservation, & the same experience was gone through by them.[48] It was either starve or steal with all of them, & they preferred not to starve.

[A short while] later, I saw those at San Carlos exhibit a wonderful patience, when they had nothing to eat & were dying in great numbers from malarial fever. It was an unusually dry & hot summer & the water in the Gila River was unfit for use on account of the presence of so much alkali in it. One could smell it hundreds of yards from the river bed. So desperate did they finally become after weeks of waiting for the off-timed promised rations, that a delegation of chiefs waited on the agent &, calling attention to their suffering through their faith in his word, said, "Give us the food that is ours, or we shall go among the white settlements & take what we need, without regard to [the] consequences. It is better to die fighting, than starve or become victims to malaria."

The situation was grave, & was brought about indirectly by fraud in causing delay in awarding the contracts for supplies, & consequently of the delivery of them. The agent was not altogether to blame in this instance, but he was under the domination of the Ring. He was a smooth, wizened, spectacled little old man, [who] always said grace before meals.[49] [He] held religious services every Sabbath in the school house to as many adults as could be induced to attend, & to as many children as the police could catch & herd into the school house; [he] really tried to issue more than half rations to his protégés & claimed great credit for his endeavors in their behalf. On meeting anyone entitled to consideration, [the agent] would "wash his hands with invisible soap in imperceptible water." [This was his] way of showing his great pleasure at forming the acquaintance of "a gentleman so well able to understand my efforts on behalf of the poor benighted heathen."[50]

[By 1878] what had been stolen from the previous year's allowance would have sustained the Indians for months & obviated the necessity of the present trouble. The agent became alarmed, & that night made his way to the nearest military post, Fort Thomas, thirty-five miles up the Gila River. His flight, when it became known to the Indians, increased their determination to get food wherever it was to be found, & about five hundred warriors were getting ready to put their threats into execution. This was reported to the Military Commander of the Department, General O. B. Willcox, who immediately ordered rations sent from Fort Thomas. Runners to all their camps carried the news that the soldiers were bringing them provisions, which would be issued on arrival at the agency, & the heads of families should come & get their shares. Never were tidings more welcome than these to a starving people, for they did not want to engage in war, [to which] necessity would have compelled them.

The military continued to feed them till the Interior Department was prepared to take them in hand again after quiet was restored. This

An Apache camp. Definite customs were observed when approaching an Apache ramada and entering a dwelling. The artwork is based upon a photo taken by A. Frank Randall, *Harper's Weekly*, April 17, 1886. From the author's collection.

was in 1878. The agency & all connected with it became so corrupt that even the powerful Indian Ring could not prevent the detail of an army officer as agent the next year. This pleased the Indians, for they got their full rations; but the contractors' consternation would not express their feelings, for they knew Major A. R. Chaffee, then of the Sixth [U.S.] Cavalry, who was to assume control.[51]

The agent for the beef provider is said to have traveled thirty-five miles in two hours, in consequence of having changed the weights of the cattle scales. He didn't fancy residence in the "calaboose." The flour men had engaged under bonds to deliver hundreds of thousands of pounds below the market price; & they delivered & were bankrupted. In a word, you never saw such a scatteration of thieves in all your life—& you never saw happier Indians.

[But] outbreaks brought money into the country, or rather into the hands of certain classes.[52] Soon after the other tribes were placed on the San Carlos [Indian] Reservation, it [was] very probable that the Apaches might have been made peaceable, not to say self-supporting, by a strong, just, & honest administration of their affairs. But the more devilment they could be made to kick up, the more money there was in it for all hands. Every outbreak required unusual expenditures by the War Department in moving troops & purchasing supplies, & furnished reasons for calling for more from the Interior Department. The greater the number of soldiers in the territory, the more money to be gotten out of the U.S., for the law required supplies to be bought in the market nearest the place where they were to be used. Those not living in towns had to be armed, & perhaps had to abandon their places & go to the towns for safety. The large cattle owner could afford to lose a few steers from his herds, if the honest settler might be prevented from taking up as a homestead a spring & one hundred sixty acres of land around it, on the immense range of public land that he claimed. It is hardly necessary to state that the barrooms flourished, for they were the council chambers of those who proposed to "clean out the varmints," but never carried their plans to the extent of "cleaning out." However, this is an old story & it is hardly worthwhile to dwell on it here. The Indians were given their reservations, but, [dear] reader, it is one thing to place them thereon & quite another to keep them there.

With occasional intervals of rest, the old-time spirit of war in these people, encouraged by certain whites, was kept alive in the breast of the braves, & the deeds of the forefathers were emulated with varying success. Except the alliance above referred to, each tribe made things lively on its own hook without regard to the doings of the others. Even when they were on their reservations, they were not peaceable. The most bitter feuds existed between families, bands, tribes & clans, & were handed down from one generation to the other. When not otherwise engaged, they would proceed to get drunk on a vile compound of their own manufacture & fight out their hereditary quarrels in a deadly manner. They called this [fiery drink] "tiswin."[53] [It] was made by soaking corn or barley until the grain had sprouted, then it was "mashed" in plenty of water, boiled to a certain consistency, allowed to cool until fermentation had begun, & drunk in large quantities after a fast of at least twenty-four hours. Pretty soon "Rome howled" & the "stiffs" were buried among the rocks. The wrongs of a great-grandfather had been avenged & the new generation had a fresh feud to start with. These drunks occasioned trouble not only to the agent & his police, but now & then their hearts would get bad against the whites &, instigated by the squaws, would sally forth among the settlers & commit the usual atrocities.

This state of affairs continued, requiring a great deal of hard work from the regular army with scarcely commensurate credit, until in 1880 the San Carlos [Indian] Reservation was made the house of all the Apaches, except the Lipans, Mescaleros, & Jicarillas with whom this sketch has no more to do. Here were gathered about five thousand men, women, & children, consisting of Chiricahuas, Warm Springs, Coyoteros, Arivaipas, Tontos, Yumas, & Mojaves. The first two named were what was left of the allies under Cochise & Mangas Coloradas, & were virtually one tribe. The last two [Yumas and Mojaves] in a peaceable way might be counted as one, [but remember, they were not Apaches]. Each hated all the others for reasons already stated. Unhappy the agent who tried to regulate that mob when the squaws "set up" the tiswin by the camp-kettle-full. Many campaigns against them were necessary, & it would be rather tedious to even mention them.

Military Commandant of the White Mountains

Willcox's tenure in Arizona was assured of its end when Geronimo, Naiche, and other Apaches raided the San Carlos Indian Reservation in April 1882. Three months later Gen. George Crook was ordered to re-place Willcox as commander of the Department of Arizona—he would not assume command until September 4, 1882.[54] Upon his arrival in the Southwest, the general toured the reservations to get an idea how bad the situation was. Shortly after meeting with the natives, he issued General Orders No. 43, which read in part: "The commanding general . . . re-grets to say that he finds among them [the Apaches] a general feeling of distrust and want of confidence in the whites, especially the soldiery."[55] Crook knew that the only way he could bring peace to the Southwest was by ending the mismanagement of the Apaches. No easy task, and he chose his subordinates with care.

Crook selected Capt. Emmet Crawford (Third U.S. Cavalry) and Gatewood as military commandants of the San Carlos and White Moun-tain Indian Reservations, respectively.[56] Both would report directly to Crook. Lt. Britton Davis (Third U.S. Cavalry), who had only arrived in Arizona in May, was assigned to assist Crawford on the reservation.[57] Becoming military Indian agents created a bond between Gatewood and Davis that would last throughout their lives. Of the three, only Gatewood knew anything about Apaches at this time.[58]

Gatewood was a perfect choice for his assignment. Not only did he understand the Apaches but he also enjoyed their company, as his words testify. His memories of the White Mountains also give a good picture of Gatewood himself. Although born a Southerner, he was able to step beyond racial prejudice and deal with the Apaches as people.

Crawford, Davis, and Gatewood accompanied Crook on his tour of the native villages, which began when he left his headquarters at Whipple Barracks on September 11. The general met with both Indians who were still "openly in hostility, and those who had not yet broken from the Reservation."[59] The councils took place near Fort Apache, in the cañon of Black River, in the Natanes Mountains, and on the San Carlos Indian Reservation.

A few days before Crook took command of the department, Philip P. Wilcox became the new Indian agent. Although Agent Tiffany had resigned on June 30, 1882, Wilcox did not assume the position until September 1. Wilcox told Crook that he "knew nothing about Indians."[60] A political appointee, "he was outspoken in his detestation of his job and his contempt for the Indians," Britton Davis wrote, and "had taken the position . . . only because of the salary."[61] Wilcox would prove to be a thorn in the military's side, as he did everything within his power to disrupt Crawford and Gatewood's efforts to improve the situation on the reservation.

In 1881–82 the White Mountains, or a part of the Coyoteros, in the north, & the Chiricahuas & Warm Springs in the south had been keeping up their warfare in an energetic manner; the other tribes, Tontos, San Carlos, Yumas, & Mojaves, remaining at peace on the reservation & furnishing scouts to the military.

In September of [1882], Gen. George Crook, having assumed command of the Department of Arizona, made a journey through the Apache country for the purpose of inspection & observation. While on his way to the San Carlos Agency from the north, near Fort Apache, he had an interview with the principal chiefs of the White Mountains who had committed no depredations for some months past, but had been hiding in the mountains ready for more war or for peace, whichever was deemed best for their interest.

The result of this consultation [was that] the Coyoteros, or White Mountains, [who] had just come in from the warpath, agreed that if allowed to occupy their old country, the northern end of the reservation, in which Fort Apache is situated, & given aid in farming implements, seed, & food enough to carry them through until they could gather their crops, they would ask nothing more of the government.[62] Forgiveness for past offences was granted, the condition being that they should at once return to their farms & by such aid as the military could give them, should rely on their own efforts for sustenance after the harvest of the first crop. They were joined by many of their kindred who had been moved to the Gila Valley near the Agency, some years before, making a total of about sixteen hundred souls, or a little less than one-third of the whole. The other tribes living in the southern part of the reservation numbered about thirty-four hundred. Captain Emmet Crawford, Third [U.S.] Cavalry, who was afterwards killed in Mexico, & who had no superior in the army in the ability to manage & control such a heterogeneous collection of savages, was assigned to duty at San Carlos.[63] General Crook placed the writer in charge of affairs at Fort Apache, near which post dwelt the Coyoteros with whom [the] general had made the above-mentioned agreement. [My assignment was to] check the consumption of tiswin, preserve the peace among them, & see that they went to work with a view to making them self-supporting. They were given to understand by General Crook that this authority was delegated by him, & the orders of the subaltern to them were those of himself, so that they fully recognized & understood my legal status.[64]

Orders were issued to the effect that all male Indians capable of bearing arms should assemble at the San Carlos Agency, to meet the new department commander, whom they had known some ten years before. Some eight hundred or more answered this call, & they presented a picturesque sight, clad as they were in all the colors of the rainbow & in all imaginable costumes from a breechclout to a stovepipe hat. The names, ages, & general descriptions of each one were entered in a book, & each was required to wear on his person a little brass tag with a letter stamped on it to designate the band he belonged to, & a numeral to show his number in the band. When the system was completed, it was easy to spot the absentees.[65] Failure to comply with this order would be punished by confinement in the "calaboose." So every morning for some days, these dusky warriors were squatted on the grounds in triple lines forming a sort of hollow square, each tribe to itself & the chiefs of each band on its right. Then Captain Crawford would count them & inspect their tags.

During the count one fine September morning, a cloud of dust up the valley of the San Carlos announced the approach of the White Mountains, who had agreed to return to the ways of peace. Suddenly horsemen began to appear on the mesa about the distance of a mile, marching in columns like cavalry. Then, by a "left-front-into-line" movement, a skirmish line of about sixty warriors was thrown across the mesa, or table land, their ponies in excellent condition, & the bright barrels of their rifles glistening in the sunshine. All had their belts full of ammunition & many of them had two belts around their waists. It was evident that their naturally suspicious nature prompted them to be ready for any emergency, for fun or for fight, as circumstances dictated. As they slowly advanced, uneasiness was plainly depicted on the swarthy countenances of the mob of their brethren who watched their approach, & doubtless the latter would have taken to their heels but for the presence of a troop of cavalry & the assurance of General Crook that the newcomers were on a peaceful errand.

[When they] arrived at about a quarter of a mile from the place where the counting was in progress, they halted, & their leader rode to the front. Being a part of [the] tribe assigned to my charge, I went out to meet their chief & soon recognized the features of Alchesay, virtual, tho' not nominal, head of the largest band of White Mountains. Upon shaking hands & grunting a mutual "An-zhoo" ("Good"), their form of salutation, he dismounted & inquired for the general. He was a fine specimen of manhood. Straight as an arrow, six feet in height, about twenty-eight years old, [he was] slender in build though muscular. [Alchesay had the] piercing black eye[s] & the high cheek bones & heavy jaw of his race. Graceful in all his movements, [he was] noted for his powers of endurance, his fleetness of foot, his skill as a hunter, & his bravery in battle. Such was the leader of this small party that looked with scorn & contempt upon the rest of the Apache nation. Upon provocation or encouragement, [he] would not have hesitated to attack the vastly superior numbers there assembled. Alchesay & some of the principal men went forward & met the department commander.

In the meantime, after a few words of explanation, the others dismounted & ranged themselves in line to be counted & have their names entered in a book. On their return to the neighborhood of Fort Apache, tags were to be issued & full descriptions recorded. All of them had served as scouts at one time or another under my command, & Alchesay had been first sergeant of my company. Consequently, there was much hand-shaking & not a little joking. For instance: "Hello, Baychen-daysen (Long Nose), your nose has grown since we saw you last."[66] "Ah! The billy-goat has kept himself thin so that he can run fast & far when the wolves get after his sheep." (They regard themselves as wolves, coyotes—coyotero, man-wolf—& the Yumas & Mojaves, a company of whom they knew I commanded in the [recent] campaign against them, as sheep.[67] Also, it was the custom of sheep owners to have a number of goats with their herds to lead the way & protect the sheep.) "Say, old goat, did you wear a bell so that your sheep could follow you?" "Ba-a-a." "Hold your head up, now that you are among men once more," & so on. All this was received with bursts of laughter & great good humor, & return of these compliments in kind only added to the general good feeling. The Chiricahuas were undoubtedly the best fighters in their way of the whole "Noo-tah-hah" nation—they had had more experience & in that experience alone lay their superiority over the present generation of Coyoteros. All others were much inferior to both; & this

Alchesay, chieftain of the White Mountain Apaches. Gatewood worked
closely with Alchesay, both in the field and during his service as military
commandant of the White Mountain Indian Reservation. Their close working relationship led to friendship. Photograph by Markey & Mytton, Fort
Grant, Arizona. Courtesy: Arizona Historical Society/Tucson, AHS #22752.

relative standing was appreciated & recognized by all the tribes, the Yumas & Mojaves as warriors being at the foot of the class.

The delicately sarcastic allusions to "billy goat" & "sheep" may be appreciated the better when it is considered that for several years my company had been enlisted entirely from Coyoteros, & the officer commanding was always considered a "Nantan," or chief, among them.[68] To hold such [a] position was an honor & a compliment to the officer; but to descend to a similar one among the Yumas & Mojaves was a disgrace, in their eyes, & perhaps a punishment. The humblest Coyotero would have disdained the offer of chieftainship of the Yuma & Mojave nations combined. It was as if the commander of Napoleon's old guard had been forced to lead a mob of France's enemies that would stampede at the first shot. While stationed with my "sheep" at Fort Apache, the [White Mountain] women, & even the children, living near there, whenever they got a chance, would point "the finger of scorn" [at] the writer & call out, "Yu-u-ma!" [&] "Moja-a-ve!" with a most exasperating sneer.

One old fellow, called Brigham, because he had eleven wives & thirty-eight children, said, "You have fallen under the displeasure of the 'Nantan Enchaw' (big chief, meaning the General), & your punishment is to be a Yuma. Leave the soldiers & Yumas & live with us. You shall have my favorite daughter for ten horses, saddles & bridles, or their equivalent in money, guns, blankets, &c." Due acknowledgments of the intended kindness were made, but the offer was not considered sufficient inducement to resign a commission in the regular army.[69]

After the Court of Justice had been established, there were no more allusions to former degradation.[70] Human nature is the same the world over. When a man is down, everybody gives him a kick, but let him get up, & he is given a lift.

The list of names having been finished & the treaty of peace ratified, the party [of White Mountains] went into camp down in the river bottom several miles from the agency. Like the others, they came & took their places to be counted & inspected—to attend a sort of roll call, in fact. They sat with their backs to the other tribes to show their contempt for & their indifference to the whole assemblage. During the few days they remained there, the general's plan was fully explained to them & agreed to, [&] they were allowed to return to their farms.

[The writer would] assume general control of them, & in fact exercise the functions of judge, jury, sheriff, & legislature in sort of "a home rule" sense. He was instructed to take all proper & legal steps necessary to preserve the peace, prevent the manufacture & consumption of tiswin, [&] encourage & aid them in agricultural & other peaceful pursuits—in other words, to keep them quiet & make them self-supporting.

Now, it is one thing to put an Indian on his reservation, & quite another to keep him there. However, with these people, the task imposed was not so difficult as it was with the Chiricahuas. Still, as time went on & difficulties arose to be overcome, it was sufficient to cause a certain second lieutenant to spend many a wakeful hour in good hard thinking, for, though allowed to exercise very considerable power & authority, yet he was held responsible for the result. An outbreak, & down would go the row of bricks & he would be the one to assume the horizontal position.

In a few weeks the different bands [under the writer's control] had selected their farms & grazing lands in the fertile valleys of White River & its tributaries, scattered over an area about eighty miles long east & west, by about thirty-five miles wide north & south, with Fort Apache situated on White River in the eastern part of it, the whole reservation being eighty miles square.[71] The squaws & children & many of the bucks set to work clearing off lands to be planted in the spring, & laying out & digging irrigating ditches. There was a great scarcity of hoes, shovels, picks, &c, although the large stone-house at the agency was filled with just [these] things. But the agent objected to so many Indians moving away from the neighborhood of his son-in-law's trading store, & declined to give them their share of what the Government had provided. After much persuasion & the expenditure of lots of red-tape & stationary, the agent kindly consented to give them one wagon out of the seven to which they were entitled, & other things in about the same proportion. They were glad to get even this small help, & went to work with a will. Miles of ditches were dug with butcher knives & sharpened sticks by those who were not lucky enough to be the recipients of the agent's bounty, or were too poor to purchase the tools for themselves. They had to travel from fifty to seventy-five miles to the agency to receive their meager rations once a week. With these short rations & with acorns, juniper berries, roots, & mescal (a species of Yucca), they managed to live & labor thru' the winter & spring, until they were rewarded with a plentiful harvest of corn, melons, & pumpkins.[72] From that time, they have been practically independent of government provisions.

The new governor had been inaugurated without ceremony other than dismounting from his mule.[73] [His] first duty was the allotment of lands to the various heads of families. Then [he] organized a kind of police court, with common law & equity sides, & made preparations for dealing out justice to all comers. It was a combination of the judicial, the legislative, & the executive, all in one. There was no right of appeal[;] it was a court of first & last resort. Fifty picked braves were enlisted as scouts, fed, clothed, & paid by the United States, with its quota of non-commissioned officers on the basis of a troop of cavalry. This body constituted the police necessary to keep order & enforce the mandates of the court. Each village had a certain proportion of these policemen among them, & a detachment of ten or twelve was kept at the post to guard the prisoners that time would bring. [They also were to] act as couriers when necessary. There was a secret service force [as well], composed of those who were willing to report the shortcomings of their neighbors, for a consideration. In this respect, women & even children were often employed.[74] They were of great value particularly in detecting & arresting the manufacturers of "tiswin" & those who committed petty offences. Crimes such as horse stealing & the taking of life interested the whole people, & the guilty could barely hope to escape. But it puzzled them how the nantan could know so much of what was going on in & around their villages. This had a good effect, for it often caused an offender to give himself up & turn state's evidence on his companions.

The chief of a band was recognized as such only for police purposes. He & the detachment of scouts quartered in his village were held responsible for the good conduct of the band, & failure on their part to maintain order was liable to [bring] punishment [down on them]. Resistance to arrest, or refusal to appear before the tribunal when summoned, were offences to be dealt with severely.

The office of chief of scouts was filled by a white man who had had considerable experience among Indians. His duties were those of a bailiff, jailer, & general assistant, as well as [a] clerk. In the execution of his various offices, he was aided considerably by the interpreters. There was no white man or red either in all the country who could interpret reliably from Indian to English. So we had to have an English-Spanish interpreter & a Spanish-Indian one. This arrangement was rather slow & tedious at times, but it was the best that could be made. The nantan spoke & understood the Apache dialect somewhat but not to an extent that would always insure accuracy of interpretation, especially in important matters. As it was, even with great care, misunderstandings arose frequently, sometimes leading to serious complications, & again with ridiculous results.

The English-Spanish expert was a native of Texas, but bore in his lineaments & disposition unmistakable evidence of Irish extraction. He had been a soldier in the regular [army] & had served on the frontier from Kansas to Arizona, before the writer was born, & left the military service soon after the [Civil] War. Drifting into Arizona, he became cowboy, farmer, mail rider, sheep-herder (as they call it), guide—whatever occupation was offered. He was most contented when he could get a "job" at a military post, especially when there were some old soldier comrades still in the service, as happened at Fort Apache, & he could be pretty sure of respectful listeners to his yarns of "the old army." He took no interest whatever in anything that happened since '65, except he conceded the superiority of the breach-loader & the Colt's revolver, & he took good care to keep his own in good order. Though well along in years & bearing on his body many evidences of the battles in which he had participated, he was quite active & energetic, & like all old soldiers, faithful to his employers. I have heard it said of him that "he would fight a buzz saw." "Old Jack" [John Conley], as we called him, represented a type of old-time frontiersman that is fast passing away.[75]

Our professor of Spanish & Indian was no less a character in his way. He was a Mexican, a native of the state of Sonora, Mexico. When quite a youth he was captured by the Apaches in one of their raids into Sonora, grew up among them, married a White Mountain squaw & identified himself with a band of that tribe of which the celebrated Diablo was chief.[76] At the time I speak of, he had spent some thirty years with the Apaches &, though he had often visited his relatives in Mexico, could never be induced to remain with them. Being sharp, shrewd, bold, reckless, & vindictive, in his younger days he exerted great influence among the people of his adoption & doubtless took part in many a horse-stealing expedition, if rumor might be credited. But finding that he could always command a fair salary as interpreter in later years, he reformed & set about making himself useful to the military. His services have been valuable, & Severiano, for such was his name, earned every dollar of his pay.[77] He was excitable, nervous, with a lively imagination

& [a] rather poetic temperament, & consequently had considerable oratorical ability. He was in his glory when a high official, such as the department commander, used him as a channel of communication with the assembled braves. On these important occasions, he could not interpret while sitting—he must be on his feet &, with bare-heart of attitude suitable to the occasion, could launch forth fiery threats or denunciations in the most terrible manner, or could utter pacific overtures with a most winning grace. Drawing a salary of one hundred dollars a month, as interpreter, he never lost a chance [to assist] his paymaster.[78]

Such were the interpreters—Old Jack & Severiano—as unlike as two mortals could be. They had one trait in common, however—each spoke his native language without regard to the rules of its grammar. Jack let his English take care of itself, while he insisted on the use of pure Castilian as between himself & Severiano; while the latter used the present tense, indicative mood, or the past participle, or even the infinitive, of Spanish, with a freelance independence that was quite startling, but was particular in his Indian. This created some confusion at first, but they soon learned to understand each other, & in a short time, the mistakes they made were few. In narration of facts & transactions of a purely business nature, their interpretations were as faithful as could be expected, but there were times when the original aboriginal speech was not adequately set forth in English.[79]

Chapter Three

Military Commandant

Throughout this chapter Gatewood refers to himself in the third person as the "judge."[1] His description of the proceedings of his court are enlightening. Not only does he show us a glimpse of White Mountain culture, but he also shows us their strong sense of justice. Apache jurors took their task seriously—to the point of violence if need be—and at times they meted out harsh punishment.

It should be noted that during Gatewood's tenure as military agent, he and Georgia began their family. Charlie Jr. was born on January 4, 1883, at Fort Apache.[2] His early years would be spent on the frontier, and the influence must have been strong, for he eventually followed in his father's footsteps and sought a career in the military. Charlie Jr.'s importance to this story stems not from the love both his mother and father had for him but from his crusade to record his father's place in the history of the Indian wars. Although he never succeeded in publishing a book on his father's accomplishments, he laid the groundwork for others to discover his father's life. His fastidious and continuous effort to document his father's participation in the last Apache war is now housed at the Arizona Historical Society in Tucson.

If the reader will pardon further digression, the narration of a few experiences among [the White Mountains] may lead to a clearer appreciation on his part of the Apache character. The writer was brought into more intimate relations with this tribe than with any other. [They] are, next to the Chiricahuas, the fiercest & most warlike [Apaches].[3]

In the fall of '82 the White Mountains were gathered together in their country according to the above-mentioned agreement [with General Crook], & the work began. They occupied farms in the fertile valleys scattered over an area of about eight x forty miles, the whole reservation being about eighty or ninety miles square. The late Captain Emmet Crawford, Third [U.S.] Cavalry, "regulated" the two-thirds near the Main Agency at San Carlos about sixty-five miles southwest from Fort Apache.

It became necessary in carrying out instructions to organize a kind of police court for the settlement of their various quarrels, adopting methods of procedure whereby both sides could be given [an] impartial hearing & just judgment rendered. This led to the introduction of the jury system. The "nantan" (literally chief but applied to the officer who commanded & who in this case was judge), having fifty scouts to act as police, arrests of offenders were made by men of [the perpetrator's] own bands, their own juries tried them, & scouts guarded those sentenced to confinement in the "calaboose." The only white m[e]n connected with the administration being the judge & chief of scouts [John Conley].[4]

Among the many who offered advice to the new ruler of this small kingdom was old Iron Tooth [Sanchez].[5] "Nantan Bay-chen-daysen (Long nose chief), in seeking for the cause of the many rows you will have to settle," he said, "remember what I say. Go to the bottom & you'll find a woman." He pointed his index finger downwards & moved it till it struck the floor, [then he] rose & walked out of the room with very solemn mien.

In verification of his dictum to tell of the mother-in-law alone would require a volume. How she & her son-in-law never look at each other, how she can stir up strife among the wives, & finally decamp with her daughter taking all the property with her, thereby stirring up all the relatives of the husband & those of the other wives & their relatives' relatives.[6] Ah! she's a holy terror. And talk! She can lay down the law to a whole tribe at once. True, the old man, her husband, may give her a beating now & then. But she will bob up serenely during his absence, or in another place, & scatter hair & rags from her luckless victims. All around the wickiup, upsetting things right & left until it looked as if a whirlwind of the first order had struck the place. It takes a great deal of courage to try to beat her off, for interference means a general row, since she is liable to have some of her relations nearby.

Once, Corporal Deer of the scouts drew his rations for ten days, & depositing them on the ground outside of the commissary store house, motioned to his three squaws to help themselves. Now, each wife had a mother present who was bent on seeing that neither of the others got the advantage of her own daughter in the division. All went well until they came to the beans. When one squaw grabbed an extra handful, [a mother-in-law] protested. Her voice pitched in a high key, she "yanked out" a solid lock of hair. [This] secured [her] a bang on the

Sanchez (Carrizo or White Mountain Apache), also known as Metal Tooth, circa 1880. During Gatewood's tenure as military commandant of the White Mountain Indian Reservation, Sanchez was vocal and firm in his defense of the White Mountain Apaches. Courtesy: Arizona Historical Society/Tucson, AHS #4546.

side of her head with a can of yeast powder, which burst & filled the air. The mother-in-law [who] lost the yeast powder reached for [the one who] had upset the beans in the mud, & the third went in on general principles. In the meantime, the wives were not idle, & the whole six rising voice & muscle, made hair, rags, & component parts of the rations fly through the air until the attention of the whole post was attracted. It is unnecessary to say that Corporal Deer didn't remain to see his rations trampled in the mud, but wisely withdrew to the other side of the building. It took a dozen men to separate the combatants & after the fracas, the Chief of Scouts exercised considerable ingenuity in improvising new costumes from gunny sacks & odd pieces of shelter tents. As for myself, I surveyed the affair safely through my office window. This was before the establishment of the above-mentioned court & when the writer simply commanded scouts.

Gatewood and the New Order

Having already served as a commander of Apache scouts for almost four years, Gatewood made the perfect choice as military commandant of the White Mountain Indian Reservation. He not only understood, and agreed with, Crook's dictum on how the reservation should be administered; he also knew and understood his wards' grasp of their situation on the reservation.[7] In 1885 he confided that decent treatment of the White Mountains would greatly enhance their chances of becoming self-sufficient while warning that "they would be equally quick to resent anything savoring of imposition of what they know to be their rights."[8] The lieutenant took his task seriously, and would spend countless hours doing everything possible to improve the natives' lifeway, as Capt. F. E. Pierce's September 11, 1885, report attests: "Lieutenant Gatewood has labored hard with these people, has ma[i]ntained their rights, and done every thing in his power to assist and encourage them."[9]

One of the first issues Gatewood dealt with was women's rights—an issue that had become national during the late 1860s and 1870s when there was a push for "woman suffrage" laws. Just how much the early advocates of a woman's right to vote influenced him is unknown, but he must have been aware of the movement. His stance met with considerable resistance from his wards, and undoubtedly would have met with just as much—if not more—resistance had he studied law and presided over an official United States court.

The years Gatewood spent in the field with Indian scouts gave him a decided advantage: the Apaches liked and respected him. Hard work, both by himself as administrator and the White Mountains as farmers, seemed to ensure eventual success for everyone. [10] That is, until Bay-chen-daysen found himself pitted, not only against the citizens of Arizona but also against his commanding officer and the White Mountains themselves. At times he had to have felt that it was him against the world.

Gatewood probably thought his new position guaranteed his ascendancy up the military ladder. It is unlikely that he ever realized that his assignment as military agent to the White Mountains also marked the beginning of the end of his military career when, against Crook's wishes, he dared to stand up for Indian rights.

In studying the condition of these Coyoteros, with a view to the adoption of measures that would [improve their lives], one thing was apparent—the necessity of securing better treatment of the women. [11] So long as they were beasts of burden, doing all the labor while the men loafed, all efforts to carry out instructions from the general would be useless. [12] When the court was organized & in good working order, it was announced officially, & with due publicity, that in the coming campaigns in the cornfields, the bucks would be expected to take a fair share in the manipulation of the hoe & the plow. [This meant] that [the] beating of women on the slightest provocation should be stopped; that the excessive labor required of female children & the unnatural cruelty to which their sex [was] usually subjected should be lessened; that when the time came for the disposal of their grain & hay to the quartermaster of Fort Apache, the women & children should receive their proportion of money paid to be expended as they chose & not [all to] be turned over to their husbands to be gambled off & squandered in drinking, & that the women were guaranteed at all times the right to lodge complaints, the same as the men.

For the purpose of securing obedience to this order, the chiefs of the different bands, & the scouts, or policemen, stationed among the different settlements, were required, under penalty of confinement in the "calaboose," to labor in the stone quarry, to supervise the farming operations, as well as to keep the peace. [They] were empowered to arrest loafers & malcontents, & produce [them] forthwith at the court room. There being no appeal, habeas corpus proceedings would not be entertained.

Of course, the bucks protested against this invasion of their sacred rights. What was the use of squaws if you could not whip them, & if they made complaints, they could not be believed, for they never told the truth anyhow. As for working in the corn fields, they, the lords, didn't know how & didn't care to learn.

It was explained to them at great length that the days of raiding were drawing to a close. White people were settling the country, & it was time for them to select permanent places of abode & secure their own means of subsistence, as the government would not always feed them. War meant final annihilation; peace offered possible race existence. To die or to adopt to some extent the ways of the white men & live—that was the question.

Their principal men saw & appreciated the drift of events. Many of them had visited the eastern cities, & their wonderful tales of the numbers of the whites & the extent of their habitations, evidences of the power of the great father at Washington, were beginning to be believed. [13] The uselessness of continued warfare with the "Indah," the white-skins, & the probable result of the anger of the great father who had so many men that might be made soldiers, were dwelt on & duly discussed in their councils. [14] The curtailment of their reservations & the encroachments on the lands they claimed as peculiarly their own were within the memories of men not very old. So the question of to be or not to be to the thoughtful was serious.

After a great deal of "talk," & the confinement of a few wife-beaters in the calaboose, along with several chiefs & scouts, whom the squaws reported as having disobeyed injunctions, they expressed their willingness to submit to the new state of things, recognizing the fact that it was [in] their own best interest. The Apache respects nothing, believes in nothing, & bows to nothing but force. And here he found himself hedged in by surroundings that convinced him of the futility of further efforts in the line of the natural bent of his mind & he must fain submit & make the best of it.

The squaws, however, welcomed this new order of things, for obvious reasons, [&] did not hesitate to complain of harsh treatment. [This resulted in] their tormentors & task-masters [spending] a turn at quarrying stone. [Nor] did they hesitate to report neglect of duty on the part of chiefs & scouts in the various camps. In fact, they "went in" for their rights with great staunchness of purpose, & contributed largely to the maintenance of order & the enforcement of regulations generally through their "Bureau of Information." An irate squaw will "give away" the doings of a whole village for a twelve-month post.

A committee of the sovereigns of the soil waited on the judge & had a "talk." After the usual recital of their wrongs & so forth, they expressed a desire to have it so arranged that their lands could not be taken from them.

"The boundary between our possessions & those of the white men has just been surveyed & marked with monuments & the flagging of trees," the spokesman said. "That line is a dam that holds back the Indah waters. Someday that dam will give way & the Apache will be engulfed in the deluge, unless there is erected a protecting lever. Cannot a wall like this be built for our protection, &c?"

The solution of the so-called Indian problem has engaged the best efforts of individuals, associating government officials, including contractors, for a very long time, & has ranged from the reading of tracts by the mild missionary to the stern announcement of the businessman that there's no good Indian but the dead one.

The Marriage of Summer Blossom

Gatewood took his task as judicial head of White Mountain affairs seriously and gave each case brought before him careful consideration before ruling. At times, he stepped beyond not only Apache mores but also the mores of the White Eye world. A case in point is that of Summer Blossom. Although he viewed her liberation as just and the only course possible to follow, in actuality her freedom and right to be treated as a human being and not just as chattel mimicked on a small scale the women's suffrage campaign, which was then in its infancy in the United States.

Many interesting cases were brought before the court, in consequence of the efforts to ameliorate the condition of the women. That of Summer Blossom [comes to mind]. She was a comely maiden who had witnessed the blossoming of flowers for perhaps eighteen summers. Her father was fairly well off in this world's goods, from the Indian standpoint, but had promised her in marriage to an old "tough" who already had four squaws, [who], like himself, were well along in years. The father, of course, according to custom, was willing to dispose of her to the highest bidder, & her aged suitor could raise the "ante" on any of her young admirers, by reason of his herd of ponies & collection of firearms, blankets, &c. But the maiden objected, & taking advantage of the new order of things, sought the judge & related her story & implored his kind offices in her behalf.[15]

If she married the old man, she would be the slave of not only himself but of his four wives. They would require her to do the cooking, fetching of wood, & drawing of water for the whole family, besides working in the fields with the five old folks [who would also take] turns in beating her. Rather than submit to such a life, she would run away & commit some crime that would cause them to put her to death in order that she might escape such a fearful fate.

She said that there was a likely young man, between whom [he] & herself [there] was [a] strong mutual affection. [He] would run away with her to the uttermost end of the mountains &, if need be, die in her defense, but she could not agree to engage in any enterprise that might bring harm to him. He was so handsome, kind, & brave. Many were the deer, bear, & mountain lions that fell before his rifle, & the trophies of the chase had been laid at her feet unknown to the "old man." He was willing to give all his possessions for her & run into debt besides, but the father was obdurate & forbade his visits. Often had she yearned to brush his long black, glossy hair at the door of the paternal wickiup, but the father & his squaws were ever on the watch.

On the one hand was misery with one she detested; on the other was happiness with one she loved. The story was told simply & unaffectedly, with maidenly coyness & modesty. The judge, being human, assured her that the thing she dreaded should not come to pass [&] she should attain her heart's desire & be the chosen wife of her own true love—or else the court would know the reason. She went away comforted.

A meeting between her father & her would-be "hubby" was arranged & the matter was discussed. The one contended that he had a right to dispose of his daughter to suit himself & that the consciousness of having brought such a big price could not fail to make her proud & happy in view of this honor she would shed on her family, no matter what her treatment might be.

The purchaser said it was simply a matter of bargain & sale, & where was the man that could offer a greater price, & that any jury of their people would decide in his favor. Whereupon the court announced that in the event of a formal trial, the aid of a jury would be dispensed with. Appeals to paternal affection, or to the sympathies of either for "young love's dream," might just as well have been made to Egyptian mummies. The law allowed the deal & the law must take its course, judge or no judge. This somewhat nettled the court, who caused the interpreter to proclaim in solemn tones its dictum, "If this [maiden] knows herself, & she thinks she does, the proposed wedding is not going to be celebrated."

The two old decrepit [men leaped] to their feet & hurled defiance at the court & all comers. Thereupon two minions of the law seized each party & they were cited to show cause immediately why both should not go to work in the stone quarry for contempt of the August Tribunal.

Being duly arraigned, old Single-Tongue, the father of the girl, said, "Many winters have passed over my head & the frosts have left their tracks in my hair. These hands have never grasped even a hoe-handle & they know not the cunning required to cause the great flat stones to leap from the bosom of the mountain in the labor yard near the calaboose. With one eye only have I looked upon this marriage of my daughter thereby seeing only one side. But now do I open mine other eye & do perceive there's something to be said against it. It is plain that the nantan's action is prompted only by the throbbing of that great heart. I am mute with astonishment."

The Court: "What astonishes you?"

Single-Tongue: "That so narrow a chest can hold so big a heart."

The Court: "Humph! Suppose we cut short these proceedings by bringing the girl & the young man in here, & let her choose whom she will serve."

The old lover here made a motion to dismiss the case, on the ground that the girl was not old enough to know what was best for her. Motion not entertained.

The young people came in, the situation was explained to them, & the maiden was told to select her lord & master. She blushed, glanced around the room at all parties, put her finger in her mouth, cast down her eyes, sidled across to her young lover, & locking her arm in his, looked at the judge with a smile of great sweetness. It only remained to fix the price, which took very little time, since the young man offered all he had & the father immediately accepted. The court then pronounced them man & wife, & asked if anybody objected, looking at the discomfited specimen of antiquity. No objection. It was then announced that whosoever attempted to interfere with the bonds wrought by the God of Nature should suffer punishment, with a jerk of the judicial thumb towards the quarry. The young couple went their way with a few farming implements to begin their new life.

More than a year afterward, the writer, in making his rounds among the people to note their progress, stopped at Y's camp, tired & hungry. The young wife bustled about & produced a very palatable meal of beef, corn, bread, coffee, & sugar, with watermelon for desert; while the husband took charge of the mule & tethered him where the grass was good & in reach of a liberal feed of barley. The chubby-faced heir to the house was brought out by the smiling mother, & exhibited with great pride, & assurances of his many fine points were received with a mother's pleasure. Indeed, a happier household I never knew. They had worked hard, & prospered as they deserved, & doubtless they are happy yet.

The Saga of Dave

Dave's case is on the opposite side of the coin for Gatewood. The warrior was guilty beyond a doubt and deserved punishment for his crime. At the same time, Judge Gatewood had no intention of allowing mob rule, and made sure he maintained control of his court. In the following court case, Gatewood presides over what appears to be an incestuous sexual assault upon a girl. Grenville Goodwin's uncanny description parallels Dave's situation and leaves little doubt of the magnitude of the crime:

When incest cases were tried publicly, the chief of the local group in which they occurred usually summoned the subchiefs and influential men living under him and informed them of what had taken place. The culprits were then sent for or, if necessary, brought by force. They were flatly accused of their crime, and if they denied it, as they were likely to do, they were strung by the wrists from the limb of a tree, just high enough to permit their toes barely to touch the ground. Culprits who would not talk could be left hanging all day, and a fire might be built under the man. . . . The man might be put to death whether he confessed or not.[16]

Dave's sister accused him of the crime, a crime that was twofold—incest and rape. Goodwin also wrote: "Certain physical aggressions on girls or women, the most serious of them being rape, could constitute punishable offenses."[17] White Mountain Apaches sometimes insisted upon the death of the rapist if he was White Mountain, but not always. Dave was lucky; he never would have lived long enough to go to trial if he had been an outsider, as his people did not hesitate to kill rapists who were not from their tribe. Although it is unknown exactly what Dave's sister accused him of doing, Gatewood's reporting of the incident without providing complete details—a maddening trait typical of his times— leaves little question.

Undoubtedly Dave's jury trial was heated, and certainly the prescribed punishment was extreme but not unexpected. If Gatewood did not take control and insist upon a slightly less harsh punishment, most likely the jury's verdict would have resulted in a death sentence.

In this, as in every other police court, the dark, as well as the bright, side of human nature appeared. The Apache jury was invariably inexorable. Certain crimes & offences merited prescribed punishments, & that was the end of it. The findings & sentences, whether by judge, or jury, or both, were never objected to, nor their justness disputed. A case in point was that of Dave, a brother of a chief [Goody-goyer]. He was arrested on complaint of his sister, accusing him of assaulting her child. He denied his guilt in emphatic terms, declaring that his sister had always hated him & had brought her child to repeat the story so that his ruin might be accomplished. It scarcely seemed probable that he had committed such a crime, but the child told her story so simply & with such apparent truthfulness that there was nothing else to do but to arraign & try Mr. Dave. So twelve good men & true were duly impaneled after much questioning, not as to whether they knew anything or were possessed of intelligence but as to relationship with the accused, it being best to have none of his own kith & kin on his jury. Old Iron Tooth [Sanchez] was appointed foreman, & the court was duly called to order. The charges against the prisoner were stated; the gravity of the offence among white men dwelt upon, & their usual severe punishment made known. "Listen to the evidence carefully & weigh it well & if you find him guilty," said the court, "you may adjudge the punishment. If you find him not guilty, why there's an end of it."

Old Iron Tooth rose from his seat on the floor, & pointing to the prisoner, hissed, rather than spoke, "He's guilty & ought to be shot, & I'd like to be detailed to do the shooting." [This] made quite a sensation for he was a man of considerable influence among his people.

Dave sat there, perfectly stolid & apparently indifferent. Of course, it was necessary to excuse Iron Tooth from his duty in the courtroom. Two-Nothings, an intelligent old chief, who said that he knew nothing as to the merits of the case, & had no particular interest in Dave, dead or alive, was made the new foreman. The trial then proceeded—after ejecting Iron Tooth from the room because he insisted on haranguing the jury.

The child told the story & no amount of questioning could shake her testimony. The accused, in his defense, attempted to prove an alibi, & brought forward many witnesses. The story seemed straight enough up to the critical moment. A young man was on the stand. In a hesitating manner, [he tried] to tell how he saw the witness more than five miles from where the crime was committed, just as the sun was in the place indicated by the child & her mother in their testimony at the time of his act of brutality. The judge noticed his manner & interrupted to say that it must be borne in mind by witnesses that the whole truth & nothing but the truth must be given & that false witness upon conviction would get six months in irons.

Two-Nothings, the foreman, said that the members of the jury would like to hold a short consultation, & they were accordingly allowed to retire. In a few minutes they returned & the spokesman said that it was the unanimous opinion of the jury that an untruth uttered in testimony before them ought to be regarded as a personal insult to each member impugning his intelligence & honesty of purpose. If they acted on lies told them, the people would know it in time & regard them as a pack of fools, & therefore they desired to deal out punishment to any lying witness with the assurance that the same individual would never do so again. It would be just as well to make an example of the first one they [caught].

This rather stampeded the young man, & he said that since he had had time to consider, he was pretty sure that it was not Dave whom he saw but a squaw with a black blanket on. At the same time, he did not think it wrong to try to get his friend out of trouble since his offense was not generally regarded as a very serious one.

"Young Man, you have made a very narrow escape," Two-Nothings said. "Take my advice & make yourself scarce," & he didn't come around again for a long time.

Dave was therefore compelled to abandon his alibi, & made a lengthy statement setting forth the troubles in his family wherein his sister always took sides against him. The sister denied all this & produced other members of the family to prove quite the reverse. The foreman glowered at the prisoner & reminded him that his status was now that of a witness & the fact that he was lying in his own behalf would not go far in palliating the great offence of trying to make fools of the jury. The prisoner still insisted on the truth of what he had said, but gave it as his opinion, however, that a defendant in a case like this ought to be allowed a little latitude in his statement, since prevarication could hurt no one.

The jury then had the victim repeat her story, & subjected her to severe questioning, but failed to find a flaw in her statements. They then retired to talk the matter over. In about half an hour it was announced that the jury was ready to announce their verdict, & the presence of the prisoner's brother, the chief of the band, was requested. [They took] their seats on the floor along the wall, all hands solemnly smoking cigarettes, for without smoke, nothing of importance can be done (& smoke, too, at the expense of the court).

With great dignity & deliberation, old Two-Nothings said: "Dave, we all have voted 'guilty.' You will be hung up by the wrists with your feet off the ground, with two ropes, one to each wrist when the first rays of the sun come over the mountain tomorrow morning, & you are to remain suspended until the last rays disappear tomorrow evening. Your brother, the chief, is to be the executioner. If he fails in his duty, he is to suffer the same punishment, the judge making details from the scouts to execute both sentences. The commanding officer of Fort Apache, the soldiers, officers & ladies—everybody—are to be invited to witness this example of Apache justice. If the prisoner & his relatives are not satisfied with this verdict, & desire to make this the beginning of a feud, the jury & their relatives are ready to accommodate them at a moment's notice."[18]

"Don't you think it would be proper to allow him a few minutes rest at the end of, say, every hour?" the judge [asked]. "The chances are that he will be dead before sundown."

"No, you left the sentence to us, & we have spoken," the foreman said. "If he chooses to die, that's no business of ours."

"Why not be merciful & put the rope around his neck & end his sufferings at once?" [the] judge [queried].

"We don't want the ropes around his neck, but around his wrists," [the] foreman [replied]. "What's the use of a jury if they are going to be interfered with?"

After much "talking," they finally consented to allow five minutes respite at the end of each hour, provided the chief of scouts, to whom was relegated the duty of master of ceremonies, kept an eye on his watch & called the time strictly on the second.

A tall juniper tree with long stout spreading branches, that stood a few hundred yards from the post hospital, was selected for the gallows.[19] The prisoner was conducted to his cell in the calaboose, & the crowd dispersed to their several homes & occupations to talk the matter over. It was the first case of importance that was settled in that way & it created a great deal of interest.

At the appointed time, the culprit was under the juniper tree, guarded by a detail of scouts. His brother stood by with the ropes in his hands. A crowd of relatives, clansmen, & the curious generally, occupied the places where the proceedings could be best witnessed, none but officials being allowed within twenty-five yards. As day began to dawn, the brother, Goody-goyer, tied the ropes to the victim's wrists, [&] threw them over a limb of the tree eight feet from the ground. As the first streak of light shot across the heavens from the tops of the eastern mountains, the executioner, with an effort that was agony to him, pulled his brother off his feet. [He] made fast the ropes, stepped back a few yards, folded his arms across his breast, & all day long stood there gazing at the torture he was obliged to inflict.

The prisoner uttered no sound, nor moved a muscle. There was an awful silence—the sentence was duly executed, except that the intervals of rest were considerably lengthened, which was never suspected by the awarders of the punishment.

About noon, quick as a flash, the wife of the suspended man rushed to him, caught him around the legs & raised him up to ease his suffering. Before the guard could interfere, his sister, the mother of the child, sailed in with a butcher knife, but was caught & disarmed before she could cause serious damage. The wife got a slight wound in her back & Dave one in the leg. It took a half dozen men to drag the enraged mother away.

In the meantime, arrangements had been made with the post surgeon to take the sufferer into the hospital & give him the necessary surgical attention. A stretcher was also provided, & when the ropes were at last cut, preparations were made to carry the sufferer to the hospital. When the attendants stepped forward to place him on the litter, he waved them back & said, "No, I'll walk to the hospital, for I scorn aid from any of you." He stalked away & actually walked fully a hundred yards when he fainted & was taken to the bed provided for him.

The surgeon took charge of him, & in twenty-four hours he was walking around, the only evidence of his experience being his bandaged wrists. He afterwards acknowledged his guilt & the justice of his punishment. He was nearly six feet tall, muscular, raw-boned, & about forty years of age. An excellent scout & hunter when he chose to be, but a drunkard & gambler, & was regarded as a dangerous man. After his recovery, he went to work in his corn patch with a will, helping his squaw, & using his sickle with great effect in gathering hay. The proceeds of this joint labor were spent on his family & he bade fair to be a model paterfamilias.

But six months of this life created a four-gallon thirst, & having laid up a store of provisions for the winter, he made a kettle of tiswin, & concluded to have a quiet little drunk all by himself. Now, if the reader will remember, even the manufacture of this stuff was prohibited, & the stone quarry was utilized for the expenditure of the extra energy that it induced. Dave intended only to fill himself with the liquor, retire to his wickiup, & dream & sleep till its effects had passed away. But the tiswin got in its usual work & good intentions went to the usual destination. Mounting his pony, with Winchester & six-shooter, he proceeded to "whoop up" the village in approved cowboy fashion, much to the consternation of the inhabitants. The settlement [consisted of] mostly old men, women, & children [as] the able-bodied men [were] away. This gave him full sway & added largely to his chances for fun. Having sobered up a little, he grew weary from exertion, & retired to his couch to take a little rest.

About [this] time, two young scouts who had just enlisted for the first time happened along that way. Learning of the doings of David, [they] proceeded to his quarters. Waking him up, [they] informed him that he was under arrest & must accompany them to the office of the nantan. [Dave] declined to [surrender. He considered them] nothing but boys & [as] it took men & a lot of them to run him in, [he told] them to "get out." They took him at his word, "lit out" for the post, & reported the matter. They were immediately discharged.

[I ordered] Juan, the sergeant of the guard, to proceed to the home of Dave, about fifteen miles from the post, & bring him in, taking with him as many men as he liked. "Nantan," [Juan said,] "there's an old feud between his family & mine, & this is the chance I've been waiting for.[20] I'll take one man. Usual orders in case of resisting arrest?"

"Yes."

He rammed a rag through the barrel of his gun to take the dust out, & with one eye to the muzzle, held it up to [the] light to observe the interior brightness, took another hitch at his cartridge belt, & was gone.

In the meantime, after the disappearance of the two youngsters that had disturbed the repose of our hero, his squaw aroused him. [She] soaked his head in cold water, & called his attention to the facts that he had not only made tiswin & created a great disturbance, but had resisted arrest by duly authorized officials—pretty soon he might expect some of his enemies. The best thing to do, in her opinion, was to hasten to the post & give himself up. Her attentions & advice brought him to in a hurry. [Dave sent] his son to the top of a peak nearby to watch for the expected comers, while the squaw saddled his pony.

When Juan rode down one gulch into the valley where Dave's abode was, the sobered man rode up another just parallel in the direction of the post. The sergeant rode into the village & was informed by the squaw that the man he was looking for had just gone out on foot westward to drive in his horses. But Juan was not to be misled, & seeing a fresh pony track, immediately set out to follow it. The squaw tried to detain him by offering him something to eat or to drink, & asking many questions, but to no purpose.

[When Juan] arrived at the crest of the mesa, he saw his man with streaming hair & applying whip & spur, fairly flying eastward in the direction of the post. He started in pursuit, & each yell he gave seemed to add to the fugitive's flightiness. Away they went full tilt. Across the valley from the post, there is a flat of about two miles in length. This had to be crossed. The writer happened to be looking in that direction when a solitary horseman made his appearance apparently bent on testing the speed of his steed. A few hundred yards behind him, soon came two more. The legs & arms of all three were flying, & their ponies were evidently being put to their mettle. As racing was a favorite amusement of [the White Mountains], it seemed to be an ordinary race. But [then I noticed] the fellow [in the lead] still urged his horse with frantic efforts, which appeared strange. The bright barrels of the rifles of the two behind, flashing out, lent it still greater interest.

What could it mean? Soon the horsemen, one after the other, disappeared down the side of the narrow valley between the post & the plain on which the race had been run, & in a very few minutes, [they] came tearing through the garrison, the leader drawing rein only at the courthouse door. Out of breath, his pony covered with foam, & both panting furiously, the rider rushed into the room & threw himself into a chair.

It was Dave. An expression of immense relief was on his face, but his voice failed him from exhaustion. In a very little while, Sergeant Juan appeared at the door in very much the same condition, but with a savage scowl on his face, & blood in his eye. He was mad all over because of his failure to catch the man he was gunning for. When he recovered his breath, he made his report, which in substance was as above narrated, expressing the hope that it would not be thought that he had not tried to discharge his duty with due diligence & energy. On this point he was assured that his energetic efforts were perfectly evident & that he needn't feel it necessary to make any apologies for his failure to make the arrest.

As the principal witnesses were near at hand, our hero was duly arraigned on the charges of making tiswin, creating disturbances in the village, & resisting arrest by the duly constituted keepers of the peace. He acknowledged it all substantially, except resisting the formal arrest. The two young ex-policemen told their story, which several eyewitnesses corroborated. The accused listened attentively, & then said, "This is strange. When I told the two men to "get out" & all that, I must have been talking in my sleep, & yet I can't recall any dreams that were bad! They were all the most peaceful & pleasant. Surely there's some mistake."

"Dreams, or no dreams," the judge [said], "David, you shall abide with us in the public house by the stone quarry for two moons, for manufacturing & imbibing ardent spirits to the terror of your neighbors.

Also, four more moons shall witness your stay with us, for resisting officials in the discharge of their proper duties. As you know by experience, honest labor on your part will secure proportionate curtailment of the period of your confinement, & dead-beating will but add thereto. Go in peace."

And Juan escorted him to his old quarters in the hostelry. There were at the time some fifteen or twenty inmates of that institution, put there for various offences. The house had been built of slabs & stone by the unwilling occupants, & when there were accommodations enough for all probable comers, work ran short, & the stone quarry was kept open for healthful exercise—a necessity. But as it was not intended for amusement & occupation there was not regarded as such by the artists that delved therein, & as the guard was not required to report malingering, you might think that an individual might take it easy & accomplish the minimum of a day's labor. Not so. Each man had his own piles of rocks taken from his own little quarry to show his progress from day to day. To prevent his squaw or friends from handling his tools, no one but the sentinels were allowed within speaking distance during working hours, & you can be sure that no sentinel would lay down his gun to pry up rocks, even for his father.

Then besides, the nantan, or the chief of scouts, was liable to appear at any time from any direction. The deadbeat, if caught, was sure to have his confinement prolonged, while the earnest laborer was as sure to have it shortened. Dave proposed to put in extra hours so as to hasten up the day of his release, but this was not allowed.

He piled up stone, however, by the wagon load, working as if he were anxious to tear down the side of the mountain, his great strength & power of endurance standing him in good stead, & placed many days to his credit.

Gatewood's Reaction to the Chiricahua Move to Turkey Creek

By early February 1884, Gatewood became aware that the Chokonen, Bedonkohe, and Chihenne Apaches living near the subagency at San Carlos wanted to move to the high country—the mountains that the White Mountain Indian Reservation provided. This did not thrill him, and he voiced his concern to Crook:

I have the honor to call your attention to the selection of farming lands for the Chiricahuas, as desired by them & as I believe approved by Captain Crawford. They want to locate as near as possible to Eagle Creek on the Eastern boundary of the reservation. With the Chiricahuas on that part of the reservation & George's band on Turkey Creek, it puzzles me to devise a system of police that will prevent an outbreak by the Chiricahuas. I have thought it over a great deal, & have endeavored to find out the temper of the Indians under my charge, & their feelings towards those people, estimating the aid in case of disturbance to be expected from the former as against the latter. They fear the Chiricahuas & will not try to spy around their camps to find out what is going on. Camped together & especially on that part of that reservation I do not believe they will stay one year, & I do not desire to have charge of them & be held responsible for their conduct. Scattered by bands among the other Indians settled here, there is some hope of managing them. Please give this your attention.[21]

Of course Crook, as appeared to be his wont when Gatewood was concerned, did not listen. The Chokonen, Bedonkohe, and Chihenne had returned to the San Carlos Indian Reservation after the general's 1883 invasion of the Sierra Madre in Mexico. However, they were not happy there. As a group they were split apart and the subgroups were dispersed over an area that provided little game and proved difficult to till. In an attempt to avoid trouble before it happened, Crook gave the go-ahead for the move. In defense of the general's decision is the fact that these people did not get along with the other Indians living at San Carlos. Over five hundred Apaches migrated in the spring of 1884—including Geronimo, Naiche, Chihuahua, and Mangus. Britton Davis, who served as their military agent, also made the move. Roughly seventeen miles southeast of Fort Apache, Turkey Creek provided pine trees, clear water, game, and a mild summer climate.[22]

It would not take long for Gatewood's fear to ferment, gather steam, and explode. For Geronimo's part, he feared being handed over to the U.S. court system, tried for his past deeds, and imprisoned. As he said to Crook in 1886, "They wanted to seize me and Mangus."[23] Geronimo rightfully feared for his life, and this would become the major factor in his deciding to run again.

Initial Pursuit and Unrest among the Apaches

After the Bedonkohe, Chihenne, and Chokonen Apaches broke out from Turkey Creek on May 17, 1885, Gatewood accompanied Capt. Allen Smith (Fourth U.S. Cavalry) and two companies of cavalry.[24] Lt. James Lockett (Fourth U.S. Cavalry) commanded Troop A while Lt. James Parker (Sixth U.S. Cavalry) commanded Troop K.[25] Lt. Leighton Finley (Tenth U.S. Cavalry) also accompanied the command.[26] Gatewood had about a dozen White Mountains scouts with him.[27] Although everyone knew that they had to move quickly if they had any chance of catching the fleeing Indians, Smith wisely remained cautious during that first night as he did not want to ride into an ambush. As the chase continued and it became more and more obvious during succeeding days that he was not going to catch up with the fleeing Indians, his subordinates became disgusted. Smith's lackadaisical pursuit, combined with the Apaches' typical mode of splitting into smaller groups and moving in different directions, produced the usual result—Geronimo, Naiche, Mangus, Chihuahua, and the people with them succeeded in gaining their freedom.

This initial hunt did result in a firefight twenty miles east of Alma, New Mexico. On the afternoon of May 22, Smith's command halted for a break in Devil's River, a cañon that opened into a small valley six hundred feet below the rim of the Mogollons.[28] Smith left Parker in charge while he and Lockett went to bathe in a creek. Gatewood sent his scouts out to reconnoiter the cañon; then he, Parker, and Finley sat down under a tree to relax. Without warning, Apaches struck from the cañon walls. Finley shared his impression of the firefight with Parker:

> You, Lieutenant Gatewood, and myself were seated under a tree on the easterly bank of the creek. All of the enlisted men, except those of the pack train, were in camp on the west bank of the creek, Troop K nearest to us and Troop A lower down. I do not believe the canyon was fifty feet wide. You, Lieutenant Gatewood, and I got on our feet at the first shot, and the quick subsequent firing immediately indicated what was up. Sergeant Warren of Troop K called to the men, "Get to the herd." . . . I heard you [Parker] say, "Never mind the herd, get your guns!" I repeated that order, and when I looked around, not three seconds later I saw you with your four or five men starting up the easterly hill. I called to the rest of the men, "Come on!"

and ran after you. The first line which reached the top of the hill consisted of about seventeen men all told, officers and enlisted men; most of the enlisted men being of Troop K, Sergeant Atkinson and Private Meyers being the only men I noticed of Troop A, although perhaps there were others of that troop. You took us up by rushes, taking advantage of various ledges of rock to rest us. The hill was particularly steep, and I cannot believe it was less than 500 feet high.

Lieutenant Gatewood came up the hill immediately behind this first line. When we got about half way up, as I remember, we met the herd being driven down; the members of the herd guard [were] doing their duty splendidly. After we passed the herd some little distance, we met the Indian scouts running down. I heard Lieutenant Gatewood shout to them and rally them, and he brought them to the summit immediately after we arrived there.

The hostiles continued their fire until we were nearly to the top. On reaching the summit . . . we discovered that the hostiles had run from the crest, scattering in every direction. In a few minutes some of the men pushed forward and discovered the hostiles on the plateau, about 500 yards from the summit. Seventeen fires were still either burning or filled with live or hot coals. The hostiles left behind them in their haste several articles of clothing and equipment and a lot of beef. . . . Between five and ten minutes, as I remember, after we reached the summit, Lieutenant Lockett got up and about five minutes later Captain Smith arrived.[29]

Even though Smith and Lockett missed the skirmish, Smith's subsequent report made it sound as if he were in the thick of the fight directing the counterattack.[30] A disgusted Gatewood later wrote, "Captain Smith appeared after the firing had ceased, and had nothing whatever to do with the fight."[31] Parker echoed Gatewood's view regarding Smith's official report: Smith "says nothing about being absent from the camp at the beginning of the fight, bathing, and leaves it to be inferred that he commanded during the fight and accompanied the men and officers who charged up the hill."[32]

The following day, Smith—after tracking the fleeing Indians only for six miles—called off the hunt, citing a need for supplies. This did not end the hunt, which dragged on without further incident until Gatewood reported to Crook at Fort Bayard, New Mexico, on June 5.

Crook sent Gatewood back to Fort Apache to oversee the enlistment of an additional two hundred Indian scouts. As he had done in 1883, the general intended to hunt the Bedonkohes, Chokonens, and Chihennes south of the border. On June 11, he ordered Capt. Emmet Crawford to take Company A (Sixth U.S. Cavalry) and ninety-two Indian scouts and enter Mexico.[33] As Crawford led his column southward, reports surmised that instead of dropping into Mexico, Mangus and those with him had gone into hiding near Sapillo Creek, New Mexico. The Chihenne chieftain had separated from Geronimo when he headed for Mexico and set out on his own. Moving southward from the Mogollons, he supposedly had "six or seven bucks and a few women and children" with him.[34] This would not do if Crook had any hope of his plan working—there could be no warring Indians remaining in the United States.

When Gatewood completed the conscription of scouts, Crook ordered him to the Black Range of New Mexico to hunt and destroy Mangus or any other warring Apaches he might encounter. After warning Gatewood to be sure that his scouts did not clash with the whites they encountered during the patrol, Crook told him: "I do not intend to take you in the field [after you return from this scout] unless you have strong reason for wishing to go."[35] By this time Gatewood and Crook had all but severed their relationship, and although Gatewood was currently embroiled in civil difficulties (see chapter 4), this was not the reason Crook gave his lieutenant the option of not campaigning in Mexico. Gatewood was a good reservation administrator, and Crook—regardless of his anger at Gatewood—realized this, and although he stated that he wanted Gatewood to "return to Apache [after this patrol] and attend to matters there," this, too, was not Crook's sole reason for his generosity. Gatewood's health had worsened over the years, and Crook knew that Gatewood's body most likely could not survive a summer of campaigning in the harsh Mexican wilderness.[36]

Gatewood set out on what would be his last patrol on June 16 (see appendix A). When he returned to Fort Apache in early July, he had found nothing. This did not mean that he had seen the last of the war, for it would come to him on the reservation that fall.

Crook ordered a second column into Mexico on July 7. However,

Mangus, chieftain of the Chihenne Apaches, circa 1885. After the May 17, 1885, breakout from Turkey Creek, Mangus split off from the other Apaches and stayed in the Black Range of New Mexico for an extended period before crossing the border into Mexico. Based on a photograph by A. Frank Randall, *Harper's Weekly*, April 17, 1886. From the author's collection.

Capt. Wirt Davis (Fourth U.S. Cavalry) was forced to wait for Gatewood to return to Fort Apache from his scout into the Black Range as he needed Bay-chen-daysen's scout company and did not enter Mexico until July 13.[37] Davis's command consisted of Lt. Robert Walsh (Fourth U.S. Cavalry), forty men from Troop F, Fourth U.S. Cavalry, two pack trains, and one hundred Indian scouts.[38] Gatewood's friend Lt. Matthias Day commanded the scouts. Because Apache scouts composed the main portion of Crook's fighting force in Mexico in 1885, some historians have erroneously placed Gatewood with Wirt Davis during the summer hunt in Mexico. He was not there, and he never left American soil. Gatewood spent that summer dealing with his civil case and preparing to hand over management of the White Mountain Indian Reservation to his successor, Lt. James Lockett.[39]

By the time Gatewood's scout ended, it was clear that most of the escapees had reached Mexico safely and that none remained north of the international boundary. With no warring Apaches behind his line of defense to warn their brothers in Mexico of his strategy, Crook placed troops and scouts at all the known watering holes and points of entry into the United States to confront the Indians if they attempted to re-cross the border. Crook's plan must have looked good on paper, but the truth of the matter is that the United States–Mexico border is just too long to prevent unwanted entry.[40]

By September 1885, Geronimo realized that for his band to survive, they had to supplement their family group. The Apache division of labor handicapped them if a portion of the family group was missing—in this case, the women. With four warriors—Gatewood put the number at six—Geronimo set out to recapture their families. Geronimo and his war party crossed the border, then onto the White Mountain Indian Reservation without being observed. They captured horses, then a White Mountain woman, whom they forced to lead them to where their relatives currently camped. At one a.m. on September 22, Geronimo slipped into the camp.[41] He rescued his fourth wife, She-gha, and a three-year old daughter, along with another woman.[42]

In the meantime, the Chiricahuas under Naiche, Mangus, & Geronimo were making their raids through Arizona & New Mexico & carrying destruction far & wide.[43] The nantan was ordered to organize a company of Coyoteros & operate in the Mogollon District in New Mexico,

where the hostiles were supposed to be hidden in the fastness of the mountains, whence they made numerous incursions through the white settlements.

Volunteers were invited from the able-bodied denizens of the house by the quarry with a promise of remission of the remainder of the sentences of all who would serve faithfully. Among others who stepped to the front was our friend [Dave,] who had caused so much trouble. Eager [to] get at the Chiricahuas, he was enlisted, made a sergeant on the spot, & sent out among the various bands to bring in recruits. He took hold with all his might & brought in a batch of fine recruits. The command took the field, & during the campaign that followed, he was always at the front, & night or day, no duty was so arduous that he was not ready to perform it.

Afterwards, in a fight with the hostiles, in the mountains of Mexico, his impetuosity cost him dearly. [44] With only four or five men, he dashed in on the enemies' flank & received a bullet through his left elbow though he killed the man [who] wounded him. His action contributed greatly to the rout that followed. This painful wound, the great heat, & the distance that had to be traveled to get to the nearest American fort, where he could receive the best treatment, would have killed most men, but Dave pulled through though worn to a mere skeleton. He finally returned to his reservation, but his left arm could be bent only a little. This was a source of great grief & regret to him. He could never again be the hunter he was, & his inability to take the field lessened his chances of killing Chiricahuas. He was still borne on the muster rolls in order to pension him, & was useful in keeping the peace among his people, for he joined the temperance procession & became an ornament to society.

The continued hostilities kept up by Geronimo & his party interfered considerably with the peaceful pursuits, not only of the remainder of that tribe, but of the others as well—especially the Coyoteros. Geronimo, himself, with [a] half dozen men one night sneaked into the Chiricahua camp, which was close to the post, & carried off one of his squaws who had remained on the reserve when he broke out a few months before, thereby creating considerable excitement among the natives. [45]

Most of the Coyotero bucks were off with the troops as scouts, & those who remained behind were so unsettled by the state of affairs that their corn & hay fields did not receive the attention that peace would have enabled them to give [them]. A man or woman would quit work & journey sixty miles to Fort Apache to inquire the news, so eager were they to know what was going on. Still, they managed to sell the quartermaster of the post large quantities of grain & hay.[46]

Pedro and the Quest for Making It in a White World

While many of the Apaches struggled to maintain their culture and revolted against captivity, others realized they could not win the fight. One such person was Pedro (Hacke-yanil-tli-din), who was originally one of the chieftains of the Carrizo Creek band of the Cibecue group of Western Apaches. In the 1850s a clan dispute erupted between him and another Carrizo Creek leader, Miguel. Pedro lost and was forced to leave the Carrizo. After two years, White Mountain chieftain Esh-kel-dah-silah allowed Pedro and his band to settle on White Mountain territory that was not far from his old home on the Carrizo, at a place that would eventually be called Forest Dale. Many members of Pedro's band intermarried with the White Mountains, and as time passed they became thought of as White Mountains. However, they also retained close ties with the Carrizo band of Apaches.

After a visit to Washington DC in 1872, Gen. George Crook named Pedro chief of the White Mountain Apaches. These were tumultuous times for the Apaches, as they watched their lifeway being destroyed. Throughout these war-torn years, Pedro and his people learned to prosper under the rule of the White Eyes. By the time Gatewood met Pedro, the chieftain was old and nearing death. Still he and his people continued to make progress conforming to the white dictum. Crook reported: "The White Mountain Indians at Ft. Apache have need[ed] no rations since July and are now self-supporting. Pedro's band of this tribe has always been self-sustaining and have never need[ed] anything from the government."[47]

Old Pedro, chief of a band of Coyoteros (or White Mountains, as they are often called) residing on the north fork of White River within ten miles of the post, kept an eye open for the chance [to profit from the white man's way]. He was very deaf, & usually carried two ear trumpets. One looked like a tin dipper, & the other was made of about a yard of hose with a copper funnel at one end in which to yell, while he stuck the nozzle at the other in his ear.

Pedro had been a great traveler. With a party of his people, he had visited Washington & other cities in the east, taking in the Centennial Exhibition at Philadelphia in '76.[48] He had shaken hands with the Great White Father in Washington & had been presented with a large silver medal as a memento of his visit, which he wore on state occasions suspended from his neck with a blue ribbon.[49] It was regarded as a sacred talisman, & will be so regarded as long as they of his family are left to inherit it, for it was shown evident respect by the few whites who were permitted to see it.

He was allowed to tell of the wonderful things he had seen on his trip. The medicine men claimed that the Great Father's Big Tum Tum put medicine in [his] eyes that made [him] believe [he] saw so many large cities, such a vast extent of country, & the white people just like blades of grass in numbers. They listened to Pedro's stories with compassion & grieved that he was entering his dotage. But in after years, others of them traveled, railroads entered the country, white settlements increased beyond imagination, many of their children went east to school & returned to repeat the wonderful stories, until now they will believe anything that is told them, & old Pedro has regained the respect of his people.

His courage & wisdom gave him great influence, which he exerted in the old days to saving the life of many a white man. When it came to a horse trade or any other business, the old fellow showed considerable astuteness, & a fair appreciation of the value of a dollar. Along the river where his band lived were extensive meadows covered with gramma grass that made excellent hay. He could have tons of it gathered, but the question of transporting it to the Q.M. corral bothered him. To pack it in bundles [& place it] on burros & squaws was a tedious process involving a great deal of labor with comparatively small return. So he induced six Mexicans with four wagons & ox teams to make an agreement in writing, which was duly recorded by the nantan.

A certain meadow was divided. All on one side of [the] line, up the river, was his & that part below was to be theirs. His working party consisting of three bucks, five women, & three children [would] cut the grass with sickles & butcher knives. The Mexicans were to be allowed to cut theirs as they chose. The contract provided that as fast as the Indians' hay was cured, it should be hauled to market by the Mexicans, & the proceeds of all they could put in from their own part of the meadow should be compensation for the use of their transportation.

Both parties started to work & made the hay fly, the Mexicans with scythes. In that dry climate, with no prospect of rain at that time of year (September), & no dew, new mown hay dries rapidly, & the next day four of the Mexicans had to begin to haul for the Indians, leaving two to turn the scythes.

For several days, the men who thought they had struck a bonanza found no chance to deliver hay for themselves, for the Indians worked as long as they could see & produced more hay than the four teams could take away. [The Mexicans] had calculated on the women only as workers [with] the bucks & children as loafers. But they soon found out their mistake. They quit work & threatened to throw up their contract if they were not given a chance to at least make enough to buy grub. The old man generously allowed them to haul a few loads for their own benefit, & they went to work again. But a few days more so greatly disgusted them that they proposed to give the Indians the rest of the hay they had cut on their own account [if they were] let off their bargain. This was accepted.

A few days after, Pedro drew all the money the Q.M. owed him in silver. [He] seated himself on the ground in front of the sutler's store, with his legs spread apart & his hat full of dollars between them, chuckling to himself in great glee. The nantan happened to pass by. "Glad to see you so happy," [he] spoke, or rather yelled, to the old man through his copper-mouthed garden hose, "contemplating your hat full of dollars. That's a fine horse you ride on," [the writer continued], pointing to [a] fine black colt that was hitched to the horse rack in front of the store.

"Yes, nantan, I ride a good horse, & if I can make another bargain with [the] Mexicans, I'll ride in a fine buggy." His unusually large mouth took the shape of the slip in a post office box.

Soldiers, Good Citizens, Geronimo, and Josanie's Raid

An Apache outbreak always struck terror in the white settlements, and nothing the military did to subdue the Indians who desired to be free could satisfy the citizenry. As far as they were concerned, the military did not have a clue how to deal with warring natives. Most of the newspapers in the territories echoed this view.

Although Geronimo's September 22 foray onto the reservation did not cost many lives, the next one would. In early November, Josanie (Ulzana, Ulzahuay, Jolsanny, Olsanny, Olzanny), a Chokonen war leader and Chihuahua's brother, reentered the United States and began a raid in the Florida Mountains of New Mexico.[50] Because he killed just about every person he came in contact with, his frequent and violent strikes struck terror. Then, as suddenly as he appeared, he vanished, only to reappear four miles from Fort Apache on November 23. That night he captured a White Mountain woman and two Chiricahua women, and he killed five men and boys, eleven women, and four children. The next morning he may have killed two herders at Turkey Creek. After questioning the Chiricahua women about recently captured Apache relatives and learning they were confined at Fort Bowie but were all right, Josanie released them on the twenty-fourth. By the time he returned to Mexico on December 27, he had traveled twelve hundred miles, killed somewhere between thirty-eight and forty-five people, yet lost only one warrior.[51]

When Geronimo left the reservation in the spring of '85, his party consisted of about forty bucks & fifty to sixty women & children.[52] There had been no outbreaks for several years, & as the news [swept] over the country the consternation among the people of Arizona, New Mexico, & the northern states of Mexico can be better imagined than described. Excitement prevailed everywhere & troops were promptly put in motion from every post.

Prior to 1886, the regular army was very unpopular with the people of the two territories, if one might judge from the general tone of newspapers, the sneering remarks of individuals, & the resolutions of mass meetings.[53] Abuse was heaped not only upon individual officers, from the Department Commander down, but upon the service as a whole. There were some exceptions among the newspapers, however— those who obtained contracts for advertising bids for government supplies. Also, many ranchers, merchants, & others, who appreciated the difficulties that the soldiers had to overcome, were friends & rendered many valuable gratuitous services to the troops. But the feeling, as a whole, was rather unfriendly. Many a contractor for the delivery of supplies, upon the failure of his attempts to corrupt the infantry or cavalry lieutenant acting as Quartermaster or Commissary, had to deliver the pounds & measurements called for in his written agreement. He was therefore wronged in that he was balked in his efforts to swindle the government, & a subsidy to the value of a steer, to a newspaper, would call down the maledictions of a whole territory upon the cowardly dudes that wore the blue.

Again, in following the trail of a hostile party, the officer would be informed by a "reliable citizen" that depredations were being committed at such & such a ranch perhaps fifteen or twenty miles off at a right angle to the direction the enemy had evidently gone. Making a forced march & arriving there, it would be found that the Indians had not been near the place but had kept on their straight course. This was considered a very good joke on the army, but it cost many innocent people their property, if not their lives, for with pursuers close behind, the Apaches never stop to depredate. The result of this practice on the part of a large proportion of the people was to create distrust in the minds of those responsible for the movements of troops. Who would want to march his command all day & perhaps all night, too, just to find himself the victim of a hoax perpetrated by "reliable citizens." [This only gave] the newspapers a chance to score [the officer] for his stupidity & for his superiors to call upon him for explanations as to his strange conduct. If he based his operations on reports that proved to be false, he was told that he ought to have known better & he lacked the qualities of an efficient campaigner. On the other hand, if he declined to be guided by rumors that were founded on truth, he was accused of too great a regard of his personal safety. If he succeeded in bringing the enemy to bay & failed to kill one half & capture the other, he ought to be replaced by a man of some energy & judgment. If he followed them night & day for hundreds of miles across deserts & over the roughest mountains on the continent—suffering from thirst & hunger & perhaps [marching] most of the way on foot, his animals having broken down—he was met with the charge that he had no desire to catch [the natives]. As they say, "He didn't lose no Indians." The final surrender was the only act in all these years of weary toil that was greeted by anything approaching general applause.

The citizens & local newspapers began their usual abuse of the military. It would become necessary for the citizen soldiery to take the field again & give the regulars more lessons in the art of fighting Indians. Barrooms echoed with loud cries of vengeance, & companies of cowherders sallied forth to wreak it on the savage foe, but with exceeding great caution. They had not forgotten the experiences of such bodies of troops in the days gone by. It was still fresh in the memories of many how a gallant band of the forty rangers had gone forth from one of the principal mining towns to do battle. [The rangers] had camped at a ranch sixty miles from home, putting their horses in the corral. Suddenly eleven Apaches appeared with their frightful yells, & the noble band, each member with his trusty Winchester, held the inside of the buildings. [This number grew to] a thousand screaming red devils, [who] opened the gates of the corral & drove off forty-five riding horses. [Although] not a single man [had been] lost, [no one had] forgotten how the forty heroes trudged back to their firesides over the mountains through the mud & snow on foot. Modesty forbade them to accept the grand reception that was tendered them on their return. All these things & more rendered the blood-thirsty avengers a little cautious when they came to carry out their dire threats.

The greater party of the Chiricahua tribe remained at peace in their camps near the post [Fort Apache]—some four hundred fifty in all, doing a fair amount of work in their fields, considering the general unsettling of affairs on the reservation.[54]

Geronimo himself left several acres of barley & corn from which was afterward taken a remarkably good yield that was divided among the tribe. He had held the plow in virgin soil till his hands were blistered, while his boy led the mule that was hitched to it, & his squaw urged the animal on with vigorous applications of a branch of tough scrubby oak. The old man showed the marks of labor, on his hands, with ostentatious pride, & seemed to desire to be considered a model granger.[55]

"Why then," you may ask, "did he leave the plow & take to the warpath?" The reader will have to answer the question for himself after reading this sketch. That he did take to the warpath is all that can be positively stated. After the old man [Geronimo] came back & took his squaw away, a party of about a dozen [led by Josanie] made a raid through the White Mountain settlements while the troops & scouts were south. [They] killed & carried away some twenty odd of that tribe. Great consternation seized the Coyoteros. They gathered their families into larger villages, hundreds of them moving to the vicinity of the post.[56]

The atrocities had been committed on isolated camps, on those who were out in the mountains gathering acorns, fruit of the cactus, &c.

At one place fifteen women & children were looked after by one old buck.[57] He had no sons, but his sons-in-law were off to the war as allies to the soldiers, & left him to take care of the families. Armed with a Sharp's rifle that had to be cocked & the trigger pulled three times before a cartridge could explode, he had spent one whole day in search of game. Returning to the camp about sundown, tired & worried over his unsuccessful hunt, he arrived at the top of a ridge near by just in time to see several of these fiends knock his little grandson on the head with a stone & cast him into a large fire they had built.

The bodies of the others lying around near the fire bore witness to the cruel sufferings they had undergone. The little grandchild was the last of the old man's blood relations. He leveled his gun, & pulling the trigger the requisite number of times, an enemy dropped with a bullet through his heart. Again another report from the fatal, though slow working Sharp's, & another threw up his arms, wheeled & ran & disappeared in the bushes. Recognizing that there was only one man & he was firing as if from a muzzle-loader, the rest of the party took to the rocks & bushes with a view of completing their bloody work on their single assailant.

But the old man succeeded in escaping, & reached the post next morning to tell his heartrending story. He exhibited his gun & begged ammunition & a new spring for the lock. With his gun repaired & his belt full of cartridges, he straightened up his bent form to its full height, held out his clenched hand till the veins stood up on his naked arm, like cords, & with the saddest expression I ever saw, said: "I am an old man, alone in the world, not a drop of the blood in my veins runs in those of a human being," & then raising his arms & face upwards, "May the great spirits protect me till I have my revenge." He turned away & disappeared.

Gatewood's Stand

At the time of Geronimo's 1885 raid on the reservation, Alchesay and Sanchez were the leading voices of the White Mountains, with Alchesay the foremost White Mountain chieftain. Both had been firebrands since the 1870s. Alchesay had had a successful career as a sergeant of Apache scouts, first during the early 1870s, for which he won the Medal of Honor, and later as Gatewood's trusted sergeant on a number of occasions during the late 1870s. Sanchez was another matter. Although Bay-chen-daysen thought highly of Alchesay and considered him a friend, he was wary of Sanchez, and Crook's insistence that he enlist Sanchez as a scout upset him.[58]

To the Apaches, a wrong always had to be righted. Josanie's violence against the White Mountains had to be revenged, and Alchesay and Sanchez would both play leading roles in their people's quest to even the score. Although Loco, the Chihenne chieftain, and his tribe remained at peace when Geronimo broke out in May, he and his people became the target of White Mountain vengeance. As we shall see, Gatewood absolutely refused to buy into the murder of Loco and his people. His stance against revenge not only hurt his working relationship with the White Mountains but also can be linked to the end of his close relationship with them.[59]

As many doubted the old man's assertion that he had killed one & wounded another of the destroyers of his family, a party of his friends [went] out to investigate. Following the trail of the murder[er]s, they soon discovered the grave of the dead man, & exhumed the body. Bloody rags & other evidence proved that one was wounded & had been carried along by the others.

[Upon returning to the writer's quarters], one of them laid a bundle on the floor, untied it, & with a great flourish placed it on the table right under the nose of the nantan as he sat there writing. It was the head of an Indian, bloody & ghastly, so placed that the face was within a foot of that of the judge, & the paper & blotting pad was smeared with clots of blood.[60]

Ugh! It gives me cold shivers to think of it. After the judge's nerves & stomach had become a little settled on the other side of the room, & orders had been issued that in future heads were not to be set up on writing desks in that fashion, the story of the finding of the body was told, & there was the head to prove that the old man had spoken the truth. It was recognized as the head of a son of Juh, a renegade chief that had died in Mexico a few years before.[61] The "cabeza" was presented to the post surgeon, & is probably now among the curiosities in the hospital at Fort Apache.

From another isolated camp, a boy about eight years old had escaped with his baby brother on his back, & made his way to the post early the next morning. The two were all that were left of the family. The heroism of the little fellow in escaping & carrying his brother nearly twenty miles drew forth compassion from everyone that heard of his exploit, & a considerable sum was contributed for the benefit of the children. They were taken into the family of a brother of the dead father, & received the kind care required by the circumstances of their orphanage.

This raid was a surprise to the Coyoteros, but it was only what might have been expected. The old-time enmity & the fact that of late years the Coyoteros had furnished the best allies of the whites from among all the tribes should have put them on their guard, although the latter had agreed to divide their lands with the former when in [May] '84 [the Bedonkohe, Chihenne, and Chokonen Apaches moved from San Carlos to Turkey Creek], & to help them in farming. [62] It is no wonder then that their hearts were "bad," & for a while there was much loud talk of revenge. [63]

Suddenly the intense excitement appeared to die out entirely. The men quietly returned to their homes after securing all the arms & ammunition possible to be had, & causing to be given out that they were going to remain there for the purpose of being ready for the next raid. An unusual number of visiting friends from the main agency were seen among the settlements but were scattered so that a casual observer would scarcely notice them. [64] They all wore empty belts & apparently had no arms.

Sanchez, Alchesay, & several other principal chiefs seemed to take turns in loafing around the post & the courtroom, eternally begging cartridges for their men on the plea of being ready for self-defense. There was an air of mystery about all this that made the nantan a little uneasy & caused a suspicion that something would soon [explode]. The interpreter swore that he knew of nothing wrong. The paid spies declared that everything was going smoothly & the medicine that was being made in every camp was "good." The chiefs, when taxed with organizing some scheme for devilment, looked surprised & said that their hearts were made sore to have it thought that they were capable of doing anything not authorized & approved by the nantan. All the same there was that unaccountable, uneasy feeling that generally forebodes evil. No bribes, threats, nor persuasion could get one man, woman, or child to even hint at what would be the result. The judicial mind was more than sorely puzzled, recognizing the fact that in case of serious trouble, someone would be held responsible, & the judge had a strong suspicion that it would be himself. Something, therefore, had to do be done—but what?

In a few days, Loco, a Warm Springs chief whose band was living with the Chiricahuas, came secretly & asked permission to move his people as close to the soldiers' barracks as would be allowed, so that in case of any disturbances arising it could be seen that he had had nothing to do with them.[65] He was brought in close to the post, & it was deemed wise to do the same with all the Chiricahuas.

Then the mystery was solved.

A delegation of White Mountain chiefs with Sanchez at the head came & protested against allowing those people to live so near the soldiers. [He] desired that they be sent back to their former camps several miles away. Their own people were now able to defend themselves & asked no protection from the military, & the others should be required to do the same. Besides, who was there to hurt them? They need not fear the hostiles, for they were kith & kin to them. To take such good care of them was a piece of uncalled-for favoritism, which was not deserved.

The nantan then informed them that he was fully aware of the plot they were hatching & could understand the motive for their protest, & advised them to go home & work, & send their friends back to San Carlos. If necessary, the soldiers would be used to prevent the massacre of innocent people, & they might rest assured that their scheme of revenge would not be carried out so long as there was a soldier present to interfere.

This brought Sanchez to the middle of the floor, & he made the smoke fly from his cigarette at a furious rate. He started in on a lengthy oration on the subject of vengeance, [to] which the court declined to listen:

> Our homes have been invaded, & our women & children outraged & massacred. Where can we get revenge? Those who committed these crimes are by this time far away in Mexico, & we can't reach them there. By our laws, their kindred here are proper victims, but you have placed them beyond our reach. Yes, more than two hundred of our braves had intended to root out their nest of hornets, counting upon your help rather than opposition. We always have looked on you as one of us, a true Coyotero, but now you've joined the Chiricahuas & act like

an enemy of ours. The mournful cries of our squaws over the
bodies of their dead seem to make sweet music to your ears.

The old man was exuding wrath, & it took some time get him quiet
enough to listen to reason. It was explained to them that so far as the
feelings of the nantan were concerned, he was proud to be a Coyotero, &
would gladly put on war paint & a breechclout & join them in carrying
out just retribution; but his orders from the department commander,
the big chief of the soldiers, forbade it. If disobeyed, the nantan would
be surely punished.

After much discussion of the situation, a compromise was finally
agreed upon to the effect that they might kill every Chiricahua caught
beyond certain well-defined limits around their camp. So they had to
be satisfied with that, which they considered a little better than having
no chances to kill any at all, & went their way casting glances at the
Chiricahuas loafing around the post.

In a few days, the committee stalked in again, squatted themselves on
the floor, & puffed away at their tobacco in [a] very apparent ill-humor.
After sitting in silence an hour or so, as they usually do when they have
an important talk on hand, [Sanchez][66] at last spoke:

We have something to say. Three days & three nights have our
warriors watched that camp, & not even a child has left it.
We've tried every inducement to get some of them out, but
to no purpose. You've gone back on us again, by notifying
them of our agreement. Now we are convinced that you are
a Chiricahua. Our hearts are bleeding.

They were informed that it had been deemed perfectly proper that
their intended victims should be notified, in the interest of peace &
their own good name. If they murdered the innocent, they would be
regarded as fiendish as their enemies, & it was to save them from the
consequences of such crimes that steps had been taken to prevent [the]
commission [of them]. It took some time to make them see it in that
light.

Before the talk ended, there was a commotion outside, & a young
Chiricahua buck rushed in & fell sprawling on the floor, gasping for
breath. [There was] an expression of fear & terror on his face, & perspi-
ration poured forth all over him. Of course, his action created consid-

erable astonishment. Before he could say a word, several White Mountains, with guns & knives, dashed in after him & there was quite [an] ado to keep them from cutting him to pieces.

In the meantime, an excited mob of men, women, & children gathered around the little building, each one eager to have a pass at the fugitive. By the aid of some half dozen scouts that were attracted by the din & excitement, the room was cleared, & the mob held at bay. The frightened youngster in the meantime [found] strength enough to ensconce himself under the table.

It took quite a little time to restore order & find out what it all meant. It seems the young fellow—taking chances of harm from the Coyoteros—went about twelve miles from the post on Turkey Creek to hunt for a horse that had strayed away. Just as he caught the horse, an unfriendly buck caught sight of him, but owing to the dense forest, could not get a shot at him. Both mounted & the race began. The unfortunate [youth] had to pass through several small villages of White Mountains, but before they could understand matters, he was beyond immediate danger, & his pursuer didn't dare to shoot through fear of hitting some of his own people though he yelled "Chiricahua! Kill him. Kill him!" as he passed in headlong pursuit. As he [continued the chase], the hue & cry was raised, & those who could took up the [pursuit].

Emerging from the narrow valley that opened on the plain above the post, he shot along in full view of his pursuers, but they still dared not shoot without [endangering] their own people, or those connected with the post. About two hundred yards from the office, his horse stumbled & fell. With a yell of triumph, they thought they had him, but he was a good runner & the swiftness of his legs saved him.

His excited enemies wanted to cut him to pieces right there in the office, but were made to understand in short order that such butchering would not be allowed. If they had succeeded in their design before he reached the post, it would have been in accordance with the compromise & nothing could be said. The hall of justice, however, was not to be desecrated by any such doings, & must be considered a veritable "city of refuge," & not a place of execution. Several of the leaders of the mob had to be arrested & threatened with severe punishment before quiet was restored. It was [not until] several hours after the crowd dispersed that the hunted man would leave the building & then only in company of the judge, who had to escort him to his tepee. [67]

Many days passed ere he left it to visit even the store. One risk was enough to last him his lifetime. The committee, whose business had thus been interrupted, soon took their leave, saying that they thought they would take a ride around towards Turkey Creek as the day was so fine, but they failed to find any more of such game in the woods. After this episode, the "game" took good care to remain inside the prescribed limits, & the hunters, in great disgust, gradually gave up the chase & disappeared each on his own business.

Thus from time to time, these little interruptions of the dull routine of the ordinary business of the police court relieved to a great extent the monotony of listening to the same stories over & over again, as brought out by the usual family quarrels. Applications for divorce on account of the mother-in-law, or incompatibility of temper, or other ground had failed to keep up the interest they had at first created, on account of the frequency with which they were made. Few decrees were issued, most of the cases being compromised, generally to the disgust of the mother-in-law, who would occasionally "sail in" & read the riot act to the court & require the best efforts of three or four scouts to remove her obnoxious presence.

The End of Gatewood's Tenure as Military Commandant

Gatewood's term as military agent of the White Mountain Apaches ended in November. On the fourteenth Crook informed Crawford: "Have instructed Lt. Gatewood to turn over the management to Lieut. Lockett."[68] The transfer of command was abrupt, unceremonious. Nevertheless, the transfer—which Gatewood had prepared for—took place without problems. Ten days later, Lockett reported that "a small band of hostiles were seen within four miles of Fort Apache."[69] We can only guess at Gatewood's reaction to the current situation. Most likely he knew that warring Indians in the vicinity of the reservation meant problems, problems that he no longer had to deal with.

Chapter Four

Civil Problems

By 1884, Charles Gatewood had established himself as both a leader of Indian scouts and military commandant of the White Mountain Indian Reservation. His close association with Crook, to whom he reported directly, labeled him a "Crook Man."[1] Actually the label was a misnomer, for Gatewood frequently confronted Crook, attempting to obtain the necessities of life for his Indian wards. The antagonism that grew between them with the passing of time set the stage for the final rift in their relationship when Bay-chen-daysen dared to stand up for Indian rights.

Crook fought his own private battle on two fronts: retain complete supremacy over the natives within his region of control and reach the absolute top of the military chain of command. They went hand-in-hand, and Crook, like his major adversary for the number one slot, Gen. Nelson Miles, knew that failure of the first almost certainly meant failure of the second.[2] And it was an uphill battle for him. Two years later Charles F. Lummis, who served as war correspondent for the *Los Angeles Times*, succinctly summarized Crook's situation:

> Since the Civil War no prominent commander has been more persistently, more savagely, more cruelly hounded by jealousy, opposition and many another masked influence than has George Crook. Almost without exception the Territorial papers have damned him—not with "faint praise," but with the bitterest invective. He has been cursed, belittled and lied about, his policy misrepresented, his acts distorted, and alleged acts of his have been made up out of whole cloth. Some of these lies—such as the one about his surrendering to the Apaches in the Sierra Madre in 1878—have already been nailed. Others have not; some never will be. He is a soldier, not a war correspondent. Let the lying go as it will, telegraphed from end to end of the country—he never opens his mouth. He is here to fight, not to justify himself.[3]

Crook himself confirmed Lummis's words in one of his reports: "While the people of this country hold me responsible for the outrages of the hostiles, the past has demonstrated that with even a much larger force than I have at my command, no human foresight can prevent their [the Chokonen, Chihenne, and Bedonkohe Apache] depredations."[4]

Gatewood's problem did not approach this magnitude. His only concern was doing his job to the best of his ability and providing for his family. Because of this, or perhaps in spite of it when one considers how structured the line of command was in the military, he also refused to back away from controversy if he thought he was in the right.

Gatewood had luckily drawn assignments that few other officers ever got the opportunity to perform: commander of Indian scouts and military commandant of a reservation. Perform well, and it would be almost impossible not to advance.

The stage was set. Even if Gatewood realized how critical his decisions would be to his career when he arrested a territorial judge named F. M. Zuck,[5] most likely he would not have altered his course. The stance Gatewood took for Indian rights would be as far-reaching as the stance he made in 1886 when he entered Mexico, found Geronimo and Naiche, and then did what was necessary to ensure they reached the United States safely. In both instances, they give us a good look at the real man.

Gatewood wrote three drafts regarding his civil problems with Zuck.[6] As all three deal with the same subject, they have been merged into one while retaining Gatewood's best selection of words.

Encroachment on Apache Land

Gatewood wrote an introduction to this chapter in two of his drafts: "The Judge's Trial" and "The Trial Chapter." The latter is more polished, and it is the basis for this section, as well as for the entire chapter, unless otherwise noted.[7]

It will be remembered that among the multifarious duties required of the "Judge" by orders & by the laws of the United States was that of protecting both red & white men in their rights on the reservation. This occasioned considerable trouble, & somewhat of [an] embarrassment too, to one who was obliged to act as a sort of buffer between two antagonistic races. One particular "embarrassment" was the necessity of having to sit in the prisoners' dock of a criminal court for several

1st Lt. Charles Gatewood in 1885. Gatewood's pride in his membership in the Sixth U.S. Cavalry is evident in this portrait. His decision to stand up for the rights of the White Mountain Apaches marked the end of any chance he had for advancement within the military. Courtesy: Western History Collections, University of Oklahoma Libraries, Rose Collection, no. 1194.

days, to answer the charge of "false imprisonment against the peace & dignity of the Territory &c.," & this was how it happened:

The mail & supplies for the military at the post & for the civilians allowed to live there had to be hauled in wagons some thirty miles across the Indian reservation, [after a sixty-mile trip] from the railroad. This caused considerable travel on the road from the railway station to the post-mail & passengers by buck-board & freight by heavy wagons. Animals used for this purpose were often allowed to trespass on the corn fields of the natives, & even herds of horses, cattle, & sheep were driven onto the reservation to graze on meadows & pasture lands which the Indians really needed for their own stock & for the hay they hoped to deliver to the quartermaster at Fort Apache to be purchased by him & fed to public animals.

It was necessary to put a stop to these encroachments. They were in violation of law & were [a] menace to the "peace of the community," for the Indians protested with vigor & bitterness. They had been informed that the lands lying within certain well defined boundaries were theirs, & [therefore why] should outsiders be allowed to intrude? That each race should remain on its own side of a line established by the dominant race was insisted on by the "non-dominants," & the former in that neighborhood disputed the proposition—they wanted all [the land] on both sides. It was in vain to point out to the trespassers that they were violating the law & were liable to suffer the punishment of a fine or confiscation of their stock.

What! Fine a white man for allowing his cattle to destroy an Indian's corn crop, or consume or trample down an Indian's hay field? Preposterous!

Yes, they had seen the notices forbidding such things posted in the towns & along the roads, but "the people won't stand it." It did not require many seizures & fines, however, to cause "the people" to understand it. Loss of dollars & cents gradually bred a respect for the law & for the rights of those who were supposed to have none. I refer more particularly to the Mormons, as aggressors on the northern side of the reservation, & could relate many instances of their endeavors to take advantage of the Indians by fair means & foul, & later to acquire an influence over them that might be used against the gentiles, but the story of this trial will suffice to point out the aims & ambitions of the Mormon Church in Arizona.

The Judge and His Proposition

Gatewood's problems began in August 1884, when he was approached by F. M. Zuck, who had a contract to deliver mail between Holbrook and Fort Apache and who wanted to build an eating house and stage station on the White Mountain Indian Reservation at the Forks of the Road. As the trip normally took twenty-three and a half hours, and as the mail delivery passed the Forks of the Road at midnight, Gatewood reasoned that an eating house was not necessary. He immediately wrote Crook, stating his reasons for denying the request, only to be overruled by his commander. Although Zuck was not a Mormon, he associated with Mormons who wielded a lot of power to the north of the reservation, and Crook was aware of the political ramifications that might accompany a denial of the request.[8]

Gatewood met with Zuck and Joseph C. Kay,[9] an Englishman, several times at Fort Apache, at which point he told them that they had to negotiate with the White Mountain Apaches for the price of cutting and hauling hay. On or about September 25, Kay, who acted as Zuck's agent, appeared at Fort Apache to work out the price, and was told he could find Gatewood at Forest Dale, one of the villages on the northern side of the reservation.

Over the years, the ownership of Forest Dale has been clouded in controversy. Located in the southern portion of Navajo County, the problem began in 1877 when white hunters discovered the land—a valley that a tributary of Carrizo Creek, Pedro's old homeland, ran through. The following year Mormons found the valley appealing as it had plenty of timber and water, and settled on the tributary (Forest Dale Creek) that ran through it. In February 1878 Mormon leaders traveled to San Carlos to find out if the land was indeed Indian land, and were assured by the Indian agent that the creek and Arizona Springs were not on Indian land, that the official boundary of the reservation was actually three miles farther south. The reasoning was simple: the natives strayed too far off their land, and the presence of whites would aid in the containment of them. Apaches who then lived in the area were removed by the military, and in March additional settlers moved onto the land. The following year, Mormon missionaries obtained permission from the military authorities at Fort Apache for native families to again live on the creek. After returning to the land, White Mountains claimed that it was really theirs and they wanted the whites to leave. Officials decided that the land was indeed on the reservation and by 1880 all the settlers had left. However, a year later rumors again hinted that the land was not part of the reservation, and settlers moved back onto the land only to flee when the White Mountains revolted in 1881 and the Bedonkohe, Chihenne, and Chokonen Apaches bolted for Mexico (see the introduction). That December, Colonel Eugene Asa Carr confused the issue when he informed the Mormons that the area in question "most likely was not on the reservation."[10] This again reversed in December 1882, when Crawford ordered Gatewood to inform the settlers that the land in question was on the reservation and they had to be off it by spring.

Kay rode out to the village and met with Pedro and his son, Alchesay, whom Gatewood had made the leading chieftain of the White Mountains back in March.[11] Gatewood, John "Old Jack" Conley, and Severiano were also present. Conley translated from English to Spanish and back, while Severiano translated from Spanish to Apache and back.[12]

The contractor [Zuck] for carrying the mail from the railroad to the post of Fort Apache was permitted to establish a station about midway between Show Low & Apache—about twenty miles from the latter, which was on the Indian reservation. There he kept relays of horses for his "buckboard" & frontier accommodations for man & beast. Of course, he needed hay for his own animals & those of others passing [by]. Being "forage agent" of the government, [he] was supposed at all times to be able to entertain all officials & animals from a general to a team mule.

Providing provender for the "mule" brought on the trouble. Men stopping there generally took the precaution to carry with them what they required [for themselves, but not their stock].

To get his hay as cheap[ly] as possible, he bargained with the Indians for the privilege of cutting the grass on certain meadows near his place, agreeing to pay [them] so much money per ton, when gathered & stacked. Having occasioned trouble before, he was distinctly & particularly warned that a failure to pay for the hay after it was stacked, duly measured, & the quantity estimated by the normal rules for such measurement & estimation, seizure of himself & haystack would surely follow, & legal proceedings against him would be instituted. It should be said that the nantan took no part in the making of this contract, but was informed of its purport by both parties, & so long as it was agreeable to them, there was no occasion [for him] to interfere.[13]

Kay Delivers the Hay

Kay was a well-liked shopkeeper, who was considered a "most pleasant and accommodating trader."[14] If he did not have an item a customer wanted, he made every effort to secure the item for his patron. He was active, constantly striving to better his lot. The first president of the Elders quorum, he dug the first irrigation ditch from the creek near the town of Taylor, which was where he opened his first store. He also grew the first garden, planned and built the first bridge, and owned the first mower and threshing machine in Taylor. Later, he owned a sawmill. When his customers could not pay in cash, he happily received payment in other ways, such as grain, fence posts, vegetables, and so on. From his home—his last was near the present-day town of Lakeside—he often "furnished meals for the traveler, and forage for their animals." He often sought contract work and, when the job was large, hired a crew to complete the work.

At the meeting at Forest Dale, Kay agreed to pay ten dollars and an ox as down payment before he began cutting the hay and an additional fifteen dollars within one month. Gatewood saw him flash a wad of bills before the White Mountains, but he did not see any money change hands. As it would turn out, Bay-chen-daysen and the natives did not fully understand the deal, or Kay misrepresented the entire negotiation.

Soon after the meeting, Kay cut the hay and delivered it to Zuck at the Forks of the Road. A broken-down ox was finally delivered to the Indians after the hay had been cut, but, as Pedro complained, it was delivered to the wrong White Mountain and the ox was not as it had been described. Bay-chen-daysen took Conley and rode out to investigate.[15] When Gatewood met with Alchesay, he discovered another disturbing fact: the White Mountains had been duped. They thought they had made a deal to sell the hay to Zuck via Kay. As it turned out, Kay bought the hay at one price, only to resell it to Zuck at a higher price—thus cutting the natives out of this extra money that should have gone to them. Not only did the Indians not receive what was owed them, but they had been cheated out of the full price. During cross-examination, the defense asked Gatewood to comment on Alchesay's unhappiness with the contract. He answered:

> The dissatisfied Indians claimed that the hay on these cienagas was worth a great deal more than was agreed on and they were therefore losing the difference of what they were getting and what it was really worth. I told the Indians that Pedro made the bargain for them, and he was responsible for selling the hay for less than it was worth. That Mr. Zuck would soon be on the reservation to buy for his stations, and then they could make their bargain with him. Since Mr. Kay was to haul his hay off the reservation, [t]hey were [anxious] to furnish Mr. Zuck with hay at the two stations on the reservation. When Mr. Kay delivered his hay at the Forks of the Road contrary to his agreement, it produced much discontent among the Indians.[16]

And then to a question regarding the Indians' complaint of a violation of the contract, Gatewood said:

> That Mr. Kay had agreed to take this hay for his own use, and not compete with them in selling hay to Mr. Zuck or to the Government, [t]hat they had to wait several days for the ox, and take one not as good as the one promised, and that they believed that Mr. Zuck wanted to get his hay for nothing and thus . . . deprive them of the market for the amount required.

After a year's supply of hay had been stacked in the corral at the station, the Indians naturally wanted their money.[17] Upon their demand for it, they were informed by the purchaser that they had already been paid in full & that he did not propose to submit to extortion. This was a surprise to them & they wanted to know to whom the payment had been made. Receiving no satisfactory reply, they hastened to complain of their treatment & to insist that now that the man had the hay, he should pass over to the representative Indians the amount agreed upon.

Full & impartial investigation was made & it was discovered that one Indian, not a member of the committee appointed by them to receive & distribute the purchase money, had been given a pair of canvas pants. Other [Indians], also not of this committee, had been the recipients of a broken-down steer left along the roadside by a Mormon freighter on his way to the post. The pants were scarcely what even a Mormon in that country would call his "Sunday best," & the steer, though he had some flesh on him, consisted mainly of hide, bones, & low spirits.

Now, when a man is offered anything, from a drink to a farm, he generally takes it—at least white men do. So with these individuals, being descendants of Adam & Eve (probably through the Chinese), accepted such evidences of goodwill & friendliness, & wondered at such munificence, considering the source.[18] To them it was simple liberality on the part of the donors, nothing having been said about hay. The [original] partners in the hay transaction, being also members of the human family, loudly & emphatically declined to consider this transfer of the pants & the steer as even a first payment on the amount due.

The steer had been killed where he lay on the roadside, & his edible parts consumed within a few hours after he had been given to them, so that there was no restitution so far as he was concerned. But the pants were recovered & were offered by the contractor's agent to the chief of the band, in the hope of pacifying them all. But the chief happened to be "Alchesay," already referred to as he appeared at San Carlos for the "round up" & count with his warriors more than a year before.[19] He considered it a personal affront to be offered the cast-off clothing of a Mormon teamster, & as chairman & spokesman of the "committee of reception," insisted on the payment of the full amount. He refused to consider the pants & steer as [any] credit on the account. [He] intimated that if they did not get their just dues in one way, they would in another. This was no idle threat, & it meant prospective "trouble," for the band lived near the northern boundary of the reservation, & just beyond [it] were numerous [gentile &] Mormon settlements. [Many had] horses & cattle at large.

Up to this time, the Indians had voluntarily driven stock off the reservation, instead of impounding them as they might have done & were instructed to do. The laws of the United States prohibit the grazing of animals on [the reservation], & provide certain punishments for such trespass—a fine of a dollar a head, or seizure & sale [of the herd] as under the [U.S.] customs laws. The statute uses the word "cattle," & certain owners of sheep undertook to appropriate all the grazing grounds because "sheep" were not "cattle" & therefore the law virtually allowed them to drive their herds on & over these reserved lands. The United States District Attorney gave his opinion to the effect that bulls, cows, & steers only were "cattle." The Attorney General of the United States decided that sheep were "cattle." [This] convinced the wool-growing trespasser—cash arguments [are] always convinc[ing].

Now Alchesay & his followers knew which ranches [belonged to] Mormons & which [belonged to] gentiles. [They also knew] the brands of each stock owner, &, if so determined, [they] could easily [exact] heavy tribute on those near the line. [Their] country was mountainous, with miles of dense forest & hundreds of secluded valleys & cañons, [and they could drive] stolen cattle without fear of discovery. Should they resort to this method of "getting even," the property & perhaps the lives of innocent people would be sacrificed, for as a rule with Apaches, [every wrong must be avenged].[20]

Gatewood Arrests Zuck and His Cohorts

After meeting with Pedro and Alchesay at Forest Dale, Gatewood, with a company of Indian police as escort, rode to the Forks of the Road station to confront Zuck.

After due consideration, it was decided that the hay should be paid for according to the agreement entered into & fully understood by all interested. The contractor declined to give further consideration—an outrage was being perpetrated. Why should a white man of his standing be made to pay for the property of a lot of ragged Indians? He was given the alternative: "Pay or arrest."[21]

"Arrest! Arrest me?" said [Zuck]. "I'm a United States mail contractor; Justice of the Peace in the town where I live & am going there now to hold my court; candidate for the territorial legislature (the thirteenth so celebrated afterwards), & an American citizen;" & slapping his breast with great dignity, [added]: "I will not pay & no one dares to arrest me."

He really believed himself to be the most important man in that county. Through not a Mormon, his political aspirations were materially encouraged by that church, being their candidate for the legislature. He also numbered among his constituency a considerable number of "toughs" and "rustlers." He therefore looked upon himself as all-powerful, a future leader of his party—in fact, an all round unapproachable.

"Jug him," was the order.[22]

The chief of scouts [Conley], who on such occasions executed the mandates of the court, had been a soldier in the regular army for many years, & when he was ordered to make an "arrest," would entertain no argument against the carrying out of his order. Result—arrest & confinement [of Zuck] in the guard house at Fort Apache, along with his Mormon agents [Kay & Jones]. A guard of scouts was placed over the hay-stack until it was paid for a few weeks afterwards.

The Zuck, Kay, and Jones Hearing

On October 21, Zan L. Tidball, who served as U.S. Marshal from July 18, 1882, until 1885, transported Zuck, Jones, and Kay to the Third Judicial District of Arizona Territory, in Prescott.[23] The trip took three days. Before leaving Fort Apache, Tidball delivered a summons that instructed Gatewood, his second in command on the reservation, Hamilton Roach (Sixth U.S. Cavalry), and Conley to appear as witnesses for the prosecution.[24] The Zuck, Kay, and Jones trial began at 10:00 a.m. on October 27, with the Honorable William H. McGrew presiding.[25] E. M. Sanford and J. T. Bostwick were council for the defense while Assistant District Attorney Edward W. Wills served as prosecutor. Gatewood was the only witness called to testify during the two days of proceedings.

Within the five days required by law, [Zuck] & his two Mormon agents [Kay & Jones], were duly delivered to United States Marshal [Tidball] to be brought before the commissioner in the capital city [Prescott]. Proper charges were preferred. In a short time an examination was held before a United States commissioner, numerous witnesses being present.

The commissioner was an old, gray-haired, partially bald man [McGrew] of great dignity, & of the same political faith as the defendant, & was also addressed as "Judge." His spectacles emitted rays of the wisest & most serenely judicial effulgence, inspiring an awe that made the beholder conscious of the presence of a mighty mentality that could convert a Webster's dictionary into an encyclopedia of all legal knowledge.

In this august presence the examination proceeded. The facts were related just as they had occurred, & the statutes bearing on the case quoted & shown to the judge. Prosecuting attorney [Wills] made his speech, reciting the law & the facts, & urged commitment of the defendant to await the action of the grand jury.

[Next], the attorney for the defense reviewed "the so-called facts as

set forth in the [written] testimony of the five witnesses for the prosecution," [then] declared that they were refuted by the simple story of
his client. [26] [He] utterly ignored the statutes, except to assert that there
was a "technicality in them," & wound up with a grand peroration in
this style:

> Your Honor sees before you here a man who's on the bench
> himself. He ought now to be holding court in his own precinct
> & running that mail line. The other candidate for the legis-
> lature is making capital out of this arrest, & if my innocent
> client don't soon get back to his county, he'll be beaten & our
> territory will lose his valuable services. Then Sir, look at that
> 'technicality!' There it is, big as life, staring out of the statute
> book, & your Honor can't get around it. I hope your Honor
> will dismiss this case at once, so that my client can get away on
> the stage tonight, for he's losing time here. We submit the case.

His "Honor" spent a few moments in profound cogitation, then
loudly blew his nose, arranged his spectacles in the fashion most becoming to oracular wisdom, &, assuming his most dignified manner,
delivered himself thus: "The most prominent citizen of that county is
here before me on these charges. It's only necessary to state that there's a
technicality here in this statute book which the accused is justly entitled
to the benefit of."

[On the stand as] principal witness for the prosecution, [I] interrupted: "Where's the technicality, judge?"

"In the law, sir," thundered the judge in deep tones of outraged dignity, glaring through those awful spectacles at the questioner.

The attorney for the accused was on his feet in an instant & with great
excitement fairly yelled, "I submit, your Honor, the witness has no right
to ask questions, not being a lawyer."

The judge, whose face was aflame with indignation at the presump-
tuous interrogation by the witness, replied to the lawyer, "You're right,
sir, witnesses don't ask questions." Then bringing to bear his judicial
spectacles, glanced around the room at all present, [&] resumed the announcement of his decision: "On account of this great technicality, the
accused & his agents will be released right off, & this court's adjourned."

That settled it, though the matter might have been laid before the
grand jury, at its next meeting. But if the present proceedings held by

one man may be taken as a pointer, a collection of them might indict the other man, & besides the only object sought was to show that there was a legal limit to imposition on the wards of the nations. However, no further prosecution was made. There was nothing for the witnesses to do, but draw their mileage from the U.S. Marshal & go home—some two hundred fifty miles distant.[27]

On the street that afternoon, [I met] one of the Mormons [Joseph Kay].[28] He informed me that he "got it straight," that he was entitled to twenty dollars damages for false imprisonment, but would be satisfied with less if a compromise could be affected. He would like half of that amount right away if there was government money available to pay it, & the check might be drawn before we left town. Upon being informed of the mode of collecting such damages from Uncle Sam, he evinced surprise & disappointment, & said, "Well, I reckon that it'll take too long, so you'll have to pay me whatever you can. You ain't got no property but a hoss, but if you'll give me that & the ten dollars, I will give it to the lawyer to retain him in my case for damages, & we'll call it square."[29]

Poor simple-minded Mormon was greatly disappointed when he finally realized that he would get no "hoss," & that he was out ten dollars for professional advice & "retainment." He had to borrow money to get home on, & he has received no damages yet, that [I] know of.

Gatewood's Trouble Begins

The newspapers had a field day at Gatewood's expense. In a news clipping entitled "Gatewood—Zuck" that was published shortly after the trial ended, Gatewood was singled out as "judge, jury, [&] witness." The slant of the article was definitely opposed to Gatewood and the natives, and it went on to say that the three defendants had been incarcerated "in the Black Hole of Calcutta, or what may be worse, the filthy Indian den at Apache."[30] It concluded that Zuck and company had been charged with stealing what they had legally contracted to obtain. It would get worse, as another article demonstrates:

> We wonder if Lieut. Gatewood, our modern Wirtz, yet thinks that Apache county is under martial law. We wonder if he will longer be permitted to command a band of savages to arrest peaceable citizens and cast them, Daniel like, into a lions den. We wonder if he will again assume the roll of the tyrant, and

practice the Shadrack, Meshack and Abednego business, for the delight or delectation of his brutal horde. The supremacy of the law has been maintained, and the people everywhere rejoice.[31]

By this time Gatewood had been on detached duty from his regiment since November 1881. The lieutenant's captain, Charles G. Gordon (Sixth U.S. Cavalry), who had been on sick leave, requested on November 22 that Gatewood rejoin his Troop D, then stationed at Fort Stanton, New Mexico.[32] The request was immediately endorsed. As Gatewood performed the duties as military commandant of the reservation as well as commanded two companies of Indian scouts (currently D and E), Crook could not afford to lose him. He ignored his anger at Gatewood's conduct regarding Zuck and made sure that Gatewood remained at Fort Apache.

If Gatewood thought he had seen the last of Zuck, he was sadly mistaken. Although there would be threats, nothing happened. Life seemingly returned to normal. Bay-chen-daysen forgot about Zuck and went about administering to his wards. He received his promotion to first lieutenant on January 3, 1885.[33]

Then in February 1885, Gatewood was subpoenaed to attend a hearing before the Grand Jury in St. Johns, the county seat of Apache County, to see if he should be indicted for felonious false arrest of Zuck, Jones, and Kay.[34] Unlike Zuck who had political clout as Crook had warned, Gatewood would face this new development virtually alone. Crook washed his hands of Gatewood in his time of need, setting the stage for ending their relationship.

The lieutenant may have faced his ordeal seemingly alone, but the question of which land belonged to the reservation and which land did not continued to plague the military personnel then overseeing the administration of the Indians. Desirous of the property rimming the perimeter of the reservation, whites persisted in their quest to reclaim the land. On February 23, 1885, the *Daily Phoenix Herald* reported: "Writs of injunction have been issued restraining Capt. E. Crawford, commanding at San Carlos, and others from further interference with rights of citizens who, he claims, are on the reservation. The plaintiff claims that the military survey does not establish the boundary as Congress enacted and that the surveys of Indian reservations should be made by the land department."[35]

[Zuck's people circulated] papers & pamphlets just before the election, setting forth the hardships of the aspirant for legislative honors, & in which were used such expressions & headlines as "Behind the Gates of the Bastille," "Disgrace to Shoulder Straps," "Modern Wirtz of Andersonville," & so on, [but it did not help]. [36] A few weeks afterward, the election was held, & our candidate was defeated. [He] got what Pete Kitchen is said to have gotten in Mexico, "Left." [37] The other man was returned.

The defeated candidate was irate. So were the toughs & the Mormon Church whom he represented. [A] mass meeting was held in a barroom [in Show Low], and his defeat was ascribed to his arrest & incarceration. [38] His friends claimed that the hay trouble had been trumped up in the interest of his opponent. [39] [They] "resolved" after several "whereases," that an invitation be extended to the author of all this mischief to visit the town where our friend resided, & receive an ovation in the shape of tar & feathers. These resolutions were duly published in the local paper & copies were sent to the intended victim with endorsements such as "Read & reflect," "Your name is Dennis," & so on.

Safely ensconced among several hundred Apache henchmen, as it were, this created no particular alarm in the heart of the recipient. [Besides], the writer [had been] assured by a written document signed by all the merchants & most of the property holders [along the northern border of the reservation who] approved of the action in the hay business as in the interest of common justice & prevention of Indian outbreaks.

A few days after the receipt of the invitation to take on a coat of tar & feathers, a telegram from the United States Marshal informed me that my presence was required as a witness in some case before the United States court. A subpoena had been issued, & in order to save him the trouble of serving it & the court the time it would take him to make so long a journey (nearly three hundred miles), [he] requested my immediate departure from the post.

To obey this summons, it was necessary to spend all night, & more than half the next day, in the town where tar & feathers had been offered—no pleasant prospect. [40] [I] put up at an opposition hotel, the landlord & landlady of which announced publicly that no guest of that house should be thus "mistreated," especially as he was an old patron & he belonged to the army. It is sufficient to say that the boys didn't have their fun, as the element of risk was too great. When the landlady said, "Ye can't molest him," that settled it, for the crowd knew she meant it. The crowd also knew that there were men who would back up Mother B.; so they went off to their barroom headquarters & voted to change it to hanging. The upshot of it was, there were no feathers & no hanging & the guest was allowed to roam around at his own sweet will. Perhaps the decided stand taken by Mother B. prevented trouble, it's hard to tell. At any rate, if she was a friend, she was a friend indeed, & her foes never came near her. She was gentle & generous to a degree to those she liked, but had no use for "enemies."[41]

The Grand Jury Indicts Gatewood

Gatewood's hearing in St. John's would begin an ordeal that would test his endurance. Zuck's friend, the Honorable Sumner Howard, presided over the Grand Jury.[42] Gatewood had probably heard of him, as he had gained fame in Utah for successfully prosecuting Mormon pioneer John Doyle Lee in 1876.[43] Using the power of his office as chief justice, on February 6, 1885, Howard, who had become chief justice of Arizona in 1884, obtained what he wanted—three separate indictments for felonious false arrest.[44] The next day, Indictment No. 49 was issued. It read:

> The said Charles B. Gatewood on or about the 15th day of October A.D. 1884 and before the finding of this Indictment at the County of Apache, Territory of Arizona, the said Charles B. Gatewood then and there being, with force and arms at the County and Territory aforesaid, in and upon one F. M. Zuck, in the peace of the Territory of Arizona then and there being, did, him, the said F. M. Zuck then and there unlawfully and injuriously, and against the will of the said F. M. Zuck and against the laws of the Territory of Arizona and without any legal warrant, and without sufficient legal authority, or lawful cause whatever imprison, confine, and detain him, the said, F. M. Zuck for a long period of time, to wit: for the period of six days next following.[45]

Two other indictments were issued at the same time: no. 50 (Jones) and no. 51 (Kay) were almost verbatim repeats of Zuck's. All were presented to the Grand Jury three days later.

In the course of time, the Grand Jury of that territorial district met, & of the many crimes called to their attention, was this one of the false imprisonment of an eminent citizen & his two Mormon tools. This Grand Jury was composed of Jews, Mexicans, Gentiles, & Mormons. At first they declined to find indictments for the alleged crimes of false imprisonment of the three innocents, & so let it be generally known. Trial would entail great expense on the county, & the treasury was already suffering from forged warrants! There were only 11,000.00 [dollars] on hand after taxes had been collected, & that amount was afterward stolen from the treasury safe. So taxes had to be collected twice, &c. But the judge was an ex-army officer, & "exited" soon after the war never having taken part in it in the field, & the manner of his exit was let down to resignation, so he had no love for any man [who] wore the blue.[46] He was chief justice of the territory & was regarded with great awe & respect by the mob generally.

Upon hearing that the Grand Jury declined to find the indictments, he had them brought into court & there delivered them a lecture the gist of which was: "now is your chance to cinch shoulder straps that are trying to turn this country." As a matter of fact, the jury went back to their room & "cinched" to the extent of their power, which was the finding of three indictments for false imprisonment. They thought the judge was displeased at their failure to find true bills, therefore true bills must "go." Thus things switched around & made the accuser a defendant with an excellent chance of getting a sentence of eighteen months in the county jail. The feelings of the governor [Frederick Tritle] were most unfriendly & therefore the hope of a pardon was slim.[47]

Gatewood's Trial Begins

As a warrant for Gatewood's arrest had not yet been issued, he hurried back to the reservation.[48] By this time, Britton Davis and the Bedonkohes, Chihennes, and Chokonens had made Turkey Creek their new home in the White Mountains, and Gatewood visited their camp whenever possible.[49] During this time, his relationship with Crook began to fall apart and he became acquainted with Geronimo. Crook's less than sterling record of backing his subordinate in obtaining necessities for his wards, combined with his continued lack of support in the Zuck affair, began to sour Gatewood on his commander.[50]

Soon after his return to the reservation, the warrant for his arrest was issued. However, it would not be served. When Sheriff J. L. Hubbell reached the northern edge of the reservation, he saw Gatewood's heavily armed Indian police patrolling the border.[51] Placing a greater value on his life than his current duty, he decided not to cross into the native reserve.[52]

Geronimo, Mangus, and other Apaches began to fear for their lives. Every time Mickey Free, a red-haired Mexican who was blind in one eye, and Chatto, a former Chokonen warrior who now served as a sergeant of Indian scouts for Davis, passed them, they drew their hands across their throats with a slicing motion, indicating that they would soon be dead.[53] The simple act of Free and Chatto drawing their hands across their throats whenever they saw Geronimo, Naiche, Chihuahua, and Mangus cannot be understated and played a major role in the Apaches deciding to run. Since Geronimo and the others were fearful to begin with, this act played upon their psyches. To cap matters, Free reported the latest news printed in newspapers regarding Geronimo, mainly that the Arizona press marked him as a "dead man walking." Geronimo, no fool, knew that if he did not run, he would soon be dead.

Geronimo later explained to Crook his reasons for leaving the reservation:

> I want to talk first of the causes which led me to leave the reservation. I was living quietly and contented, doing and thinking of no harm, while at the Sierra Blanca [the White Mountain Indian Reservation]. I don't know what harm I did to those three men, Chatto, Mickey Free, and Lieutenant Davis. I was living peaceably and satisfied when people began to speak bad of me. I should be glad to know what started those stories. I was living peaceably with my family, having plenty to eat, sleeping well, taking care of my people, and perfectly contented. I don't know where those bad stories first came from. There we were doing well and my people well. I was behaving well. I hadn't killed a horse or man, American or Indian. I don't know what was the matter with the people in charge of us. They knew this to be so and yet they said I was a bad man and the worst man there; but what harm had I done? I was living peaceably and well, but I did not leave on my own accord. Had I so left it would have been

right to blame me; but as it is, blame those men who started this talk about me. Sometime before I left, an Indian named Wadiskay had a talk with me. He said, "They are going to arrest you," but I paid no attention to him, knowing that I had done no wrong; and the wife of Magnus, "Huera," told me that they were going to seize me and put me and Magnus in the guardhouse, and I learned from the American and Apache soldiers, from Chatto, and Mickey Free, that the Americans were going to arrest me and hang me, and so I left. I would like to know now who it was that gave the order to arrest me and hang me.[54]

Citing Britton Davis, Crook reported the military take on the unrest:

The opposition of the chiefs Mangus and Geronimo to the punishment of members of their bands for offences committed on the reservation. Mangus is under the control of his wife who has been a captive in Mexico and consequently is able to speak Mexican and has sufficient intelligence to be troublesome. Mangus insisted that the[y] had been promised immunity from punishment for all offences not capital and denied the right of Lieut. Davis to interfere with their tiswin drunks unless killing resulted. Geronimo joined Mangus in opposition when Davis refused to release a squaw belonging to his band whom he had confined for making tiswin.[55]

The threat as well as what Geronimo, Mangus, and others considered as hostile living conditions was clear, and Geronimo had no intention of waiting around until it worsened or someone murdered him. Certain that treachery could not be far off, Geronimo and Mangus, along with Naiche, and those of their people who chose to follow them bolted the reservation on May 17, 1885. Although the initial report placed the number of Apaches on the run at 50, later reports ranged anywhere between 40 to 50 men and 96 to 103 women and children to 143 of the 550 Bedonkohes, Chokonens, and Nednhis under Britton Davis's control at Turkey Creek.[56]

Gatewood joined the initial pursuit, and afterwards he led a patrol into the Black Range of New Mexico to ensure that all the Apaches who had bolted the reservation had left the region and moved into Mexico (see chapter 3 and appendix A for additional information on this patrol).

His participation in the last Apache war ended early in July. By this time, Gatewood's relationship with Crook had deteriorated to the point where Bay-chen-daysen just wanted out. Citing his trouble with Zuck as the reason, he submitted his resignation from Indian Command. Crook denied the request.[57]

Bay-chen-daysen continued to work with and administer to the White Mountain Apaches. However, his ongoing problems with Crook and government bureaucracy seemed to be a never-ending hell. Finally, on August 5, in a letter to the adjutant general of the army, he went above Crook and asked "to be relieved from my present duties in connection with the management of Indian affairs."[58] He wanted to rejoin his regiment, which was then stationed in New Mexico. Crook finally acquiesced on August 14 and forwarded the paperwork to the Division of the Pacific "with recommendation that this request be granted."[59] But then a month and a half later Crook changed his mind and sent a telegram: "Lt. Gatewood, now on duty in charge of White Mountain Apaches[,] has been relieved by orders of the War Dept. and ordered to join his regiment without delay. Lt. Gatewood has been indicted for a matter in connection with his administration of his duties[. H]is trial has been set for Dec[ember] seventh and it will prejudice his case if he is obliged to leave before trial. I therefore request that I may retain him until his matter is decided."[60]

Before Crook changed his mind, a warrant was issued for Gatewood's arrest, but it was never served. In telling the story, Gatewood became confused as to who actually was sheriff and who was deputy sheriff. J. L. Hubbell, who owned Hubbell's trading post, was sheriff, not deputy sheriff, at this time and it was he who first attempted to serve the warrant. Not daring to cross the reservation, he later sent his brother, F. A. Hubbell, who was a deputy sheriff, to Fort Apache, to speak with Gatewood and ask him to give himself up. When Gatewood appeared at St. Johns soon after, J. L. Hubbell, via F. A. Hubbell, served the warrant for his arrest.[61]

The sheriff's deputy [actually J. L. Hubbell] attempted to serve his warrant on the Indian reservation & was sent about his business. He had neglected to serve it when he might have enforced it, off the reserve, & in consequence an attempt was made to oust him from his office. He asserted in his defense that the man [to be served] was down there

among the Apaches with several hundred well-armed bucks around him & it would take more than the whole county to get him, since the legality of the warrant is denied & its service will be resisted. But that made no difference; they wanted to fire him out of his office anyhow.

He sent his brother [Deputy Sheriff F. A. Hubbell] to explain matters & say it would be a great favor if the wanted [man] would appear & deliver himself up, a favor he would never regret. So it was deemed best to surrender & have done with the business especially as the goodwill of the sheriff might & would indeed prove to be valuable since he had considerable influence [with] the average juror.

Six months [had] passed by [since the indictment], &, with wife & six shooter & mounted on a mule, the seventy-five miles to the hall of justice were made in two days. [62] Turning up on the day the court met [September 5], capitulation was arranged & settled with an 1500.00 dollar bond.[63] The case was set among the first on the docket, & was very promptly called [September 7], & the prisoner duly arraigned, the judge commanding: "Prisoner at the bar, stand up!" & he stood up. The clerk read a great long rigmarole of "to-wits," "did falsely imprison," "against the peace & dignity of the Territory," &c, &c.

"How say you, guilty or not guilty?"

"Not guilty."

The courthouse was crowded with a heterogeneous collection of cowboys, Mexicans, Mormons, toughs generally, along with quite a number of farmers, cattle owners, & other decent people. Nearly everybody carried a six-shooter, & so as not to be out of fashion the prisoner had one, too, but carried it concealed.

The plea of "Not guilty" made quite a stir in the crowd. Some hissed & others applauded, as their feelings prompted them. A fight [broke out] in the back part of the room, which created quite a commotion. It was only fisticuffs, but it bade fair to bring on a general row, when it was cut short by an order from the court to the sheriff to clear the room. It took some minutes to drive everybody out, but no sooner was the door shut on the last of the evicted, when everybody returned & that took several minutes more. When quiet was finally restored, the judge lectured the mob & announced that the next offenders would be sent to jail.

The trial proceeded. The prosecution announced that they were not ready & asked for a continuance. One of the attorneys for the prisoner was the same [one] that had appeared before the commissioner for the other prisoner [Zuck] & made that unanswerable argument.[64] He was just as zealous now as then & transferred his apparent feelings from one side to the other with great ease. [He] spread [himself] in a stirring appeal to the court to have the trial proceed to the end that justice might be administered & the prisoner's mind be relieved of the great strain that bid fair to shatter it. "Either he should go to jail for eighteen months," yelled the speaker, "or he should be free & able to hold his head up among his peers in this sun-kissed land." Although it was a "greatest effort of his life" speech, it did no good, for it was not intended that the case should be tried. They had formed an unbreakable trust on fees & the market was cornered. Of course the case was continued for another six months. It looked as if this business would never end till the surplus in the treasury was exhausted & the territory placed in the hands of receivers.

The case was continued to the next term of the court just six months from that time. But before the victim was allowed to leave, his lawyers [proposed] to change the bonds & give more dignity to the bonded, thereby increasing the chances of acquittal. But the "bonded" couldn't see it in that way, strongly protested against further change, & intimated that he would appeal to the court to head off this fee-making. When called upon for [further] explanation of his reason for raising the bonds [of] his own client, [counsel] said: "A mere formality required by practice. The sureties are here & we'll go right away to the clerk's office & fix the matter up," & [the] bonds were increased to 1800.00 dollars.[65] The U.S. paid him 30.00 dollars for his services in the bond business & his client hurried out of town for fear they would be raised again.

Gatewood's Trial Continues

Since his last court appearance, Gatewood had relinquished his position as military commandant of the White Mountain Indian Reservation and severed his relationship with the White Mountain Apaches. Lt. James Lockett had replaced him as commandant. Even though the war raged all around him, Gatewood sat; he no longer commanded a company of Indian scouts. Finally in December, Crook released him and he was ordered to Fort Stanton, New Mexico Territory, where he would rejoin his regiment.[66]

Unfortunately for Gatewood, his stay at Stanton was short-lived. His experience with Indians was too valuable, and he received orders to report to Fort Wingate, in northwest New Mexico, to command a company of Navajo scouts. This assignment did not please Gatewood as it separated him from Georgia, who remained at Stanton. Even though he never saw action with the Diné, as the Navajo call themselves, because the government never got around to issuing them weapons, he considered them little more than "loafers."[67]

Crook may have seen the last of Gatewood, eliminating what must have amounted to little more than an irritation when considered in the overall picture of the general's agenda—bringing the warring Apaches to bay—but he had not seen the last of Miles's quest for his position, which he had been aware of dating back to at least November of the previous year when he complained to Sheridan about the matter. On January 8, 1886, the *Arizona Journal-Miner* reported: "The President has decided to relieve General Crook from his command in Arizona, and will probably" replace him with "General Miles within the next week or ten days."[68] Continuing, the *Journal-Miner* stated, "the pressure upon the President to make a change is very strong and comes both from friends of General Miles—who is anxious to try his hand at the job—and the people of Arizona, who have lost confidence in Crook." Luckily for Crook, Sheridan did not make the change in leadership.

In March 1886, Gatewood again headed for St. Johns. Although he was not aware of it when he left Fort Wingate, the Honorable Sumner Howard had been replaced by the Honorable John C. Shields.[69] Shields, whose honesty and integrity were unquestioned, was one of the youngest men ever to hold the position of chief justice of Arizona Territory. This did not mean that Gatewood had seen the last of Howard, not by a long shot. Howard now served as the prosecution's chief counsel. Gatewood's case generated considerable interest about town as people voiced their views to convict or acquit. The staunchly drawn sides guaranteed a packed courthouse.[70] As soon as the court came to order, Zuck attempted to impose his clout, only to be reprimanded.

Once again the half-yearly session opened & all the bars, including that of justice, [ran] under a forced draught that made the town red-hot. Cattle & sheep men, gentiles & Mormons, white men & Mexicans, & various political cliques—all contributed fuel to the furnace, & the ship of state scudded along at a furious speed. Now & then a man

Brig. Gen. Nelson A. Miles during the last Apache war. *Harper's Weekly*, September 18, 1886. From the author's collection.

fell overboard & was lost in the waves; but that made no difference as everybody expected to go over the rail sooner or later, with the help of his neighbor.

The judge [Howard] in the meantime had been removed, & a new man [Shields] from an eastern state sat in the chair, or rather on the bench. He had not become accustomed to the ways & methods of the country, for he greatly offended the principal witness on the other side of this case. It [happened thusly]: The defeated political aspirant naturally wanted revenge, especially when the territory could be made to pay for it, & for this purpose, proposed to leave no stone unturned. Upon the arrival of the judge, my friend [Zuck] called on him, introduced himself, & stated that he wanted to tell him the whole story so that the judge might get it straight & render his decisions properly, for on starting in, it was necessary to be on the popular side. Otherwise, he might as well not open his court. The judge considered this speech an insult to his integrity & [Zuck,] the eminent exponent of the art of [coercion,] rapidly skipped out of the door with a milder estimate of his power of persuasion.

It would perhaps be as well to state here that a new occupant [Conrad M. Zulick] of the gubernatorial chair had arrived a few months before [October 1885], who was known to be a personal friend of the justice now holding court.[71] [Zulick] also received a visit from the persecuted one [Zuck], listened to the tale of his woes, & was requested to use his influence with the judge [in order] that justice might be done a wronged & prominent citizen. The door of the governor's office was slammed against the coat tails of the persuader.

Learning [of] these things from the gentlemen themselves, the prisoner at the bar felt that the court was not prejudiced against him but would be impartial, & that if the worst came to the worst, it would not be difficult to obtain a pardon. So there was reasonable hope, if this business could be ended during the incumbency of these two officials, there'd be no incarceration in the county jail.

Well, the case was again called one day [March 24, 1886] just before noon adjournment, but the district attorney had had time to announce that their side was ready, having all their witnesses present, & was anxious to go ahead & finish by placing this man where he belonged—in gaol.[72] He then introduced as associate council the man [Howard] who had previously occupied the judge's seat & had caused the finding of the "true bills." The defense would rather have him prosecute than run the whole court. The Mormon Church had presented him with a handsome retainer with a promise of a substantial bonus in case of conviction. The last postponement was made at the instance of the prosecution & it was now our turn. You see, it was only fair to alternate in these courtesies. So the prisoner was informed during the recess that it would be best to wait till the next term of the court, as the council felt sure that conviction would surely follow a trial at this term. [73] By delaying six more months immunity from punishment was assured: by going on now at least eighteen months languishing in a prison cell was certain. "We have examined the list of jurors to be drawn," said they, "& you are sure to be convicted. We propose, when the court meets, to ask for a continuance."

"And I propose to be tried," answered the prisoner, "even if I have to conduct my own case, & will state to the court that we are ready."

This decisive answer was prompted by a belief that a plea to the jurisdiction of the court would be sustained, for the arrests were made on a United States reservation, & this was a territorial court; & even in case of conviction, a pardon would be promptly granted. So, when court opened, it astonished the prosecutors to hear it announced: "We are ready for trial, your honor."

Then came the tedious process of impaneling a jury. [74] We did not object to a single Mexican, because the sheriff was "solid" with them, & "our" appearance on time saved trouble for the sheriff, so we were "solid" with him. Finally, the territory had one more peremptory challenge, the name of the juror was called, & he was notified to step to one side as he was excused.

"Why, Judge," said he, "I can try this case according to the law & the evidence, not having any bad feelings against anybody, & I want to stay right here. I'm a square man," & he gazed around with an expression that said: "Who objects?"

It was not till the sheriff was ordered to remove him that he would consent to go. He went out exceedingly wrathy, stopping to whisper to the prisoner that he'd "get even with those scoundrels yet." He had been a member of the legislature & so on, & had a grudge against the principal witness, the man in whose behalf all these proceedings were had. That morning accosting him on the street with: "How are you Mr. M.?" (just as well to be polite to possible jurors), he turned his back, &

jerking his thumb over his shoulder, replied, "You go on; don't speak to me. I'm liable to be on your jury, & if that friend of yours sees us talking, I'll be fired off. Oh! the ———" & he applied a series of appellations that are not fit for ears or eyes polite, & he passed on. If he had been on the jury, a plea of "guilty" would not have been able to cause him to vote "guilty,"—he hated the other man too much.

Well, the case went on. The fact of arrest & confinement was conceded, but before the plea to the jurisdiction of the tribunal could be entered, all the evidence for the prosecution had to be given. It is unnecessary to relate the tales of suffering & hardship that had been undergone by these victims of military despotism. Now & then during the recital, "liar" would come out from the crowd, answered by "you're another," & then a scuffle. The intervention of the sheriff would produce order & the witness would proceed.

Although Gatewood did not provide details of the testimony against him, a reporter for the *Prescott Morning Courier*, did:

> Mr. Zuck detailed his arrest and subsequent alleged cruel and inhuman treatment, incarceration in an Indian guard house without bed or bedding and in the midst of vermin; his forced march to Show Low, under guard of eight or ten armed Indians, and thence his trip to Prescott, in charge of Marshal Donovan; his trial and discharge there before and by U.S. Commissioner McGrew. His testimony was very long and, in the manner of its giving, very dramatic. He stated his repeated and vain efforts to learn the cause of his arrest. He was severely cross-examined by Sanford, with good result to the defense. Mr. Kay was called to corroborate him, and his testimony, being important, occupied [the] balance of [the first] day.[75]

The court adjourned at 5:30 p.m. that day.

The Second Day of the Trial

The court reconvened at 9:00 a.m. the next day. "Mr. Zuck was recalled, and after opening communications as to the cutting of hay on the White Mountain reservation from Gen. Crook, Lieutenants Gatewood and Roach, &c., the prosecution rested."[76] Howard presented for the prosecution, and after he finally relinquished the floor, J. C. Herndon, speaking in Gatewood's behalf, "addressed the court in a concise, legal argument of fifteen minutes, covering the only legal proposition involved—jurisdiction." The court adjourned for dinner, and after re-assembling, Shields made his decision.

Next day all their evidence having been presented, the argument as to jurisdiction began. Then the fun commenced. The lawyers on both sides abused each other with great eloquence, & several times would have come to blows except for the interference of the sheriff. The ex-judge [Howard] sailed into the character & antecedents of the prisoner & his lawyers in fine style, & was interrupted by a cutting piece of frontier sarcasm aimed at the principal witness & his council. This brought the four lawyers, the prisoner, the witness, the sheriff, & the judge to their feet all at once, each one claiming the floor, & desiring to be heard. The jury sat still, but the mob that had come to see the show took part in the discussion, & showed symptoms of a determination to fight it out. The judge, finally securing the ear of the sheriff, got the floor by threatening to send the whole outfit to jail if they didn't shut up. Everybody was ordered to sit down & be quiet, too, which order was obeyed.

The court [Shields] then called attention to the fact that he didn't care if the father of one of the attorneys had spent ten years in the penitentiary, or the brother of another was hanged for horse-stealing, or if the father of the prisoner had been a traitor to his country, & the principal witness had tried to die in defense of his sutler wagon. "The point to be argued, gentlemen," [Judge Shields] said, "is purely one of law, & that is, is the trial of this case in this court legal? Argument will be confined to that question."[77]

The ex-judge arose again & tried to convince the judge that he could legally try that case or any other brought before him.[78] Like the resumption of specie payment, the best way to try a case was to try it. After reading extracts from various law-books for perhaps half an hour, he turned & pointed his finger at one of the opposing counsel who had had his hair cut short with a clipper leaving his ears rather prominent, & said, "that gentleman's ability may be gauged by the amount of hair on his head, & from the size of his ears, you'd think he was one of a car-load of Missouri "shaved-tail" government immigrants." (Mules brought there have close-cropped tails, & "shaved-tail" is equivalent to "tender foot"—new comer, green horn.) Everybody appreciated the joke, & laughed & applauded. The "immigrant" got on his feet right away, his face all ablaze with indignation, but the judge called the debating society to order, & reminded them that personalities must be left out of the discussion, & the jail was on the adjoining lot.

So several hours were spent in speech-making if in dryly legal character, which considerably thinned out the audience.

The Decision

Not having arrived at a decision, the court adjourned for dinner. Afterwards, it reassembled and the case continued. Herndon made the matter on jurisdiction clear to Shields, and the judge addressed the jury: "[T]he evidence introduced on behalf of [the] Plaintiff discloses that this court has no jurisdiction of the offense charged in the indictment and you are therefor[e] instructed to render a verdict discharging the defendant."[79] The jury did. Their decision ended Gatewood's ordeal, an ordeal that should never have happened but did because he dared to stand up for Indian rights.

Finally the decision was rendered, & it was to the effect that the court had no jurisdiction & the prisoner might go free—complaint must be made before the grand jury of a U.S. court. That practically settled a trouble that had lasted a year & a half, with great expense to the territory, the United States, & the two prisoners, all because of an effort to defend the Indian in his rights & to bring wrong-doers to justice.

Chapter Five

Gatewood and Geronimo

While Gatewood's civil difficulties with Zuck dragged to a conclusion in St. Johns, Crook met with Naiche, Chihuahua, and Geronimo at Cañon de los Embudos, Sonora, Mexico, on March 25–27, 1886.[1] During the first day of the meeting, Geronimo explained why he left the reservation. He then said:

> The Earth-Mother is listening to me and I hope that all may be so arranged that from now on there shall be no trouble and that we shall always have peace. Whenever we see you coming to where we are, we think that it is God—you must come always with God. From this [time] on I do not want that anything shall be told you about me even in joke. Whenever I have broken out, it has always been on account of bad talk. From this [time] on I hope that people will tell me nothing but the truth. From this [time] on I want to do what is right and nothing else and I do not want you to believe any bad papers about me. I want the papers sent you to tell the truth about me, because I want to do what is right. Very often there are stories put in the newspapers that I am to be hanged. I don't want that any more. When a man tries to do right, such stories ought not to be put in the newspapers. There are very few of my men left now. They have done some bad things but I want them all rubbed out now and let us never speak of them again. There are very few of us left. We think of our relations, brothers, brothers-in-law, father-in-law, etc., over on the reservation, and from this [time] on we want to live at peace just as they are doing, and to behave as they are behaving. Sometimes a man does something and men are sent out to bring in his head. I don't want such things to happen to us. I don't want that we should be killing each other.[2]

Crook apparently took a hard line when dealing with the old warrior, something that Geronimo realized almost immediately. Continuing, he said:

> What is the matter that you don't speak to me? It would be

better if you would speak to me and look with a pleasant face.
It would make better feeling. I would be glad if you did. I'd be
better sati[s]fied if you would talk to me once in a while. Why
don't you look at me and smile at me? I am the same man; I
have the same feet, legs, and hands, and the sun looks down on
me a complete man. I want you [to] look and smile at me.

Geronimo tried to convince the general that his heart was good, but to
no avail. Not only did Crook refuse to listen to Geronimo, he took a
firm stance with him—unconditional surrender or fight until you are
dead. To which Geronimo said: "I am a man of my word. I am telling
the truth [about] why I left the reservation." Crook disagreed: "You
told me the same thing in the Sierra Madre, but you lied," to which
Geronimo replied, "Then how do you want me to talk to you? I have
but one mouth; I can't talk with my ears." But Crook refused to back
off, saying, "Your mouth talks too many ways." Geronimo then snapped,
"If you think I am not telling the truth, then I don't think you came
down here in good faith." Crook had the upper hand and knew it. He
said: "I come with the same faith as when I went down to the Sierra
Madre. You told me the same things there that you are telling me now.
What evidence have I of your sincerity? How do I know whether or not
you are lying to me?" Crook's short replies, interspersed with probing
questions that almost became accusations, kept Geronimo constantly
on the defensive. The old warrior was "nervous and agitated; perspira-
tion, in great beads, rolled down his temples and over his hands; and he
clutched from time to time at a buckskin thong which he held tightly
in one hand."[3] At the conclusion of the first day, tension ran high. That
night Crook sent former Chihenne war leader Kaytennae and Alchesay
(who had accompanied him into Mexico) into Geronimo and Naiche's
camp to talk about surrendering. [4] They found the warriors agitated
and heavily armed, and not being fools, they did not broach the subject. Geronimo was suspicious. If the White Eyes showed even a hint
of treachery, he gave orders to "kill all they could, and scatter in the
mountains."[5]

Geronimo and Crook did not meet on the twenty-sixth. When the
peace talks continued on the afternoon of the twenty-seventh, Geronimo blackened his face with pounded galena. Instead of taking part in
the negotiations, he and another warrior sat off by themselves. [6] Unlike

Detail of a drawing made of Geronimo during the surrender talks with
Gen. George Crook at Cañon de los Embudos, Sonora, Mexico (March
25, 1886). A translation of Geronimo's words at the conference reveals an
unparalleled depth of understanding and persuasive ability regarding his
people's situation. Based upon a photograph by C. S. Fly, the drawing
appeared in *Harper's Weekly* on April 24, 1886. From the author's collection.

the first day of the negotiation, Crook did not antagonize the other Apache leaders; instead, he made it clear:

> I have told them that they must decide at once upon uncon-ditional surrender or to fight it out; that [in the] latter event hostilities should be resumed at once and the last one of them killed if it took fifty years. I told them to reflect upon what they were to do before giving me their answer. The only propositions they would entertain were these three: that they should be sent east for not exceeding two years, taking with them such of their families as so desired, leaving at Apache Nana, who is seventy years old and superannuated, or that they should all return to the reservation upon their old status, or else return to the war path with its attending horrors.[7]

Chihuahua did most of the talking on the second day of negotiation. After he surrendered, Naiche followed suit. Finally Geronimo came for-ward and also surrendered. But this was not an easy decision, and he later said: "It was hard for me to believe him at that time. Now I know that what he said was untrue, and I firmly believe that he did issue the orders for me to be put in prison, or to be killed in case I offered resistance."[8]

This should have ended the last Apache war. Should have, but did not for two reasons. First, Crook's harsh attitude ate at some of the Apaches' psyche and undermined the peace talks. And second, per Sheridan:

> The President cannot assent to the surrender of the hostiles on the terms of their imprisonment east for two years with the understanding of their return to the reservation. He in-structs you to enter again into negotiations on the terms of their unconditional surrender, only sparing their lives. In the meantime on the receipt of this order you are directed to take every precaution against the escape of the hostiles which must not be allowed under any circumstances.[9]

Unhappy over their situation and frightened of what the future held—probable deportation to a far-off land—Geronimo, Naiche, and most of their band gave into their weakness for alcohol. That night they drowned their sorrow with mescal bought from Godfrey Tribolet, a trader who had a contract to sell beef to the U.S. military. Naiche became so inebri-ated that he could not stand the next morning.[10]

From left: Perico (holding his son), Geronimo, Naiche, and Tsisnah. C. S. Fly took this photo during a break in the surrender talks between the Apaches and Gen. George Crook at Cañon de los Embudos, Sonora, Mexico (March 26, 1886). Courtesy: National Archives, 111-SC-83615.

Crook should have heeded this as a sign that all was not well with the prisoners. He did not. Instead, he departed for Fort Bowie, Arizona, with his entourage and left Lt. Marion Maus (First U.S. Infantry) and the Indian scouts to begin the homeward march with the Apaches on the twenty-eighth.[11] Unhappy with Crook's treatment of him, Geronimo's fears continued to grow as the day passed. On the night of the twenty-ninth, Maus camped near San Bernardino Springs, Mexico. Although he tried, he failed to prevent the natives from procuring more alcohol. Triblet not only sold the Apaches mescal, he filled their heads with horror stories of what their future might be. Geronimo had no intention of being locked in a cell, or worse, hung. He decided to run and kept at his companions until a number of them agreed to join him. Geronimo waited until almost everyone had gone to sleep, then he, Naiche, and thirty-four men, women, and children slipped quietly into the night and vanished. The remaining seventy-seven to eighty-two Apaches refused to join the new outbreak and continued on to Fort Bowie with Maus.[12] Among those who did not rejoin the escape were Naiche's mother, Dosteh-seh, his second wife, E-clah-heh, and their daughter, Dorothy.[13]

As news of the escape spread, terror and outrage gripped the Southwest. On April 1, Crook asked to be relieved as commander of the Department of Arizona, and the next day Lt. Gen. Philip Sheridan, the commander in chief of the army, followed President Cleveland's direction and accepted the resignation.[14] On April 2, prior to the acceptance of his resignation, Crook said: "The hostiles who did not leave with Geronimo arrived to-day—about eighty. I have not ascertained the exact number. Some of the worst of the band are among them. In my judgement they should be sent away at once, as the effect on those still out would be much better than to confine them after they got to their destination."[15]

Geronimo's escape and the end of Crook's tenure in the Southwest generated mixed feelings on the current state of affairs. On April 5, the *Arizona Journal-Miner* pointed out that the *Tucson Citizen* "has never been in harmony with General Crook's policy and . . . has never missed an opportunity to critici[z]e him." Then quoting the *Citizen*, they printed: "No reasonable man can find any cause for rejoicing in this deep calamity on account of his desire to see the military forces humiliated, as many do."

Geronimo and Naiche's flight ended all hope for the refugees who remained true to the surrender terms. His race from captivity under the cover of night gave Sheridan the freedom to state: "The proposed terms not having been agreed to here, and Geronimo having broken every condition of surrender, the Indians now in custody are to be held as prisoners and sent to Fort Marion without reference to previous communications and without in any way consulting their wishes in the matter."[16] Two days later, on April 7, Crook reported, "The Chiricahua prisoners numbering fifteen men, among them Chihuahua, Nana and Josanie, thirty-three women and twenty-nine children left Bowie Station, about four p.m. to-day."[17] Their destination: Florida.

Crook's tenure in the Southwest came to an end. "On the 11th of April," Crook wrote, "in obedience to the orders of the War Dept., dated April 2nd, 1886, I turned over the command of the Department to General Miles."[18] Miles discarded Crook's strategy of using Indians to fight Indians. Although he retained natives on the active roster, he reduced their activities to little more than scouting duty. Assembling between five and six thousand U.S. troops, he intended to hound the warring Apaches relentlessly until they either surrendered or were annihilated. While guarding all the usual entries into the United States, he began sending patrols into Mexico.

Even though Gatewood and Georgia lived at different posts when the sudden turn of events erupted like wildfire across the Southwest, they actually enjoyed a time of peace and quiet. The turmoil of his civil ordeal had barely passed when there was another change in their lives. On April 13 Georgia gave birth to their second child, Hugh McCulloh Gatewood.[19]

Before Miles sent columns into Mexico to find and destroy the fugitives, Geronimo struck first—raiding Arizona on April 27. He and Naiche split into small groups as they spread terror and destruction across the Southwest. The raid lasted twenty-three days and claimed fourteen lives. Desperate, the raiders continued to kill when they returned to Mexico. When asked about the rampage later, Naiche said: "[W]e were afraid. It was war. Anybody who saw us would kill us, and we did the same thing. We had to if we wanted to live."[20]

On May 3, the House of Representatives introduced a "JOINT RESOLUTION Authorizing the President to offer a reward of twenty-five thousand dollars for the killing or capturing of Geronimo."[21] The next day, Capt. Henry Lawton (Fourth U.S. Cavalry) received orders to lead Miles's primary punitive invasion force into Mexico.[22] His command initially consisted of Troop B, Fourth U.S. Cavalry (twenty-five men), Company D,

Eighth U.S. Infantry (twenty men), two pack trains, and twenty White Mountain Indian scouts. During the course of the next four months his personnel would change drastically as the unforgiving terrain and harsh environment rendered men and livestock unfit for duty.[23]

Days turned into weeks and then months. The Americans, along with three thousand Mexican soldiers, gave the Indians no rest night or day. A number of engagements took place during this time. They looked good on paper, but they did not come close to ending the war.[24] Although Geronimo, Naiche, and their people were shot up, hungry, and worn out, they somehow continued to avoid death or capture.

During this time Gatewood must have felt trapped at Fort Wingate. Apparently Georgia's recovery from the birth of Hugh was slow and he must have worried about her condition. Also he had nothing to do as the government had still not supplied his Navajo scouts with weapons so they could take the field. He viewed the Navajos as little more than "coffee coolers."[25] The weapons never arrived, and Gatewood never took the field with his new Indian scouts. At the same time, he had no desire to return to the war front in charge of a company of Apaches. If orders arrived, reuniting him with the White Mountains, he intended to protest "on the ground that they no longer have any liking for me, & the best interest of the service would require that I be not connected with them in any way."[26] In a letter dated June 13, Gatewood replied to a letter Georgia wrote to him, opening his letter with, "Yours of the 10th is just to hand & right (glad) am I to hear from you, to the effect that you are getting along better."[27] He then goes on to state: "So you have named the boy Hugh McC. Well, well, well! I have no objection but am rather glad that the poor little cus knows what to be called."

There are no records of Gatewood obtaining leave to be with his wife at Fort Stanton during the time their second son was born. With nothing to do, a lonely and bored Gatewood moped about the post. After reading an apparent accusation from Georgia that he was spending too much time in the company of women on the post, Gatewood wrote back defending himself. He asked if it was better he accept the invitations to socialize rather "than that I should sit around the stove?"[28] Continuing, he wrote: "I am behaving myself, though appearances are against me." This letter and others from this period make it very apparent that the separation from his family seemed to weigh heavily on him, and that he missed his children and Georgia dearly. Talking about the newly born

Hugh, he wrote: "As I have told you already, he bids fair to eclipse Tough 1 [Charles Jr.], & that's saying about as much as can be said of anybody's baby." He soon nicknamed Hugh "Tough 2," and proudly spoke of Hugh at every opportunity. [29] Gatewood also made it clear of his feelings in regard to not living with Georgia: "What pleasure is it to retire & wake up alone?"[30]

Although thrilled with the arrival of his second son, the addition of a new family member added pressure to Gatewood's financial difficulties, which were bleak at best. [31] Trying to support his family on a first lieutenant's pay was a never-ending battle, and he constantly juggled bills to make ends meet.

Georgia's sister, Nannie McCulloh, had traveled to Fort Stanton, undoubtedly to help with Hugh's arrival. As Georgia recovered from the delivery, she decided to return home. Leaving in early June, she took Charlie Jr. with her, presumably to enable Georgia to devote all of her time to her newborn, and they arrived in Frostburg on July 14.[32]

Gatewood thought he had seen the end of his active participation in the Apache war, but he was mistaken. Miles did not intend to fail. Charles Lummis, who reported on the last campaign, had a very telling observation: "General Miles has, I am frank to say, done everything possible; but things in the Territory are a thousand-fold worse than when Crook left them."[33] While continuing to hunt the warring Apaches, Miles made up his mind to send an officer into Mexico to negotiate peace. Since none of his officers knew Geronimo or Naiche, he decided to use one of Crook's officers as emissary. Crawford was dead, killed by Mexicans in January, and Britton Davis had resigned his commission.[34] This left the man who dared to stand up for Indian rights in 1884, Gatewood, the Crook outcast.

On July 13, 1886, Miles summoned Gatewood to his office in Albuquerque, New Mexico, and ordered him to find Geronimo and Naiche in Mexico and demand their surrender.[35] Gatewood knew his health could not handle a prolonged campaign in Mexico. Besides, he wanted nothing to do with what he considered a fool's errand. Miles would not be denied and offered to make him his aide-de-camp upon successful completion of the mission. [36] This appealed to Gatewood, and he accepted the assignment.

Way too often Geronimo has been crucified as the Devil Incarnate, a bloody butcher, and a blot on mankind. This is a cliché and a half-truth at best. Even though this image is still all most people know of him, it is not a fair assessment. He had a family. Over the years, his family would be taken from him, raped, and killed. In 1850, his mother, wife (Alope or Gee-esh-kizn), and three children were murdered near the pueblo of Janos, Mexico. [37] This was only the beginning. During the next thirty-five years, he would lose additional wives and children and, finally, his homeland. For him everything was at stake in his battle with the White Eyes: his religion, his language, his culture, his lifeway, his freedom. He fought back in the only way he knew how—with violence. As the years passed, freedom meant war, for leaving the reservation turned him and those with him into "hostiles," a target for anyone, soldier or civilian. To survive, Geronimo had to constantly keep on the move, he had to find shelters that were unknown. As the U.S. army used Apache scouts to hunt him, this became harder and harder, as some of the scouts knew of the rancherías he had used in the past or had the skills to track him wherever he went. For Geronimo it became a war of kill or be killed. Years later, just before he died, he "expressed his regret for having surrendered. He wished that like Victorio he might have died fighting his enemies." [38] By the 1880s, his name struck terror on the borderlands of two countries, but for him and those with him it was a totally different situation. Depressed, desperate, and probably harboring a feeling that death was near, Geronimo's hatred for the people who had taken his land must have been consuming him as he contemplated his next move to stay alive. [39] It was this atmosphere Gatewood and his handful of followers dared to enter when he found the old warrior in Mexico.

Gatewood wrote two drafts of his trek into the Sierra Madre to find Geronimo. [40] Whenever a section appears that is only in one of the drafts, it is so noted. At times Gatewood wrote two versions of the same event, two versions that do not lend themselves to being merged. When this happens, one version appears in the text while the other becomes a note.

The Assignment

Three people would play key roles in Gatewood's search for the Choko-nen, Bedonkohe, Nednhi, and Chihenne Apaches in Mexico. Two of them, Ka-teah, who was either a Nednhi or Chokonen, and Martine, a Nednhi, had already agreed to the assignment before Gatewood entered the picture. [41] Miles wrote a letter of safe conduct for them on July 9. [42]

They would join Bay-chen-daysen at Fort Bowie on the fifteenth.[43] Luckily, the lieutenant bumped into the third, George Wratten, on the street before leaving Albuquerque, and the young Apache interpreter agreed to join his party.[44]

Ka-teah had served as a scout under Britton Davis at the time of the 1885 breakout and took part in the hunt for Geronimo and Naiche. His father, Bish-to-yey (or Bishtoyyeh), became chief by appointment of Naiche's people who opted not to return to the war trail in 1885. As the war wore on, Ka-teah quietly tended to his plot of corn and beans.

Mexicans captured Ka-teah's cousin, Martine, when he was a young boy and sold him to a family that lived near Casas Grandes, Chihuahua. He was lucky; his owners took to him and made him part of the family, even baptizing him in the Catholic church. When his master neared death, he freed Martine, who joined Juh's Nednhi Apaches. Sometime after marrying, he and his wife decided they wanted to live peacefully and moved to Fort Apache, where at various times he served as an Indian scout.

The Apaches claimed Wratten spoke and understood their language better than any other White Eye.[45] While still a teenager in the early 1880s, Wratten left home and began working at a trading post on the San Carlos Indian Reservation. Befriending the Apaches who came in for supplies, he made every effort to communicate with them in their native tongue. The hard work paid off, and he learned the White Mountain, Chokonen, and Chihenne dialects—no easy task.

Both Ka-teah and Martine, who had been friends since childhood, were related to members of the warring band. This gave them the opportunity to get within speaking distance of Geronimo and Naiche and opened the door for negotiation without being shot. Typically conversations between the races were translated from English to Spanish to Apache and back. As many interpreters did not have a good command of their native language, translations were oftentimes suspect. Wratten would give Gatewood the accuracy he needed if and when a meeting took place.

In July 1886 General Miles, after an interview with some of the friendly Chiricahuas at Fort Apache, Arizona Territory, determined to send two of them, Ka-teah & Martine, to the hostiles with a message demanding their surrender, promising removal to Florida, or to the East. The final

disposition of them was to be left to the President of the United States [Grover Cleveland]. I was selected to accompany them. Written authority was given [to] me to call upon any officer commanding U.S. troops, except those of several small columns operating in Mexico, for whatever aid was needed. In his verbal instructions, General Miles particularly forbade my going near the hostiles with less than twenty-five soldiers as escort, fearing that I might be entrapped & held as a hostage as had been done before by other Indians.[46]

My command organized at Fort Bowie, Arizona Territory, & consisted of the two Indians [already] mentioned, George Wratten as interpreter, Frank Huston as packer, three pack mules, & myself. Later on "Old Tex" [Whaley], a rancher, was hired as courier.[47] The twenty-five soldiers were not taken, because a peace commissioner would be hampered with a fighting escort, & besides, that number of men deducted from the strength of the garrison.

Having all that was necessary to our health & comfort, & everybody mounted on a good riding mule (do you know that all mules are not good riding mules?), we set out [on July 16] & in three days arrived at a camp [at Cloverdale] near the Mexican line, where I had been persuaded that twenty-five mounted men could easily be obtained.[48] A company of Infantry, about ten broken down cavalry horses, & a six mules team—and you could have knocked the commanding officer [Capt. John F. Stretch, Tenth U.S. Infantry] down with a feather when I showed my order & demanded my escort. However, as he had been my instructor at West Point, I took another dinner with him & didn't disturb his "mixed command," but journeyed along into Mexico. [We] landed in the wild Sierra Madres several weeks after.[49]

Into Mexico

Gatewood and his five companions reached Carretas, Chihuahua, Mexico, on July 21. Here he met Lt. James Parker, who had been ordered to wait for him, and who supposedly followed Geronimo's trail. By this time, Gatewood's health had deteriorated to the point where he could barely walk. Although he made no mention of it in his reports or his drafts, his joints ached, he suffered from dysentery, and soon he would have an inflamed bladder. Parker had news that did not help matters— Geronimo's tracks had been washed out by the rains three weeks before.[50]

Gatewood's route through Mexico in search of Geronimo, July and August 1886. By Louis Kraft (© 2004).

Undoubtedly sensing his mission was doomed to failure, Gatewood said, "Well, if that is so I will go back and report there is no trail!"[51]

"Not at all," Parker replied. "If Gen[eral] Miles desires that you be put on a trail[,] I will find one and put you on it." Parker offered his entire command as escort. This was just the push Gatewood needed; instead of quitting, he decided to continue. After a forced rest of six days to recover his health, Gatewood resumed his hunt for Geronimo, and only began looking for Lawton—whom he thought would probably know the Indians' location—when it became obvious that his chances of finding the warring Apaches might end in failure. Gatewood and his escort left Carretas on July 27 and did not find Lawton until August 3.[52]

Lawton was not open to having Gatewood join his command, and Parker described the situation thusly:

> "I get my orders from President Cleveland direct," [Lawton] said. "I am ordered to hunt Geronimo down and kill him. I cannot treat with him." I said, "Lawton, you know as well as I do, that now General Miles has made up his mind to open negotiations for Geronimo's surrender, that that is the way he will be brought in. As for finding him and killing him, it is as difficult to find him in this immense mass of mountains as to find a needle in a hay stack." I said further, "[I]f I keep Gatewood with me, I may in the end effect the surrender of Geronimo. But my scouts are worthless, while yours are good; and furthermore you are liberally supplied with transportation, money, guides and spies—your command is larger and your facilities are much superior—I, myself, am nearly out of rations. And again if there is any honor to be gained from this surrender you, after all you have done, deserve it."
>
> I stayed three days with Lawton. Before I left him he agreed to take with him Gatewood and his Indians. "But," he said, "if I find Geronimo I will attack him—I refuse to have anything to do with this plan to treat with him—if Gatewood wants to treat with him he can do it on his own hook."[53]

By this time, an inflammation of Gatewood's bladder made riding difficult.[54] While Parker bent Lawton's ear, the lieutenant again considered quitting, then changed his mind. By now, Gatewood knew that his chances of finding Geronimo and the others "on his own hook" was almost nonexistent. Since Lawton had Miles's complete support, he reasoned that if anyone had a chance of finding Geronimo, it would be the captain. Gatewood decided that he needed to remain with Lawton if he wanted to complete his mission and badgered the captain until he gave in and allowed him to join his command.[55] So sealed their alliance— an uneasy one at best, as both officers had their own agenda.

Soon after crossing the line, we were escorted southward by [Lieutenant] Parker, Fourth [U.S.] Cavalry, whose command consisted of a troop of cavalry & infantry detachments under Lieutenants [Wilds P.] Richardson, Eighth [U.S.] Infantry, & [Robert] Bullard, Tenth [U.S.] Infantry.[56] Their whole outfit didn't number more than thirty or forty men, so that a deduction of the escort ordered would have put them "out of the fight."[57]

We finally arrived at [Captain] Lawton's camp on the Aros River well up in the Sierra Madres above the junction of the Yaqui & Aros rivers & perhaps two hundred & fifty miles below the boundary line.[58] Having no escort, which was my own fault of course, for I should have taken it from Fort Bowie, I put myself under Lawton's orders, with the understanding, however, that whenever he approached the hostiles, & circumstances permitted, I should be allowed to execute my mission.[59]

It was extremely hot, the thermometer registering 117 degrees in the shade, not a breath of air stirring, the river barely fordable, the water muddy & almost hot, too warm to drink or even bathe in. The heavy rains in the mountains had swollen it so that it was almost out of its banks. To cool the water so as to render it fit to drink, we filled canteens, soaked the heavy woolen covering & hung them in the shade. The atmosphere being dry & rare, evaporation was rapid, & thus water was cooled in a short time.[60]

If you had seen those officers & soldiers, you would never have taken them for regulars of the U.S. or of any country. Their attire consisted of a tattered woolen shirt, canvas trousers whose original color had long since disappeared & whose variety of patches would put to shame the celebrated coat of Joseph, a kind of moccasin for the feet made by Mexicans [out] of oil-tanned leather & [with] rawhide soles, a hat—well, any kind of a hat you chose, from a high crowned broad-brimmed, straw sombrero a la Spanish hidalgo, to the well ventilated floppy-brimmed government woven headgear. [The men] were of both [the] cavalry &

infantry arms of the service, & [as] for their numbers, as fine a lot of soldiers as any nation could boast. Although the excessive heat fermented their beans & made them sour, only a few moments of sunshine liquefied their bacon & made rancid the rind & the tissue; & the bread became hard, & even hard tack became harder; the sugar seemed to lose it sweetness; & the few mouthfuls of beef they got would emulate a Georgia razorback hog in its toughness, yet never a murmur.

Week after week & month after month, from fifteen to as much as thirty miles in one day, they toiled along the trail over mountains [Sierra Madres] that are the roughest, have the deepest cañons, the most impetuous streams in the rainy season, on this continent. Wading, swimming, & rafting the rivers—across the arid sandy plains that became hot [enough] under the scorching sun to blister the feet & [making it] exceedingly uncomfortable to rest on at night. The wind, when it blew, was like the breath of a furnace. [The men's] arms & faces & breasts were as brown as white skin can become. There was no murmur of discontent. The truth is, the American soldier was on his metal. He had heard & seen so much of the Apache, & now that he had a chance to measure himself with the Indian, he made use of it, & the result was that the wily, fiery, red man with all his boasted wariness & endurance gave up the fight & made his bow to the only foe that ever conquered him. There is only one thing that I could ever discover which Apaches respect & that is force [&] power superior to his own, which [make] him fear[ful].

The Hunt for Geronimo Heats Up

During the course of the next two weeks, Lawton's command meandered first one way, reversed directions, before changing directions yet again—sometimes only traveling two or three miles in a day. They found nothing.[61]

Finally Geronimo appeared fifteen miles south of Fronteras, Sonora, on the main road to Nacosari on August 17, but Lawton and Gatewood did not know this.[62] They did not hear of Geronimo's whereabouts until the eighteenth, when they spoke with some Mexicans who packed acorns onto their burros at an old mine. After making camp that afternoon, Gatewood and Lawton decided that Gatewood would make a forced march to Fronteras after nightfall.

Chihuahua, subchieftain of the Chokonen Apaches, circa 1885. Chihuahua did most of the talking with Gen. George Crook at Cañon de los Embudos after Geronimo blackened his face and pulled out of the negotiations on March 27, 1886. Based on a photograph taken by A. Frank Randall, *Harper's Weekly*, April 17, 1886. From the author's collection.

That day surgeon Leonard Wood, who served as Lawton's second in command, and who had earlier denied Gatewood's request for a medical discharge, wrote that Gatewood "was far from well." [63] Bay-chen-daysen's health had failed him again. He stalled his departure, hoping that somehow his condition would improve. It did not. As the hours passed, Lawton became angry and even considered arresting Gatewood and replacing him. Then somehow in the early hours of August 19, Gatewood found the strength to press onward. Ka-teah, Martine, Wratten, a few packers, and six of Lawton's men accompanied him. [64]

A prefect, or prefecto, was an elected head of a Mexican district, or distrito. He wielded considerable power. In 1886, the Mexican state of Sonora was divided into nine distritos, each having its own prefect. The cabecera was the administrative capital of each distrito, and gave each official his name. For example, the Villa de Arispe was the cabecera of the Distrito de Arispe, which included the pueblo of Fronteras. Jesus Aguirre, the prefect of Arispe, was in Fronteras when Gatewood rode into the pueblo on August 20. [65]

To return to my narrative, information was obtained to the effect that the hostiles were several hundred miles to the northwest of us, so the command moved in that direction. About the middle of August, [we] arrived at a point about seventy-five miles southeast of Fronteras. [Here] we learned definitely that Geronimo's party was in that vicinity carrying on negotiations with the Mexican authorities with a view to surrendering to them. [66]

My small party, with an escort of six soldiers, all well mounted, left Lawton's command about 2:00 a.m. [We] marched about sixty miles [67] that [night &] day, [finally camping] eighteen or twenty miles south of Fronteras. The next morning after arriving [at Fronteras], I learned that several [Apache] squaws had been in the town, & that Lieutenant [Wilbur] Wilder [Fourth U.S. Cavalry] of our army, belonging to another column, had had some conversation with them, in which they said there was a disposition to surrender if their terms could be accepted. [68] The squaws departed with three extra ponies loaded down with food & mescal, a drink the Mexicans make, distilled from the mescal plant, with a pretty high percentage of alcohol.

In the meantime, the prefecto of the district, whose office includes both military & civil functions, had assembled about two hundred

Mexican soldiers in the town, they having arrived in detachments at night under cover of darkness, & hid them in various dwellings in the town. He hoped to play the old trick of getting the hostiles into the town, giving them plenty of mescal, so as to get [them] drunk & then massacring the whole party.[69] But this [trick] had been played before, & the Apache was not to be caught.

[The prefect] was very much annoyed at the appearance of the American troops. Wilder's command was in camp about six miles west of Fronteras & Lawton's about twenty [miles] south, with other troops in various places. But, as the treaty between the two republics [gave] the Americans [the] right to be there, he could do nothing towards getting them away, & his requests to that end availed not.

Duping the Prefect and Tracking Geronimo

Aguirre ordered Gatewood to leave Fronteras and make no attempt to track the Apache women, who had left the pueblo to return to Geronimo around midnight on August 20.[70] Gatewood agreed, telling the prefect that he would rejoin Lawton's command. Before leaving the American camp, which was three miles below Fronteras and returning to Lawton, Bay-chen-daysen added two additional interpreters to his detachment: Tom Horn, a former packer who could translate from English to Spanish and back, and Jesus María Yestes, a local who could translate from Spanish to Apache and back.[71]

[During my meeting with the prefect], he insisted that the Americans should not move in the direction the squaws had taken, because they would interfere with his well laid plans. [I agreed to this, and] while the Mexican commander contented himself over his wine, in the belief that he was master of the situation, [&] while Lieutenants [Thomas] Clay [Tenth U.S. Infantry], Wilder, & others were trying to control the supply of wine [in the American camp], I took my small outfit of six or eight men [that] Wilder gave me, [along with] Tom Horn & a Mexican as interpreters, & started in the direction of Lawton's camp, causing them to believe we were going there.[72]

After proceeding south five or six miles, & out of sight of the town or ranches along the river, we darted up an arroyo about dark so as to not be seen by the Mexicans & made for the mountains in which Geronimo was supposed to be encamped. If the Mexicans had known of our move, they probably would have taken steps to head us off.

Early next morning, by "circling" toward the north, we struck the trail of the squaws five or six miles from Fronteras. We followed it until dark, bivouacking about fifteen miles east of the town. Lawton was notified of what had been done, & which direction the trail was leading, by one of the escort who was to act as guide until his scouts could take up the trail.

The next day we proceeded slowly & cautiously, with a piece of flour sack to the fore as a white flag, because of the risk of an ambuscade. This peace commission had no desire to run amuck of the Chiricahuas in any hostile manner. Proceeding thus, on the third day, [we] struck the trail of the whole band, about four miles west of the Bavispe River. The country was very rough, & as we approached dangerous looking places, Artemus Ward's magnanimity in sacrificing his relations in the war was nothing [compared] to my desire to give Ka-teah & Martine a chance to reap glory several hundred yards ahead.[73] The trail was decidedly hot & at the head of a cañon leading into the Bavispe valley, the two Indians halted.

The cañon was uninviting, as one might say, severely unattractive, & besides there was a pair of faded canvas pants hanging on a bush nearby.[74] The two friendly Indians declined to travel in advance any further. A cañon like that with such a banner on its head would make anybody halt. In the discussion of the matter, everybody gave his opinion, but nobody knew how to interpret what the pants had to say. My idea was that the two Indians should proceed several hundred yards ahead as usual, then several soldiers & George Wratten with the pack mules & Frank Huston following should come next; two more soldiers & myself, & a hundred yards in rear, two more soldiers. I still think that was the best plan. But the two Indians said that they would go as far as I dared, & no farther—they were not greedy, but willing to divide the glory equally among the whole party. Then everybody else volunteered to go ahead with the Indians, & I volunteered, too, so we all proceeded together.

That proved to be a very innocent cañon, & I was sorry after we got through that I had not gone ahead. A few miles further on, we reached the Bavispe River where, after flowing northward, it makes a bend & turns to the south. [We] crossed the river, & went into camp in a canebrake [that was] just under a peak that commanded the surrounding country for half a mile or so.

Not caring to run [the] risk of surprise, [I sent] a picket, or look out, [up] a round hill near us. I [then] sent the two Indians to follow the trail further on, & examine the country within a few miles of us. With a picket on the peak & the Indians following the trail for several miles beyond, together with the hiding places the canebrake offered in case of emergency, we felt pretty safe, though this peace commission business was getting decidedly tiresome. The white flag was high up on a century plant pole all the time, but that don't make a man bulletproof. As it turned out, Geronimo saw us all the time, but [he] never noticed the flag although he had good field glasses, & he wondered what fool small party dogged his footsteps.

About sundown that day, August [24], 1886, [Martine] returned to me with the information that the hostiles occupied an exceedingly rocky position high up in the [Teres] Mountains in the bend of the Bavispe, some four miles from our camp.[75] They had both been up there & had delivered General Miles's message. Geronimo had sent [him] back to say that he would only talk with me, & that he was rather offended at our not coming straight to his ranchería, where peaceably inclined people were welcome.[76]

Naiche, their real leader, sent me word that I should have no fear of harm from them, as it was perfectly evident from the size of our party that we were not there to fight, & as they had no old scores with me to settle, he desired me to visit him right away.[77] Knowing that Naiche's influence was greater than any other one man among them, his message took the keen edge off of [my] uneasiness. [But] as we had already begun our evening meal & made preparation for the night, & as it was growing dark, I decided to remain where I was till morning & then meet them & talk it out.

[Shortly after Martine returned,] about twenty [of] Lawton's [Indian] scouts under Lieutenant R. A. Brown [Fourth U.S. Cavalry] arrived & camped with us.[78] [As Lawton's] command was supposed to be nearby, [we felt] completely secure from any molestation by the hostiles.

Bedonkohe, Chokonen, Nednhi, and Chihenne Apaches

Gatewood had sent several messengers back to Lawton, updating him on the situation. Anticipating the coming meeting, and knowing the Apaches' need to smoke when making important decisions, Gatewood requested tobacco. Lawton, in return, wrote:

> I have just arrived in Brown's camp, and have rec[eive]d your notes. My pack train got off the trail yesterday, and will not be in until . . . night. I have sent Lt. [Abiel] Smith back on [a] fresh horse to bring up your tobacco and some rations and will send them over to you as soon as they arrive.[79] I have ordered them to come forward if it kills the mules. It will be too late for me to go over tonight, and besides I do not wish to interfere with you, but will come over if you wish me. Send a man back to conduct pack mules over, and write me what you want. I hope and trust your efforts will meet with success.[80]

Gatewood supplied the guide, and fifteen pounds of tobacco arrived during the night.

Even though Gatewood said he felt secure because Lawton's command was in the vicinity, he and those with him spent an uneasy night. Bay-chen-daysen awoke before dawn, packed the tobacco, and, anxious to meet the Apache leaders, moved out at first light on August 25. Martine led the way, and Brown's scouts served as escort. Gatewood traveled several miles along the cañon floor before he reached the base of the rocky crag that Geronimo held.[81]

The next morning, on the strength of Naiche's message & not Geronimo's, I took the whole force & moved up into the mountains, feeling somewhat safer. Within a mile of the hostile camp, we met an unarmed Chiricahua who came to repeat the message & assurance of the day before. A few yards further on, we met three armed warriors, who brought the suggestion from Naiche that my party & theirs should meet & discuss matters down in the bend of the river where there was plenty of wood, water, grass, & shade. [They] also [said] that Brown & his scouts should return to the place where we had bivouacked the night before, & that any troops that might join him must remain there.

These conditions were complied with. I sent Brown & his scouts back to the camp of the night before to await the coming of the main column

of American troops & to inform [Lawton] of the status of affairs with [the] request that he come no nearer our place of conference than my last camp.

In the meantime, a dozen or so of the bucks joined us, & the usual handshaking & offer of tobacco took place. Then a shot was fired up in their camp, answered by my party. A smoke was sent up, also answered by us. Thus were passed salutations of mutual respect & unity. The white flag that we had been marching behind was lowered, & the party adjourned some two miles to the place designated in the river bottom.

Geronimo, Naiche, and Their Band

It was somewhere between 8:00 and 9:00 a.m. when Gatewood and his party arrived at the meeting spot. None of the other Apaches had yet arrived. Minutes slowly ticked by as everyone waited for the remainder of the band to appear. Then, suddenly, armed warriors appeared above them and began their descent. "We were very anxious for a few minutes[,] thinking that maybe Geronimo had changed his mind and meant trouble for us," Martine remembered. [82] Surrounded, it was too late to run.

Gatewood knew most of the people he was about to meet. He also knew that they were a tight-knit group whose bonds through birth and marriage were strong. The Bedonkohe Ahnandia, who married his second wife, Tah-das-te (a Chokonen), while riding the war trail for the last time, was a second cousin to Geronimo. [83] Beshe (a Chokonen) was related to Naiche by marriage: his daughter, Ha-o-zinne (a Chokonen) was the chieftain's third wife.[84] Another Chokonen, the warrior Zhonne, was Beshe's stepson and Ha-o-zinne's half brother. [85] Fun (Bedonkohe) and his brother, Tsisnah (Bedonkohe) were half brothers of Perico (Bedonkohe) and second cousins of Geronimo. [86] Kanseah (Chokonen and Bedonkohe) had a number of relatives in the band.[87] His uncle was Geronimo, and he was related to one of Fun's wives. Chappo (Bedonkohe), Geronimo's son by his second wife, Chee-hash-kish, and Chappo's wife, Noh-chlon (Bedonkohe), anxiously awaited the arrival of their first child. [88] Two women known as "warrior women" traveled with the band: Siki Toclanni (Chihenne) and Lozen (Chihenne). [89] A number of Nednhi Apaches also remained with Geronimo and Naiche until the end: the warrior Yahnosha; La-zi-yah and his brother, Nah-bay, who had his two-year-old daughter with him; Garditha; Hunlona; a nine-year-old boy named Alchintoyeh; and Charlotte See Lo Sahnne, who may have been aged anywhere between six and nine.[90] Eyelash, a Chokonen–White Mountain Apache, also rode with Geronimo, who only had one wife with him at this time, She-gha.[91] Gatewood claimed that Perico had his children with him, one of which is in the famous Fly 1886 photograph.[92]

By squads the hostiles came in. [We] unsaddled our horses & mules & turned [them] out to graze on the little provender the place offered, placed our arms & accoutrements as convenience dictated, & put our food into one common mess. Both sides had very little to eat. We had some panocha & perrola, with a little flour, bacon, & coffee.[93] They had some jerked horse meat & some mescal cakes. I [also] had fifteen pounds of tobacco on my saddle with a sufficient quantity of cigarette papers & matches, [&] put [it] into [the] commissary depot.[94] The first thing was to have something to eat. While this was being prepared by our cook & the squaws [who] gave us several very good meals, we sat around smoking cigarettes & chatting in a very friendly way.

Among the last to arrive was Geronimo. I was sitting on his brother-in-law's saddle[,] which had been thrown on a log, & another Indian was sitting on mine, both with the owner's arms attached.[95] Geronimo appeared through the canebrake about twenty feet from where I was sitting, laid his Winchester rifle down, & came forward offering his hand & repeating their salutation, "Anzhoo," which [means] "How are you? Am glad to see you." [We] shook hands. He remarked [about] my thinness & apparent bad health & asked what was the matter with me. After an answer to this question, [he took] a seat alongside [me] as close as he could get (gentle reader, turn back, take another look at his face, imagine him looking me square in the eyes & watching my every movement, twenty-four bucks sitting around fully armed, my small party scattered in their various duties incident to a peace commissioner's camp, & say if you can blame me for feeling chilly twitching movements).

I asked [Geronimo why he had opened peace negotiations in Fronteras] with the Mexicans. [He] informed me that it was done to gain time to rest a little while, for he knew the American soldiers were at a great distance, & he expected by making the Mexicans believe he wanted to surrender to them, to get food & this mescal & have a regular good time in the place they selected for camp. So far as the Mexicans were

Asst. Surgeon Leonard Wood photographed at Fort Huachuca, Arizona, just prior to joining Capt. Henry Lawton's command, which left for Mexico to hunt the warring Apaches on May 5, 1886. Wood went on to enjoy a long and successful military career. Courtesy: Arizona Historical Society/Tucson, AHS #1125.

concerned, his plans were successful, but he said that the Americans turned up sooner than he had anticipated & that rendered it necessary for them to sober up & be prepared to move at a minute's notice & at a rapid gait. [96]

Then Naiche came [in], much in the way Geronimo did, & the party was complete—twenty-four bucks with fourteen women & children on their part, & ours, five soldiers & interpreters. [97] After breakfasting, tobacco [was again] passed around [&] the ever necessary & ever present cigarette was resumed. The warriors took their seats in a sort of circle, & the "talk" began. Geronimo announced that the whole party was now assembled, & with open ears, would listen to what I had to say. I want to say that in this talk I used interpreters because of the importance of the occasion, that although I could carry on an ordinary conversation with them in their own dialect, I was too liable to make mistakes that might occasion misunderstanding & it was a poor time to risk anything. It took but a few minutes to deliver my message, which was, "Surrender, & you will be sent to join the rest of your people in Florida, there to await the decision of the President of the United States as to your final disposition. Accept these terms, or fight it out to the bitter end."

They all listened very attentively, watched my every movement & every man that could look me in the eyes, did so, & a silence of several weeks fell on the party, at least so it seemed to me. Geronimo sat on the log beside me, as close as he could get. I could feel his six shooter against my hip, & he was the closest watcher of all.

Then Geronimo passed a hand across his eyes, & extending both arms forward & making his hands tremble, asked if I had anything to drink. "We have been on a three days' drunk," he said, "on the mescal the Mexicans sent us by the squaws who went to Fronteras. The Mexicans expected to play their usual trick of getting us drunk & killing us, but we have had the fun; & now I feel a little shaky. You need not fear giving me a drink of whiskey, for our spree passed off without a single fight, as you can see by looking at the men sitting in this circle, all of whom you know. Now, in Fronteras there is plenty of wine & mescal, & the Mexicans & Americans are having a good time. We thought perhaps you had brought some with you." He seemed to know what was going on, but it was explained to him that we had left the town in such a hurry that we had neglected to provide ourselves with desirable drinkables.

After a silence of a few moments, Geronimo proceeded to talk business; [he] said that they had a proposition to make as a result of a council & medicine making the night before:

> They would leave the warpath only on condition that they be allowed to return to the reservation, occupy the farms held by them when they left the last time, be furnished with the usual rations, clothing, farming implements, seeds, etc., that they be placed as they formerly had been with guaranteed exemption from punishment for what they had done.

If I was authorized to accede to these modest propositions, the war might be considered at an end right there. Well, I pointed out the apparent disagreement of the two propositions, & since I was not authorized to modify ours, a settlement would necessitate a modification of theirs to suit ours. I explained that the big chief, General Miles, whom they had never met, had ordered me to say just so much & no more, & that they knew it would make matters worse if I exceeded my instructions. This would probably be their last chance to surrender, & if the war continued they must all be killed eventually, or if surrendered or captured, the terms would not be so liberal.

The matter was thus discussed for an hour or two. Geronimo recited the history of their troubles ever since the white man had penetrated what he was pleased to consider their country—the injustices, frauds, thieving, &c., that Indian agents had perpetrated on their reservations. [Finally, he] pointed out they must have a right to some part of the country since they were the oldest settlers. To give up the entire Southwest to another race was asking too much. They were willing to divide but not to give up all.

They withdrew to one side in the canebrake & held a private conference for an hour or so. It being about noon when their caucus adjourned, we all had something to eat with a cup of coffee. After lunch the bucks [returned to] their places, [&] the talk resumed. Geronimo said that to expect them to give up the whole Southwest to a race of intruders was too much. They were willing to cede all of it, except the reservation.[98] They would move back to that land, or fight till the last one of them was dead. "Take us to the reservation, or fight," was his ultimatum, as he looked me square in the eye.[99]

I couldn't take him to the reservation & I couldn't fight, neither could I run, nor yet feel comfortable. Naiche, who had taken little part in the proceedings, here said that whether they continued the war or not, my party would be safe so long as [we] did not begin hostilities. They came as friends, not as enemies, & would be allowed to depart in peace. Knowing his influence among them, I felt considerably easier in my mind.

Gatewood's Trump Card

Unsure what to do next, Gatewood gambled. Although he knew that roundup of the Chokonen, Bedonkohe, and Chihenne Apaches still living on the reservation was planned, it had not taken place yet—which made what he told Geronimo, Naiche, and their people a lie.[100] His words would eventually be true. They would also be the key to him convincing the Apaches to return to the United States and ending the war.

You will remember that between four & five hundred of their people yet remained on the reservation. I had learned a few days before that they were to be removed to Florida by General Miles. It was with these people, they wanted to live. [I] informed [them] that the rest of their people—the mother & daughter of Naiche were among them—had been removed to Florida to join Chihuahua's band, & their going back to the reservation meant living among their hereditary enemies, the Coyoteros.[101]

I have spoken of the feeling of animosity existing between this tribe & their kindred—the Coyotero, or White Mountains. This put a new [face] on the matter.

Geronimo looked me in the eyes & asked me if I was telling the truth or only meant it as a trick to get them in the white man's clutches. He wanted to know the source of my information, & how it was brought about. Had his people been asleep that this new commander had been able to surprise & capture them & remove them without some getting away to inform him? It was incredible. I could not inform him how it was done, & it surprised me, too, for I knew how wary & wide awake & suspicious these people were, but the fact remained all the same that it had been done, & it was hard to say what might be done if things kept going on in this way. Here was the unexpected with a vengeance, & [it] required a reconsideration of their unalterable decision to quit the warpath only on their own terms. The all-knowing medicine man had failed to apprise them of this startling item of ghastly news. They therefore retired into the canebrake to discuss the subject in its new bearing, & the conference was not resumed for perhaps an hour.[102]

After the reassembling of both parties, Geronimo announced that they adhered to their terms. [He then] requested me to listen to an amplified statement of their history, &c., with a view of presenting it to General Miles in the hope of at least being able to persuade him not to send them to Florida, but to some place in the West where they might all be together, & where they could in time, with the aid of the government, become self-supporting.

They wanted me to go alone [on] mule-back, or with one man, several hundred miles across the country to the nearest American post, & communicate again with the general with a view to getting a modification of the terms.[103] No harm should come to me from any source [as] they would send a number of their warriors to protect me. An invisible posse of their bucks [would] spread out around me & warn me of any danger that threatened from the Mexicans or others that might bode harm to me.

This I declined to do for the reasons that I did not know the whereabouts of General Miles at the time; that it would do no good, for he had made up his mind as to what he would do, & no further discussion would alter his determination. Besides I was sick & a few more days of hard riding would [make] me unfit for service for a time.

Thus passed several more hours, in what appeared to be further "talk."

During this time, we ate, & smoked, & joked, & drank muddy warm water from the river. They again retired to think & talk it over. [By then, it was] late in the afternoon. Upon re-assembling after an hour, Geronimo announced that they could not & would not surrender on those terms.

In view of this, they wanted to "talk" all night if they could find a beef to kill to furnish the necessary meat. I objected to talking all day & all night, too, but would have had to agree to it. The beef was to be killed & then paid for by the quartermaster, but luckily no beef could be found & the project had to be abandoned. Thus the afternoon was spent in each trying to argue the other into his own position.[104]

After considerable smoking & general conversation, Geronimo asked what kind of man the new general was. They knew General Crook very well & might surrender to him. He wanted to know General Miles's age, size, appearance, color of his eyes & of his hair, whether his voice was harsh or agreeable to listen to, whether he talked much or little, & if he meant more than he said or less. Does he look you in the eyes, or down on the ground, when he talks? Has he many friends among his people, & do they generally believe what he says? Do the soldiers & officers like him? Has he had experience with other Indians? Was he cruel or kind-hearted? Would he keep his promises? [Does] he [have] a large heart or a small one? In fact, his questions required a complete description of the general in every respect.

I did my best to answer these questions truthfully & without exaggeration. They all listened intently to the answers I gave & nodded their [heads] & grunted "Anzhoo."[105]

Then Geronimo said: "He must be a good man, since the Great Father sent him from Washington, & he sent you all this distance to us."[106]

About sundown I concluded to repair to the American camp—Lawton had arrived that day—for the night, & so announced my intention. That night they could discuss the matter further among themselves, & their medicine men might take a few glances into the future. To this they agreed.

[Before I left], they asked me to remain a few minutes to listen to a request they had. After the usual amount of taffy setting forth large-hearted friendship & so on, Geronimo said: "We want your advice. Consider yourself one of us & not a white man. Remember all that has been said today, & as an Apache, what would you advise us to do under the circumstances. Should [we] surrender, or should [we] fight it out?"

It did not take long to make up my mind as to that. This was a peace commission, a regular Quaker outfit, & the very thought of war was exceedingly distasteful. "I would trust General Miles & take him at his word."

Had not we had enough of it? Besides, we were in their power, & who would advise fight under such circumstances? So, in the most earnest manner possible, I reminded them of the fact that I had always been a friend to them, & if I thought it was best, I would advise them to fight it out (a small white fib), but my heart was drawn to them in brotherly yearning (another fib), & it was only for their good that I must council peace on the terms offered. They listened very solemnly, & said that they would retire to their mountain stronghold, hold a council, & make some more medicine. Geronimo said he would let me know the result of their council in the morning. We shook hands all around with a hearty grip, & then I mounted my mule & rode toward the camp about three miles down the river, with feelings better imagined than described.[107]

Having gone about a mile, I was overtaken by Geronimo's son, Chappo, a young man about nineteen or twenty years old.[108] After riding a mile or so, I asked him where he was going.

"With you," he replied. "I'm going to sleep close to you tonight & tomorrow I'll return to our camp. I have my father's permission to do so."

No, I would not allow that for fear he might meet with harm, not from the American soldiers, but from our allies, the Indian scouts—[with whom] Chappo's people never had been on friendly terms. He insisted, however, that no harm would be done him if he ate & slept with me, & besides, he had permission from his father, who was satisfied that even if they finally decided to continue on the warpath, he would be allowed to return to his people.

The risk of getting a knife stuck in him during the night was too great to take, & I did not want to take any chances of having the day's proceedings marred. It is easy to understand that injury to him in our camp would never do. [After] explaining [this] to him, I told him to explain the reasons why he was sent back to his father. He reluctantly turned back, saying he would be over at the camp the next morning.

Sending the boy back in that way had a good effect on them as I learned afterwards.

Geronimo Agrees to Surrender

By the time Gatewood returned to his camp in the canebrake, Lawton had arrived.[109] After reporting to him, Gatewood—who was done in—went to bed.

So, I went on. [After] arriving at camp, I narrated to [Lawton] all that had happened. The next morning, the scout pickets announced the approach of a small party of the hostiles, who were calling "Bay-chen-daysen," my pet name, meaning "Long Nose." With the interpreters, I met our handsome friend & four or five of his bucks a few hundred yards from camp. When they saw us coming, they dismounted, unsaddled their ponies, & laid their arms on their saddles—all but Geronimo, who wore a large pistol under his coat in front of his left hip—& advanced to shake hands.

Geronimo asked me to repeat my message, [&] also the description of General Miles. He then said, the whole party, twenty-four bucks & fourteen women & children, would meet the general at some point in the United States, talk the matter over with him, & surrender to him in person—provided the American commander would accompany them with his soldiers & protect them from Mexican & other American troops that might be met on the way. [He insisted that] they must be allowed to retain their arms until they did meet [the general &] had surrendered formally. I was to march with them & camp with them at night. Individuals of each party [would] have the freedom to enter the other's camp. In short, they desired friendly commingling all the way. This was agreed to.

Geronimo said that he would now like to meet the American commander, & all hands repaired to the camp. On being introduced to Captain Lawton, he gave him a regular hug—a Mexican salutation. Lawton invited him to sit down & produced something [to] eat & smoke by way of showing good will. We lacked nothing in the smoking line, for I had brought in all [of the] pounds of tobacco [that remained from the previous day], a quantity of which was brought out. In the talk which followed, a repetition of what had already been said, of course the [inevitable] cigarette had to be smoked, & it was amusing to see Lawton try to smoke one that I rolled for him in brown, stiff straw paper. Not being a smoker, he struggled with it as best he could, & it fell to pieces just about the time he was getting a little sick. Having agreed to Geronimo's propositions, there was nothing to do but inform General Miles & proceed to the point selected for the meeting—Skeleton Cañon, about sixty miles southeast of Fort Bowie.[110]

The rest of the hostiles then moved down near us, & everybody was happy. They had very little food, & as our pack train wandered off on the wrong trail, it was a sort of starvation camp for several days, much to the amusement of the Indians.[111]

Although all seemed fine on the surface with the surrender already a reality in all but the final handshake, dark clouds hovered just out of sight. An incident that would soon happen on the trail back to the United States, and which has since been shuffled into obscurity, took seed—

the proposed murder of Geronimo and the Apaches. Thomas Clay discussed the incident with Gatewood Jr.: "Pending the arrival at our camp [Gatewood's original camp in the canebrake] of the Indians, some of the officers proposed that when they arrived that we throw a guard around them and if they would not surrender that we shoot them down. Your father, Wood and I, and others whom now I do not recollect, objected at once to such an act of treachery."[112] As we shall see, Wood's opinion regarding what action should be taken would change. The proposal had to have alerted Gatewood of what the future might hold. Although Clay later stated: "No attempt whatever was made to molest the Indians," the future actions of other officers would prove him wrong.

The Prefect of Arispe

While the Bedonkohes, Chihennes, Nednhis, and Chokonens moved their camp close to the American camp, Gatewood settled back and began a letter to Georgia.[113] This letter, along with the Wood journal and Gatewood's October 15, 1886, report to Miles, settle the controversy of the dating of these events. In his two drafts, Gatewood totally confuses the situation, not being able to consistently date the events he writes about.

Although Gatewood thought he had duped Aguirre in Fronteras, the prefect either had good sources or else he quickly surmised that all had not gone according to plan. Not wanting to lose his prey, he set out in pursuit.

We broke camp August 28th & [began our homeward journey].[114] We had just halted to go into camp [that afternoon] when the disappointed Mexican commander [the prefect of Arispe] suddenly came down on us from the west with two hundred infantry. [Lawton] sent an officer out to meet [the prefect &] explain the situation & ask them not to come nearer.[115] But no, the Mexican was on his own territory & proposed to take our prisoners from us.

[This] created quite a stampede among our new friends. Geronimo, the suspicious, began to believe that there was an understanding between the two commanders whereby his party were to be caught in a trap, & made preparations to take to the hills. But he was satisfied when [I] informed [him] that I was going to run with him towards our territory while the command would stand off the Mexicans even to the extent of fighting if necessary. You may be sure that it did not take the squaws long to saddle up & pack their property & children. Then away we went—our prospective prisoners & myself made a "run for it" northward—at an eight or ten mile gait, through the bushes & over gulches, scrambling up the side of a ridge & down the other, with a skirmish line of warriors behind us. Flankers & a small advance guard were thrown out, the rear guard being composed of most of the bucks under Naiche. After about an hour's run, we halted so as not to be too far from the command, for in case there should be serious trouble with the Mexicans, our wards proposed to take the side of the Americans. Having made about ten miles, I remained behind with a squad of bucks to await news from Lawton.

Soon a courier [Leonard Wood] arrived from Lawton informing us that the Mexican would not be satisfied until he heard from Geronimo himself that he intended to surrender to the United States authorities.[116] A compromise had been made—an interview between the two was arranged in a new camp to be established near our present position, the Mexican force to remain several miles away. The prefect was to be accompanied by seven of his men as escort, & Geronimo by the same number, all armed. The rest of the Mexicans [would] remain a mile off.

It took not a little persuasion to induce the Indians to agree to this. They wanted nothing to do with that party, fearing some treacherous plot against them. But finally they consented, as the meeting was to be among the American soldiers who they knew from experience could be trusted. So we went into camp.[117]

The Mexican party arrived first & were received with due formality & hospitality [from Lawton & his officers, after which] the [prefect &] his followers sat down under a large cottonwood tree. Then Geronimo dismounted, [&] at the head of his party came through the bushes, dragging his Winchester rifle by the muzzle with his left hand, & his six-shooter handy in front of his left hip. The suspicious old rascal would take no chances. The Mexican rose from the ground, [&] I introduced [Geronimo] to the prefect, whose name I have forgotten.[118] After shaking hands, the Mexican shoved his revolver around to his front & Geronimo grasped his & drew it half way out of the holster—the whites of his eyes turning red, & a most fiendish expression on his face. As I happened to be standing a little in rear & to the left of the Mexican & being unarmed & a man of peace anyhow, with praiseworthy celerity, I slid to one side out of the line of fire & brought up alongside of a little old Mexican soldier whose rifle I proposed to wrestle for. The prefect had sense enough to put his hands behind him & [Geronimo] dropped his right hand by his side. Having returned his pistol [to its holster], the whites of [Geronimo's] eyes resumed their normal yellowish color. [Even though] serious trouble [had been] averted, I purposely neglected to take up my former position, but took one a little to the side.

The prefect asked why he had not surrendered at Fronteras. Geronimo replied that he did not want to be murdered, that he never had any idea of doing a thing so foolish & fraught with such dire results.

Prefect: "Are you going to surrender to the Americans?"

Geronimo: "I am, because I can trust them. Whatever happens, they will not murder me & my people. [I have] nothing further to say."[119]

Prefect: "Then I shall go along & see that you do surrender."

Geronimo: "No. You are going south & I am going north. I'll have nothing to do with you nor with any of your people."

And so it was. A Mexican soldier came with us & finally returned to his country with official notice from General Miles that the much dreaded Apaches had been moved to Florida.[120]

The Lost Command

That night Gatewood realized that Geronimo still believed that the Americans might join forces with the Mexicans and kill him. After discussing the problem with Wratten, Ka-teah, and Martine, he suggested to Geronimo that the Apaches make a run for the border. Next he sold the plan to Lawton. The group moved out that night. When daylight arrived on August 29, everyone was worn out, but still they pressed onward until Lawton (who had left Smith in charge of his command), Wood, their orderlies, and Clay caught up to them.[121]

At a makeshift camp, everyone waited for Lawton's command—but it never appeared, as Smith had missed Geronimo's trail when it veered away from the Río San Bernardino. Lawton became nervous and sent Wood's orderly back to find the troops. Several more hours passed. The orderly never returned, and a nervous Lawton, accompanied by Wratten, rode out to find his command.[122] Clay described the Apaches' march toward the international border: "The order of march of the Indians the day we were with them was as follows: [Naiche] with the main band started out first, with his men deployed in a skirmish line about a mile in length. After he had been gone about half an hour, Geronimo, with the old men, women, children and pack horses, followed in the rear of the center of the line. This order of march was kept up all day."[123]

The next day we resumed our journey, keeping a good look out [lest] we run into troops of either nation, or Indian scouts, & the hostiles be fired on. A day or two afterward, having marched about a day's journey (fifteen to twenty miles), we halted at a good camping place, & to our surprise the command failed to materialize.[124] Hour after hour passed & no command & no rations—the command & pack train failed to follow us, our tracks being so scattered that they naturally took an old trail that seemed to lead in the direction in which we had gone. We sent out parties to hunt up the outfit, & found that they had gone a considerable distance in the wrong direction.

Lieutenant T. Clay, Tenth U.S. Infantry, & Dr. L. Wood, U.S.A., were with us [in the Indian camp]. One can of condensed milk was all we guests could muster, when the "outfit" had concluded to have something to eat & then move to a good place for our bivouac for the night. Wandering around among the people, I noticed the squaw of Perico, brother-in-law of Geronimo, preparing a meal for the family.[125] Thereupon I presented her with the can of milk, with a smile & a bow, & entered into conversation with [Perico]. Some venison had been obtained that morning, & with the flower, sugar, & coffee the thrifty woman had brought with her, she was cooking a toothsome repast. Perico invited me to partake, with considerable grace & dignity, &, motioning to Clay & Wood, requested their presence also. Being very hungry, we needed no second invitation. The squaw made everything clean, the edibles were well cooked, & it pleased her to see us eat so heartily.[126]

American Treachery

After Lawton left to find his command, Gatewood and Geronimo waited until after night fell. Then, under the cover of darkness, they broke camp and moved northward. After traveling eight miles, Geronimo found a defensible position to the east of the Río San Bernardino and called a halt.[127] On the morning of August 30 they moved out at first light, reaching Alias Creek by mid-morning.[128] Everyone was tired and hungry. Gatewood and Geronimo decided to halt for the day.[129]

Soon after camp was set up, Wood left to find the missing command.

Night Watch, a painting of Gatewood and Geronimo during the trip back to the United States in 1886 by Louis Kraft (© 1999). Here they keep a vigilant eye for trouble while discussing the next day's march. Originally published in *Gatewood & Geronimo*, University of New Mexico Press, 2000.

By the time he reached it, Lawton, who had previously found it, had told Lt. Abiel Smith that he was nervous that he may not be able to keep his promise and deliver the Apaches safely. To which Smith replied: "I haven't promised them anything. You . . . communicate with Miles, and I'll take command."[130] Lawton agreed and set out for the nearest heliographic station.

Smith and Wood decided not to wait for Lawton to return, and pushing onward they caught up to the Indians later that day. On August 31, the Americans broke camp at roughly the same time as the Apaches. That morning, a courier overtook Smith and Wood after they had traveled three miles. It is unknown what the message said, but perhaps Lawton forwarded copies of two communiqués he had received from Miles— both of which urged the capture of Geronimo by any means.[131] Whatever Smith and Wood received, it changed their outlook on the current status of the Indians.

Gatewood handled the wording in this portion of his manuscript very carefully for obvious reasons. However, his memory was again off on the timing of events. The proposed murder of Geronimo happened at this camp and not at a later camp. Also, Lawton had not yet rejoined his command—he would not arrive until after the incident had occurred.

Breakfast next morning [August 30] was served for us in much the same manner [as previous meals], though, as one of the interpreters expressed it, "grub's getting short." The command & the pack train joined us, having been piloted by a party sent out to hunt them up, & [we] resumed our journey [on August 31]. We would march early in the morning, lay over during the day, & resume the march late in the afternoon, camping sometimes several hours after dark.

[When we reached] Guadalupe Cañon, considerable uneasiness was manifested by the Indians.[132] They had killed some of Lawton's troopers at this place some months before, & Lawton was away the better part of the day.[133] The next officer in command [Smith] expressed a desire to pitch in with the troop & have it out right there.[134] We had stopped there, because there was no other water within seven or eight miles. The Indians began to mount their ponies & get out of the cañon, the squaws & children going first.

Seeing Geronimo among them going up the trail, I immediately rode after him. Out of the cañon, I noticed them taking up a lively trot, &

had to gallop my mule to overtake the old man. The troops having followed leisurely, we came down to a walk, & after some conversation, Geronimo asked me what I should do in case they were fired on by the troops. I replied that if possible I would proceed toward the troops & endeavor to have the firing stopped; otherwise I would run away with them.

Naiche, who had joined us, said, "You must go with us, for fear some of our men might believe you treacherous & try to kill you."

I cautioned them again, as [I] had all along the road, to keep a good look out all around as there were many small columns of American troops in that region, & I must have notice of their approach so that a collision might be prevented by my going ahead & explaining matters to the officers. The Mexican troops had gotten close to us by their not keeping up their usual watchfulness. We camped a few miles further on where Lawton joined, & spent a rather uneasy night. It was in this camp or the next one that several young officers proposed to kill Geronimo during one of their talks.

Gatewood was wrong when he stated the incident happened after Lawton rejoined the command. Also, there was only one incident. When it happened, Gatewood took Wratten and Geronimo and rode back to confront Smith and Wood, who led their men forward in single file. Smith stated he wanted to meet with the Apaches. When Gatewood refused to allow a meeting, Smith cited his seniority of rank over Gatewood and demanded a meeting. Tempers flared, and Gatewood, after saying he knew Smith intended murder, "threatened to blow the head off the first man if he didn't stop."[135] Both Smith and Wood backed down, ending the tense situation.

Gatewood Wants Out

Obviously murder hung heavily on everyone's mind that evening of August 31. Even though those who commented felt that it was Gatewood—and Gatewood alone—who held the Indians together, he had lost faith in his ability to deal with the Apaches.[136] Fearing failure or worse, he wanted out, Lawton refused to release him.

It was also while coming to this camp that Geronimo & Naiche proposed to me to run away from the troops, with all their people, into the mountains near Fort Bowie, & they would remain there while I went into the post to communicate with General Miles & arrange for their immediate surrender to him. But I knew the general was not at Fort Bowie, & by the time I could go there & communicate with him I feared they might be attacked & run out of the country & leave me to "hold the bag." So I advised strongly against such a proceeding.

It was about this time also that I wanted to take my baggage & join some other column, stating to Lawton that I had been ordered simply to see that the two Indians [Ka-teah & Martine] went to the hostiles & delivered their message. More than that was not expected. He pointed out the necessity of my remaining, the "trouble" we would both be in if the Indians got away, & said he would use force to keep me if necessary. I remained.[137]

Skeleton Cañon

Gatewood, Lawton, and the Apaches arrived at their destination without further incident late in the afternoon on September 2.[138] Skeleton Cañon is at the western edge of the Peloncillo Mountains, which are just inside New Mexico on the Arizona–New Mexico border. The entrance to the cañon is narrow, then widens, splits into two, and again narrows as the two branches wind their way into the Peloncillos.[139] Regulars from several U.S. commands already bivouacked at the agreed-upon location, and then before the Apaches had a chance to set up camp, more soldiers arrived.

The alarming number of U.S. troops unnerved the Apaches, and Gatewood informed Lawton that he and his wards intended to move away from the soldiers and farther into the cañon. Geronimo camped above the confluence of the two branches, on a rocky precipice that gave him a good view of the San Bernardino Valley and the soldiers down on the flat. Just as he had at Cañon de los Embudos, the old warrior had chosen well—he would not be surprised by White Eye treachery. Naiche camped farther up in the mountains.[140]

September 3 brought a swirl of activity on the flat below the Apaches, but no Miles. "A perfect epidemic of couriers," Wood wrote.[141] "No news. Everybody trying to do something and doing nothing." As the soldiers milled about below, Bay-chen-daysen and Geronimo watched from their perch up in the cañon. Finally, Miles and his entourage arrived at 3:00 p.m.

Finally we arrived at Skeleton Cañon, where the general came a day or

two later. The general's arrival created quite a stir in the camp. The Indians naturally were very anxious to meet him &, you may imagine, were extremely interested in finding out what he had to say. Geronimo lost no time in being presented. In few words, General Miles told them what he would [do], the gist of which was that they would be sent to Florida & there await the final action of the President of the United States. Then, to the interpreter, [Miles said:] "Tell them I have no more to say. I would like to talk generally with them, but we do not understand each other's language."

That settled it. I was sitting a little behind. [142] Geronimo turned to me, smiled, & said in Apache, "Good, you told the truth." He then shook hands with the general & said he himself was going with him, no matter what the others might do. He followed our commander wherever he went, as if fearing he might go away leaving his captive behind.

In the meantime, Naiche was out in the hills several miles away, mourning for his brother who had gone back into Mexico to get a favorite pony, & he began to fear the Mexicans had killed him. [143] The next day, [at] Geronimo's suggestion, he & myself with interpreters walked over to [Naiche's] mourning place, to try to persuade him to come in & surrender. He had with him his own band of twelve or fifteen bucks & their families, quite a large portion of the whole party. The situation was explained to him, & as the big white chief had arrived, the presence of Naiche was necessary to complete the formalities of surrender. Among the whites, such delay for the reason stated was never made, & it would appear better in him to control his grief, which indeed elicited the sympathies of his white friends, & conform to the usual custom on such occasions as the present. He said that it was hard for him to do so before he learned the fate of his brother, but as he did not wish to show disrespect to the big chief, he would go immediately. He gathered his band together, brought them in, & was as much pleased with the general as was his secretary of state, Geronimo.

The next thing was to get the two Indian chiefs to agree to accompany the white chief into Fort Bowie ahead of the main body, for they were very suspicious, or had been up to that time. [144] With a little diplomacy, this was accomplished. They made the sixty miles in one day, the rest of us taking three. [145] From Bowie, they were sent to Florida, after some delay in Texas, & finally removed to Alabama.

The General's Word

Geronimo, Naiche, and four other warriors rode to Fort Bowie with Miles, while the remainder of the prisoners of war followed at a less rapid pace.[146] Miles took no chances and issued orders to "kill any one who attempted to escape."[147] Per Miles's instructions on September 6, Field Orders no. 89 read in part:

> In obedience to telegraphic instructions from the Acting Secretary of War, dated Washington, September 4, 1886, Captain H. W. Lawton, 4th Cavalry, accompanied by 1st Lieutenant A. L. Smith, 4th Cavalry, 1st Lieutenant T. J. Clay, 10th Infantry, Assistant Surgeon [L]. M. Wood, U.S. Army, Interpreters George Wratten, W. M. Edwardy, J. M. Montoya, and twenty men of Troop B, 4th Cavalry, will take charge of the surrendered Chiricahua Indian prisoners of war, and proceed with them to Fort Marion, Florida.[148]

Exactly how many surrendered and were exiled is unclear. However, it may have been thirty-two: eleven married males, seven unmarried males, eleven married females, and three unmarried females. This count did not separate children from the adults.[149] A further breakdown lists the captives, their guessed ages, and their marital status (I have added the wives' names whenever possible), and includes Geronimo (47 years old) and wife (She-gha, 35); Naiche (35) and wife (Ha-o-zinne, 17); Perico (37) and wife (Bi-ya-neta Tse-dah-dilth-thlilth, 28); Fun (20) and wife (19); Ahnandia (26) and wife (Tah-das-te, 21); Nah-bay or Nahi (45) and wife (35); Yahnosha (32) and wife (20; perhaps Rachel Tsikahda, a Chihenne); Tishnolth Touzee, meaning Tsisnah? (22) and his wife (14); Bishi, meaning Beshe (40) and his wife (U-go-hun, 35); Chappo (22) and his wife (Noh-chlon, 16); Lazaiyah or La-zi-yah (46) and his wife (37); Molzos (35); Kilthdigal or Kilthdigai (30); Sephonne, or more likely Zhonne (20); Lonah, or perhaps Hunlona (19); boys Skayocoarnet (11), Garditha (10), Eslichinauntoya, or perhaps Alchintoyeh (7); and girls Laeswani (6), Nah-bay's infant (2), and Chappo's newborn (less than a month old).[150] It is obvious that the listing and subsequent reports are terrific attempts by the military authorities to document the captives. At the same time, a lot of guesswork went into these lists and reports. For example, Geronimo is listed as 47 years old. This would make his birth

Geronimo at Fort Sam Houston, San Antonio, Texas, in 1886, shortly after surrendering. This photo tells all: here is a man on the edge. His people's lifeway has just ended, and he is fearful of the future. Courtesy: Western History Collections, University of Oklahoma Libraries, Rose Collection, no. 854.

Geronimo's signature. Early on Geronimo realized that the artifacts he made to sell while a prisoner of war always sold out quickly. He began selling artifacts made by others as if they were made by him and shared the profits. Seeing that photographs of himself also sold well, he added them to his list of sale items. Then, realizing that his autograph added value to photographs or pieces of paper, he learned how to sign his name. From the E. C. Young Collection (Massachusetts), which dates to 1900 and was dispersed at Williamsport, Pennsylvania, in the early 1990s. From the author's collection.

date sometime during the year 1839. Since it has been fairly well accepted that he was born in 1823, this is an obvious mistake. The only thing we can surmise from his age stated in these documents is that his health was terrific and that his physical condition was superb.

H. Henrietta Stockel, who has written a series of marvelous books on the Chiricahua Apaches, found the same (or similar report) in a Senate Executive Document, and after stating, "It is not unusual that she (referring to Dahteste/Ta-des-te) was unnamed in the telegram, given the perspective of the day about women," raised an important question: "But one wonders why the warrior woman Lozen was not mentioned by name and/or marital status. It is virtually certain that the army knew of her exploits and acknowledged that she was indeed a worthy foe."[151] Another question mark in the missing category is Geronimo's youngest warrior, Kanseah, who stood guard on the rocky perch in the Teres Mountains just prior to the Gatewood-Geronimo negotiation. His name and approximate age do not match any of the above names. Also missing, although this omission might be accounted for via the poor judgment of age, is Charlotte See Lo Sahnne. She surrendered with the old warrior and Naiche in 1886, and one can only conclude that she was listed as Laeswani (age 6).

The prisoners headed for Florida included two surprise additions: Ka-teah (30 years old) and Martine (28). They had served Gatewood and the United States superbly, tracking the Apaches and then opening negotiations with Geronimo. There is no doubt that without their assistance, Gatewood would never have located the Apaches in Mexico or, if he did, would not have gotten close enough to speak with them. This accomplishment cannot be understated—they played a major role in the end of the last Apache war. Their reward was imprisonment. For whatever it is worth, their wives were already prisoners housed in that far-off land known as Florida.[152]

This final perfidy does not reside on Miles's shoulders, and it must be made clear that he did everything within his power to ensure that the prisoners were not murdered and were shipped safely to Florida. Miles put his career on the line to do this.[153]

Epilogue

Slow Fade to Oblivion

Gatewood's return to the United States marked the end of his relationship with the Apaches. Knowing that his rheumatism would soon limit his ability to serve in the field, he applied for a position in the Quartermaster Department, but there were no openings. Nevertheless, he still secured an all-important desk job. On September 14, as promised, Miles issued General Orders no. 24: "1st Lieutenant C. B. Gatewood, 6th Cavalry, is hereby appointed aide-de-camp to the Brigadier General commanding, and will be obeyed and respected accordingly."[1] Bay-chen-daysen jumped at the opportunity to work with Miles. He rightfully assumed that his career now moved in a direction that would propel him up the military ladder.

Two months later the lieutenant assumed the responsibilities of the judge advocate's office of the Department of Arizona.[2] This, along with serving as aide to Miles at Whipple Barracks, Arizona, did not end his quest for the rank and position he really wanted—captain in either the Quartermaster or Subsistence departments.[3] However, before he heard an answer on his application, he went into Prescott, a town near the barracks, for a night out. By chance, he met packer Henry Daly, who had previously served with him.[4] They decided to have a drink in a bar and the talk became lively, too lively, especially when it turned to Crook and Miles. Afterward, when they stepped outside, their conversation turned to Geronimo's surrender. Suddenly Miles pulled up in an ambulance and ordered Gatewood to climb aboard. Gatewood refused; he would return to the barracks when "good and ready."[5] Miles, who was a much larger man, climbed down, grabbed him, pushed him onto the ambulance, and drove off. Gatewood was no fool; he knew someone had alerted the general, and he had come to personally silence him. Surprisingly, the incident did not prevent Miles from seconding his application for the Quartermaster Department.[6] But there still were no vacancies available.

The altercation made Gatewood wary of Miles. But more so, it woke him up to the fact that a scramble had begun and to the victor would go the credit for ending the war. Lawton's September 9 report had singled out all the officers in Mexico for exceptional service—all of them except

Gatewood.[7] Most likely the importance of his exclusion did not strike him, as he was not a member of the Fourth and probably figured that it was just factionalism and loyalty to one's own regiment. Besides, he had received credit in some of the newspapers reporting on the surrender, including the *San Francisco Chronicle* and the *Kalamazoo Telegraph*.[8] Still, recent events were ominous harbingers of what the future might hold.

That fall, he and Georgia lived through one of the hardest things parents ever have to deal with: the death of a child. On October 6, Hugh—the infant that Gatewood had affectionately called "Tough No. 2"—died. Georgia claimed that "Little Mac" (as he was also known) was not cared for properly, and she blamed the attending physician.[9] Gatewood did not want his son buried in the Southwest, and he contacted Marcus E. Taylor, the assistant surgeon at Fort Stanton, regarding exhuming Little Mac for the purpose of having him reinterred, most likely back East. Taylor's response put a hold on the project: "I do not think you can remove the body of your baby for some time—perhaps two or three years. Decomposition, under ground, in this climate, proceeds very slowly."[10] The good doctor then went on to give an example for his opinion.

Gatewood did not fully recover from his ordeal in Mexico. By December it was obvious that his health had worsened. He applied for a leave of absence. When his request was granted on December 8, Gatewood, Georgia, and Charlie Jr. visited her family in Frostburg, Maryland. The time off did not improve Gatewood's health, and in February he requested two additional months of leave. His request was granted.[11]

During Gatewood's absence, the Department of Arizona moved its headquarters to a small coastal suburb of Los Angeles named Santa Monica. During the 1870s, Los Angeles had thrived on tourism, but now an ever-increasing flow of people from the East turned the city and its surrounding communities into el pueblo grande.[12] Finally Gatewood's health improved enough for him to return to duty on March 22.[13] The change of climate from the Southwest to the Pacific Coast probably pleased him.

The joy did not last long. Time had changed his world during his absence. Those who had served in Mexico during the closing months of the Apache campaign had begun to reap the rewards and climb the military ladder. The infighting Gatewood had observed in the army at the end of 1886 had blossomed into a full-scale war, with the victor claiming all the glory for the capture of Geronimo. He saw—as did everyone else—what the outcome would be, and kept his opinions to himself, although it is possible that he seriously began considering writing a book on his experiences with the Apaches. If completed, the book would certainly provide the perfect medium for presenting and preserving his participation in the final surrender, and once published it could not be dismissed.

Gatewood's silence did not help matters. As a member of the Sixth he found himself surrounded by the officers of the Fourth, such as Wood, and as it had been in Mexico, he again found himself an outsider. Using his wits, he had outmaneuvered the Mexicans and Americans and had talked Geronimo and the remnants of the Apaches into surrendering. Soldiers who had never heard of him, much less seen him, cheered him for his success, which brought them home from what had been a never-ending war.[14] Not so with Miles's officers. In their minds they had tramped through Mexico: they had earned the victory—and Miles made sure it remained their victory. W. P. Richardson, who had accompanied Gatewood during his search for Lawton, wrote that "there appeared to be a concerted effort to give Lawton all the credit for bringing Geronimo in."[15]

Gatewood's contribution to the final surrender shrank and came alarmingly close to disappearing. He ignored the controversy as much as possible while he performed his duties as aide to Miles. But the controversy, along with the daily confrontations with officers from the Fourth, ate away at him. His self-esteem suffered, and he withdrew further and further into himself. A stoicism hid the pain that he tried to conceal. Georgia saw the change in him and blamed Miles and Wood.[16]

That summer Arizona Territory announced that it would host a celebration in honor of those who had rid them of the dreaded Apaches. This lifted Gatewood's spirits, as he supposed his accomplishment would be recognized. In anticipation of the coming event, he ordered new wardrobes for himself and Georgia.

The celebration began in Tucson on November 8. Gatewood had no idea that he would not attend the fête until just before it was time to leave for Arizona. Miles dropped a bombshell: Gatewood would remain in Los Angeles to perform clerical work. So, while the citizenry of Arizona cheered on the conquering heroes, while all the officers—save himself—were praised, and while Miles accepted an ornamental sword at a ball held at the San Xavier Hotel, Gatewood performed tasks an ordinary clerk could have completed.[17] Undoubtedly this ultimate snub gnawed deeply at him.

It also set a dangerous stage upon which Gatewood would again dare to tread.

As had occurred with Crook and the Zuck debacle, Gatewood again found himself confronted with fraud. This time, however, it did not concern Indian rights. Nevertheless, he would again confront his commanding officer.

Miles employed a number of servants in his household as well as in another household.[18] Not wanting to pay the expenses out of his pocket, the general submitted the paperwork for the salaries to the government. Since the government did not cover the cost of retaining personal servants, Miles listed them as packers.

The request for payment progressed through the regular channels until it reached the final authorization, a signature to certify that the named employees were employed as packers. With Miles celebrating in Tucson, the task of signing the request fell to his aide, Gatewood. The lieutenant had always been known as "cool, quiet, courageous; firm when convinced of right but intolerant of wrong."[19] Signing would be a fraudulent act; therefore, Gatewood refused to sign.

Livid when he heard of Gatewood's refusal, Miles ordered Gatewood to sign the paperwork. The lieutenant held his ground: he would not break the law. He would not sign. The servants did not get paid.

Gatewood's morality once again put him in an unenviable position. He was no longer the outsider from the Sixth lurking within Miles's inner circle. He had become a pariah within that circle.

Unhappy with the situation, Miles looked for ways to eliminate his errant lieutenant. But Gatewood was careful. When the general set him up to contradict one of Lawton's reports from the recent campaign, he refused, knowing full well that such a statement could result in his court-martial.[20]

Although Miles supposedly continued to hunt for Gatewood's head unofficially, he did not shortchange the lieutenant in his efficiency reports.[21] Still Gatewood knew that his future was precarious, and actively sought the position he originally wanted in the Quartermaster Department. He had plenty of documents supporting his capability to fill the position, including letters of recommendation from former commanding officers Lt. Col. A. P. Morrow and Brig. Gen. Orlando B. Willcox.

Even Miles had previously written a letter of recommendation. When Gatewood asked Crook for support, the general replied: "I have already made recommendations for the vacancies which will occur in the near future in both the Quartermaster and Subsistence Departments, and therefore do not feel justified in recommending you for either of these vacancies."[22] Nothing had changed. The so-called "Crook man" was still out in the cold.

On June 4, 1890, Gatewood, Georgia, and Charlie Jr. left for Frostburg, Maryland, to spend a four-month leave of absence with Georgia's family. Even though he claimed he needed time to take care of business matters in the East, undoubtedly the main reason for the trip was so that Georgia could be near her mother, Sarah Ellen McCulloh, and her sister, Nannie McCulloh, when she gave birth to their third child.[23] Georgia did not want a repeat of the tragedy of little Hugh's death and probably did not want to depend upon another military physician. There is also a possibility that Gatewood needed time again to improve his health. Gatewood and Georgia's daughter, Emily Natalie, was born in Frostburg on July 28.[24] While still in Maryland, on September 13, his tenure as aide to Miles ended. He was officially relieved from Miles's staff and ordered to rejoin his troop (H, Sixth U.S. Cavalry), then stationed at Fort Wingate, New Mexico, when his leave ended on October 4.[25]

To this point in his career, Gatewood had performed admirably despite his human frailties. Yet he was becoming painfully aware that his career was on hold. He was still a first lieutenant, the position he held years before when he had negotiated with the Apaches in Mexico. By this time officers in the Fourth had begun to enjoy ascension in rank. Parker had become a captain and Lawton a lieutenant colonel. In the future most of the other officers who served in Mexico during the summer of 1886 would see their rank within the army rise.[26] But not Gatewood. The only change he saw was the continual deterioration of his health.

Eighteen-ninety saw a lot of change. Crook's unexpected death (March 21) resulted in Miles assuming command of the Division of the Missouri. When the Ghost Dance religion that had begun in Nevada spread to the northern plains, Miles anticipated trouble and ordered Gatewood's regiment to the Dakotas in December. Although officially listed as serving "in the field in South Dakota, in operations against hostile Sioux Indians at Pine Ridge Agency," Gatewood did not take part in two tragedies that quickly ended the Indian wars: the murder of Hunkpapa Sioux medicine man Sitting Bull (December 15) at the Standing Rock Reservation and the butchery of Big Foot's Miniconjou Sioux at Wounded Knee Creek (December 29).[27]

The winter of 1890–91 was extremely harsh, and Gatewood suffered an attack of rheumatism in January. Fearing the worst, but hoping for the best, he refused to apply for leave, believing that somehow his condition would improve. It did not. His condition deteriorated to the point where he could not move either of his arms. Not able to report for duty, on February 16 he wrote the post adjutant at Fort Meade, South Dakota, requesting a one-month leave of absence as soon as he was able to travel. The military granted his request seven days later.[28] Soon after this, the military officially recognized Gatewood's contribution to the end of the last Apache war. In April 1891, the military circulated the following: "The Major General commanding takes pleasure in publishing in orders to the Army the names of the following officers and enlisted men who, during the year 1886, distinguished themselves: . . . Lieutenant Charles B. Gatewood, 6th Cavalry, commanding Chiricahua Indian scouts: For bravery in boldly and alone riding into Geronimo's camp of hostile Apache Indians in Arizona and demanding their surrender."[29]

Painfully aware that the end of his military career neared, Gatewood increased his search for another assignment within the army. He excelled in three areas: He knew and understood Indians, especially Apaches; he was well-versed in the duties of a cavalry officer; and he was an experienced aide-de-camp. He applied to be either an instructor at West Point or a recruiting officer. Nothing materialized, and Gatewood returned to frontier duty when his leave ended.[30]

When warring cattlemen in Wyoming threatened to annihilate each other in the Johnson County war, Miles sent the Sixth U.S. Cavalry (troops C, D, and H—Gatewood's troop) to Fort McKinney to prevent excessive bloodshed.[31] The lieutenant traveled to his new station at the conclusion of his sick leave on June 8. The following winter was worse than the previous one. A succession of blizzards, combined with extreme temperatures, played havoc with Gatewood's health. Still he held on, fighting to remain in the army. Tensions between the ranchers continued to escalate until the following May when the rich landowners decided to end the problem. They hired an army of gunmen and sent them off to wipe out the small ranchers. Aware of the situation, a combination of small ranchers and rustlers rode out to find the gunmen. The hunted became the hunters and soon cornered the gunmen in a cabin. The army heard of the confrontation and, acting quickly, rushed to the besieged cabin, arriving in time to save the would-be killers from annihilation. They then escorted the mercenaries to Fort McKinney. Angered at being thwarted, the small-time ranchers slipped into the fort on May 18, 1892, and set the portion of the post where the gunmen were incarcerated on fire. The fire spread quickly, threatening to destroy the entire post. In an effort to save the rest of McKinney, squads of volunteers rushed to blow up the burning buildings. Gatewood entered one of the doomed structures with a keg of gunpowder. He managed to work his way into the smoke-filled inferno and place his charge. However, before he finished setting up the explosive, a part of a wall gave way without warning and a section of roof fell. The fire spread quickly. Gatewood refused to quit and hurried to complete his task. He never did. Flames reached a can of powder, ignited it, and the room exploded. The blast flung Gatewood against a wall. Soldiers managed to drag him to safety before the inferno reached him.

The lieutenant lived, but his body would never be the same. The explosion completed what rheumatism had begun twelve years before: it crippled him. "Besides suffering extensive superficial burns," his hip, shoulder, and shattered left forearm never healed properly. The left arm suffered "severe angular deformity in its upper portion."[32] From that day forward, Gatewood had very restricted movement in these joints, and any movement in the affected areas caused him considerable pain. His right side was almost as bad.

Gatewood's career was now in jeopardy. Yet he refused to give up his quest to become a captain and again submitted his application. In his efficiency report, he had some heady recommendations, which perhaps could have become the deciding factor in his promotion. Carr wrote: "Fitted for college and recruiting detail," and later added, "Summary is Very good."[33] Miles also gave him a boost, stating: "Is efficient in all that pertains to the duties of his office. Attention to duty, conduct and habits, Excellent; is qualified to fill any detail to which his rank makes him available. Is well qualified for the management of Indians. 'A brave officer and a gentleman of integrity and good character.'" Finally Col. J. J. Van Horn (Eighth U.S. Infantry) wrote: "Professional zeal and ability, conduct and habits, capacity for command, Good; attention to duty, Excellent; would make a good recruiting officer."[34] But then Van Horn mentioned the ailment that forever haunted Gatewood: "Suffers from rheumatism almost constantly." An examination for promotion took place at Fort Custer, Montana, on October 3, 1892, and resulted in the following diagnosis: "Permanently disqualified physically to perform the duties of a captain of cavalry."[35]

His quest to become a captain had ended. On November 3, Special Orders no. 258 directed Gatewood to travel to his home in Denver, there to await further orders.[36] Nineteen days later he reached his home and as ordered reported to the adjutant general. The move initiated what he knew would be the beginning of the end of his military career.

Gatewood returned to work on his dream of writing a book based on his Indian experiences that were now so far in the past. His perseverance paid off. A periodical named *The Great Divide* published an article he wrote about the Victorio campaign in their April 1894 issue. In the article he states: "Victorio was a palsied, aged and decrepit chief, who was barely able to accompany the squaws and children in their forays."[37]

Unfortunately, the thrill of being published did not amount to much when compared to his ever-growing problems. On the plus side, he was still a member of the Sixth U.S. Cavalry. Although nothing had changed, his situation remained desperate. The army had been his life and his livelihood. It had never paid much, but now, more than ever, he had to secure his family's future. He needed to find a way not only to prove his worth but also to increase his earnings.

In June the sheriff of El Paso County, Colorado, contacted him and requested his services as military adviser in civilian difficulties brewing at Cripple Creek.[38] A thrilled and hopeful Gatewood immediately forwarded the request to the secretary of war, who just as quickly rejected the idea.

Gatewood's downhill plunge continued. By September he could no longer juggle his bills. Then, adding to his already stressed condition, one of his creditors complained to the military about his failure to pay a bill. As Gatewood took pride in his honesty, he fought back the only way he could—with pen and paper.[39] Soon afterward, he moved to Fort Myer, Virginia. The last years had not been kind, and even though his efficiency reports constantly stated that he was more than qualified to teach native history, he never came close to securing a position in academia.

His future gone, Gatewood reached back to claim that one shinning moment of his career. He wanted to hold onto the memory of when he met Geronimo and Naiche in Mexico. In May 1895 he applied for the Medal of Honor. Miles endorsed his request, and so did others. But it did no good. On June 24, the acting secretary of war informed him that since he had not distinguished himself in action, he was not worthy of the honor.[40] Putting his life on the line and dealing with an enemy with honesty and integrity did not count. The verdict decimated Gatewood. His accomplishment meant nothing. He made no further attempt to save his career.

Gatewood spent the last year of his life nursing his health. Although depressed at his state of affairs, he was also grateful. The military could have ended his career at any moment. Instead of forcing him into retirement, they allowed him to remain on the payroll. By now he was the senior lieutenant of his regiment, and it was just a matter of time before he made captain. But it never happened. On May 11, 1896, with his body a mere shell of what it was just ten years earlier, he entered the post hospital at Fort Monroe, Virginia. He never came out. On May 20, a malignant tumor of the liver killed him.[41]

Georgia did not have enough money to bury her husband and petitioned the army to inter him at Arlington National Cemetery. For once, the official response was positive and Gatewood was buried with full military honors. Georgia survived the next twenty-four years on the paltry pension of $17 she received from the government. Then, around 1920, she moved in with her eighty-nine-year-old mother, who owned her home free of mortgage, and her sister, Nannie, who was single, in Frostburg. At this time, Nannie earned her living as a high school teacher. After her mother died, Georgia moved to California to live with Charlie Jr. and his wife. Georgia died at her son's home in La Mesa on November 13, 1946.[42]

Without a doubt, the frailties of Gatewood's body contributed to his failure to advance in "this man's army."[43] At the same time, the lieutenant dared to stand up for what he felt was right. His stance on Indian rights and justice severed his relations with Crook and Miles. Both were supposedly in his court and supposedly backed him for promotion. At the same time, both were angered by actions he took regarding what he considered right that were in stark contrast to their requests. Gatewood's stand against his superiors' wishes guaranteed that his exceptional skills at native management on the reservation, his magnificent success in the field commanding native scouts, and finally his ability to talk Geronimo and Naiche into ending the final Apache war would be ignored.[44] Over the years much has been said about men who were able to bridge the racial gap and treat Native Americans as humans. Gatewood has seldom been included in these discussions. The reason is simple: he did not get along with his two commanding officers.

His problems with Crook were directly related to his efforts to treat his native wards fairly and the general's goal of becoming the commander in chief of the army. To Gatewood's credit, he refused to budge when he knew he was right. Looking back, this was a costly error on the lieutenant's part: if he had conceded to the general's request and dropped the charges against Zuck, perhaps his relationship with Crook would have taken another path. Although Gatewood was a highly skilled commander of Indian scouts before Crook assumed command in 1882, it was the combination of leader of scouts and military commandant of the reservation that pushed him to the fore of a small percentage of skilled officers. Since Crook elevated him to this position, Gatewood became known as a "Crook man." With the staunch factionalism that predominated military thought at that time, this sobriquet would hurt Gatewood more than it would help him. If anything, the exact opposite was true— Gatewood was not a "Crook man." He must have found the situation ironic. Once he even snapped in anger: "I [don't] owe my commission to General Crook."[45] Nevertheless, the moniker stuck, making him an outsider; a position from which there would be no escape.

Not once, . . . twice.

After his association with Crook ended and he became Miles's aide, nothing changed. He was still an outsider. The problem with Miles was twofold. Miles commanded the Department of Arizona when the last Apache war ended in 1886, and he made sure that he and the Fourth U.S. Cavalry received credit for the victory. This is understandable and returns us to the idiocy of Gatewood being labeled a "Crook man." At the same time, he was not a "Miles man." Most certainly if he had been a member of the Fourth's mess instead of the Sixth's, he would have been a "Miles man" and would have received his due at the conclusion of the war. That aside, or perhaps because of it as he was hurt by the exclusion of his participation in the final capitulation, Gatewood had no intention of committing an illegal act for his commanding officer, Miles. Gatewood's stance on Miles's fraudulent requisitions while Miles and the Fourth celebrated the victory in Tucson in 1887 all but ended his military career.

Gatewood came from a "Confederate-inclined family," but he never turned his back on his race and culture.[46] At the same time, he controlled whatever racial prejudices he was born with and accepted the people of a race and culture totally foreign to him as human beings and coworkers. In his manuscript he used words that today are totally unacceptable, such as "squaw" and "buck," but we must remember that when he wrote these words they were totally acceptable. That aside, there is nothing in Gatewood's writing that even hints at him looking down on the Apaches. Actually, his relationship with the native warriors was just the opposite. A perfect example is when he introduced Alchesay for the first time—the rough-and-tumble word play between himself and the White Mountains clearly illustrates the type of relationship he had with the Apaches. It was loose enough that they could joke and play around with each other as only friends can. Sad to say, this is still a major accomplishment in today's world; in Gatewood's time, it was an extraordinary achievement. Perhaps that is why white men on the frontier who dared to stand up against racial prejudice—men such as Charles Gatewood and Cheyenne agent Edward Wynkoop—are either forgotten or regulated to the role of minor player.

Gatewood's knowledge of the Apaches, especially the White Mountain Apaches, was unique. A handful of Apache researchers of the twentieth century, who through years of hard work befriending and then interviewing—such as Morris Edward Opler and Eve Ball—have documented a cultural and historical oral tradition that could have been so easily lost if not for their persistence. Even though Gatewood predated their work and did not make a systematic study of his wards and coworkers, his words are a valuable contribution to our further understanding of the people known as Apache.

His writing attempts to flesh out the reports he wrote. Although incomplete, his words and anecdotes give us an insight into what he felt was important with regard to his management of the reservation, including his absolute refusal to back away from Zuck, as well as his take on his quest to find Geronimo and his people and return them to the United States. Although only a lieutenant, we see a man who did not shy away from command, who could make decisions, and whose morality never left him regardless of the situation and consequences. At the same time, he has given us a glimpse into a life most extraordinary—even more so when we consider the frailties of his health, which at times pushed his fortitude to the extreme.

Bay-chen-daysen succeeded as a commander of Indian scouts, succeeded as military commandant of an Indian agency, and finally succeeded in peaceably talking Geronimo, Naiche, and the rest of the warring Apaches into returning to the United States in 1886. This success can probably be attributed to many factors, with his ability to lead and manage topping the list. However, without a doubt, the underlying root of his success stems from his ability to accept the Apaches as fellow humans, gaining their trust, respect, and, in their own way, love.[47]

Bay-chen-daysen, watercolor of Charles Gatewood by Louis Kraft (© 2004).
Knowing he had to learn all he could about the Apaches, Gatewood talked
with his scouts daily and listened to their views. This openness allowed
him to excel both as a field commander of Indian scouts and as military
commandant of the White Mountain Indian Reservation.

Appendix: Old Black Joe's Devil

When Geronimo, Naiche, and the Bedonkohes, Nednhis, Chokonens, and Chihennes broke out on May 17, 1885, Gatewood and twelve of his Apache scouts joined the initial pursuit that was led by Capt. Allan Smith (see chapter 3). Afterward Gatewood returned to Fort Apache to enlist an additional two hundred Indian scouts. As soon as he completed the conscription, he again entered the field, this time in pursuit of Mangus and his band in the heavily forested Black Range of New Mexico, which has also been called Sierra Diablo, the Devil Range.[1] As we shall see, they are aptly named. Gatewood marched out of Fort Apache on June 16. By the time the scout neared its end, a totally disgusted Bay-chen-daysen wrote Georgia:

We are still aimlessly wandering around these mountains hunting for Indians that are not, & examining all sorts of rumors that have no shadow of foundation of truth in them.

Some of the settlers are wild with alarm & raise all kinds of stories to induce us to camp near their places, to protect them and buy grain & hay at high prices. Others are quiet & sensible, & laugh at the fears of the timid.

The whole thing has turned out just as I put it up before leaving the post—no truth in any of it. The other day a prospector was fishing near our camp, discovered some tracks made by our scouts, [&] let out for parts unknown. He is probably now spreading dismay through the country.

Another one was going to make it his chief business in life to kill scouts, but he changed his mind when they appeared at his place. Few are friendly toward the troops, unless they can sell things.

Our trip has been without interest. Up one hill and down another would sum up the whole thing.

I sent a report to Gen. Crook today setting forth the condition of things, & will have to wait for orders till July, which will be the earliest date they can reach me. I think their purport will be to send me back home, & that can't be too quick to suit this chicken.[2]

El Diavolo

While Gatewood dealt with the futility of tracking Apaches after the final breakout from the reservation in his letter to Georgia, he created a totally different description of the scout when he wrote the draft, mainly as the result of seeing an animal that was not a figment of anyone's imagination.[3]

In the summer of 1885, I happened to command a military expedition scouting through the Black Range of New Mexico for hostile Indians. It was the start of the Geronimo–Apache campaign that has been so much written about. I had been sent from Fort Apache, in southeastern Arizona, with my company of enlisted Indian scouts, to search thoroughly all that rough and mountainous region lying around Silver City, New Mexico, to as far east as Hillsboro—country which at that time was one of the favorite retreats and strongholds of renegade Apache Indians. Wild and rugged, most of it was then unknown to white men; but there were many pleasant and fertile little meadows in the deeper cañons, where game of many kinds abounded.

Between Silver City and Fort Bayard, [New Mexico], there lived an old half-breed Mexican trapper and hunter who was familiar with all that wild country; and he was often employed by the military at Fort Bayard as a guide. I never knew his right name, but, on account of his grizzled hair, his very dark complexion, and his age, we called him "Old Black Joe," or, more officially when necessary, "Joe Black." I employed old Joe to help guide us on our present trip. Then we proceeded to scout laboriously through the Black Range, visiting all the known waterholes and searching out all other sources of water we could find, observing carefully at each place for the tell-tale signs of hostile Indians.

The third day after leaving Fort Bayard, we camped well out in the mountains near a little spring whose overflow made a shallow pool in soft ground. Encircling the pool were many and various animal tracks, and among them I noticed some large wolf tracks, so unusually large that I spent several minutes in examining them. It dawned on me that there was something puzzling about them, [an] unusual grouping of the feet I thought, and I called Old Black Joe, who was near, to look at them. He came closer, but with evident reluctance, and at first would not look at the tracks or give any but evasive and indirect replies to my comments and questions. Finally, somewhat annoyed at his manner, I remarked sharply that he was not very attentive or courteous and asked him point-blank if he saw the tracks.

"Sí, sí, Señor," he burst out, "seguro lo miro; pero es El Diavolo!" ("Yes, Sir, of course I see them; but it is the Devil!")

Knowing him for a fearless hunter and scout, I was amazed that he should be so upset over the tracks of any animal, and I questioned him at length, but could get only vague, rambling talk about the Evil One and the various ways in which he could appear at will upon this Earth for his fell purposes. I gave it up and forgot the incident—for the time being.

The next day, and for twelve or fifteen more, we struggled through those rough mountains, searching every possible route and mountain pass for Indian trails and examining all springs and wells, but to no purpose, for Geronimo and his gang of land pirates were already far down in Old Mexico, though none but themselves then knew it. At last we started back towards civilization—or as much of it as was represented by the rough towns and camps of that period. But we still kept up a careful watch for hostile Indians. On the march, each day, a number of the scouts would spread out for miles in front and to each side of the main body, spying out the country in advance in every direction. To keep in touch with them and to get the first possible news of anything they might discover, I usually rode with the small advance party half a mile or more ahead of the main body.

We were within three days' march of Fort Bayard. As we had been going that day since dawn, about three o'clock, as was usual, I sent out word that we would camp, and then halted by the trail until our advance scouts could locate a good camping place and notify the rest of us. I sat down under a small tree, along with Old Black Joe and one of my scout sergeants, an old sub-chief of the White Mountain Apaches named Bartis, an intelligent and dependable man who, in spite of his many years, was still the best hunter and trailer of the whole company. We were at the mouth of a large cañon with a broad, level floor over which we could see for three or four miles. The day was warm and bright, with every bush and rock for miles standing out clear in every detail.

Suddenly, Bartis stiffened and pointed up the valley, and at the same time I heard a stifled gasp from Old Joe. I turned, and there, about four hundred yards away, a black kangaroo was making his way in calm, unhurried leaps across the valley floor. I rose up to see better. There was no mistake: the long, powerful hind legs and massive hips, the short fore legs held with the paws curving downward, the tapering forequarters and neck, the erect head and up-standing ears—in every aspect a kangaroo. It was black all over. Sometimes it crouched low for a moment at the end of a leap; sometimes it continued on erect in a succession of bounds without pause. Old Joe, beside me, was muttering and stirring uneasily, and with a side glance I saw that he was on his knees, crossing himself and praying.

The creature continued on in plain sight for several minutes and at length gained the opposite cañon wall, perhaps a thousand yards away, and disappeared among the rocks at the mouth of a little side cañon. Then Bartis seized his rifle and started to go in pursuit.

"No, no!" screamed Old Joe, desperately grasping Bartis by the arm.

Bartis, surprised, shook him off, turned and looked him over, and then glanced at me as though for instructions. Joe was plainly in a bad funk about something and so excited and shaken that he could not talk coherently; but he made it evident enough that he was in deadly fear lest Bartis follow the creature. I signed to Bartis to give up his intended pursuit, and we finally calmed Old Joe down a bit. But his talk was still rambling—all about "El Diavolo" and a varied assortment of the superstitious terrors [that] he inspired. I then remembered the incident of the waterhole and the strange wolf tracks. But it all seemed too foolish: the tracks of a wolf, Joe's fear of the Devil, and now a black kangaroo apparently native to the mountains of western New Mexico— the facts did not fit together in any logical way.

That night, by the camp fire, I talked the matter over with Bartis. Several years before, he had been sent East with a delegation of Indians for a talk with President [Ulysses S.] Grant, and, among other experiences, had visited a circus and its menagerie, which included kangaroos; but neither of us had ever before seen a black kangaroo, or heard of any kangaroo running wild in America. In view of Old Joe's perturbation and strange behavior, we both felt that there was more mystery here than appeared on the surface, a mystery that called for explanation. Bartis, contrary to what might have been expected of one of his race, did not seem to share any of Joe's superstitious fears regarding the unknown beast; and he was as curious as I to learn more about it. So finally it was arranged that he should take one other man, trail the black kangaroo, and capture it or bring in its body if he could.

The rest of us went on to Fort Bayard, waited there a few days for orders from Department Headquarters, and, when they came, returned to our home station [Fort Apache] where the company was disbanded.[4] Bartis failed to overtake us at Bayard, nor did he reach Fort Apache during the next several days after our arrival there. I might have worried lest the hostile Indians had caught him; but I knew his ability to take care of himself in the wildest country, so merely wondered what he might be doing for so long a time.

Then, after about ten days, Bartis sent me word, from his little home in the village of the band he ruled, several miles from Fort Apache, that he had something there to show me privately, and would I come over? I lost no time in going. He met me with cordial hospitality, which the Apache is capable of showing when he wants to, and led me out behind his wickiup, to a little brush corral. There, in the shade, pegged out on the ground and in process of the Apache method of tanning, was a large pelt with the fur side down. I noticed that black hair protruded from around the edges. The skinning had been carefully done and the hide was complete, without the legs or any other parts missing. Bartis removed it from the pegs and turned it over, and I examined it closely. He also produced a skull, boiled and neatly cleaned, saying that it had belonged to the same animal as the skin.

Skull and pelt were those of a wolf, beyond any doubt; but such a wolf! The hair was black, thick and rather short, which was remarkable; but the astounding thing was the extreme shortness and slenderness of the front legs and the length and great over-development of the hind ones which had evidently been very powerfully muscled. The animal had been of great size, too, larger than any other wolf I had ever seen; its head and forequarters look small only in comparison with the large, powerful lower body and hind quarters. A strange freak indeed; and a formidable beast it must have been—this veritable "kangaroo wolf."

Bartis started the tale of his adventure, and I sat down in the shade to listen. He told of the almost supernatural intelligence and cunning of the creature; how it eluded him and his companion time and again when they expected to come up with it; how they followed and read the signs of its trail where it had most skillfully stalked deer or other game; how it ran alone and how the other wolves, and even the cougar, avoided it and showed fear of it; how, in spite of its deformity, it traveled on those immense hind legs with tireless ease and speed over the roughest ground; and how, at length after many days, when [he] had cornered it in a cañon pocket tearing at the recently killed body of a heifer, [he] had overcome it only after a terrific fight. Truly, Old Black Joe had had good excuse for thinking the creature to be the Evil One.

Just what the start was of Joe's fears and superstitions regarding the strange wolf I never learned; but I always felt that somewhere back of it all there was a story, though perhaps a bloodcurdling one, that was worth knowing.

I wanted that wolf skin; its scientific value, I felt, was very great; but I could see that Bartis wanted it too, and there was an earnest appeal in his eyes that I could not disregard. After all, it was he who had done all the hard work, and the trophy was really his. So, after hearing his story and discussing the marvel with him and with his family and the neighbors who dropped in to join us, I bade them all good-bye and returned to the post.

The wolf skin became greatly venerated by the people of Bartis's tribe, and its owner thereby acquired much increase in his importance among them. Years later, after old Bartis passed on, the skin still remained a treasured possession in the tribe, and it may be there yet for all I know.

Kangaroo or Kangaroo Wolf?

Since no such creature exists, Gatewood's sighting of the Kangaroo Wolf and his later viewing of the pelt raise the question of what he actually saw. As it is also doubtful that a wolf could be malformed to this extent and move about as Gatewood described, one naturally wonders about kangaroos. Again, the answer is negative. Nevertheless, Georgia Gatewood attempted to lend credence to the idea that perhaps a few kangaroos existed at least for a while in the Southwest. Supposedly she once saw a kangaroo while riding with Gatewood. Discounting the "wolf" portion of her husband's story, she shared what she claimed to have seen years earlier with her son:

> I forgot about the kangaroo. Your father & I were driving west of Apache some miles—which is a dangerous thing to do for it is a succession of low hills with a narrow way between. . . . [Y]ou can turn and turn, even keeping the same direction ap-

parently[,] and surely & hopelessly get lost. . . . [A]mong them [the hills] the troops never caught the Indians. Going down one little valley, a black kangaroo thing emerged ahead of us and hopped at right angles across in front of us, in a leisurely way, never noticing us. It was small—four or five feet at most, jet black all over, with all the kangaroo characteristics, pouch, long strong hind legs, short arms held in front, and hopped just like the real thing. We saw it close & for some time, as it crossed and went between two of those bewildering round foot hills.

We inquired all about & no one had ever heard of them, except the Indians, who said they saw one now & then, very few, & didn't know what they were. . . .

The kangaroo bore no resemblance to a wolf. [T]he head [was] entirely different—a kangaroo head [is] small, no long snout. The Indians won't talk of what is strange to them, & they won't skin a coyote.[5]

Gatewood Jr. wrote the following note: "Britton Davis says he had heard of the 'Kangaroo Wolf.' [H]e thought it was said to have been a cross between a wolf and a bear. [T]he Indians accounted for it by saying it was the returned spirit of a man who had killed his mother—the worst crime they knew of."[6]

I have found no instances of kangaroos in the Southwest. None of the educated institutions I have contacted have an answer to the mystery Gatewood created when he described his kangaroo wolf. The only animal that is indigenous to both South and Central America, as well as the U.S. Southwest, is the coatimundi (coati), which is related to the raccoon. Indeed, its features could perhaps be construed as wolflike: yellow-brown, red-brown, and grey-brown to black in color, with a pointed snout and fluffy (banded) tail.

Here the similarity to wolves ends. Coatimundis forage on the ground and in trees, where they prefer to sleep. Although they eat plants, invertebrates, and small animals, they prefer soft fruit when it can be obtained. There does not seem to be any relationship to marsupials, nor have I found references to them having the capability to travel on their hind feet, although males will rear up on their hind legs and bear their teeth in warning. And, finally, they range in size from 16 to 28 inches with their tail accounting for another 12.5 to 27 inches (for a grand total of

6 to 30 pounds), which is a far cry from the so-called oversized wolf (kangaroo wolf?) that Gatewood described. Nevertheless, they are the leading candidate for being the animal that Gatewood saw. Bill Hilton Jr., executive director of the Hilton Pond Center for Piedmont Natural History in York, South Carolina, wrote: "I know from having observed them in Arizona that Coatimundis—and the somewhat smaller Ringtails—give the impression of being much larger than they actually are."[7] U.S. scientists did not begin documenting their findings on specimens they collected from the borderlands of the American Southwest until the 1920s and 1930s, even though sightings were reported in the early 1900s.[8] Perhaps this is why Gatewood was confused by the animal he saw.

Notes

Introduction

1. Headquarters Sixth Cavalry, General Orders no. 19 (May 23, 1896), letter 54, Gatewood Collection, Arizona Historical Society, Tucson.

2. Shenandoah Co. VA Marriage Bond (fiche 6093445 #4), 304; National Archives Collection of Census: 1850 Shenandoah Co. VA 58th Dist. Census, 18; 1860 Shenandoah Co. VA Woodstock Census, 851; 1870 Rockingham Co. VA, Harrisburg Twp Census, roll 1676, 161; 1880 Shenandoah Co. VA Stonewall Census, roll 1390, 362 (hereafter listed by particular census). Emily A. Bare (1824–86) lived with her daughter Julia and son-in-law H. C. Allen by the 1880 census, as John Gatewood (b. 1819) had probably died. John's parents were Charles Gatewood (c. 1791–94, d. after 1830) and Susannah McKay (c. 1793–1800, d. after 1830), and Emily's parents were Samuel Bare (c. 1781–90, d. 1842–43) and Christina (c. 1784–85, d. 1850–60). Mary Frances was born in 1843, Julia McKay was born November 24, 1845, Cornelia Susan was born in 1848, Samuel Deyerle was born September 26, 1855, and DeWitt Clinton was born May 18, 1859. Cornelia Susan is listed in the 1850 census but then disappears, leading me to believe she died at a young age. Dixie Smith to author (February 4, 2003), Louis Kraft Papers, Fray Angélico Chávez History Library, Palace of the Governors, Santa Fe, New Mexico. See also the "Gill Family of Baltimore County, Maryland, and Canada" (www.rootsweb.com, updated December 22, 2002), entries for Charles B. Gatewood, Georgia Gatewood, and Charles B. Gatewood Jr. (hereafter cited as Gatewood entries on rootsweb.com—there are a number of entries for Gatewood, but some are obviously inaccurate.

3. Gatewood efficiency report (November 25, 1895), National Archives Microfiche Publication M1395 (five fiche relating to Gatewood's career), Letters Received by the Appointment, Commission, and Personal Branch of the Adjutant General's Office, 1871–94 (hereafter cited as NA, M1395). See also Bvt. Maj. Gen. George W. Cullum, *Biographical Register of the Officers and Graduates of the U.S. Military Academy at West Point, New York since Its Establishment in 1802, Supplement, Volume 4, 1890–1900*, edited by Edward S. Holden (Cambridge: Riverside Press, 1901), 281; 1870 Rockingham Co. VA, Harrisburg Twp Census, roll 1676, 161; Dixie Smith to author (February 4, 2003), Kraft Papers; and Constance Wynn Altshuler, *Cavalry Yellow and Infantry Blue: Army Officers in Arizona between 1851 and 1886* (Tucson: Arizona Historical Society, 1991), 138.

4. Gatewood acceptance letter (June 30, 1877); Gatewood to AG, U.S. Army

(February 12, 1878); and Gatewood Statement of Military Service (June 5, 1896), all in NA, M1395. Fort Wingate, so named in 1862 for Capt. Benjamin Wingate, who died at the Battle of Valverde, is near today's San Rafael, New Mexico. Camp Apache, located in the heart of Apache territory on the White River, was originally called Camp Ord after Gen. Edward Ord in May 1870, became Camp Mogollon in August 1870, then Camp Thomas in September 1870, and Camp Apache on February 2, 1871. Robert Julyan, *The Place Names of New Mexico* (Albuquerque: University of New Mexico Press, 1996), 137; Byrd H. Granger, *Arizona Place Names* (1960; repr., Tucson: University of Arizona Press, 1982), 233.

5. Lori Davisson, "Fort Apache, Arizona Territory, 1870–1922," *Smoke Signal* 33 (Spring 1977): 68.

6. Headquarters Sixth Cavalry, General Orders no. 19 (May 23, 1896), letter 54, Gatewood Collection. This letter mistakenly claims that Gatewood remained in command of native scouts until January 13, 1886. See George Crook to John Pope (October 2, 1885), NA, M1395, for the end of Gatewood's tenure as commander of Indian scouts. He was ordered to rejoin his regiment, which was stationed in New Mexico Territory, in October 1885, and although he did not immediately report for duty at his new station, he relinquished all duties dealing with Indians.

7. Gatewood efficiency report (November 25, 1895), NA, M1395.

8. Thomas Cruse, *Apache Days and After* (1941; repr., Lincoln: University of Nebraska Press, 1987), 55–56; Louis Kraft, *Gatewood & Geronimo* (Albuquerque: University of New Mexico Press, 2000), 2.

9. Henry Daly to Gatewood Jr. (Apr 25, 1924), Gatewood Collection, letter 581; William Harding Carter statement on Gatewood, Gatewood Collection.

10. Gatewood to Georgia (June 25, 1886), Gatewood Collection, letter 12.

11. Gatewood to Georgia (August 26, 1886), Gatewood Collection.

12. Kraft, *Gatewood & Geronimo*, 2.

13. Matthias W. Day (August 8, 1853–September 12, 1927) graduated from West Point with Gatewood in 1877. After his first assignment with the Tenth U.S. Cavalry, he transferred to the Ninth U.S. Cavalry in March 1878. In an engagement with Apaches at Las Animas Cañon in New Mexico Territory on September 18, 1879, he earned the Medal of Honor when under heavy fire he rescued a fallen comrade after the order to retreat had been given. In 1894 Gatewood proudly recounted Day's heroic action in "Campaigning against Victorio in 1879," *Great Divide* 11 (April 1894): 102. See Marcos E. Kinevan, *Frontier Cavalryman: Lieutenant John Bigelow with the Buffalo Soldiers in Texas* (El Paso: Texas Western Press, 1998), 246, for Day's placement (70) in the graduating class. According to Britton Davis, Day had a nickname, "Daisy." See Davis to Gatewood Jr. (April 25, 1926), Gatewood Collection microfilm, reel 7. The Gatewood Collection, Arizona Historical Society, Tucson, has nine reels of microfilm. Unfortunately, some of the microfilm pages are pieced together haphazardly and are incomplete, espe-

cially in several of the longer documents. Also, some have been copied with no attempt to darken what must have been faded handwritten text, making them totally unreadable.

14. Victorio (c. 1825–October 15, 1880), also known as Lucero, Bidu-ya, and Beduiat, has been described as short, stout, burly, and a good horseman. Coming to the attention of the whites in 1853, he remained a warrior-chieftain until his death when he and his band were ambushed by Mexicans under Lt. Col. Joaquin Terrazas at Tres Castillos, Chihuahua, Mexico. Seventy-eight Apaches died in the fight and sixty-eight women and children were taken prisoner, whereas the Mexicans suffered only three dead and ten wounded. Dan L. Thrapp, *Encyclopedia of Frontier Biography*, 3 vols. (Glendale CA: Arthur H. Clark, 1988), 3:1483–84.

15. For background on the Chihenne, see Gillett Griswold, comp., "The Fort Sill Apaches: Their Vital Statistics, Tribal Origins, Antecedents," manuscript on microfilm, Family History Center, Salt Lake City, Utah, 1970, catalogue # XLIB 7–102 (order no. 0928251), item 8 on the roll, 2; Morris E. Opler, *An Apache Lifeway: The Economic, Social, and Religious Institutions of the Chiricahua Indians* (1941; repr., New York: Cooper Square, 1965), 1; and Thomas E. Mails, *The People Called Apache* (1974; repr., New York: BDD Illustrated Books, 1993), 251.

16. Dan L. Thrapp, *Victorio and the Mimbres Apaches* (Norman: University of Oklahoma Press, 1974), 190; Woodworth Clum, *Apache Agent: The Story of John P. Clum* (Boston: Houghton Mifflin, 1936), 230. Thrapp uses many citations, whereas Clum uses none. Thrapp is well respected, whereas Clum's prose is questionable. The San Carlos Indian Reservation was created by executive order on December 14, 1872. Dan L. Thrapp, *The Conquest of Apacheria* (Norman: University of Oklahoma Press, 1967), 111. Gen. O. O. Howard initiated the selection of San Carlos as a reservation earlier that year. Ralph Hedrick Ogle, *Federal Control of the Western Apaches, 1848–1886* (Albuquerque: University of New Mexico Press, 1970), 105. See NA, RG 94, M689, Letters Received by the Office of the Adjutant General, 1881–89: 1066 AGO 1883, roll 184, for "Brief of Papers Relating to the Police Control of the San Carlos Reservation." San Carlos became an Indian reservation on November 9, 1871, by Executive Order, and became "a catch-all for the various bands of Apaches as well as other Indians. Included were the Mojaves and the Yumas. Apache bands included the Arivaipa, Chiricahua, Coyotero, Membre[ñ]o, Mogollon, Pinaleno, San Carlos, Tonto, and Tsiiltaden. The total acreage was 1,834,240." Granger, *Arizona Place Names*, 116. In the preceding quote, substitute the word *tribe* for *band*. Also, the word *Chiricahua* actually represents the Bedonkohe, Chokonen, and Nednhi Apaches.

17. Thrapp, *Victorio*, 193. See 195 for the breakout. Named after Arizona's first territorial governor (John N. Goodwin), Camp Goodwin became a military post in 1864 at "a spring in Goudy Canyon" and provided protection for "Americans at the end of the Gila Valley." But, "[u]nscrupulous contractors put up a few

poorly built adobe houses at a cost estimated at $150,000. . . . Malaria-carrying mosquitoes swarmed and the soldiers sickened." This led to the abandonment of the post and the eventual establishment of what would become Fort Apache. Located six miles east of where Camp Goodwin had been and three-quarters of a mile south of the Gila River, Fort Thomas began as Camp Thomas in August 1876, but became Fort Thomas the following May. Granger, *Arizona Place Names*, 127, 132.

18. Loco (1823–February 2, 1905), a Chihenne Apache chieftain (sometimes listed as a Warm Springs or Mimbreño Apache), is usually referred to as "old" and "ancient" by historians at this time, which is surprising as he was probably born the same year as Geronimo, who was just coming to the fore of the Apache resistance. What is also surprising is that historians usually refer to him as decrepit but still able to walk the war trail when he chose to follow it. Beginning in the 1850s, he and Victorio shared the leadership of the Chihenne Apaches; however, he held the senior position as leader. He was the sole leader of the Chihennes after Victorio's death in 1880. Griswold, "Apaches," 87. See also Thrapp, *Frontier Biography*, 2:865–66.

19. Apache historian Ed Sweeney thinks that Gatewood did come in contact with Victorio at this time. Sweeney to author (January 26, 2002), Kraft Papers.

20. Thrapp, *Victorio*, 201–9.

21. Thomas Cruse to Gatewood Jr. (December 14, 1927), Gatewood Collection, letter 186. Cruse did not have anything nice to say about Merritt, whom he called "a drunken, worthless, irresponsible man, afterwards dismissed and later on, about 1883, a suicide." If Gatewood did return some Chihennes to Ojo Caliente and did turn them over to Merritt, it most likely happened in 1879, for that is when Merritt commanded at Ojo Caliente. Merritt died at the age of thirty on December 12, 1879, of undisclosed causes after his November 26, 1879, dismissal from the army when a court-marital found him guilty of conduct unbecoming to an officer. See also Thrapp, *Frontier Biography*, 2:976–77.

22. Gatewood, "Campaigning against Victorio," 102.

23. Gatewood, "Campaigning against Victorio," 102.

24. Tomas and Torivio died in 1879, leaving Nana, whom Gatewood called "Nanye," as the only capable leader. Gatewood, "Campaigning against Victorio," 102. Ed Sweeney reviewed this book in an early draft in October 2001, and he supplied the following information: Tomas, who may have been one of Mangas Coloradas's sons, was also known as Tomaso Coloradas and Tomascito. Torivio (Turivio) seems to have been the son of Cuchillo Negro, a Chihenne chieftain during the 1840s and 1850s, as he received his rations with him. Torivio was also Victorio's son-in-law. Sweeney October 2001 review of Kraft ms, and Sweeney to author (January 26, 2002), both in Kraft Papers.

25. Augustus Perry Blocksom (November 7, 1854–July 26, 1931) graduated

twenty-second in the West Point class of 1877. Like Gatewood, he was assigned to command Indian scouts almost immediately after reporting for duty in January 1878, taking charge of his first company in July. As scout commander, he saw a lot of action during the Victorio campaign. Blocksom, who retired as a brigadier general in 1918, made first lieutenant on January 15, 1884. Altshuler, *Cavalry Yellow,* 35–36; Thrapp, *Frontier Biography,* 1:128.

26. Albert Payson Morrow (March 10, 1842–January 20, 1911) was wounded in the hip in March 1865. The ball was never removed and caused him a lot of pain. In July 1866, he received a commission as captain in the Seventh U.S. Cavalry. A year later he became major in the Ninth U.S. Cavalry, seeing duty in Kansas and Texas before moving on to New Mexico. Altshuler, *Cavalry Yellow,* 238–39; Thrapp, *Frontier Biography,* 2:1019.

27. Alchesay (c. 1853–August 6, 1928), who was also known as Alchisay, played a prominent role in Gatewood's career in the Southwest, first as a scout and later as chieftain of the White Mountain Apaches. He first came to the fore when, through heroic action as a scout during Crook's Tonto campaign of 1872–73, he won the Medal of Honor. Although he would be arrested for supposedly taking part in the 1881 Cibecue affair, he would be released, as there was no proof that he joined the revolt. By the time Crook returned to the Southwest in 1882, Alchesay was well acquainted with Gatewood, having served as his sergeant of scouts. Gatewood would later play an instrumental role in making him one of the head chieftains of the White Mountains. Thrapp, *Frontier Biography,* 1:12–13; Charles Collins, *Apache Nightmare: The Battle at Cibecue Creek* (Norman: University of Oklahoma Press, 1999), 258n23.

28. Charles D. Beyer (1842–September 15, 1898), who saw service with African American troops during the Civil War, transferred to the Ninth U.S. Cavalry on January 1, 1871. Beyer wanted to court-martial Day for his heroic action, but instead Day won a gold medal. Thrapp, *Frontier Biography,* 1:104; Thrapp, *Victorio,* 240. Animas Creek, amid a maze of cañons, flows eastward from the Continental Divide (the Black Range) to the Río Grande.

29. Thrapp, *Victorio,* 241.

30. Created in 1863, Fort Cummings was named after Maj. Joseph Cummings, who died that year while serving under Kit Carson during the Navajo campaign of 1863–64. Abandoned in 1873, it was reestablished in 1880 only to be abandoned a second time in 1886. Julyan, *Place Names,* 134.

31. Gatewood, "Campaigning against Victorio," 102. Apparently "Mimbres" was spelled "Miembres" at one time. See Memorandum of Services of Charles B. Gatewood, Late of the U.S. Army, NA, M1395, which spells the word the same as Gatewood did.

32. Gatewood, "Campaigning against Victorio," 102, for this quote and Gatewood's next quote.

33. The Black Range is a "conspicuously dark and foreboding" range of forested mountains that extend southward from the Plains of San Agustin in New Mexico for one hundred miles. "[T]he steep slopes permit few clearings or meadows, and the mountainsides are densely covered with conifers." Julyan, *Place Names*, 41.

34. Named after Baishan, or Cuchillo Negro (c. 1816–May 24, 1857), a Chihenne (Mimbres) Apache chieftain, Cuchillo Negro Creek enters the Black Range of New Mexico southwest "of Chloride and flows [southeast] to join the Rio Grande just [north] of Truth or Consequences." Julyan, *Place Names*, 103. See also Thrapp, *Frontier Biography*, 1:352.

35. Morrow to AAAG, Santa Fe (November 5, 1879), as cited in Thrapp, *Victorio*, 242.

36. Gatewood, "Campaigning against Victorio," 102.

37. Gatewood, "Campaigning against Victorio," 102.

38. Pronounced "muggy-YOHNZ," the Mogollons range southeast from roughly the present town of Reserve in the north to Cliff in the south. Julyan, *Place Names*, 231.

39. The San Mateo Mountains are west of the Río Grande and range northward from the current town of Monticello, New Mexico.

40. Thrapp, *Victorio*, 244–48.

41. Matthias W. Day to Gatewood Jr. (August 3, 1926), Gatewood Collection, letter 278, for this quote and Day's next quote. Charles Harrod Campbell (July 12, 1845 or 1847–March 6, 1915) may have been drunk during the engagement. He had a drinking problem that landed him in trouble on numerous occasions and eventually led to his resignation from the military in 1881. Altshuler, *Cavalry Yellow*, 55; Thrapp, *Frontier Biography*, 1:215.

42. Thomas Cruse to Gatewood Jr. (March 3, 1926), Gatewood Collection, letter 181; Cruse, "Notes concerning Al Sieber as I recollect him" (January 6, 1934), Gatewood Collection, letter 188.5.

43. Charles Gatewood, Record of Events on Muster Roll of Company "A" Indian Scouts for March and April 1880; Memorandum: Service of Charles B. Gatewood, Late of the U.S. Army, both in NA, M1395.

Thomas Cruse (December 29, 1857–June 8 or 9, 1943) graduated from West Point in 1879. However, unlike Gatewood and other graduates of earlier years, he did not have to wait until the following year to report for active duty, joining the Sixth U.S. Cavalry at Fort Apache, Arizona, on October 28, 1879. Assigned to command Indian scouts, he immediately came in contact with Gatewood. Like Gatewood, he saw a lot of action during the Victorio war. Altshuler, *Cavalry Yellow*, 88–89; Thrapp, *Frontier Biography*, 1:351–52.

44. Cruse to Gatewood Jr. (December 14, 1927), Gatewood Collection, letter 186. Cruse appears to be in error in a number of places in his statement, which

can probably be blamed on the length of time that had passed since the scene he describes occurred. However wrong he may be in some of his facts, I am certain he is accurate in his main point, that Gatewood met Victorio. It does not appear that any of the Chihennes were at Fort Apache, and I cannot find any time wherein Gatewood spent six months with them. If he did spend time with them, it most likely happened during his first assignment at Fort Wingate in January 1878, or during 1879 when some Chihennes were escorted back to Ojo Caliente. Cruse's words "six months" and "Fort Apache" are questionable. Regardless of which natives the "shavetail" first came in contact with, he undoubtedly spent as much time with them as possible, for they were no longer just words in a textbook but rather living and breathing reality.

45. Gatewood, "Campaigning against Victorio," 102.

46. Thrapp, *Victorio*, 364n24.

47. Edwin R. Sweeney, ed., *Making Peace with Cochise: The 1872 Journal of Captain Joseph Alton Sladen* (Norman: University of Oklahoma Press, 1997), 31.

48. Julyan, *Place Names*, 309.

49. Cruse, *Days*, 78–79, for this quote and the next two quotes, ending with no one being killed.

50. Gatewood, March-April 1880 Record of Events; Memorandum: Service of Charles B. Gatewood, Late of the U.S. Army, both in NA, M1395. See also Memorandum: Brevet Case of Captain Gatewood, 6th Cavalry, NA, M1395, which discusses confusion over when the skirmish actually occurred. The second fight, although it took place on the sixteenth, as Gatewood recorded, was supposedly recorded as the twelfth. This seems very strange, as Gatewood's action on the sixteenth was part of a concerted military operation to force the Indians back onto the reservation. It goes on to state: "Lieut[enant] Gatewood thus gets a brevet for a fight in which he took no part and for a date on which there was no fight, and fails to get a brevet for a fight in which he did take a gallant part." These reports are vague at best and for the most part were recorded long after the fact. There is additional controversy surrounding this skirmish. C. L. Sonnichsen, in *The Mescalero Apaches* (Norman: University of Oklahoma Press, 1958), 180, states that the Mescaleros were not running off stock, that they had permission to be where they were, and that only two died, and they had been sent out to bring in strays. This does not fit in well with Gatewood's orders or his participation in the action. Over the years, Sonnichsen's work has been well received. However, it is obvious that some of what he wrote in this book is questionable, to say the least. Finally, it seems that if innocent Apaches were killed by Gatewood that day, there would not have been any question regarding a brevet rank.

51. Cruse, *Days*, 83.

52. Special Orders no. 152 (November 24, 1880), NA, M1395. Orlando Bolivar Willcox (April 16, 1823–May 10, 1907), a West Point graduate (eighth in a class of

thirty-eight) and a veteran of the Civil War, became commander of the Department of Arizona, headquartered at Whipple Barracks, near Prescott, Arizona, in March 1878. Altshuler, *Cavalry Yellow*, 370–71; Thrapp, *Frontier Biography*, 3:1566.

53. Gatewood to AG, U.S. Army (February 2, 1881). AG to Gatewood (September 7, 1881) confirms the date that Gatewood's leave actually began. See also a note regarding Gatewood's sick leave (June 24, 1881), which states: "When last heard from, Ap[ri]l 30, he was at Woodstock VA." All in NA, M1395. Woodstock was the only forwarding address that Gatewood supplied the military at this time.

54. Norris certificate of disability (May 5, 1881), NA, M1395.

55. Gatewood to AG, U.S. Army (May 5, 1881), NA, M1395.

56. General Orders no. 114 (June 29, 1881) certifies Gatewood's disability and grants him sick leave until July 7. NA, M1395.

57. There seems to be a discrepancy regarding the year of Georgia's birth. The 1860 and 1870 censuses list her birth year as 1855–56, the 1880 census lists her birth year as 1857–58, the 1900 census lists her birth year as 1855, and the 1920 census lists her birth year as 1856–57. The split in the years presents the question of whether the census took place before her birthday or after, because the question asked was "How old are you?" rather than "When were you born?" See 1860 Allegany Co. MD, Frostburg District Census, 357; 1870 Allegany Co. MD, Frostburg P.O. Census, roll 566, 158; 1880 Allegany Co. MD, East Frostburg Census, roll 493, 278; 1900 Norfolk Co. VA Western Branch Dist. (ED44, SHT12, LN15), 37; and 1920 Allegany Co. MD, Frostburg Elect. Dist. 32 (ED53, SHT2, LN61), 280. George Huddleston, comp., *Huddleston Family Tables* (1933; repr., Concord NH: Rumford Press, 1973), 60, removes the confusion, listing her birth year as 1855. "My Southern Family" at freepages.genealogy.rootsweb.com (printout in Kraft Papers) lists Georgia's birth as October 6, 1854. October 6 seems to be the correct day. However, considering the above census records and *Huddleston Family Tables*, four records point at her birth year as 1855, three as 1856, two as 1857, one as 1858, and none as 1854. Undoubtedly her parents reported her birth year correctly during the 1860 and 1870 censuses. When 1880 arrived, Georgia found herself in an unenviable situation for a young lady—she was twenty-five or twenty-six years old and still unwed—which might have led her to shed a couple of years off her age. By 1900 there was no reason to alter her birth year, and she answered 1855. By the time 1920 arrived, she had aged and perhaps suffered a memory lapse. This leads me to believe that most likely her birth occurred in 1855. The 1880 census listed her as "Georgiana" and the Preston Co. WV, Will for Thomas McCulloh of Allegany Co. MD (probated December 11, 1896), listed her as "Georgie."

58. Thomas McCulloh (1817–before December 11, 1896) and his wife, Sarah Ellen Huddleston (October 16, 1831–after 1920). The 1860 census lists Thomas's birth year as 1817–18, whereas the 1870 and 1880 censuses list his birth year as 1816–

17. Again, the split in the years presents the question of whether the census took place before his birthday or after. The 1860 census lists him as forty-two, whereas the 1870 and 1880 censuses list him as fifty-three and sixty-three, respectively. This leads me to believe that the 1860 census took place before his birthday, while the others happened after it. In conclusion: he was born in 1817. McCulloh's second daughter, Mary, died in 1863. See the 1860 Allegany Co. MD, Frostburg District Census, 357; 1870 Allegany Co. MD, Frostburg PO Census, roll 566, 158; 1880 Allegany Co. MD, East Frostburg Census, roll 493, 278. See also Preston Co. WV, Will for Thomas McCulloh of Allegany Co. MD (probated December 11, 1896); *Huddleston Family Tables*, 60.

59. Gatewood to Georgia Gatewood (June 25, 1886), Gatewood Collection, letter 12.

60. The Cibecue Apaches, one of the tribes of the Western Apaches, lived on the upper reaches of Cibecue Creek, a short distance west of Fort Apache. "Cibecue" has been spelled as "Cibicu" and "Cibecu" over the years.

61. Eugene Asa Carr (March 10 or March 20, 1830–December 2, 1910), an 1850 graduate of West Point (nineteenth in a class of forty-four), rose to the rank of brevet major general during the Civil War. After the rebellion, he continued his career, seeing extensive duty against Indians on the plains. He scored a major victory when he, as major of the Fifth U.S. Cavalry, attacked the Southern Cheyenne Tall Bull's Dog Soldier village at Summit Springs, Colorado, on July 11, 1869. By 1881, he was a colonel in the Sixth U.S. Cavalry, stationed in Arizona. Altshuler, *Cavalry Yellow*, 60–61; Thrapp, *Frontier Biography*, 1:230–31.

62. Mails, *People*, 28–30.

63. Of the twenty-five scouts in Company A, twelve belonged to Pedro's band of White Mountains and thirteen were Cibecue Apaches. Only twenty-two or twenty-three scouts (depending upon the source) accompanied Carr because one was in the guardhouse and one was sick, or two were sick and one was on leave. Before leaving Fort Apache to make the arrest, Cruse wanted the scouts discharged, as he doubted their loyalty. Although Alchesay and his White Mountains did not take part in the incident, they went into hiding and joined the outbreak. Cruse wrote: "Alch[e]say never turned renegade nor any of his band, although the hostiles tried to involve him in killing and burning four Mormons at One Mile Hill." Cruse to Gatewood Jr. (January 19, 1926), Gatewood Collection, letter 179; Collins, *Apache Nightmare*, 32–33, 36, 238n5. The battle site is approximately two and a half miles south of the current town of Cibecue. Granger, *Arizona Place Names*, 237.

64. AG to Gatewood (September 7, 1881), NA, M1395.

65. These bands belonged to the group of tribes that spoke the Yuman dialect. They were not Apaches, and ranged from the upper portion of Baja California to the very southern tip of California and into Arizona from the east side of

the Colorado River all the way to the north where the Colorado joins the Little Colorado River and then south to the Salt River. The Yuman people have been divided into four groups: California, Upland, Delta, and River. The Yumas (or Quechan) and Mohave belong to the River subdivision. They live along the lower Colorado River where it divides Arizona and California. Kenneth M. Stewart, "Yumans: Introduction," in Alfonso Ortiz, ed., *Handbook of North American Indians*, vol. 10: *Southwest* (Washington: Smithsonian Institution, 1983), 1, 8.

66. The Cibecue is perhaps thirty miles northwest of Fort Apache, and the Black River is to the south of Fort Apache.

67. In Keith H. Basso, ed., *Western Apache Raiding and Warfare* (1971; repr., Tucson: University of Arizona Press, 1993), 137, John Rope, one of Grenville Goodwin's informants, called Sanchez a "Carrizo" chief. Regardless of his conspicuous role in the Cibecue uprising, Sanchez was certainly aligned with the White Mountains, and he would play a prominent role in Gatewood's dealings with the White Mountain Apaches during his tenure as military commandant of the White Mountain Indian Agency. Gatewood himself grouped Sanchez with the White Mountains and not with the Cibecue, as some historians have done. Gatewood was well acquainted with the firebrand; although having been forced by Crook to take Sanchez on as a sergeant of his scouts at one time, Gatewood later considered him a friend. See Gatewood to Georgia Gatewood (March 1, 1893), Gatewood Collection, letter 50. In stark contrast to Gatewood's opinion of Sanchez, Thomas Cruse to Gatewood Jr. (February 9, 1926) wrote: "Sanchez was the only Indian I ever thought deserved hanging for the Cibicu, and the only one I ever ardently wished to shoot on sight. I have always claimed that he was the fellow who started the Cibicu fight, and did it through a malignant desire to square up with my Scouts and get them in bad—rather than love for the medicine man."

68. John F. Finerty, "On Campaign after Cibicue Creek," in Peter Cozzens, ed., *Eyewitnesses to the Indian Wars, 1865–1890: The Struggle for Apacheria* (Mechanicsburg PA: Stackpole Books, 2001), 244–46. Finerty was a correspondent for the *Chicago Times*. He was in San Francisco when news broke of the firefight at Cibecue. He quickly took a train to Tucson and then traveled on to Fort Apache, where he joined Carr's command on September 17. Oliver Knight, *Following the Indian Wars* (Norman: University of Oklahoma Press, 1960), 304, 309. His dispatches regarding the uprising appeared in the *Times* between September 18 and October 21, 1881. See also Collins, *Apache Nightmare*, 114, 117, 121–23.

69. Tullius Cicero Tupper (September 23, 1838–September 1, 1898) rose through the Union ranks from enlistee to an officer during the Civil War.

70. Finerty, "On Campaign," 247, as well as 249–50 for Finerty's next quote.

71. Edward Everett Dravo (November 23, 1853–July 30, 1932) graduated from West Point in 1876, nineteenth in a class of forty-eight.

72. Carr to AAG, Department of Arizona (November 5, 1881), Letters Received by the Commissioner of Indian Affairs (1882–86), National Archives, letter 20507. See also Collins, *Apache Nightmare*, 182–83, 185; Finerty, "On Campaign," 252. Gatewood returned from the scout on November 5. Indian agent J. C. Tiffany would complain about these deaths, writing, "The Indians killed were not hostiles but friendly ones, old and crippled, who had gone to try and gather the remnant of the crop of corn not destroyed by the military on the Cibicu Creek." See Tiffany to Commissioner of Indian Affairs (December 6, 1881), Letters Received by the Commissioner of Indian Affairs (1882–86), National Archives, letter 21916. Tiffany claimed that four old women were also killed during this patrol. See Alch[e]say et al., "The Apache Story of the Cib[e]cue," in Cozzens, ed., *Eyewitnesses*, 301, for Alchesay not being at the Cibecue.

73. Since there were 346 Chiricahuas listed on the 1880 census and all but 30 left the reservation, we can assume that the number of people who broke out of the reservation on September 30, 1881, was somewhere above 300–74 men and the rest women and children. Ed Sweeney clarifies just which bands left the reservation: "The Chokonens, Nednhis, and part of the Bedonkohe bands went out. Only Loco's group, mostly Chihennes with some Bedonkohes, remained on the reservation." Sweeney, October 2001 review of Kraft ms, and Sweeney to author (January 26, 2002), both in Kraft Papers; and Gatewood to Carr (October 2, 1881), Records of U.S. Army Continental Commands, 1821–1920, NA, RG 393, Department of Arizona, 1870–93, Letters Received.

74. Opler, *Life-way*, 1–3; Geronimo, *Geronimo: His Own Story*, edited by S. M. Barrett; newly edited by Frederick W. Turner III (New York: E. P. Dutton, 1970), 66, 68; Mails, *People*, 251; Eve Ball, with Nora Henn and Lynda Sanchez, *Indeh: An Apache Odyssey* (Provo UT: Brigham Young University Press, 1980), 11; Sweeney, ed., *Making Peace*, 130n5.

75. Griswold, "Apaches," 2.

76. Naiche (c. 1856–1921), also known as Nachee, Nachite, Nahche, Nahchi, Natchez, Nachez, and Christian Naiche, was both Chokonen and Chihenne. His parents were Chokonen chieftain Cochise and Dos-teh-seh, daughter of Chihenne chieftain Mangas Coloradas. His older brother was Taza (Tahza, c. 1843–September 26, 1876). Naiche became the last hereditary Chokonen chieftain when Taza died of pneumonia while visiting Washington DC. Dan Thrapp wrote, "He was less able than Cochise or Taza, but was a fine warrior and held the respect of his people." See Thrapp, *Frontier Biography*, 2:1038. Thrapp was opinionated, and he constantly boosted those whom he felt worthy and denigrated those who did not measure up in his mind. This is unfortunate, as he has influenced future generations with what is in reality only his opinion. Comparing Naiche with his brother is unfair to both men. Naiche definitely held the respect of his people, even though Jay Van Orden (director, Field Service Division, Arizona Historical

Society) claims he never did. Van Orden believes that Naiche shot his wife for refusing to break out in 1885 and that his mother disowned him. Jay Van Orden review of Kraft ms (May 2, 2002). A terrible accusation; unfortunately, Van Orden has shared no supporting documentation for his statements, and I have yet to confirm them. During the last years of freedom for the Chokonens, Bedonkohes, and Nednhis, Geronimo may have been the power behind the throne, but there is no doubt who was chieftain. Continuing that thought, there is no doubt who was chieftain during all their years of captivity: Naiche. Griswold, "Apaches," 106. Gatewood used the Anglicized spelling of Naiche's name, Natchez. Throughout this text, he is referred to as Naiche.

77. Geronimo (c. 1823–February 17, 1909), who was also known as Goyahkla, Goyankla, Goyathlay, Go-Khla-yeh, and Gokliya, all of which mean "One Who Yawns," is probably the most famous of all the Apaches. Thrapp, *Frontier Biography*, 2:547, lists Geronimo's birth year as 1823, whereas Griswold, "Apaches," 41, lists his birth year as 1829.

78. Ball, *Indeh*, 11. Although Griswold, in "Apaches," 61, claims that Ishton was a first cousin of Geronimo and not his sister, Daklugie states in Ball, *Indeh*, 3, that Ishton was "dearly loved by her brother Geronimo."

79. Geronimo, *Geronimo*, 69.

80. Gee-esh-kizn (d. 1858) was Geronimo's first wife. A Nednhi Apache, she was also known as Alope. Geronimo married her after he and his mother, Juana, joined the Nednhi after his father (Taklishim) died in the 1840s. Griswold, "Apaches," 41. According to Angie Debo, *Geronimo: The Man, His Time, His Place* (Norman: University of Oklahoma Press, 1976), 31: "The two had long been in love."

Juana (d. 1858), a Bedonkohe Apache, married Taklishim (the Gray One), son of Mahko, the last chieftain of the Bedonkohes. After he died of an illness, Juana and Geronimo joined Juh and the Nednhi Apaches in Mexico. Griswold, "Apaches," 71. Even though Juana had a number of children by Taklishim, Griswold claims only Geronimo and one sister's name (Nah-dos-te) have been remembered by time.

81. Griswold, "Apaches," 5, 18, 41, 58, 111, 124, 148; Geronimo, *Geronimo*, 136; Debo, *Geronimo*, 244, 246–47; Crook to AG, Division of the Pacific (August 17, 1885), no. 223, and Crook to AG, Division of the Pacific (September 22, 1885), no. 234, both in George Crook Collection, Rutherford B. Hayes Memorial Library, Fremont OH; Ball, *Indeh*, 102–3; Kraft, *Gatewood & Geronimo*, 108.

82. George Crook (September 8 or September 23, 1829–March 21, 1890), a West Point graduate, saw duty in Indian wars before serving in the Civil War, from which he emerged a brevet major general. He became a major in the Third U.S. Infantry in the reorganized army at the close of the war. His star soon rose, as he proved to be one of the military's best Indian fighters. His circumventing

the seniority rule, leap-frogging over a number of officers with longer terms of service, and becoming a brigadier general caused considerable animosity among his peers. Although his star had been tarnished somewhat by his performance during the Sioux war of 1876–77, he was nevertheless a good choice to replace Willcox. Altshuler, *Cavalry Yellow*, 86–88; Thrapp, *Frontier Biography*, 1:348–50. Altshuler and Thrapp are not close with the birth dates they list for Crook.

83. Sherman to Secretary of War (August 2, 1882), as cited in Collins, *Apache Nightmare*, 210–11.

84. Kraft, *Gatewood & Geronimo*, 12–13.

85. Gatewood to Georgia Gatewood (August 26, 1886), Gatewood Collection.

86. "Nantan" is an Apache word that means captain, leader, or chief.

87. Britton Davis, who also served as a military Indian agent in Arizona Territory during the 1880s, stated that Gatewood was "Cool, quiet, courageous; firm when convinced of right but intolerant of wrong; with a thorough knowledge of Apache character." Britton Davis, *The Truth about Geronimo*, ed. M. M. Quaife (1929; repr., New Haven: Yale University Press, 1963), 223. In 1890 Maj. Gen. Nelson A. Miles evaluated Gatewood: "Is efficient in all that pertains to the duties of his office. Attention to duty, conduct and habits, <u>Excellent</u>; is qualified to fill any detail to which his rank makes him available. Is well qualified for the management of Indians. 'A brave officer and a gentleman of integrity and good character.'" Gatewood efficiency report, NA, M1395. The underline is in the original text.

Prologue: The Adventure Begins

1. Gatewood Collection microfilm, reel 3. The draft is 3 pages in length.

2. Kinevan, *Frontier Cavalryman*, 245; Altshuler, *Cavalry Yellow*, 373.

3. Percheron are powerful and rugged draft horses that originally came from the Perche region of France.

4. When Gatewood drafted the chapter he could not remember the name of the post and called Camp Apache "Fort" Apache twice in this section. Camp Apache did not become Fort Apache until 1879.

5. Although this is a racially tainted statement by today's standards, it was not considered such during the nineteenth century. Nevertheless, it is a rarity and seldom found in Gatewood's writing.

1. Mismanagement and the Last Outbreak

1. Charles B. Gatewood, "Gatewood on the Control & Management of the Indians (including the Outbreak of May 1885)," Gatewood Collection, box 3, folder 50, contains 8 unnumbered pages.

2. Gatewood speaks in general terms when naming the Apaches, and he com-

bines four Apachean tribes and calls them Chiricahuas. These tribes are the Chokonen, Bedonkohe, Nednhi, and Chihenne Apaches.

3. This news terrified the Apaches because they were aware that the white population of Arizona would like nothing better than to see them dead.

4. Gatewood refers to Crook's 1883 invasion of the Sierra Madre in Mexico to round up warring Apaches. See Kraft, *Gatewood & Geronimo*, 25–35, for Gatewood's role in the expedition. He reached Fort Apache about the middle of June. At that time, 325 Chiricahuas (Chokonen, Bedonkohe, and Nednhi Apaches) and Warm Springs (Chihenne Apaches) returned to the reservation, including Bonito, Mangus, Nana, and Loco. During the surrender talks with Crook, Geronimo had requested additional time to gather his people and their belongings. Crook granted the request. Naiche and those with him returned to the United States in December, and Chatto and his people returned to the United States early in February 1884. Geronimo did not return until the end of February 1884. For Mangus's return in 1883, see see Crawford to AAG, Dept. of Arizona (June 24, 1883), Records of U.S. Army Continental Commands, 1821–1920, NA, RG 393, Department of Arizona, 1870–93, Letters Received. After returning from the expedition, Crawford met with some of the Apache leaders on the reservation. He reported that after ten Western Apaches verbalized their views, Loco, Bonito, Nana, and Mangas spoke, assuring the Western Apaches that they would behave themselves and not cause trouble.

5. Geronimo was a shaman, warrior, and leader of his own band of Bedonkohe Apaches, but he was never an elected chieftain.

2. The Apache Indians

1. NA, M1395.

2. Frederick Webb Hodge, ed., *Handbook of American Indians North of Mexico*, Smithsonian Institution Bureau of American Ethnology, Bulletin 30, 2 vols. (Washington: Government Printing Office), 1912, 1:66.

3. Hodge, *Handbook of American Indians*, 1:109.

4. Coronado is quoted in Curtis F. Schaafsma, *Apaches de Navajo: Seventeenth-Century Navajos in the Chama Valley of New Mexico* (Salt Lake City: University of Utah Press, 2002), 211. See also 210. This volume has many citations related to early Spanish encounters with Apaches. Although some "experts" take offense at the term "Apachean," it appears in numerous publications.

5. Schaafsma, *Apaches de Navajo*, 216. See also Ogle, *Western Apaches*, 5.

6. Hodge, *Handbook of American Indians*, 1:63. See also Grenville Goodwin, *The Social Organization of the Western Apache* (Chicago: University of Chicago Press, 1942), 1; Richard J. Perry, *Apache Reservation: Indigenous Peoples and the American State* (Austin: University of Texas Press, 1993), 63; and Mails, *People*, 25.

7. Perry, *Apache Reservation*, 29.

8. This chapter is based upon two drafts; both drafts are called "Gatewood on Experiences among the Apaches" and are in the Gatewood Collection: box 3, folder 48 (hereafter cited as Gatewood, "Apaches"), and box 3, folder 49 (hereafter cited as Gatewood, "Experiences"). The draft in folder 49 (23 pages and a second 6 pages) is a rewrite of the draft in folder 48 (34 pages, extra page, 7½, and pages 1–2 to be added). In the folder 49 draft, Gatewood expands upon what he already wrote, while maintaining much of his text in folder 48. See also Kraft, *Gatewood & Geronimo*, 210.

9. The reservations are the White Mountain Indian Reservation, which was headquartered at Fort Apache, and the San Carlos Indian Reservation, which was south of the Black River. Both were created in 1872, but by 1882 were considered one reservation. See Kraft, *Gatewood & Geronimo*, 14.

10. The Apaches are descended from the "most southerly group of the Athapascan [or Athapaskan] family" of people, which are, according to Hodge, "The most widely distributed of all the Indian linguistic families of North America, formerly extending over parts of the continent from the Arctic coast far into N. Mexico from the Pacific to Hudson bay at the N., and from the Rio Colorado to the mouth of the Rio Grande at the S.—a territory extending for more than 40° of latitude and 75° of longitude." Hodge, *Handbook of American Indians*, 1:63, 108.

11. Most of the Apache scholars, using early Spanish documents, feel that the people now known as Apaches did not migrate to the Southwest until after the beginning of the sixteenth century. Their reasoning is straightforward. Spanish accounts do not mention the Apaches at the beginning of the 1500s, but then do so soon after 1540. At this time, the Spaniards referred to these people, who would soon be called "Apaches," as "Querechos" and "Teyas." Perry, *Apache Reservation*, 40, 43; Schaafsma, *Apaches de Navajo*, 6, 210–12; and Hodge, *Handbook of American Indians*, 1:63, 108.

12. Although the names that the Apaches called themselves at this early date are unknown, we do know that by the mid-1600s the Spanish called them by various names, including "Apaches del Perrillo," "Xila Apaches," "Apaches de Quinia," and "Vaquero Apaches," as well as the "Apaches de Nauajò." Schaafsma, *Apaches de Navajo*, 208.

13. Gatewood called these Indians "Yukis" in the manuscript, but it is clear that he refers to the Yaqui Indians of northwestern Mexico. Because Yaqui land was fertile, the Mexican government decided it should become part of the hacienda land system with the former owners serving as laborers. This did not sit well with the Yaquis, who, like the Bedonkohe, Chokonen, Nednhi, and Chihenne Apaches, had no intention of giving up what they considered theirs. They fought back, and mostly succeeded until 1887, when Mexican president Porfirio Díaz initiated his costly and yet successful "pan o el palo" (bread or the club) campaign against

them. Through death or deportation, the Yaquis population swiftly declined from 20,000 to 3,000. See Edward H. Spicer, "Yaqui," in Ortiz, ed., *Southwest*, 250–51; and Shelley Bowen Hatfield, *Chasing Shadows: Indians along the United States–Mexico Border, 1876–1911* (Albuquerque: University of New Mexico Press, 1998), 6–7.

14. The Spanish called towns "pueblos."

15. Perry, *Apache Reservation*, 48: "Athapaskan peoples did, however, have a long-standing pattern of taking advantage of subsistence opportunities. This strategy arose from generations of survival in harsh and uncertain environments. Livestock and other food stores in the villages of the Southwest were potential resources. Raiding in that sense was as much a transformation of their existing mode of subsistence as it was an innovation." Perry continues: "This does not mean that anyone who was not kin was necessarily subject to attack. The Apache traded and interacted on a friendly basis with many other groups in the Southwest, but such relationships tended to be uncertain" (63).

16. This sentence is only in Gatewood, "Apaches."

17. Goodwin, in *Western Apache*, 9, wrote: "Scalping enemies who were killed in the occasional blood and clan feuds which sprang up between families of different groups was unthinkable because 'they were really one people.' But, when a slain Navajo, Mexican, or American was scalped, it was different, and even a Chiricahua might meet the same fate, although here the feeling of closer relationship made the practice unlikely."

18. This paragraph only appeared in Gatewood, "Apaches."

19. In Gatewood, "Apaches," his text differs: "Coming & going like the whirl-wind, they naturally terrorized the country, & continued to do so until the surrender of Geronimo in 1886, in spite of the increase of the other races who settled there & against whom they bore enmity almost implacable. Incessant warfare, carried on through centuries, prevented their natural increase in population & in later times produced a decrease. Cochise & Mangas Coloradas, when forty years ago, they effected an alliance between their respective tribes, could muster fifteen hundred warriors. This was when Geronimo was a budding warrior. Today, Geronimo can scarcely count a hundred men of the same people, & they are in captivity far away in Alabama." Apache historian Ed Sweeney places the combined Cochise–Mangas Coloradas force at roughly four hundred men in 1850 and three hundred a decade later. As Sweeney wrote, "These are just estimates based on probable population of the four Chiricahua bands, whose numbers, I think, were usually overestimated. I have been analyzing their population in the early 1870s when they were on reservations, and in 1872 the four bands totaled about 1,250 individuals, with 22 percent being men." Sweeney to author (January 26, 2002), Kraft Papers. See also Sweeney October 2001 review of Kraft ms, Kraft Papers.

20. Goodwin, in *Western Apache*, 351–52, wrote: "Polygyny was accepted as a rich man's prerogative and the outcome of personal desires." He adds that "there could be important economic advantages. A wealthy man who periodically brought in game and booty from raids was extremely desirable in marriage, and more than one set of parents-in-law could be partly supported by him. At the same time more than one wife in the family meant that certain economic duties could be shared and lightened. It is said that a man who still loved his first wife would sometimes take a second one to spare his first wife the burden of all the family tasks. Some women were reconciled to this, since it lessened their labors." Opler, in *Life-way*, 417, quotes a story that discusses the number of wives a man might have: "Most men have one wife. . . . The limit is about five. If a man can afford it, he might have more, because there is no rule, but the greatest number of wives I ever heard of is four or five, and the greatest number I've actually known about is only two or three." The division of labor—male and female tasks were well defined—became more important when Apaches lived in the wild and even more so when they were at war. See also Kraft, *Gatewood & Geronimo*, 6–7.

21. Goodwin, *Western Apache*, 69.

22. Morris E. Opler, "The Apachean Culture Pattern and Its Origins," in Ortiz, ed., *Southwest*, 368, 381–82. See also Mails, *People*, 22, 29; and Sonnichsen, *Mescalero Apaches*, 12. Richard J. Perry, in *Western Apache Heritage: People of the Mountain Corridor* (Austin: University of Texas Press, 1991), 6, wrote: "Their presence after that [their arrival during the sixteenth century] was felt throughout the region. Had they been there much before 1500, it seems likely that they would have been noted by other groups and mentioned to the earliest Spanish expeditions of the 1540s."

23. Keith H. Basso, "Western Apache," in Ortiz, ed., *Southwest*, 463. See Opler, "Apachean Culture Pattern," 368, for the linguistic link between these people.

24. Hodge, *Handbook of American Indians*, 108.

25. Goodwin, *Western Apache*, 2–3. See Goodwin's map of the various Western Apache groupings (4).

26. Although the draft in Gatewood, "Experiences," continues to remain the main draft, the text from Gatewood, "Apaches," offered a better lead-in and has been retained.

27. War and raiding was just as significant as hunting for survival. One of Opler's informants, in *Life-way*, 333, said: "They went on raids because they were in need. They divided their booty among the poor in camp." In other words, the wealth was shared all around. This statement does not agree with Gatewood's that the people argued over how the recently acquired goods would be divided, leaving the modern reader in limbo as to the real reason why a war erupted that

split the people apart. It is a shame that Gatewood did not dig deeper. See also Opler, 332.

28. According to Goodwin in *Western Apache*, 71, the White Mountains called the Navajos "yú·ùdàhá," which means "people above" because the Navajos lived on higher ground.

29. Gatewood spelled this word Aravaypas. Although he names the San Carlos and the Arivaipas as one and the same, Mails, *People*, 47, classified them as separate. Basso, "Western Apache," 488, citing Albert H. Schroeder's 1974 research, lists the Arivaipas as a subgroup of the San Carlos Apaches, as does Goodwin, *Western Apache*, 2.

30. Geronimo was a Bedonkohe Apache.

31. Nelson Appleton Miles (August 8, 1839–May 25, 1925) replaced Crook as commander of the Department of Arizona on April 11, 1886, when Geronimo and Naiche decided not to return to the United States because they did not trust Crook's words. Miles abandoned Crook's strategy of using Indians to defeat Indians. He assembled five thousand U.S. troops to patrol the Mexican border and to guard all the known water holes. Then, using the Fourth U.S. Cavalry as his primary weapon, he began sending columns into Mexico to hunt the Apaches. The cost was high, the results were minimal, and soon, desperate to end the war with the Apaches, he approached Gatewood to find Geronimo and deliver his surrender terms. Gatewood considered Miles's request a fool's errand and balked. The stakes were high (a major general rank) for the general, and Miles dangled the position as his aide-de-camp before the lieutenant. Gatewood accepted the assignment. See Louis Kraft, "Assignment: Geronimo," *Wild West* 12, no. 3 (October 1999): 36.

Apache Kid (c. 1860–94?), an Aravaipa Apache, served as an Indian scout on a number of occasions, eventually obtaining the rank of sergeant. His trouble began when his father, Togo-de-chuz, was murdered in 1887. The killer also met his demise, but the Kid was not satisfied, and he killed the dead man's brother, which illustrates what Gatewood says about feuds and inner-fighting among the Apaches. The Kid, along with some of his fellow Indian scouts, went AWOL and had a tiswin drunk. After five days he and his cohorts returned to the reservation to see how bad the punishment would be. Captain Pierce ordered them to surrender their weapons, which they did, but someone from the crowd began shooting. Scout Al Sieber was wounded, crippling him for life, and the Kid ran, becoming a fugitive, only to surrender and be convicted and sentenced—a sentence that was later reduced. In 1889, in a new trial the Kid was sentenced to seven years at Yuma Territorial Prison. During the trek to the Arizona prison, the Kid and five others killed their guards and escaped. The Kid's death is still unknown; he may still have been alive in 1899, 1915, or even as late as 1935.

Sherry Robinson, *Apache Voices: Their Stories of Survival as Told to Eve Ball* (Albuquerque: University of New Mexico Press, 2000), 79–81, 84.

32. Francis Edwin Pierce (July 6, 1833–November 4, 1896) received the assignment to replace Capt. Emmet Crawford as military commandant of the San Carlos Indian Reservation on February 22, 1885. Although he arrived at San Carlos on March 4, he did not assume command until March 28. Beginning his military career as a captain in the 108th New York Infantry in 1862, he received a brevet as brigadier general of volunteers before the Civil War ended. After the rebellion, Pierce remained in the military and was commissioned second lieutenant (First U.S. Infantry) in 1866. He became a first lieutenant in 1867 and a captain in 1880. In 1891 Gen. Nelson Miles appointed him military agent of the Pine Ridge Reservation in South Dakota, but an illness prematurely ended his assignment a month later. See Kraft, *Gatewood & Geronimo*, 56; Thrapp, *Frontier Biography*, 3:1144.

33. Albert Sieber (February 29, 1844–February 19, 1907) arrived in the United States while still a boy. After serving in the Civil War, he migrated westward and eventually reached Arizona in 1868. He soon gained fame as a scout in campaigns against the natives of the Southwest.

34. Col. H. B. Wharfield, *Apache Indian Scouts* (El Cajon CA: privately printed, 1964), 51–53.

35. Although Petone's date of death is unknown, we do know how he died. See Wharfield, *Apache Indian Scouts*, 6. Wharfield reports: "During a tulapai drinking spree at Petone's camp south of Show Low[, Arizona Territory,] the two [Alchesay and Petone] got into a drunken brawl over a card game of monte. They started pommeling each other and tearing out hair, which caused intoxicated followers of both men to join the melee. It ended in a general gun fight with the two principals shooting each other through the body. Petone was killed as well as several others, but Alchesay was only badly wounded."

36. This entire section was only in Gatewood, "Experiences."

37. Although a small amount of the text in this section is from Gatewood, "Apaches," the bulk of the text comes from the rewrite in Gatewood, "Experiences."

38. This sentence is from Gatewood, "Apaches."

39. Cochise (c. 1805–June 8, 1874) rose to prominence as leader of the Chokonens during the 1840s, and by the late 1850s he had become the most powerful chieftain of the central Chiricahuas. Although he had mostly remained peaceful with the Americans up until this time, his attitude would change in January 1861, when he was seized during a negotiation regarding stolen livestock and a missing boy. He eventually escaped—amid a flurry of bullets—but both sides executed prisoners, and a decade of bloody warfare followed. Anson P. K. Safford, governor of Arizona Territory (1869–77), met Cochise near the end of the chieftain's

life in November 1872, and wrote this verbal description of him: "His height is about six feet; shoulders slightly rounded by age; features quite regular; head large and well-proportioned; countenance rather sad; hair long and black, with some gray ones intermixed; face smooth, the beard having been pulled out with pincers as is the custom of the Indians. He wore a shirt, with pieces of cotton cloth about his loins and head, and moccasins covered his feet, which constituted his costume." Safford, "Something about Cochise," from Tucson *Arizona Citizen* (December 7, 1872) as cited in Cozzens, ed., *Eyewitnesses*, 127.

Mangas Coloradas (c. 1795–January 18, 1863), the Chihenne chieftain, earned a fearsome reputation in Mexico as a war leader who ravaged the northern states of Sonora and Chihuahua before first contact with Americans. In contrast to the bloody war he waged south of the border, he tried to befriend the Americans—only to be murdered by them. Even though *Tombstone Epitaph* editor John Clum never met "Red Sleeves," as he was sometimes called, he wrote that Mangas Coloradas was "powerful physically, intelligent, resourceful, fair minded, assumed seriously the task of leading his people. He was a great thinker." Clum, *Apache Agent*, 11.

The alliance that Gatewood refers to began when Cochise accompanied Mangas Coloradas on raids in the 1830s. It was cemented in the late 1830s or early 1840s when Cochise married the latter's daughter, Dos-teh-seh, who became his principal wife. Edwin R. Sweeney, *Cochise: Chiricahua Apache Chief* (1991; repr., Norman: University of Oklahoma Press, 1995), 45. Sweeney explains: "Chiricahua custom required a man to live with the local group or band to which his wife belonged; in Cochise's case, perhaps following a brief six- to eight-month trial period, he returned to live with his Chokonens because his status among his people made him too valuable to be gone very long. According to one anthropologist [Keith Basso], 'the sons of prominent men were obliged to stay close at home.' In any event, the relationship between Cochise and Mangas Coloradas developed and was nurtured in the years that followed." For a biography on Mangas Coloradas, see Edwin R. Sweeney, *Mangas Coloradas, Chief of the Chiricahua Apaches* (Norman: University of Oklahoma Press, 1998).

40. Mangus (1846–February 9, 1901), a Chihenne Apache, was also known as Mangas and Carl Mangus. His family intertwines with Apache chieftain blood. His father was the famed and feared Chihenne chieftain Mangas Coloradas, who was murdered by whites on January 18, 1863. Of his two sisters, Nah-ke-de-sah and Dos-teh-seh, and brother, Seth-mooda, Dos-teh-seh married Cochise and was the mother of both Taza and Naiche. One of Victorio's daughters, Dilth-cley-ih (b. 1846), a Chihenne (both Mimbreño and Warm Springs Apache), became his wife. She had a daughter (Elsie Vance Chestuen) by a previous marriage. Their union produced five children: Cora, Frank, Lillian, Faith, and Flora. Dilth-cley-ih was luckily in the Black Range in New Mexico Territory when Victorio

died at Tres Castillos, Chihuahua, Mexico, on October 15, 1880. Little is known of another of Mangus's wives, Huera (Chihenne Apache), who was captured at Tres Castillos and sold into slavery in Mexico. After escaping with several other women and returning to the reservation, she pushed Mangus into speaking out against government rule on May 14, 1885, which led to the last Apache outbreak. She may have been captured west of Casas Grandes, Chihuahua, Mexico, when Capt. Wirt Davis's Indian scouts attacked Geronimo's camp on August 7, 1885; however, Thrapp claims she escaped. During the latter years of the Apache struggle for freedom, Mangus spent more time with the Chokonens (Chiricahuas) than he did with his own people. Although he made the final escape from captivity in May 1885 with Naiche and Geronimo, he broke away and did not surrender with them. Mangus and his small band surrendered in October 1886, and he was imprisoned at Fort Pickens, Florida, while the women and children were sent to Fort Marion, Florida. Mangus became a member of the Twelfth Infantry (Company I) after the prisoners of war were transferred to the Mount Vernon Barracks in Alabama. After the U.S. government moved the prisoners to Fort Sill, Oklahoma, he headed what became known as "Mangus's Village." Enjoying military service, he enlisted in the Seventh Cavalry (Troop L) and then in 1897 served as a scout. He died at Fort Sill and was buried in the Post Cemetery. Griswold, "Apaches," 30, 92. See Robinson, *Voices*, 224n5, for Dilth-cley-ih in the Black Range. For information on Huera, see Eve Ball and James Kaywaykla, *In the Days of Victorio: Recollections of a Warm Springs Apache* (Tucson: University of Arizona Press, 1970), 168–74; Kraft, *Gatewood & Geronimo*, 85, 103; and Thrapp, *Conquest*, 311, 331n8. Thrapp mistakenly thought Huera was Mexican. For a word portrait of Mangus in the 1870s, see Sweeney, ed., *Making Peace*, 31. Lt. Joseph Alton Sladen met Mangus at Fort Tularosa, New Mexico Territory, in 1872 and called him a "fine looking young Indian of not more than 21. He was held in high esteem, by his people. . . . He was a favorite, too, among the soldiers of the garrison on account of his handsome appearance and good nature, and through this intercourse had acquired a fine vocabulary of profanity and vulgarity which he used on all occasion to show his acquirements, without the slightest idea of the meaning." Daklugie (1872–April 14, 1955), a Nednhi and Bedonkohe, who as a boy experienced the last Apache war and surrendered with Mangus, told an interesting story of the train ride from Arizona to captivity. He awoke one night, saw Mangus take a swig of whiskey, which Dilth-cley-ih had hidden, open the car's window, and leap out while the train was in motion. Soon after his leap, soldiers realized what had happened, stopped the train, and captured him. The reason for the aborted escape: Mangus thought the soldiers planned to attack the women, and he could not bear the thought of not being able to protect them from the coming horror. Ball, *Indeh*, 134–35.

Daklugie is key to Geronimo's story because the old warrior was his uncle, and in the later years of Geronimo's confinement he became not only Geronimo's confidant but also his translator. Referring to the trouble his mother (Ishton or Ish-key; who was Geronimo's sister) had with his birth, he has been called "One Who Grabs" and "Forced His Way Through." His father was the Nednhi chieftain Juh. He had two brothers (Dah-se-gau and unknown; both who were captured by Mexican troops and supposedly died in Mexico City) and two half sisters (Jacal, who died sometime before 1886, and Cheuleh, of which nothing is known). Daklugie traveled with Mangus after the 1885 breakout, and it was with him that he surrendered in 1886. In captivity he was called "Asa." He attended the Carlisle Indian School in Pennsylvania from December 8, 1886, until November 7, 1895. After leaving Pennsylvania he rejoined his people at Fort Sill, Oklahoma, and in 1898 he married Chihuahua's daughter Ramona (their marriage would last over fifty years). In later years he served as scout and was a leading proponent of settling at the Mescalero Indian Reservation in New Mexico. One of his daughters (Maude) married Geronimo's son (Robert) and another daughter (Lydia) married a non–Fort Sill Apache (Shanta). Griswold, "Apaches," 28; Kraft, *Gatewood & Geronimo*, 82, 203, 205, 210.

41. In Gatewood's other version of this chapter (Gatewood, "Apaches"), he added: "When the Chiricahuas 'broke out,' scouts could be easily obtained from the White Mountains, who generally made the best, or from others, & so on."

42. In Gatewood's other draft (Gatewood, "Apaches"), his comment gives a better reason for why so many enlisted: "They jumped at a chance for revenge— 'eye for an eye & tooth for a tooth' is their religion, if they have any at all— especially when armed, paid, rationed, & clothed, by the government & backed up by the regular troops."

43. Whites often mistook Apaches scouting for the army as the enemy. For example, on June 3, 1885, during Gatewood's first scout after Geronimo and Naiche broke out that May, Jim Cook and Charlie Moore prepared to ambush the lieutenant and his scouts on the Eagle Creek trail, about sixty miles northwest of Silver City, New Mexico. Luckily, the white men asked Gatewood to halt and identify himself before they began shooting. James H. Cook, *Fifty Years on the Old Frontier as Cowboy, Hunter, Guide, Scout, and Ranchman* (1923; repr., Norman: University of Oklahoma Press, 1980), 145–46. See also Crook to Major Beaumont (June 3, 1885), Crook Collection, no. 163.

44. For an interesting discussion on fraud and Indian rings during the 1870s, see Francis Paul Prucha, *The Great Father: The United States Government and the American Indians*, 2 vols. (1984; repr., Lincoln: University of Nebraska Press, 1986), 1:586–92.

45. James H. Toole, "Agent Tiffany Torn to Tatters," *Arizona Star* (Tucson), October 24, 1882, in Cozzens, ed., *Eyewitnesses*, 319–20. Toole served as foreman

of the United States Grand Jury (First Judicial District) that investigated the misconduct of Indian agent J. C. Tiffany in 1882.

46. This agreement between the United States and Mexico was signed on July 29, 1882. The eleven articles of the document allowed a pursuing army to cross the international border if in hot pursuit of Indians, but only in "unpopulated or desert parts" of the country being entered. The other key article stated: "The pursuing force shall retire to its own territory as soon as it shall have fought the band of which it is in pursuit or have lost its trail. In no case shall the forces of the two countries, respectively, establish themselves or remain in the foreign territory for any time longer than is necessary to make the pursuit of the band whose trail they follow." U.S. secretary of state Frederick T. Frelinghuysen and Mexican minister plenipotentiary Matias Romero signed the document. The agreement was in force for two years, and both countries had the right to terminate it with four months' notice. Frederick T. Frelinghuysen, "Mexico: Reciprocal Right to Pursue Savage Indians across the Boundary Line," as cited in Cozzens, ed., *Eyewitnesses*, 343–45.

47. Gatewood is speaking in general terms here. The Apaches did not smoke peace pipes; they preferred cigarettes, which they rolled themselves.

48. As a result of a Department of Interior decision to concentrate all the Western Apaches, Yavapai, and Chiricahuas (Bedonkohe, Chokonen, Nednhi, and Chihenne Apaches) on one reservation, over 1,400 Tonto Apaches and Yavapai were relocated on the San Carlos Indian Reservation in February 1875. Several months later the White Mountain and Cibecue Apaches were moved from their homes near Fort Apache to San Carlos, and in June 1876, 325 Chiricahuas also joined the unhappy mix of people on the arid land. By the time Victorio and 400 four hundred of his people had been relocated at San Carlos in 1877, the population had exploded to over 5,000 people. Several years after being transferred to San Carlos, the White Mountain and Cibecue Apaches were allowed to return to their homes near Fort Apache. Basso, "Western Apache," 481; Collins, *Apache Nightmare*, 14.

49. The "wizened, spectacled little old man" was Henry L. Hart, who assumed the role as agent of the San Carlos Indian Reservation in August 1877. He held the position until mid-1879.

50. This marks the end of Gatewood's rewrite (Gatewood, "Experiences"). The remainder of this chapter is from Gatewood, "Apaches."

51. Adna Romanza Chaffee (April 14, 1842–November 1, 1914), a Civil War veteran, became acting military agent at San Carlos on July 6, 1879. The assignment lasted until May 31, 1880, when he was replaced by Joseph Capron Tiffany, a civilian.

52. This paragraph includes text pulled from "Gatewood on Apache Indians, Government Relations, Reservation Courts & Scouts," Gatewood Collection,

box 3, folder 39 (hereafter cited as Gatewood, "Indians"), 9. The concluding paragraphs in the section are from Gatewood, "Indians," 9–11.

53. Tiswin is sometimes spelled as "tizwin." It is an intoxicating drink made from corn or fermented mescal stalk and root. Dahteste, a Chokonen Apache woman who was with Geronimo in 1886, shared her recipe: "To make tiswin you grind corn fine on metate. Build a big fire, boil meal twenty minutes. Take it out, squeeze mash out good. Throw grounds away. Put in jar and let ferment with yeast twenty-four hours. It took much longer when we had no yeast." Robinson, *Voices*, 168. See also Mails, *People*, 123. He discusses a longer preparation that was made with mescal: "Tiswin was made from the 'heart' or center of the unopened cluster of leaves of the mescal plant. The heart was cooked for about fifteen days until the roots were of a semi-gelatinous consistency. Then they were crushed and the liquor was poured off into retaining receptacles, where it was kept until fermentation set in." It was Eve Ball's opinion, based upon what she was told, that tiswin was not very intoxicating. Perhaps her informants only tasted the corn recipe, for Mails continues: "At this point friends and relatives in great numbers assembled for a dance that often resulted in a drunken and obscene brawl." The Apaches had another intoxicating drink that they made from corn: tulapai.

54. Crook to AG, Military Division of the Pacific (September 27, 1883), Crook Collection (hereafter cited as Crook, *1883 Annual Report*), 1; Davis, *Geronimo*, 29. Dan L. Thrapp, in *The Conquest of Apacheria* (Norman: University of Oklahoma Press, 1967), 256, contradicts Crook and places the return on September 3, 1882. See also 250n43.

55. General Orders no. 43, Whipple Barracks, Prescott, A.T. (October 5, 1882), in Crook, *1883 Annual Report*, appendix A, 18. Collins, in *Apache Nightmare*, 261n6, correctly surmises that "the soldiery" Crook accuses of mistreatment of the natives is the Sixth U.S. Cavalry and Twelfth U.S. Infantry. However, he also implies that this is why Thomas Cruse in a letter to Gatewood Jr. (January 19, 1926), Gatewood Collection, letter 179, said: "General Crook did not have any use whatsoever for any of our Regiment [the Sixth]—Gatewood included." Here he is mistaken. By ignoring Cruse's words that precede the above quote: "In regard to Gatewood's experience with the hay thief mail contractor, and Gen[eral] Crook's refusal to support him," he has missed the crux of Gatewood's problems with the general. But this was still to come (see chapter 4, "Civil Problems"). The falling out between general and lieutenant did not begin until Gatewood dared to stand up for Indian rights in 1884. In September 1882, Gatewood's record with the Apaches was sparkling, and that is why Crook chose him as one of his key subalterns to bring peace to the Southwest.

56. Emmet Crawford (September 6, 1844–January 18, 1886) enlisted in the U.S. Army at the beginning of the Civil War. After the rebellion ended, he became a second lieutenant in the Thirty-ninth U.S. Infantry (1867). Three years later

he transferred to the Third U.S. Cavalry, and in 1871 reported to Camp Verde, Arizona Territory, but by the end of the year he reported to the Department of the Platte, where he saw action against the Sioux on the northern plains (1876). Promoted to captain on March 20, 1879, Crawford returned to the Southwest in 1882. Altshuler, *Cavalry Yellow*, 84.

57. Britton Davis (June 4, 1860–January 23, 1930), a Texan, graduated West Point in June 1881. He would excel in his position as military agent. In fact, when the Third was transferred out of Arizona, Gen. George Crook petitioned to keep Davis on Indian duty. Charles B. Gatewood Jr., "Britton Davis, Class of 1881," unpublished article, Gatewood Collection, letter 382; Thrapp, *Frontier Biography*, 1:379.

58. Davis, *Geronimo*, 30, 32; Crook, *1883 Annual Report*, 2–3.

59. Crook, *1883 Annual Report*, 1.

60. George Crook, *Annual Report* (September 9, 1885), Crook Collection, 4. See also Collins, *Apache Nightmare*, 222.

61. Davis, *Geronimo*, 34. The situation with Wilcox continued to deteriorate until July 1883, when Crook met with Secretary of War R. T. Lincoln and Secretary of the Interior H. M. Teller and worked out a memorandum that gave the military control over recently surrendered Apaches. Pleased with the outcome, Crook issued General Orders no. 13, which left Crawford in overall command of the two reservations. Gatewood, who retained control at White Mountain, would report to Crawford. Unfortunately, Crook did not think through the situation completely. He considered the San Carlos and the White Mountain reservations one, and failed to include the White Mountain Apaches in the memorandum. This oversight gave Wilcox the opening he needed to continue to disrupt Crook's plans to make the natives self-sufficient. See Memorandum signed by Teller and Lincoln (July 7, 1883) and General Orders no. 13 (July 24, 1883), NA, RG 94, M689: 1066 AGO 1883, roll 174.

62. Gatewood is referring to the aftermath of the Cibecue affair.

63. Crawford led a column of Apache scouts into Mexico on December 11, 1885. On January 10, 1886, his scouts attacked and captured Geronimo's camp at Espinosa del Diablo (the devil's spine) near the Río Aros in Sonora. Later that day, Geronimo sent two women, Lozen (a Chihenne) and Dahteste (a Chokonen), to set up a meeting between the two sides. However, at dawn on January 11, a Mexican force of irregulars attacked the American force. Santa Ana Perez gave the Mexican side of the incident, claiming they thought they attacked "a great number of wild and tame Indians." Perez named the location as Teepar or Sierra del Bavis. The Mexican force included Tarahumara Indians. Crawford was shot while attempting to end the attack; he fell and smashed his head on a rock. He died eight days later. Some feel that it was the head injury and not the bullet that killed him. "Mexican Treachery," *Charles Lummis Scrapbook*, MS.1

Scrapbook 5, 43, Autry National Center–Southwest Museum of the American Indian, Los Angeles. See the *Arizona Journal-Miner* (February 8, 1886) for the Perez quote. See also Crook to AG, Division of the Pacific (April 10, 1886), 8 (hereafter cited as Crook, *1886 Annual Report*); Ball, *Days of Victorio*, 182, 208n1 (Surrender chapter); Marion P. Maus to C. S. Roberts (April 8, 1886), appendix I in Crook, *1886 Annual Report*, 47; Robinson, *Voices*, 12; and H. Henrietta Stockel, *Women of the Apache Nation: Voices of Truth* (Reno: University of Nevada Press, 1991), 31.

64. This paragraph also includes text from Gatewood, "Indians," 12.

65. This sentence is from Gatewood, "Indians," 12.

66. Most of Gatewood's nicknames referred to his nose, which was large and Roman in shape. He preferred the name the Apaches gave him, Bay-chen-daysen. Even though Gatewood translated it to mean "long nose," others have translated it to mean "beak" or "the chief with the crooked nose." See John Upton Terrell, *Apache Chronicle* (New York: World, 1972), 384; and *Prescott Courier*, November 23, 1886. He has also been called "Shonbrun," which also means long nose. "Geronimo: Details of His Submission to the Inevitable," *Mississippi Republican*, November 22, 1886. Odie B. Faulk, *The Geronimo Campaign* (New York: Oxford University Press, 1969), 38, found yet another name, "Nantan Bse-che," which means big nose captain.

67. Gatewood refers to the White Mountain–Cibecue outbreak that happened when the Apache scouts turned on Col. Eugene Carr's command when he arrested the Cibecue Apache medicine man–chieftain, Nock-ay-det-klinne.

68. Gatewood uses both "nahn-tahn" and "nan-tan" in his text. As "nantan" is the generally accepted spelling, it is used. This paragraph and the next two paragraphs are from Gatewood, "Apaches," pp. 1–2 to be added.

69. Gatewood forgot to mention that he was already happily married.

70. Gatewood refers to the Apache judicial system he set up on the reservation.

71. Gatewood refers to the entire reservation (White Mountain and San Carlos) here and is stating the approximate square of the reserve. He is not talking about the actual square miles, which would be 80 miles x 80 miles = 6,400 square miles.

72. The Indians on the White Mountain Indian Reservation harvested crops in the following amounts during 1883: 2,625,000 lbs. of corn; 200,000 lbs. of barley; 180,000 lbs. of beans; 135,000 lbs. of potatoes; 100,000 lbs. of pumpkins; 20,000 lbs. of watermelons; 12,600 lbs. of wheat; 10,000 lbs. of muskmelons; 10,000 cantaloupes, along with a small amount of onions, cucumbers, lettuce, and cabbage. Crook, *1883 Annual Report*, appendix I, 43.

73. Here Gatewood speaks of himself taking command of the White Mountain Indian Reservation at Fort Apache.

74. Davis, in *Geronimo*, 38–39, wrote: "In addition to the regular scout enlist-

ments seven secret scouts were enlisted from the most trustworthy Indians we could find to take the dangerous job. Two of these were for Gatewood at Fort Apache. Of those at San Carlos, two were women. . . . The duty of these scouts was to report to us every indication of discontent or hostility that might arise among the Indians on the Reservation. . . . Their method of communicating with us was, of course, secret. A tap on a window pane shortly after our lights were out would bring the occupant of the room to the door."

75. Conley would also serve as Gatewood's chief of scouts.

76. Gatewood called Diablo, a Cibecue Apache, "Diabolo." Shortly after his brother Miguel was killed in the 1870s and during the Cibecues' struggle to remain on their own land, Diablo came to prominence as a chieftain. Forced onto the San Carlos Indian Reservation in the mid-1870s, his relationship with the White Mountains and Pedro's band worsened to the point where Diablo led an attack on the White Mountains on August 30, 1880, which resulted in his death. Collins, *Apache Nightmare*, 8–10.

77. Gatewood called Severiano (c. 1841–post 1883) "Serviana," but I have chosen to use Severiano, as that is the name most commonly used. Thrapp, *Frontier Biography*, 3:1289, lists two other variations on his name: Sibi-ya-na and Gracias. See also Kraft, *Gatewood & Geronimo*, 27. After living with the Apaches for thirty years, Severiano, who was a Mexican, became employed at Fort Apache translating Spanish to Apache and back.

78. Gatewood refers to himself here.

79. Gatewood's text has one final sentence, which is incomplete: "For instance, once when Gen[eral] Crook, the Department Commander, visited Fort Apache—" One can only surmise that he either did not complete this draft or pages are missing.

3. Military Commandant

1. "Gatewood on Apache Indians, Government Relations, Reservation Courts & Scouts," Gatewood Collection, box 3, folder 39 contains 54 numbered pages, which begin on p. 9 and end on p. 62. Unfortunately, the first eight pages of this draft are missing. Pages 9–11 of Gatewood's text have been moved into chapter 2, "The Apaches Indians."

2. Charles B. Gatewood Jr. (January 4, 1883–November 13, 1953) graduated from the Military Academy at West Point on June 12, 1906. He became a first lieutenant in 1907 and a captain by 1909. On November 11, 1911, he married Charlotte Cushman Pierce (November 11, 1880–November 13, 1952) of Brownsville, Texas, in New York City. Although there has been some confusion over the date when Charlotte passed on, some articles even placing her death in the 1940s, she died one year to the day before Gatewood Jr. died. They had one child, Charlotte Josepha (b. January 28, 1923). "Gate," as he was known, eventually changed the

spelling of his middle name from Bare to Bhaer or Baehr (the spelling more often seen), which should shed light on why Gatewood's middle name has constantly been spelled differently.

In 1912, his rank reverted to first lieutenant for one year before returning to captain. Gate made the rank of major in 1916 and lieutenant colonel in 1917, but returned to the rank of major—the rank at which he retired—at the end of World War I. He would eventually be granted his wartime rank of colonel in 1930, but this did not increase the small amount of pay he received in retirement. While still in the military, he began researching his father's participation in the Apache wars, and his efforts continued after retirement. Although he did have a few articles published and at times spoke about his father's exploits before such organizations as the Order of the Indian Wars, he could not find a publisher for a book about his father. Perhaps this was because most of the officers who fought in Mexico in 1886 had become colonels and generals and did not want the story of Geronimo's "capture" changed. Nelson Miles eventually became commander in chief of the army (1895) and Leonard Wood became chief of staff (1910). In 1909 Georgia Gatewood wrote her son concerning his efforts to write about his father. Calling Wood "that Wood man, or thing," she wrote: "I realize your position in regard to Wood and I tell you, cautious as you may be, you will incur his enmity if you say a word without mentioning him, for he don't want the subject uncovered at all, & I seem to stand alone in my opinion of his unscrupulous vanity, & as he perjured himself for Miles, for his own advancement, so will Miles perjure himself now to uphold them both, & others will keep quiet."

Gate had a hot temper and supposedly once threatened his wife, Charlotte, with a gun and said he would kill her. "His mother[,] Georgia, lived in the house that all of them had once occupied and Charlotte fled to Georgia's apartment. She told her mother-in-law what Gate was going to do and Georgia left the apartment locking the door behind her. She talked to her son in a 'casual and calmly manner.' Shortly after he left the premises," ending the episode and eventually the union. Sometime after his divorce from Charlotte (about 1937), he married an English widow named Lilbian Luck (d. December 17, 1977).

Gate moved to San Diego shortly after retiring, and like his father suffered from numerous illnesses. At the time of his death he lived in Ramona, some forty miles east of San Diego. Lilbian and Charlotte Josepha (whose last name was Oakland at the time of her father's death) played major roles in the placing of his research at the Arizona Historical Society in Tucson. For Georgia's comments about Miles and Wood, see Georgia Gatewood to Gatewood Jr. (April 4, 1909), Gatewood Collection, letter 79. For the background on Gatewood Jr., see Gatewood entries on rootsweb.com; Charles G. Mettler, "Charles Baehr Gatewood," *Assembly* (April 1954): 1001–2.

3. Gatewood groups the Chokonens, Chihennes, Nednhis, and Bedonkohes as Chiricahuas.

4. One of Gatewood's duties as military commandant of the White Mountain Indian Reservation included presiding as judge for all the trials held in the native court. His new duties did not relieve him from his regular duty of commanding Company A Apache scouts. Conley also served as Gatewood's interpreter.

5. Goodwin, in *Western Apache*, 578, names Sanchez as chieftain of clan 57 of the White Mountains who were tagged as "M" at Fort Apache; calling him "Metal Tooth" (béˑcbìyòˀán). Goodwin, in Basso, ed., *Western Apache Raiding*, 137, states that "Metal Tooth" was a name given to Sanchez by white men. There is no mistaking that Metal Tooth and Iron Tooth, as Gatewood called Sanchez, are one and the same man. He is not to be confused with the Chihenne Apache Tah-ho-klisn (Falls in the Water), who was James Kaywaykla's grandfather. The Mexicans who captured him when he attempted to rescue his son (Kaywaykla's father) and made him a slave (as opposed to killing him) gave him the name Sanchez (Sánchez). He learned Spanish and served his captors as a *vaquero-ra* (cowboy) and scout against his own people. Eventually he and his son escaped captivity and returned to the Chihennes. Tah-ho-klisn's birth and death dates are unknown. Kaywaykla's father was killed in a fight south of Deming, New Mexico, in 1879, and his name has not been remembered. The Chihenne war leader Kaytennae (Kaahtenny) became Kaywaykla's stepfather. Ball, *Days of Victorio*, 20–21; Griswold, "Apaches," 130–31; Jason Betzinez with W. S. Nye, *I Fought with Geronimo* (Harrisburg PA: Stackpole, 1959), 53; Robinson, *Voices*, 17–18, 224n2. See Rubén Cobos, *A Dictionary of New Mexico and Southern Colorado Spanish*, 2nd ed. (Santa Fe: Museum of New Mexico Press, 2003), 235, for the spelling and meaning of *vaquero-ra*.

6. See Goodwin, *Western Apache*, 127, for the way that men traditionally behaved around their mothers-in-law.

7. Historian Francis Paul Prucha sums up Crook's take on Indians: fight them aggressively while espousing "a philosophy of Indian relations based on honesty, justice, and concern for Indian civilization." Prucha defines Crook's policy during the 1880s when he writes that the general "worked out a positive program for the economic welfare of the Apaches that sought to convert them into capitalistic farmers." See Prucha, *Great Father*, 1:545–46.

8. Gatewood to F. E. Pierce (September 8, 1885), appendix O in Crook, *1885 Annual Report*, 40.

9. Pierce to C. S. Roberts (September 11, 1885), appendix N in Crook, *1885 Annual Report*, 37. Pierce's comment refers to Gatewood's performance at the end of his tenure as military commandant of the White Mountain Indian Reservation.

10. See Kraft, *Gatewood & Geronimo*, 23, 100–101, 105, for the gains that he

and his wards made in the their attempts to make the reservation a successful farming community.

11. "Coyoteros" was widely used as a generic term for the Western Apaches during the nineteenth century, usually referring to the White Mountains. Gatewood considered the Coyoteros and White Mountains as one and the same. So did Morris E. Opler, in "Chiricahua Apaches," in Ortiz, ed., *Southwest*, 405. Keith Basso, in "Western Apache," 488, divides the White Mountain Apaches into two groups: Sierra Blanca (White Mountain) in the north and Coyotero in the south. Goodwin, in *Western Apache*, 2, claims that at the end of the nineteenth century, Coyoteros referred to White Mountain Apaches who lived south of the Black River. As Gatewood's White Mountains lived north of the Black River, he perhaps used the term generically. Davis, contrary to Gatewood, Goodwin, and Opler, considered the Coyoteros and the White Mountains as two separate tribes. See Davis, *Geronimo*, 106.

12. Regarding the division of labor, Goodwin, in *Western Apache*, 332–33, wrote: "A man made and cared for his own clothes and sometimes those of his children; made and repaired the tools, weapons, and accoutrements which he used. He hunted game, skinned and butchered it, and transported home the meat and hides. He raided enemy peoples to secure such things as livestock and blankets. In times of war and feud he fought. It was his continual duty to guard the safety and health of his wife and children. . . . In the building of wickiup and ramada, principally woman's work, he might help erect heavy frame poles or cross-beams. . . . A woman made and cared for her and her children's clothing; made and repaired the household utensils such as baskets and pottery; gathered the material for wickiup and ramada; made and repaired these; and kept the camp swept. She gathered and prepared wild plant foods; cared for all meat brought into camp; attended to the storing of foods in caches; cooked, cleaned up after eating, and brought in the necessary supply of wood and water. She ordinarily did all the work in preparation of skins. In moving camp, she gathered and bundled the family property. To her fell the care of the small children. . . . This division of labor meant that women were more continually occupied than men, and it was said of a good woman that she was never still but always doing something. . . . Men's work was more dangerous and entailed great physical hardship at times, but it left them leisure for relaxation at sweat baths, gambling places, and parties."

13. White Mountain chieftains Es-kel-te-ce-la, Meguil (who only had one eye), and Pedro (who dreamed of a civilized life even at this early date), Pima chieftain Antonito, the Pima Louis, Papago chieftain Ascencion, two Date Creek Indians (José and English Charlie), and Santo traveled to Washington DC in 1872. Maj. Gen. O. O. Howard, *My Life and Experiences among Our Hostile Indians* (Hartford CT: A. D. Worthington, 1907), 164–65, 169. Chokonen chieftain Taza

(Tahzay), White Mountain chieftain Diablo and his son, Aravaipa chieftain Eskiminzin (Hashkibanzin) and his wife, Yuma chieftain Sagully, Casadora and his wife, Pinal subchieftain Captain Chiquito and his wife, Captain Jim and his wife, plus nine warriors and a twelve-year-old boy visited Washington DC in 1876. Clum, *Apache Agent*, 187.

14. Gatewood definitely spelled the word as "Indah." His spelling, along with his definition, apparently hit the mark, for "Indah" also caught Eve Ball's attention. She wrote: "I had long been familiar with the Apache word *Indah*, which military officers and historians have interpreted as meaning *White People*. That translation is indirect; the literal meaning of *Indah* is *The Living*." What is more interesting is the word she discovered during her time with Daklugie, one of her primary informants. She continues: "Until Ace Daklugie (Ace was the first name bestowed upon him when he attended the Indian school at Carlisle, Pennsylvania, shortly after the last Apache war) used the term *Indeh*, I had not encountered it. Literally it means *The Dead*, and it is the term by which Apaches, recognizing their fate, designated themselves." At this late date in time, one can only muse over the similarities between the two words. See Ball, *Indeh*, xix.

15. Goodwin, in *Western Apache*, 315, wrote: "Marriages which were the outcome of courtships were probably no more common than those arranged without any preceding courtship. The latter type of marriage is said to have been satisfactory and lasting and shows the influence which parents and older siblings had in the individual's life. The young couple were sometimes ignorant of the arrangement until the girl was sent to the boy's camp."

16. Goodwin, *Western Apache*, 419–20.

17. Goodwin, *Western Apache*, 388. If a person was beaten, the aggressor could make a payment to the injured party. "Compensation payments for either accidental or nonaccidental injuries were not always made," Goodwin wrote, "however, and, if thought unnecessary, could be omitted entirely, depending on the disposition of the two families concerned. In all compensated cases the relatives of the injured person made the demands and accepted the payments, the injured one never dealing directly with the individual causing the injury" (395). See also Goodwin, 289, 389.

18. For background on retaliation or feud killing, see Goodwin, *Western Apache*, 403–15.

19. The hospital stood at the west end of the Fort Apache parade ground, just above the gouge of the east fork of the White River, which wrapped around the north end of the post. Davisson, "Fort Apache," 71.

20. One can only guess at the reason for Juan's desire to go after Dave; however, there is little doubt that he was bent upon more than a payback retaliation killing. Goodwin, *Western Apache*, 396, 403.

21. Gatewood to Crook (February 10, 1884), Records of U.S. Army Continen-

tal Commands, 1821–1920, NA, RG 393, Department of Arizona, 1870–93, Letters Received.

22. Britton Davis, "A Short Account of the Chiricahua Tribe of Apache Indians and the Causes Leading to the Outbreak of May, 1885," 3–4, Gatewood Collection; Davis, *Geronimo*, 102–3. However, Emmet Crawford to AAG, Whipple Barracks, A.T., cited as appendix A in George Crook's 1884 annual report to the AAG, Division of the Pacific, stated that the move took place in May. Crook Collection, no. 27. See also Kraft, *Gatewood & Geronimo*, 41–42.

23. See Kraft, *Gatewood & Geronimo*, 122, for quote. See also 59.

24. The son of Gen. Charles F. Smith, Allen Smith (April 21, 1849–October 30, 1927) became a member of the First U.S. Infantry after his graduation from the U.S. Naval Academy in 1866. After becoming a first lieutenant in 1868, he married Julia Stephens on July 2, 1874. He was promoted to captain on May 1, 1880, and in December transferred to the Fourth U.S. Cavalry. Assigned to Arizona Territory in 1884 (stationed at Fort Apache), he spent a good part of 1885 in the field after Naiche and Geronimo broke out. He became a major in 1897 (First U.S. Cavalry), lieutenant colonel in 1901, and colonel in 1902 (Sixth U.S. Cavalry), and he retired as a brigadier general in 1905. Altshuler, *Cavalry Yellow*, 307.

25. Georgia-born James Lockett (October 31, 1855–May 4, 1933) was not on Gatewood's best-liked list. Gatewood thought him a fool and nothing more. See Georgia Gatewood to Gatewood Jr. (January 15, 1928), Gatewood Collection, letter 176. Possibly Gatewood's opinion was based upon this patrol. A member of the Fourth U.S. Cavalry, Lockett married Helen Grant on January 19, 1881. He served in both Colorado and New Mexico before being assigned to Arizona Territory in 1884. Lockett replaced Gatewood at military commandant of the White Mountain Indian Reservation in November 1885, a position he held less than six months. At the end of his tenure as military agent he was transferred to Troop I (at Fort Bowie, Arizona Territory) and promoted to first lieutenant (March 1, 1886). Lockett became a captain in 1894, major in 1903, lieutenant colonel in 1911, and colonel in 1912 before retiring in 1919. After Helen died in 1908, he married Helen W. Healy in 1911. Kraft, *Gatewood & Geronimo*, 111, 240n38; Altshuler, *Cavalry Yellow*, 203–4.

James Parker (February 20, 1854–June 2, 1934) graduated thirty-first in the 1876 West Point class of forty-eight, and as a second lieutenant joined the Fourth U.S. Cavalry after graduation. Parker saw considerable action in the Southwest, including Col. Ranald MacKenzie's illegal 1878 strike into Mexico and the 1885–86 Apache war. He became a first lieutenant in 1879, captain in 1888, major in 1898 (Twelfth New York Infantry), and then lieutenant colonel the same year. In 1899 he was mustered out of the regular army, but a few months later, in August, he became a lieutenant colonel of volunteers (Forty-second U.S. Volunteer Infantry). Mustered out of the volunteers in 1901, he rejoined the Fourth U.S.

Cavalry (as major). He received a promotion to lieutenant colonel (Thirteenth U.S. Cavalry) in 1903, colonel (Eleventh U.S. Cavalry) in 1907, brigadier general in 1913, and major general (National Army) in 1917 (his official rank did not advance to major general until 1930), retiring in 1918. Altshuler, *Cavalry Yellow*, 255–56; Thrapp, *Frontier Biography*, 3:1113.

26. Leighton Finley (June 9, 1856–February 12, 1894), a Southerner, graduated Princeton University in 1876 and received a commission as a second lieutenant in the Fifteenth U.S. Infantry in 1879, but quickly transferred to the Tenth U.S. Cavalry. Beginning in 1880, he saw extensive service against the Apaches in the Southwest, including both the Victorio and Geronimo campaigns. Finley became a first lieutenant on October 5, 1887. Two years later he married Ida May Davis (July 2, 1889). He broke his leg on October 26, 1893, while drilling horses at Fort Custer, Montana. The bones in his leg were crushed and never healed properly, and he died in St. Paul, Minnesota, the following year after additional surgery was performed on his leg. Altshuler, *Cavalry Yellow*, 130–31.

27. James Parker, *The Old Army: Memories, 1872–1918* (Philadelphia: Dorrance, 1929), 152–53; Crook to Col. Luther Bradley (May 22, 1885), Crook Collection, no. 148; James Wade report quoted in Robert Walsh to AAG, Department of Arizona, Whipple Barracks (May 18, 1885), Gatewood Collection; Allen Smith to Crook (June 15, 1885), appendix B in Crook, *1886 Annual Report*.

28. There has been confusion over the actual date of the skirmish. In Gen. James Parker, Retired, "Service with Lieutenant Charles B. Gatewood, 6th U.S. Cavalry," Arizona Historical Society, Tucson, Gatewood Collection, 2, Parker placed the date on May 21. However, in Parker, *Old Army*, 156–57, he stated the date was May 22. See also Smith to Crook (June 15, 1885), appendix B in Crook, *1886 Annual Report*, 13–15. It is worth noting that although Thrapp, in *Conquest*, 319, cites Parker's *Old Army*, his description of the fight is totally different from Parker's. For a full account of the patrol, see Kraft, *Gatewood & Geronimo*, 87–94.

29. Finley to Parker (September 7, 1885), as cited in Parker, *Old Army*, 157–59.

30. For Smith's account of the skirmish that upset Parker and Gatewood, see Allen Smith to Crook (June 15, 1885), Attachment B in Crook to AG (April 10, 1886), Crook Collection, no. 344, 13–18. In the report, Smith praises not only Finley, Gatewood, and Parker but also Lockett. There is no mention that he and Lockett were away from the command bathing when the engagement took place.

31. Parker, "Service with Gatewood," 2.

32. Parker, *Old Army*, 162.

33. Thrapp, *Conquest*, 328; Crook to Luis E. Torres (June 12, 1885), Crook Collection, no. 200.

34. Crook to AG, Division of the Pacific (June 7, 1885), Crook Collection, no. 184.

35. See Crook to Gatewood (June 11, 1885), Crook Collection, no. 198, for this

quote and the quote regarding returning to Fort Apache, as well as the beginning date of the scout.

36. By 1885, Gatewood had already accumulated an extensive amount of sick leave. In 1881 alone he was absent from duty from May through September, and as the rheumatism grew, his capability to perform in the field diminished. The following year when Gatewood hunted Geronimo in Mexico, he constantly found himself bedridden and considering quitting. See Kraft, *Gatewood & Geronimo*, 139, 141, 146, 150, 152, 163, 180, 187, 209–10. His health never recovered from the 1886 ordeal in Mexico and spiraled downward until an examining board at Fort Custer, Montana (September 4–October 8, 1892), found him "physically incapacitated." See Adjutant General's Office statement of the military service of Charles B. Gatewood (May 23, 1896) for a summation of his career, including the October 1892 decision that put him on inactive duty awaiting retirement; and Gatewood's efficiency report, for a listing of his lengthy absences from duty for medical reasons. NA, M1395.

37. Virginian Wirt Davis (May 28, 1839–February 10 or 11, 1914) enlisted as a private in the First U.S. Cavalry in 1860, which would eventually become the Fourth U.S. Cavalry, an act that severed his relationship with his family until after the Spanish–American War. He received his discharge three years after enlisting, only to accept a commission as a second lieutenant in the Fourth. After the Civil War, he served on the plains and in the Southwest. He became a first lieutenant in 1865, captain in 1868, major in 1890 (Fifth U.S. Cavalry), lieutenant colonel in 1898 (Eighth U.S. Cavalry), and colonel in 1900 (Third U.S. Cavalry), before retiring in 1901. Three years later he received a promotion to brigadier general. Davis married Anna J. Berry in 1884, was considered one of best marksmen in the military, and played a major role in the final Apache war. Thrapp, *Frontier Biography*, 1:382–83; Altshuler, *Cavalry Yellow*: 98–99.

38. Robert Douglas Walsh (October 14, 1860–August 15, 1928) received a commission in the Twenty-second U.S. Infantry in 1883 after graduation from the Military Academy (thirty-seven in a class of fifty-two), but quickly transferred to the Fourth U.S. Cavalry. He arrived in the Southwest in 1884, and beginning in the spring of 1885 he commanded Indian scouts. The following year he served in Mexico with Lawton during the hunt for Geronimo. He became a first lieutenant in 1890 (Fifth U.S. Cavalry), captain in 1899 (Ninth U.S. Cavalry), major in 1899 (Thirty-fifth U.S. Volunteer Infantry), lieutenant colonel in 1899, major in 1910 (Eleventh U.S. Cavalry), lieutenant colonel in 1914 (Eighth U.S. Cavalry), colonel in 1916, and brigadier general in 1917 (National Army). He retired in 1919 at his regular army rank of colonel. Altshuler, *Cavalry Yellow*, 350–51.

39. Crook to AG, Division of the Pacific (July 7, 1885), Crook Collection, no. 208; Crook to Luis E. Torres (June 12, 1885), Crook Collection, no. 200; and Crook, *Autobiography*, 255. See also Robert M. Utley, *A Clash of Cultures: Fort*

Bowie and the Chiricahua Apaches (Washington DC: National Park Service, 1977), 60, and Wharfield, *Apache Indian Scouts*, 33, for inaccurate examples of Gatewood being in Mexico in 1885. Lockett succeeded Gatewood as military commandant on November 14, 1885. Crook to Emmet Crawford (November 13, 1885), no. 244, and Crook to Crawford (November 14, 1885), Crook Collection, no. 245.

40. Not much has changed with the passing of time. To this day illegal entry into the southwestern portion of the United States continues to be a major problem.

41. Crook to AG, Division of the Pacific (September 22, 1885), Crook Collection, no. 234; Debo, *Geronimo*, 245–46. The loss of perhaps a third of the women and children with Geronimo had been devastating not only to the family circle but also in the division of labor between males and females.

42. Very little is known about She-gha, a Chokonen-Nednhi Apache. After an unsuccessful raid into Mexico in the fall of 1861 in which Geronimo was wounded, Mexican troops ventured into Arizona, attacked, and destroyed his ranchería. Many women and children died in the attack, including Geronimo's third wife, Nana-tha-thtith, and their child. Destitute and with winter near, Geronimo and other Bedonkohes began living with the Chokonens. It was probably at this time that Geronimo and She-gha met and married. Geronimo's fourth wife, She-gha, was Yahnosha's sister and related to Cochise and Naiche. She was with Geronimo when he and Naiche decided to return to the United States and surrender in 1886. Griswold, "Apaches," 41–42; Debo, *Geronimo*, 49–50.

43. Gatewood refers to Chokonen, Bedonkohe, Nednhi, and Chihenne Apaches here and throughout this section.

44. Gatewood enlisted scouts for both Crawford and himself, and Dave entered Mexico with the Crawford–Davis column. Davis wrote: "My scouts, unattended by me or by any officer or civilian of our (Crawford's) command, jumped them [the warring Apaches] about fifteen miles N.E. of the town of Opoto, Sonora. Casualties [included] one squaw killed, one squaw and one small child wounded (a little boy about four years of age) and my 2nd Sergt., Dave[,] shot through the elbow. Captured 17 squaws and children, who were sent back to the Reservation. The bucks as usual escaped[;] one however was reported to have been wounded." Britton Davis to Gatewood Jr. (April 25, 1926), Gatewood Collection microfilm, reel 7. Chatto commanded this independent command, taking thirty scouts with him. The attack on the ranchería took place in a heavy rain on June 23, 1885. A Chokonen member of Naiche's band named Kutle or Cathle was wounded in the skirmish. The prisoners were shipped to Fort Bowie, where they remained from July 3, 1885, until April 1886, when they were shipped to Florida. Thrapp, *Conquest*, 328–29; Sweeney October 2001 review of Kraft ms, Kraft Papers. Thrapp put the number of captured at fifteen, which is correct.

45. Gatewood speaks of Geronimo's rescue of his wife She-gha. But he is

mistaken; she had not been left behind during the breakout on May 17, 1885, but had departed the reservation before that day. Hoping to enlist additional recruits for the escape, Geronimo sent She-gha and another woman to speak with the Mescaleros. However, after they arrived at the Mescalero Reservation on May 26, Indian police arrested them and turned them over to Mescalero agent W. H. H. Llewellyn, who delivered them to the commanding officer at Fort Stanton, Maj. James J. Van Horn. On June 16, Van Horn sent them to Fort Bowie. According to the *Arizona Weekly Citizen*, the women "both had 5 guns and [a] large quantity of ammunition" when they were captured. They were eventually escorted back to the White Mountain Indian Reservation. When Wirt Davis's scouts attacked Geronimo's camp on August 7, 1885, which was west of Casa Grandes, Chihuahua, Mexico, one woman and a boy were killed. Although casualties were low, it was a devastating blow—dried meat, saddles, blankets, thirteen horses and mules, Perico's wife (Hah-dun-key) and children, Mangus's wife (Huera), along with two, perhaps three, of Geronimo's wives (Shtsha-he and Zi-yeh), and five of Geronimo's children (Zi-yeh's infant son; Dohn-say, a girl who had just reached womanhood; a three-year-old girl, and two of Geronimo's grandchildren) were captured. Although She-gha has been listed as captured during Davis's attack, this could not be as these prisoners spent the duration of the war at Fort Bowie. When Geronimo raided the reservation at one a.m. on September 22, 1885, he rescued She-gha and their three-year-old daughter, along with another woman. Geronimo, *Geronimo*, 136; AAG, Headquarters, District of New Mexico, to AG, Department of the Missouri (June 22, 1885), Records of U.S. Army Continental Commands, 1821–1920, NA, RG 393, microcopy M1072 (roll 7), Letters Sent, Ninth Military Department, Department of New Mexico and District of New Mexico, 1849–90; *Arizona Weekly Citizen* (June 20, 1885); Sweeney to author (January 26, 2002), Kraft Papers; Sweeney October 2001 review of Kraft ms, Kraft Papers; Crook to AG, Division of the Pacific (August 17, 1885), Crook Collection, no. 223, and Crook to AG, Division of the Pacific (September 22, 1885), Crook Collection, no. 234; Debo, *Geronimo*, 244–46. Llewellyn began his duties as Mescalero agent on June 16, 1881. Sonnichsen, in *Mescalero Apaches*, 209–10, described Llewellyn as "a frontier adventurer, who had come to the Southwest from Nebraska not long before. People learned to discount his stories of his own exploits, but his ideas about Indian management were definitely constructive. He had a suave and quietly polite manner. He considered the welfare of his charges, went hunting with them, subjected them to discipline, and won their respect. They called him 'Tata Crooked Nose.'"

46. Concerned by how the current war affected his wards, Gatewood wrote F. E. Pierce: "I also desire to invite your attention to the peculiar state of affairs on the reservation existing at just the time the Indians were working at their crops and which to a great extent has prevented a greater yield. I refer to the Chiricahua

outbreak and the consequent excitement of the remaining Indians, and to the fact that a great proportion of the male adults were taken away as scouts. It is a mistaken idea that the men do not work, and thus their absence has retarded the agricultural process of these people for this year in two ways, first, the loss of their manual labor, and second, the moral effect of their presence so far as their families are concerned." Gatewood to Pierce (September 8, 1885), appendix O in Crook, *1885 Annual Report*, 40. In the same report (39, 41), Gatewood presents a positive picture of the White Mountains' attempt to succeed at farming in 1885. They had 2,120 acres under cultivation and had raised 80,000 lbs. of barley (of which they sold the government 65,000 lbs.) and 3.5 million lbs. of corn. In addition, they sold the government 700,000 lbs. of hay, with an estimated 1 million lbs. still to be sold to the U.S. before year's end. Also, the tribes' flock of sheep had grown to 1,156.

47. Crook to AG, Division of the Pacific (November 3, 1882), Crook Collection, no. 51. See also Collins, *Apache Nightmare*, 6; Thrapp, *Frontier Biography*, 3:1128–29. Thrapp gives Pedro's dates as c. 1835–c. 1885, making him roughly fifty at the time of his death. This seems too young if we listen to what Gatewood and others say about the chieftain during the 1880s. According to them, Pedro was ancient, had wobbly legs, was almost deaf, and so on. In comparison, Geronimo was born about 1823, making him some twelve years older than Pedro. And yet at this time Geronimo was not close to his deathbed. Just the opposite—he had become the most feared warrior in two countries.

48. Gatewood is mistaken here. Clum, in *Apache Agent*, 187, names the Apaches who visited Washington DC in 1876. Pedro is not on the list. However, Pedro did visit Washington in 1872 with Gen. O. O. Howard. See Howard, *My Life and Experiences*, 165. Howard wrote that Pedro "constantly longed for civilized life." See also Howard, 168.

49. Ulysses S. Grant was president (1869–77) at this time.

50. In 1881 Josanie (1821–December 21, 1909) served as a scout in the war against the Chihenne chieftain Nana. After surrendering to Crook in March 1886, he returned to the United States with his brother, Chihuahua, a Chokonen chieftain. Over the course of his life, he had two wives and seven boys, two of which outlived him and eventually moved to the Mescalero Reservation in New Mexico after the years as prisoners of war ended. Thrapp, *Frontier Biography*, 2:745; Griswold, "Apaches," 66.

51. Crook to AG, Division of the Pacific (November 24, 1885), Crook Collection, no. 249, and (November 25, 1885), Crook Collection, no. 251; Cyrus S. Roberts to Emmet Crawford (November 25, 1885), and Crook to CO of detachments at Mud Springs, Silver Creek, San Bernardino, Guadalupe Canyon, Langs Ranch (November 25, 1885), in Records of U.S. Army Continental Commands, 1821–1920, NA, RG 393, Department of Arizona, 1870–93, Letters Received, at Arizona

Historical Society, Tucson; Sweeney October 2001 review of Kraft ms, Kraft Papers; Thrapp, *Conquest*, 334–39. Josanie had between nine and eleven warriors.

52. See chapter 4 for the number of Apaches who broke out.

53. This and the next paragraph are from Gatewood, "Apaches," 19–21.

54. Again, Gatewood refers to the Chokonen, Bedonkohe, and Nednhi Apaches.

55. This is the opposite of what Britton Davis said about Geronimo's efforts to become a farmer. Davis, in *Geronimo*, 136–37, wrote: "Geronimo's efforts at self-support were typical of the efforts of many. He came to me one day with the request that I visit his 'farm.' I could not go at the moment but went the following morning. He had shown me a small blister on the palm of one of his hands, of which he was very proud. When I arrived at the section of river bottom that had been allotted to him and his band, he was sitting on a rail in the shade of a tree with one of his wives fanning him. The other two were hoeing a quarter-acre patch of partially cleared ground, in which a few sickly looking sprouts of corn were struggling for life." See also Crook to AAG, Division of the Pacific, 1884 Annual Report, appendix A, 7, Crook Collection. The general supports Gatewood's point of view. He wrote: "Although it was late in the season [of 1884], [the Bedonkohes, Chokonens, and Chihennes] set to work to raise such crops as could at that time be planted. Those that had distinguished themselves most in their desultory warfare in times past set them the example, for to-day *Geronimo* and *Chat[t]o* have the best farms belonging to the tribe" (italics in original).

56. The post was Fort Apache.

57. The chronological placement of this incident and its aftermath is inaccurate in Kraft, *Gatewood & Geronimo*; see 107–10. Although I originally thought that Geronimo's raid initiated the old man's heroism and the White Mountains' quest for revenge, in actuality it was Josanie's raid that set the stage for Gatewood's confrontation with his wards. It took many readings of Gatewood's words before I finally understood the real order of events.

58. See Thomas Cruse to Gatewood Jr. (February 9, 1926), Gatewood Collection, letter 180. Many years later, Gatewood would consider Sanchez a friend. Gatewood to Georgia Gatewood (March 1, 1893), Gatewood Collection, letter 50. For Alchesay's service as a scout, see Kraft, *Gatewood & Geronimo*, 17, and Thrapp, *Frontier Biography*, 1:12–13.

59. While commanding Navajo scouts in New Mexico in 1886, Gatewood thought there was a possibility that he might be reassigned to again command White Mountain scouts, something he did not want to do. He wrote Georgia "that they no longer have any liking for me, & the best interest of the service would require that I be not connected with them in any way." Gatewood to Georgia (June 25, 1886), Gatewood Collection, letter 12.

60. Sanchez led the group that went out to check on the old man's story. The head of the dead Apache was identified as belonging to Agaiequclch (sp?). See Crook to AG, Washington DC (November 28, 1885), NA, RG 94, M689, Letters Received by the Office of the Adjutant General, 1881–89: 1066 AGO 1883, roll 180. The death count at this point had reached eleven White Mountain women, five men, and four children.

61. Juh (c. 1825–November 1883), also known as Ho, Whoa, and Long Neck, was a Nednhi chieftain who married Geronimo's sister (or cousin; there is some confusion here), Ishton (or Ish-keh). When Ishton had trouble during childbirth (about 1870), Geronimo prayed to Ussen (Creator of Life, God) to spare his sister and her child's life. Juh and Ishton's son, Daklugie, would live through the last Apache war as a teenager, then become Geronimo's confidant in captivity. Until Juh's death, Geronimo and his band of Bedonkohes often lived near Juh and his band of Nednhis in Mexico. See Kraft, *Gatewood & Geronimo*, 5; Griswold, "Apaches," 71. The name of this other "son of Juh" is unknown.

62. Crook, 1884 Annual Report, 7, Crook Collection.

63. Feuds and revenge cannot be understated when studying the White Mountain Apaches. Gatewood had a major problem on his hands when his wards decided to kill Loco and his people to avenge the raids on the reservation by Geronimo and Josanie, and from what I have seen, he solved it himself. For an extensive discussion on revenge and feuding, see the chapter entitled "Social Adjustments," in Goodwin, *Western Apaches*.

64. Gatewood refers to San Carlos.

65. Gatewood did not consider the Chihenne (Warm Springs or Mimbreño Apaches) as one of the bands of Chiricahuas (Chokonen, Bedonkohe, and Nednhi Apaches), and this is in agreement with Griswold, "Apaches," 2. Gatewood also combines the Bedonkohe, Chihenne, and Chokonen Apaches as Chiricahua Apaches.

66. In the manuscript, 58, Gatewood calls the White Mountain speaker "Said." I have not found any other references to Said, so I believe that Gatewood meant Sanchez, as the tone and word usage matches the earlier speech.

67. Gatewood had a note in the margin to "change this sentence." What he wanted to change is unknown. However, although others have also referred to tepees in the Southwest, for the most part they did not exist there. The reason was simple: depending on the size of the tepee, it could take between twelve and eighteen buffalo hides to create just one tepee. As buffalo did not range into the Southwest, obtaining that many hides would be difficult. It would be not only unusual but unlikely that any Warm Springs had tepees at this time. Most likely Gatewood only referred to the boy going home, which more than likely was to a wickiup. See John Newton, ed., *The Buffalo Hunters* (Alexandria VA: Time-Life Books, 1993), 127, for information on tepees.

68. Crook to Crawford (November 14, 1885), Crook Collection, no. 245.

69. Crook to AG, Division of the Pacific (November 24, 1885), Crook Collection, no. 249.

4. Civil Problems

1. The military was cliquish, and officers and men were loyal to regiments, for example, the Fourth U.S. Cavalry or the Sixth U.S. Cavalry. Since Gatewood came to prominence as military commandant of the White Mountain Indian Reservation during Crook's tenure, his name became linked with the general and would remain so even after they severed their working relationship. Being known as a "Crook man" became more noticeable in 1886 when Gatewood (a member of the Sixth) searched for Geronimo in Mexico surrounded by officers of the Fourth, Nelson Miles's chosen regiment to end the war.

2. Like Crook, Miles knew that soon one of the major general positions would become available. As there were only five such positions and they only became available when a major general died or retired, Miles began to seek Crook's position as commander of the Department of Arizona. As time passed, Miles became more and more aggressive, even taking his campaign to the newspapers. As he was also the son-in-law of William T. Sherman, commander in chief of the army, the pressure he exerted had to have pressed Crook to concentrate on only one thing—defeating the warring Apaches. See "Probably a Mistake," *Arizona Journal-Miner*, January 8, 1886.

3. Charles F. Lummis, *General Crook and the Apache Wars,* edited by Turbesé Lummis Fiske (Flagstaff AZ: Northland, 1966), 11–12. A writer-editor, Lummis (March 1, 1859–November 25, 1928) had recently been appointed city editor of the *Los Angeles Times* when he was assigned to travel to the Southwest to cover the Apache war in March 1886. Becoming interested in the natives of the Southwest, he studied their culture and collected artifacts. In 1907 he founded the Southwest Museum in Los Angeles (which is currently called Autry National Center, Southwest Museum of the American Indian). See also Lummis, viii; Thrapp, *Frontier Biography*, 2:884–85.

4. Crook to AG, Division of the Pacific (September 19, 1885), NA, RG 94, M689, Letters Received by the Office of the Adjutant General, 1881–89, roll 179.

5. In Kraft, *Gatewood & Geronimo*, I identified Zuck as "Thomas," following a conversation with Cynthia Wood, a research assistant at the Arizona Historical Foundation, Arizona State University, Tempe, on January 8, 1997, and mistakenly transcribing the *F* on the some of the handwritten documents as a *T*. See also Cynthia A. Wood to Jay Van Orden (March 12, 1996), Arizona Historical Society, Tucson. Researcher Gayle Piotrowski, of Tucson, has helped me correctly identify Zuck not as "T. M." but as "F. M.," which stands for Francis M. Zuck. Born in Greensburg. Pennsylvania, Zuck (b. July 21, 1838) migrated to Iowa

with his parents in 1850. Eight years later he moved to Indiana and earned his living in merchandising. At the outbreak of the Civil War Zuck enlisted in the Third Iowa Volunteer Infantry, but did not serve until war's end. After he fought bushwhackers in northern Missouri, his health deteriorated, and he received an honorable discharge (November 20, 1863). Zuck resumed his life as a salesman. The following year he married Jennie Brobst (January 21, 1864) of Knoxville, Iowa. In the coming years they had four children: Frank A., Harry Z., Myrtle J., and Grace May. In 1882 he moved his family to Arizona, eventually settling in Holbrook. Within two years, he owned a large percentage of the town as well as numerous ranches in the area. "For many years [he] has been one of the leaders of the Republican party of Navajo county and he is well known among the prominent members of that party throughout the territory." *Portrait and Biographical Record of Arizona* (Chicago: Chapman, 1901), 661–62.

6. All three drafts are contained in box 3, folder 40 in the Gatewood Collection: "How the Judge Was Arrested & Tried" contains 23 pages (hereafter cited as Gatewood, "Arrested"); "The Judge's Trial" contains 9 pages (hereafter cited as Gatewood, "Judge"); and "The Trial Chapter" contains 13 pages (hereafter cited as Gatewood, "Trial").

7. See Gatewood, Gatewood, "Judge," 1–2, and "Trial," 1–3.

8. M. Barber, AAG, to Gatewood (August 22, 1884); Gatewood to Barber, AAG (August 28, 1884); and Barber to Gatewood (August 28, 1884), all in F. M. Zuck, T. F. Jones, and J. C. Kay Trial, RG 21, Records of the District Court of the United States for the Territory of Arizona, Third Judicial District, 1869–1910, Criminal Cases A-83–5 to A-85–19, box 4, #52, National Archives—Pacific Southwest Region, Laguna Niguel (hereafter cited as Zuck Trial). See Gatewood, "Trial," 3–4; Gatewood, "Judge," 2–3; and Gatewood, "Arrested," 1, for the text.

9. Joseph Chatley Kay (July 1, 1844–early July 1891) moved to the United States with his parents, John and Sarah Chatley Kay, in 1851. They immigrated to Wellsville, Utah, where he spent his youth. Almost nothing is known of his first wife other than that he lived with her in Idaho where she bore him three children before she died. While still in Idaho, he met and married Margaret Ann Walker (December 17, 1847–June 22, 1924), whose father, John B. Walker, served as a captain in the militia at Grantsville, Utah. Married in 1869, their union eventually produced at least eight additional children. James Petersen, "Joseph C. and Margaret A. W. Kay," Joseph C. Kay biographical file, Arizona Historical Society, Tucson, 4 unnumbered pages including a supplement.

Kay's death was unusual and apparently unpleasant. The *Arizona Enterprise* reported: "Joseph C. Kay, of Taylor, in the western portion of this county died in a very peculiar manner a week or ten days since. His bowels became constipated and refused to act for seven or eight days but seemed to give him no trouble, as he was cheerful and lively as usual. But one afternoon, while in the co-op store at Snowflake, he was taken with a severe pain in the chest, which rapidly grew worse in spite of every effort to alleviate it. In a short time his body and one side of his face began to swell and continued to do so until he burst open along the backbone, fully eighteen inches. After death ensued, he burst again clear across the stomach. Those who were present describe his sufferings as something terrible to witness." *Arizona Enterprise*, July 11, 1891.

10. James H. McClintock, Arizona State Historian, *Mormon Settlement in Arizona: A Record of Peaceful Conquest* (Phoenix: n.p., 1921), 172. See also 170–71, 173.

11. Wharfield, in *Apache Indian Scouts*, 5, states that Alchesay was Pedro's nephew, not his son.

Gatewood wrote: "Monday I am going to Forest Dale to depose old Pedro as chief and put in someone else, probably Alchesay. As it is now, no one is really responsible. Pedro is so old and deaf and feeble that he can do nothing with [his band]. They sneak off the reservation and buy arms and whiskey from the Mormons, and it is almost impossible to get them to report on each other. But if there is a chief with get up, he can be calaboosed for not reporting those who do wrong[,] which will have a tendency to check their going off." Gatewood to Emmet Crawford (March 1, 1884), Records of U.S. Army Continental Commands, 1821–1920, NA, RG 393, Department of Arizona, 1870–93, Miscellaneous Records, as quoted in Collins, *Apache Nightmare*, 225.

12. Gatewood testimony (October 27, 1884), Zuck Trial. Gatewood placed the September meeting some fifteen to twenty days before he arrested Zuck and his cohorts. As the warrants for the arrests were signed on October 1, and time was necessary for the negotiation, cutting and stacking of the hay, and a delivery that the Indians refused to accept, it follows that the meeting took place on or about September 25. See Indictments for False Imprisonment of F. M. Zuck (no. 49), Thomas F. Jones (no. 50), and Joseph C. Kay (no. 51) by Charles B. Gatewood; all filed in the District Court of the United States for the Territory of Arizona, Third Judicial District on February 10, 1885. RG 1, Apache County, SG8, Superior Court. Phoenix AZ: Arizona State Archives, Department of Library, Archives, and Public Records (hereafter cited as Gatewood Trial).

13. Gatewood is not completely truthful here. Although he did not take part in the negotiations, he was present during the negotiation.

14. Petersen, "Joseph C. and Margaret A. W. Kay," 2, for this quote, and 4 for the next quote. See also Petersen, 1.

15. Gatewood testimony (October 27, 1884), Zuck Trial.

16. Gatewood testimony (October 28, 1884), Zuck Trial, for this quote and the next quote.

17. Again, "The Trial Chapter" is the basis for this section, with only a few words used from "Judge." See Gatewood, "Trial," 4–8; Gatewood, "Judge," 3–6;

and Gatewood, "Arrested," 1–2. Although Gatewood claimed that it was a yearly supply of hay in "Trial," in "Arrested" he placed the figure at "50 tons," and in "Judge," he upped the figure to "75 tons." However, in Zuck Trial, October 27, 1884, Gatewood testified that it was either ten or fifteen tons of grass or hay.

18. See chapter 2 for a discussion of the early migration from Asia.

19. See chapter 2.

20. See Goodwin, *Western Apache*, 412, 414, for a discussion on reprisals and revenge.

21. Although the text again is from Gatewood, "Trial," 8–9, this quote is from Gatewood, "Judge," 6, which also includes 7 in this section. In "Trial," 8, Gatewood said, "Pay or arrest," and in "Arrested," 3, Gatewood said, "Pay or be jugged."

22. This sentence is from Gatewood, "Arrested," 3.

23. A popular choice for the marshal position, Tidball took part in the investigation of San Carlos Indian agent Joseph Tiffany in 1882. Tiffany was eventually charged with embezzlement and perjury, but the case was dropped when a judge ruled on December 3, 1883, that federal marshals and the district attorney were prejudiced against the agent. The following year Tiffany testified before a congressional committee on the performance of federal officials in Arizona, including Tidball. For information on Tidball, see Larry D. Ball, *The United States Marshals of New Mexico and Arizona Territories, 1846–1912* (Albuquerque: University of New Mexico Press, 1978), 165, 167–70; Zan L. Tidball, MS 820, Arizona Historical Society, Tucson; and Collins, *Apache Nightmare*, 222–23.

24. Hamilton Mitchell Roach (October 9, 1857–January 24, 1923), who was also known as "Hampton," did not graduate from West Point. He enlisted in the Fifth U.S. Cavalry in 1876, and three years later received a Medal of Honor for his participation in an engagement against the Utes at Milk Creek, Colorado (September 29–October 5, 1879). By 1883, he had risen to the rank of second lieutenant (First U.S. Infantry) and married Cora Reader. Their son, Hampton Jr., was born at Fort Apache (September 19, 1884). Although he was not Gatewood's assistant at the White Mountain Indian Reservation in the same way that Britton Davis was Emmet Crawford's assistant at the San Carlos Indian Reservation when Crook appointed his military commandants, Roach would soon join Gatewood. Altshuler, *Cavalry Yellow*, 283.

25. See the three separate arrest warrants for Zuck, Jones, and Kay issued on October 1, 1884; Gatewood testimony (October 27–28, 1884); see also a single summons for Gatewood, Roach, and Conley to appear at Third Judicial District, Territory of Arizona, Commissioner's Court, on October 27, 1884. It was signed by the Honorable William H. McGrew and delivered on October 21, 1884. All in Zuck Trial. "The Trial Chapter" is again the basis for this section, with only a few words pulled from "Judge" and "Arrested" with the exception of Kay going after Gatewood for money. See Gatewood, "Trial," 9–12; Gatewood, "Judge," 7–9; and

Gatewood, "Arrested," 3–7. This section marks the end of Gatewood's draft of "Judge."

26. Gatewood established that there were five witnesses in "Arrested," 4.

27. This sentence is from Gatewood, "Arrested," 6. Gatewood is off on the distance. As the crow flies, the distance is about 120 miles. Assuming he traveled on roads, the distance most likely was considerably longer. However, it is unlikely to have been 250 miles.

28. This can only be Joseph Kay: Kay was Mormon and Zuck was not, and since most of Gatewood's interaction had been with Kay and not with Zuck or Jones, it follows that Kay was the one who tried to shake Gatewood down for money.

29. This entire section is only in Gatewood, "Arrested," 6–7.

30. "Gatewood–Zuck," undated and unknown newspaper that was published sometime after November 12, 1884, as it quotes the *Albuquerque Democrat*, which was published on that date. Clipping in the Gatewood Collection.

31. "Judge Zuck's Acquittal," undated and unknown newspaper. Clipping in the Gatewood Collection. The article refers to Capt. Henry Wirz, commandant of Andersonville Prison, who was convicted and executed for war crimes during the Civil War.

32. Charles Garnet Gordon (September 28, 1837–October 26, 1898) served in California during the Civil War, but was discharged on disability before the war ended (April 25, 1864). He reenlisted in the Sixth U.S. Cavalry in 1867, and in 1881, upon Capt. Edmund Hentig's death at Cibecue during the Indian scout revolt, he assumed command of Hentig's company. At the present time, Gordon was on a sick leave from which he would never return, remaining on it until he retired on October 5, 1887. Altshuler, *Cavalry Yellow*, 141.

Gordon to AG, U.S. Army (November 22, 1884); First Endorsement for Gatewood to rejoin troop (November 22, 1884), both in NA, M1395. Even though Fort Stanton was Troop D's official post, it was currently stationed at South Fork NM.

33. Statement of Service, and Adjutant General's Office (June 5, 1896), NA, M1395; Gatewood Biography, and Headquarters Sixth U.S. Cavalry, General Orders no. 19 (May 23, 1896), letter 54, Gatewood Collection.

34. Indictments for False Imprisonment of F. M. Zuck (no. 49), Thomas F. Jones (no. 50), and Joseph C. Kay (no. 51) by Charles B. Gatewood, Gatewood Trial.

35. "A Restraining Order," *Daily Phoenix Herald*, February 23, 1885. Although the paper is dated February 23, 1885, the lead-in begins with "Globe, February 27."

36. This sentence is from Gatewood, "Arrested," 7; however, the rest of this section is a mix from both Gatewood, "Trial," 12–13, and Gatewood, "Arrested," 7–9, until Gatewood's draft of "Trail" ends.

37. Not much is known of Pete Kitchen's (1819–August 5, 1895) early life in Kentucky and Tennessee. He arrived in Arizona in 1854 and began supplying beef to the army. In 1861, Indians destroyed his ranch, about twenty-five miles south of Tucson, ending his supply business. At the end of the 1860s, Kitchen fortified his new ranch-farm, located in the Santa Cruz Valley, to rebuff Indian attacks, and although a succession of raids decimated his herds of sheep, oxen, and horses, he held on and by 1870 he sold produce in Tucson. Between 1873 and 1876 he served as a local mail carrier. During this time he added the army to the list of clients to whom he sold produce. As time passed, his sales expanded to include Prescott and San Carlos. When the railroad arrived in 1882 at Nogales, a border town to the south of his ranch, his business shrank, and a year later he sold out. Thrapp, *Frontier Biography*, 2:790. Zuck lost the election and was "left out." Gatewood is undoubtedly referring to Kitchen's supply business to the military dwindling or ending with the arrival of the railroad in Nogales, and Kitchen being "left out."

38. Although Gatewood does not name Show Low as the town, it is the most obvious location for Zuck's hometown because his destination was not Prescott, as he implied in "Arrested," 8, when he said his destination was not the "capital city" but St. Johns.

39. In "Arrested," 7, Gatewood wrote: "They decided that the cause of his defeat was his arrest & incarceration & claimed with loud voices that it was a 'put up job' in which the 'arrestor' stood in with the Gentile candidate to route the 'arrestee.'"

40. Gatewood's draft of "Trial" ends here. The rest of this chapter is from "Arrested."

41. Georgia claimed: "I returned from M[arylan]d just then, when he [Gatewood] was warned not to go to Holbrook [she means St. Johns, as Gatewood never had to go to Holbrook]. My presence saved a lynching there." Georgia Gatewood to Gatewood Jr. (January 15, 1928), Gatewood Collection, letter 176. Could this be true? Was it a combination of the landlady and Georgia that prevented mob rule?

42. Sumner Howard (May 2, 1835–September 6, 1890) was born in Brockport, New York. A year later, his parents moved to Flint, Michigan, and it was here that he first gained fame as a criminal lawyer—perhaps the best criminal trial lawyer in the state at that time. In 1857 he married Lucy R. Mason (1837–95); they had one daughter and adopted a son. Over the next ten years, through a series of elections and appointments, his career continued to advance. Although he had been elected prosecuting attorney as a Democrat in 1858, after a short stint in the military during the Civil War (spring of 1861–September 1863) in which he saw no action, he served three additional terms as prosecuting attorney, this time running on the Republican ticket. Changing political parties paved the way for his next career advancement, when in 1876, President Grant appointed him the

U.S. attorney for Utah. John S. Goff, *Arizona Territorial Officials, Volume 1: The Supreme Court Justices, 1863–1912* (Cave Creek AZ: Black Mountain Press, 1975), 100–101, 103.

43. Illinois native John Doyle Lee (September 12, 1812–March 23, 1877) became a Mormon in 1838 at Ambrosia, Missouri. Soon after his baptism, he joined the Danite, a band of Mormon militants, and served as bodyguard for Joseph Smith and Brigham Young. Lee played an active part in the war between Mormons and non-Mormons before the Mormon move westward. He also bought into the belief of multiple wives, having, it was said, nineteen wives over the course of his life. He took part in the exodus to Utah and helped found Provo. After the move, he held a number of positions, including Indian agent at the Iron County agency, probate judge, and clerk and assessor of Washington County. However, it was his role in the so-called Mountain Meadows Massacre (September 11, 1857) for which he will be forever remembered. During the action, he persuaded some 140 emigrants on the Fancher train, which he and some sixty Mormons had stopped, to step from the safety of the train. When they did, they were butchered. Afterwards, it was life as usual. Then, a year and a half later, he went into hiding after being named as one of the suspects in the infamous incident. Nothing happened, and he continued to prosper for another decade. Then in 1870 Brigham Young asked him to move away. Shortly thereafter, he was excommunicated from the Mormon Church. In 1875 he was tried for the murder of the people of the Fancher train, but only one Mormon testified against him, and a hung jury (eight Mormons for acquittal and four gentiles for conviction) resulted in him remaining in prison. In May 1876 he was released on bail pending a second trial, which began in December 1876. After much testimony, an all-Mormon jury convicted him of the crime—the only one convicted of the sixty or so men (this number may have been as low as forty) who took part in the heinous act. The following year he was executed while sitting on his coffin at the site of the tragedy. Thrapp, *Frontier Biography*, 2:832–33; M. M. Rice, "Judge Sumner Howard," in Reminiscences of M. M. Rice, MS 684, Arizona Historical Society, Tucson.

44. District Court of the Third Judicial District of the Territory of Arizona in and for the County of Apache, Territory of Arizona vs. Charles B. Gatewood, defendant (February 6, 1885), Gatewood Trial. Howard was appointed chief justice of Arizona on March 18, 1884, commissioned on March 26, and on May 20 officially assumed the position during a ceremony in Prescott. Living in Prescott, he presided over three counties: Apache, Yavapai, and Mohave. Goff, *Supreme Court Justices*, 102.

45. False Arrest Indictment no. 49 (dated February 7, 1885). See also False Arrest Indictments no. 50 and no. 51 (also dated February 7, 1885). All in Gatewood Trial.

46. Gatewood was aware that Howard had enlisted in the spring of 1861 as a second lieutenant, was promoted to first lieutenant, and should have seen action at Gettysburg (July 1–3, 1863), but missed the battle due to sickness. It also sounds as if Gatewood was aware that Howard did not serve his country until the completion of the war; he resigned his commission in September 1863. See Goff, *Supreme Court Justices*, 101. Gatewood hints that Howard may have been forced to resign and that this was the reason for his hatred of the military.

47. Tritle, a Republican, served as governor of Arizona Territory from 1882 until 1885.

48. Warrant for Gatewood's arrest (February 18, 1885), Gatewood Trial.

49. Gatewood and Davis became close at this time. Davis later wrote that it was "at Turkey Creek where the long friendship existing between your father and myself was cemented into something so dear to me that I feel it still exists." Britton Davis to Gatewood Jr. (September 3, 1925), Gatewood Collection microfilm, reel 7.

50. Thomas Cruse to Gatewood Jr. (January 19, 1926), letter 79, and Crook to Gatewood (January 22, 1885), letter 4, both in Gatewood Collection; M. Barber, AAG, to Gatewood (August 22, 1884), Zuck Trial; Kraft, *Gatewood & Geronimo*, 21–22, 46–47, 53–54.

51. New Mexican John Lorenzo Hubbell (November 21, 1853–November 11, 1930), who is still famous to this day for the trading post he established in Ganado, Arizona (on the current Navajo Indian Reservation), became sheriff of Apache County in 1882 and served two terms. Thrapp wrote: "Hubbell had a reputation for honest dealing with the Indians, spoke Navajo fluently (and, being half Spanish, that language as well), claimed to be a friend of several important Indians, including Victorio and Geronimo among the Apaches, Ganado Mucho, Manuelito and others among the Navahos." Thrapp, *Frontier Biography*, 2:687.

52. Kraft, *Gatewood & Geronimo*, 55.

53. Ball, *Days of Victorio*, 168. Mickey Free (c. 1847–1915) of Sonora, Mexico, had parents whose names definitely sound Hispanic (Santiago Tellez and Jesusa Martinez), and yet it has been said that he also had Irish blood. After his father's death in 1858, his mother moved her family to Arizona. When he was fourteen, Apaches abducted him and he spent a year living with the White Mountains. In December of 1872, Free became an Indian scout, and within two years he became a sergeant. As scout, and later interpreter, he served the U.S. government off and on until 1893. Thrapp described Free, who was married four times: "Blinded in his youth in his left eye, he was of disreputable appearance, light complected with long reddish-blond hair and grey eyes, and always was a controversial figure. He was considered 'mean' by many who knew him, but never dangerous. He is never known to have killed a man, despite yarns to the contrary." Thrapp, *Frontier Biography*, 1:518.

Chatto (1854–August 16, 1934), a Chokonen who later called himself Alfred Chatto, lived through these tumultuous times, seeing his life change from a feared warrior to a scout (and traitor in his brethren's eyes) to someone who survived many years in exile as a prisoner of war after faithfully serving the United States. Views on Chatto are strong, and they are always pro or con. During the summer of 1886, Chatto, with a number of other Apaches, visited Washington DC, supposedly to discuss the Apaches' situation. Officials presented him with a medal, but he never returned to his homeland. While en route, he and those with him became prisoners of war and were shipped to Florida, a perfidy that turned him into a bitter man. Britton Davis later wrote: "Chat[t]o was one of the finest men, red or white, I have ever known." Davis quoted in William Hafford, "Chat[t]o the Betrayed," *Arizona Highways* 69, no. 2 (February 1993): 17. See also Hafford, 16. Thrapp, *Frontier Biography*, 1:259.

54. Geronimo's comments to Crook during the first day of their peace negotiation at Cañon de los Embudos, Mexico, on March 25, 1886. Sen. Exec. Doc. no. 88, 51st Cong., 1st sess., 11.

55. Crook to AG, Division of the Pacific (May 21, 1885), Crook Collection, no. 129.

56. Crook to CO, Fort Bayard NM (May 18, 1885), Crook Collection, no. 112; James Wade report quoted in Robert Walsh report (May 18, 1885), Gatewood Collection; Parker, "Service with Gatewood," 1; Davis, "A Short Account of the Chiricahua Tribe," 5; Davis, *Geronimo*, 101; Britton Davis report quoted in Pierce report (May 17, 1885), Gatewood Collection; and Crook to AG, Division of the Pacific (May 19, 1885), Crook Collection, letter 115. Britton Davis claimed that over four hundred Bedonkohe, Chokonen, Nednhi, and Chihenne Apaches remained on the reservation. Davis to Gatewood Jr. (April 25, 1926), Gatewood Collection microfilm, reel 7.

57. Georgia Gatewood to Gatewood Jr. (January 15, 1928), Gatewood Collection, letter 176.

58. Gatewood to AG, Washington DC (August 5, 1885), NA, M1395.

59. Crook endorsement, NA, M1395.

60. Crook to AG, telegram, Washington DC (October 3, 1885), NA, M1395. Crook later sent a letter (October 25, 1885) to the AG, Washington DC, which stated virtually the same thing.

61. Three separate warrants for Gatewood's arrest (September 5, 1885, filed on September 8, 1885), District Court, County of Apache, Territory of Arizona (hereafter cited as Gatewood Warrants). Gatewood Trial.

62. It is assumed that Gatewood traveled winding roads through the mountains, which logically could almost double the distance as the crow flies (forty miles) between Fort Apache and St. Johns.

63. Three separate bail bonds (September 5, 1885) for indictments (September

6, 1885) charging Charles B. Gatewood with false imprisonment, District Court of the Third Judicial District of the Territory of Arizona (hereafter cited as Gatewood Bail Bonds). Gatewood Trial. These bonds were filed on September 8, 1885.

Gatewood's bail seems exceedingly high. See Gatewood Warrants and Gatewood Bail Bonds. On all these documents, the bond to guarantee his appearance at court was listed at $500 per issuance, which totals $1,500. See the various summons to appear in court on September 7, 1885, for the date of Gatewood's trial. All in Gatewood Trial.

64. Gatewood's attorney was E. M. Sanford. He and J. T. Bostwick had been Zuck's attorneys. Zuck Trial. Bryan W. Tichenor, "Correspondence," *Prescott Morning Courier*, March 31, 1886, 2, confirms that Sanford represented Gatewood at this time, along with J. C. Herndon, who was an assistant U.S. attorney. See Gatewood Trial for Herndon's initials and official title.

65. Three separate bail bonds (September 10, 1885) for indictments (September 6, 1885) charging Charles B. Gatewood with false imprisonment, District Court of the Third Judicial District of the Territory of Arizona (hereafter cited as Gatewood Bail Bonds 2). Gatewood Trial. On these documents, the bond to guarantee his appearance at court was listed at $600 per issuance, which totals $1,800. These ball bonds were actually numbered (no. 49, no. 50, no. 51) to coincide with the separate indictments. Note that part of this text is pulled from an earlier section of Gatewood, "Arrested," 14, as he placed it in the wrong location. On the same page, Gatewood also said, "So the subject was dropped," which was not true, because the bond was increased.

66. Gatewood Jr. (January 26, 1929), Gatewood Collection, letter 347; Davis, *Geronimo*, 222; Crook to Crawford (November 13, 1885), no. 244, and Crook to Crawford (November 17, 1885), no. 245, both in Crook Collection. Lockett replaced Gatewood as military commandant of the White Mountain Indian Reservation on November 14, 1885.

67. Gatewood to Georgia Gatewood (June 25, 1886), Gatewood Collection, letter 12.

68. "Probably a Mistake," *Arizona Journal-Miner*, January 8, 1886. Grover Cleveland was the president at this time (1885–89). This news came via a telegram from Washington DC dated January 4. See also Thrapp, *Conquest*, 335; Utley, *Clash*, 60.

69. John Calhoun Shields (January 21, 1848–May 2, 1892) of Alpena (sometimes spelled Alpina), Michigan, was sworn in as chief justice of Arizona on November 9, 1885. Howard had resigned his post as chief justice to help facilitate the confirmation of Shields as chief justice. But even though Shields was respected, the U.S. Senate did not confirm his appointment: a Republican senator from his home state cast the final political and deciding vote against him. An

uproar resulted as people from both within and without Arizona protested the vote. It did little good, and even though President Cleveland resubmitted his name for the position on July 1, 1886, the Senate again refused to confirm the appointment. Luckily for Gatewood, he held the position for sixteen months, through March 1887, and sat on the bench for the lieutenant's final court appearance. The territorial bar in Arizona would later resolve: "As a Judge he was firm and possessed a mind peculiarly suited to the position, active and analytical and well grounded in all the principles of the law." After the fiasco in Arizona, Shields returned to Alpena, where he continued to practice law. Just five years later, he became ill with the grippe, suffered a stroke, and never recovered. Goff, *Supreme Court Justices*, 115, for the quote. See also 102, 112–13. For the exact date of his death and additional background information, see the *Arizona Enterprise*, May 12, 1892.

70. Tichenor, "Correspondence," 2.

71. Conrad Zulick, a politician from New Jersey, became governor of New Mexico Territory in 1885. However, before he could assume office, he had to be rescued from Mexican laborers, who held him prisoner in Nacozari, where he managed mining property. Ball, *United States Marshals*, 165–66.

72. Summons to appear in the District Court of the Third Judicial District on March 24, 1886, and signed by Honorable J. C. Shields on March 22, 1886. Gatewood Trial. Note that in the various documents dealing with the end of the Gatewood trail, Shields's name is at times also spelled "Sheilds."

73. In "Arrested," 13, Gatewood also had another comment out of order. He became sarcastic when he realized what was happening, and wrote: "The legal lights drew their fees from a sure source; the one side from the Territory & the other from the United States. They knew a good thing when they had it & didn't propose to let go."

74. Although Gatewood does not mention it, the impaneling of the jury was difficult, as both sides challenged the jurors. Tichenor, "Correspondence," 2.

75. Tichenor, "Correspondence," 2. Tichenor seems to be in error as to the marshal who transported Zuck and company to Prescott; the marshal was Tidball.

76. Tichenor, "Correspondence," 2, for the first quote and the quote concerning Herndon.

77. Shields held firm that this was the only point to be debated. Gatewood Trial.

78. According to Tichenor in "Correspondence," 2, Howard gave an "exceeding[ly] eloquent and logical speech of an hour, in which the whole proceeding was reviewed in a very able manner."

79. Gatewood Trial.

5. Gatewood and Geronimo

1. Chihuahua (1822–July 25, 1901), a subchieftain of the Chokonen Apaches, played a major role during the last years of his people's freedom and was often associated with Geronimo. Brother of the warrior Josanie and related to Chihenne war leader Kaytennae by marriage, Chihuahua began his association with Geronimo and Juh in the early 1880s. He took part in the raid on San Carlos, which resulted in breaking Loco and the Chihenne Apaches out in 1882, led a raid of terror into the Southwest in March 1883 (which is sometimes called "Chatto's raid"), broke out from Turkey Creek with Mangus and Geronimo in May 1885, was the leading Apache negotiator with Crook at Cañon de los Embudos on March 27, 1886, and returned to captivity at the conclusion of the conference. Thrapp, *Frontier Biography*, 1:262. See also Griswold, "Apaches," 18, 66; Kraft, *Gatewood & Geronimo*, 24, 123. Historian Marc Simmons, in *Massacre on the Lordsburg Road: A Tragedy of the Apache Wars* (College Station: Texas A&M University Press, 1997) makes a convincing argument that it was Chatto who led the March 1883 raid. See 84, 86. See John G. Bourke's record of the surrender (March 25 and 27, 1886), Crook Collection, no. 359. Bourke's record of the meeting can also be found in Sen. Exec. Doc. no. 88, 51st Cong., 1st sess., 11–17.

2. Sen. Exec. Doc. no. 88, 51st Cong., 1st sess., 11–14, for this quote and the following quotes from this meeting.

3. John G. Bourke, *On the Border with Crook* (1891; repr., Lincoln: University of Nebraska Press, 1971), 476.

4. Kaytennae (1861–January 1918), who was also known as Kaahteney, Kaatena, Kaatenny, Looking Glass, and Jacob Ka-ya-ten-nae, participated in the Victorio war (1879–80), joined the Geronimo-Juh 1882 raid on San Carlos which broke out Loco and the Chihenne Apaches, and roamed free until 1883 when he came into the reservation after Crook's invasion of the Sierra Madre. While on the reservation, he plotted to kill Britton Davis. However, before he actually attempted to assassinate the lieutenant, he was arrested, tried, and incarcerated at Alcatraz, an island fortress prison in San Francisco Bay, California. His stay was short-lived as Crook made sure he was able to observe whites in San Francisco. What he saw changed him; he never again rode the war trail. Thrapp, *Frontier Biography*, 2:761.

5. Crook, *1886 Annual Report*, 10.

6. Bourke, *Border*, 478.

7. Crook to Sheridan (March 29, 1886), NA, RG 94, M689, Letters Received by the Office of the Adjutant General, 1881–89: 1066 AGO 1883, roll 179.

8. Geronimo, *Geronimo*, 138.

9. Sheridan to Crook (March 30, 1886), NA, RG 94, M689, roll 179.

10. Kraft, *Gatewood & Geronimo*, 124.

11. Marion Perry Maus (August 25, 1850–February 9, 1930) graduated from the Military Academy in 1874 (thirty-seventh of a class of forty-one), and as a member of the First U.S. Infantry saw his first action against Indians on the northern plains when the Nez Percé made their dramatic march for freedom in 1877. He received a promotion to first lieutenant in 1879. Three years later he transferred to the Southwest, where he saw extensive duty; first in the signal corps and later in the field tracking Apaches. He became a captain in 1890, a major in 1899 (Second U.S. Infantry), lieutenant colonel in 1902, colonel in 1904 (Twentieth U.S. Infantry), and brigadier general in 1909. He also served as Nelson Miles's aide twice (1890–95, 1897–1902). Altshuler, *Cavalry Yellow*, 225; Thrapp, *Frontier Biography*, 2:960.

12. Howard to Drum (February 24, 1887), Sen. Exec. Doc. 117, 49th Cong., 2d sess., 35; Crook, *1886 Annual Report*, 10; T. J. Clay to Gatewood Jr. (May 29, 1930), Gatewood Collection, letter 392; Bourke, *Border*, 480–81; Davis, *Geronimo*, 217–18. Davis put the number of natives who ran at thirty-nine (twenty men, thirteen women, three girls, and three boys). See also George Whitwell Parsons, *The Devil Has Foreclosed: The Private Journal of George Whitwell Parsons*, vol. 2, *The Concluding Arizona Years, 1882–87*, ed. Lynn R. Bailey (Tucson: Westernlore Press, 1997), March 29, 1886, 200–201, 204, 207 (*San Francisco Chronicle*, April 1 and 3, 1886); and Leonard B. Radtke, "Sons of Two Famous Indian Scouts Are Now Boy Scouts," *El Paso Times*, December 18, 1927, *Gatewood Scrapbook*. See also Matthias Day to Gatewood Jr. (September 27, 1926), Gatewood Collection, letter 278. Day wrote: "Geronimo & his [I]ndians started north with Maus, but got drunk, got scared & escaped and went back to the Sierra Madres."

13. Dos-teh-seh, a Chihenne, was Cochise's primary wife and Mangas Coloradas's daughter. Griswold, "Apaches," 106.

A Bedonkohe, E-clah-heh's (1859–1909) name can be translated as "Under the Century Plant." Fun and Tsisnah, two warriors with Geronimo and Naiche, were her cousins. Her great-grandfather was the Bedonkohe chieftain Mahko. Griswold, "Apaches," 34, 107.

Dorothy (1876–1946), a Chokonen-Bedonkohe-Chihenne Apache, was also known as Deh-kluh-kizhee, Dorothy Dekhliksch, Dorothy Naiche, and Dorothy D. Naitches. She had three sisters (Bah-nas-kli, Jane Naiche, and May), one half sister, one brother (Bah-nash-kli), and five half brothers. Her ancestors included grandfather Mangas Coloradas (Chihenne) and great-grandfather Mahko (Bedonkohe) on her mother's side. (Griswold reported that Mahko was her grandfather; he also reported that he was her mother's grandfather. But he can only be one of their grandfathers.) After the exile to Florida as a prisoner of war, she entered the Carlisle Institute in Pennsylvania on December 8, 1886. After leaving the school, she worked in West Grove, Pennsylvania. After rejoining her people at

Fort Sill, Oklahoma, she married James Kaywaykla. Griswold, "Apaches," 79–80; Ball, *Days of Victorio*, xiv.

14. General Orders no. 15 (April 2, 1886), 10, Sen. Exec. Doc. 88, 51st Cong., 1st sess.

15. Crook to Sheridan (April 2, 1886), NA, RG 94, M689, roll 179.

16. Sheridan to Crook (April 5, 1886), NA, RG 94, M689, roll 179.

17. Crook to Sheridan (April 7, 1886), as quoted in Brig. Gen. George Crook, *Resumé of Operations against Apache Indians, 1882 to 1886* (1886; repr., London: Johnson-Taunton Military Press, 1971, with notes and introduction by Barry C. Johnson), 21.

18. Crook, *Resumé*, 21.

19. Gatewood entries on rootsweb.com. Although Kraft, *Gatewood & Geronimo*, 131, reported that Hugh was born on April 6, it now appears that his actual birthday was April 13.

20. See notes from Crook's January 2, 1890, visit to Mount Vernon Barracks, Alabama, Sen. Exec. Doc. 35, 51st Cong. 1st sess., 33, for Naiche's quote. See also Geronimo, *Geronimo*, 140; Georgia Gatewood to Gatewood Jr. (April 4, 1909), Gatewood Collection, letter 79; William A. Thompson report (October 7, 1886) and Miles report (September 18, 1886), Sen. Exec. Doc. 117, 49th Cong., 2d sess., 39; Terrell, *Apache Chronicle*, 382; and Thrapp, *Conquest*, 351. In his memoirs, Geronimo talks of going as far east as the mountains in New Mexico. Thrapp did not know that Gatewood had rejoined his regiment, which was stationed in New Mexico, at the end of 1885 and mistakenly placed him at Fort Apache when the raid took place.

21. House of Representatives Joint Resolution (May 3, 1886), NA, RG 94, M689, Letters Received by the Office of the Adjutant General, 1881–89: 1066 AGO 1883, roll 184.

22. Henry Ware Lawton (March 7, 1843–December 19, 1899), a Civil War veteran, chose to make the military his career at the close of the rebellion. In July 1866, eight months after his muster out of his Civil War service, he became a second lieutenant in the Forty-first U.S. Infantry, which in 1869 became the Twenty-fourth U.S. Infantry. Promoted to first lieutenant in 1868, he served as regimental quartermaster until January 1871, when he transferred to the Fourth U.S. Cavalry. He again served as regimental quartermaster (May 1872–March 1875, September 1876–March 1879), attaining the rank of captain on March 20, 1879. During this time he saw action against the Comanches in 1874 at Palo Duro Cañon, Texas, and against the Northern Cheyennes in 1876 on the Powder River, Montana. He married Mamie Craig on December 12, 1881, in Kentucky, and they would eventually have four children. By 1883 he was stationed at Fort Stanton New Mexico Territory, and in 1884 at Fort Huachuca, Arizona Territory. During the early days of the final Apache breakout from the reservation in 1885,

five of Lawton's men were killed when fleeing Apaches attacked his command near Guadelupe Cañon on the United States–Mexico border on June 8. During the final pursuit of Geronimo and Naiche, he led Miles's primary command in pursuit of the Apaches. After Geronimo and Naiche surrendered in September 1886, his star continued to rise: he became a major in 1888, lieutenant colonel in 1889, brigadier general of volunteers on May 4, 1898, colonel in the regular army on July 7, 1898, and major general of volunteers on July 8, 1898. Lawton died during action east of Manila in the Philippines. Altshuler, *Cavalry Yellow*, 198–99; Thrapp, *Frontier Biography*, 2:821–22.

23. Crook to Sheridan (April 1, 1886), Crook, *Resumé*, 19, 21; Nelson A. Miles, *Serving the Republic: Memoirs of the Civil War and Military Life of Nelson A. Miles* (New York: Harper & Brothers, 1911), 225; Howard to Drum (February 24, 1887), Sen. Exec. Doc. 117, 49th Cong., 2d sess., 35; William A. Thompson report (April 20, 1886), Sen. Exec. Doc. 117, 49th Cong., 2d sess., 2; James Parker orders to Lawton (May 4, 1886), Sen. Exec. Doc. 117, 49th Cong., 2d sess., 45; Leonard Wood, *Chasing Geronimo: The Journal of Leonard Wood, May–September 1886*, ed. Jack C. Lane (Albuquerque: University of New Mexico Press, 1970), May 4–5, 1886, 26–27. Wood, who remained with Lawton during the entire time in Mexico, claimed they started out with thirty Indian scouts. Interestingly, Matthias Day stated that Miles offered him this command before he offered it to Lawton, but Day had financial difficulties with the military at that time and refused the assignment. Day to Gatewood Jr. (August 9, 1926), Gatewood Collection microfilm, reel 7.

24. See Howard to Drum (February 24, 1887)), Sen. Exec. Doc. 117, 49th Cong., 2d sess., 35; Thompson report (October 7, 1886), Sen. Exec. Doc. 117, 49th Cong., 2d sess., 24, for the various engagements.

25. Gatewood to Georgia (June 25, 1886), Gatewood Collection, letter 12.

26. Gatewood to Georgia (June 25, 1886). Gatewood mistakenly thought that Alchesay, Sanchez, and the other White Mountains wanted nothing more to do with him because he had refused to allow them to kill Loco's people to avenge the raids made against their people on the reservation. Nothing could have been further from the truth, as he would learn many years later when he revisited Fort Apache and the surrounding area, writing Georgia: "Many of my old Indian friends came in to see me and inquired about you and Charley—Sanchez, Alchesay, Cooley & others, & Suviana [interpreter Severiano] as well." Gatewood to Georgia Gatewood (March 1, 1893), Gatewood Collection, letter 50.

27. Gatewood to Georgia (June 13, 1886), Gatewood Collection, letter 11, for this quote and the next one.

28. Gatewood to Georgia (June 12, 1886), Gatewood Collection, letter 10,

29. Gatewood to Georgia (July 1, 1886), Gatewood Collection, letter 14. See also Gatewood to Georgia (June 25, 1886), Gatewood Collection, letter 12. Gatewood's

correspondence at this time makes you aware of his devotion and love not only for Georgia but also for his two sons.

30. Gatewood to Georgia (July 1, 1886), Gatewood Collection, letter 14.

31. Gatewood to Georgia (June 12, 1886), Gatewood Collection, letter 10.

32. *Frostburg Mining Journal*, June 12, 1886, and July 17, 1886.

33. Lummis, *Apache Wars*, 142.

34. After Crawford's Indian scout command attacked and captured Geronimo's camp near Sierra del Bavis, Sonora, Mexico, on January 10, 1886, the captain agreed to meet with the Apache leaders. However, before the council took place, Mexican irregulars and Tarahumara Indians under the command of Santa Ana Perez attacked Crawford's scouts on January 11. When Crawford tried to stop the firefight, he was shot. He fell and banged his head. He never recovered and died on January 18. See Maus to C. S. Roberts (February 23, 1886), Crook Collection, no. 352; *Arizona Journal-Miner*, February 8, 1886 (which printed the Mexican version of the firefight); and Ball, *Days of Victorio*, 182.

Davis, like Gatewood, was not happy with Crook. He accompanied Crawford's initial pursuit of the Apaches into Mexico during the summer of 1885, and in August led an independent command into Chihuahua. After an exhausting chase that proved fruitless, he reentered the United States in September 1885. Sick of the army, Crook, and the war, he tendered his resignation, remaining on leave until his request became official on June 1, 1886. Davis, *Geronimo*, 187, 192–95; Gatewood Jr., "Britton Davis, Class of 1881," unpublished article, Gatewood Collection, letter 382; Cruse to Gatewood Jr. (January 19, 1926), Gatewood Collection, letter 179; Thrapp, *Conquest*, 332.

35. Gatewood to Miles (October 15, 1886), Gatewood Collection.

36. Gatewood to Georgia (August 26, 1886), Gatewood Collection.

37. Griswold, "Apaches," 41; Debo, *Geronimo*, 34–35; Thrapp, *Frontier Biography*, 2:547; Kraft, *Gatewood & Geronimo*, 223n20. Debo points out that the date is certainly in question and that she thinks Geronimo's dating of summer of 1858 is inaccurate.

38. Ball, *Indeh*, 181. See also 104.

39. Kraft, *Gatewood & Geronimo*, 144, 149, 164.

40. Charles B. Gatewood, "The Surrender of Geronimo," box 4, folder 59, 53 pages (hereafter cited as Gatewood, "Surrender"); and Charles B. Gatewood, "Gatewood on the Surrender of Geronimo," box 4, folder 61, 50 pages, which also includes a page numbered as 14½ and two pages numbered 45 (hereafter cited as Gatewood, "Surrender 2"). Both are in the Gatewood Collection. As in previous chapters, his words are very similar in many sections of both drafts. "Surrender" is by far the superior draft and is probably a rewrite of "Surrender 2." As such, it is the base draft for this volume. "Surrender 2" text has been merged into "Surrender" whenever it improves Gatewood's words and meaning. "Surrender"

has been printed and is the copy most often quoted. See *Journal of Arizona History* 27, no. 1 (Spring 1986), which was later reprinted as C. L. Sonnichsen, ed., *Geronimo and the End of the Apache Wars* (Lincoln: University of Nebraska Press, 1990). In 1929, Gatewood's son, Charles B. Gatewood Jr., compiled a shortened version of Gatewood's text and presented it before the Order of the Indian Wars. It has been printed in *The Papers of the Order of Indian Wars* (Fort Collins CO: Old Army Press, 1975): 103–13. "Surrender" begins with an introduction that is shortened and similar to Gatewood's introduction to the Apaches (see chapter 2). It has been cut. "Surrender 2" begins with an outline that leads one to believe that Gatewood's scope was much larger than what he actually got down on paper. As it adds nothing to this publication, it has also been cut. As both drafts refer to Capt. Henry Lawton as colonel and lieutenant colonel, they had to be written sometime after February 12, 1889, the date Lawton obtained this rank. See Altshuler, *Cavalry Yellow*, 199, for Lawton's rank.

41. Although Kayitah (1856–February 15, 1934) is the spelling of his name most often used, I have opted to use Gatewood's spelling of his name for this volume. He was also known as Kieta, Kaytah, Ke-ta, Kayihtah, Keyehtah, and Martin Kayitah. His wife, Sahn-uhshlu (b. 1860), a Nednhi, was also known as Sahn-uh-shlu and Mary. They had five children: Mary, Gsorn, Nat, Kent, and Rachel. After moving to Fort Sill, Oklahoma, with the prisoners of war (which they also became after the surrender), Ka-teah again served as a scout (1897–1900). During this time the village he lived in was known as "Ka-teah's village." See Sweeney to author (January 26, 2002), Kraft Papers; Sweeney October 2001 review of Kraft ms, Kraft Papers; Maj. James Wade to AAG, Department of Arizona (June 27, 1886), Gatewood Collection, Arizona Historical Society, Tucson; Griswold, "Apaches," 77, 121; Miles report (September 18, 1886), Sen. Exec. Doc. 117, 49th Cong., 2d sess., 40; Davis, *Geronimo*, 220; Betzinez, *Geronimo*, 143; and Debo, *Geronimo*, 270n13. Miles and Davis claim that after he (they called him Ka-teah) was wounded in an engagement (May 12, 1886) east of Santa Cruz, Sonora, while fighting to remain free with Geronimo, he returned to the reservation. Betzinez and Debo disagreed; they thought the warrior in question was Massai, a Chihenne. Ed Sweeney disagrees with everyone. His research proves that the wounded warrior who returned to the reservation was a member of Naiche's people, a Chokonen named Tah-ni-toe (also Tah-ni-to, Tametoe). See also Dan L. Thrapp, *Encyclopedia of Frontier Biography*, vol. 4. (Spokane WA: Arthur H. Clark, 1994), 269–70; Radtke, "Sons of Two Famous Indian Scouts Are Now Boy Scouts."

Martine (1858–July 31, 1937), who was also known as Martin, Martinez, Marteen, Nahteen, Martino, Old Martine, and Charles Martine, was Ka-teah's cousin and lifelong friend. His wife, Cah-gah-ahshy (b. 1866), a Nednhi also called Cah-gah-ashen, had a son by another father (Chinches or Chin-chee) who was also named Charles Martine (Martine the Younger). Martine and Cah-gah-ahshy had seven children: Bertha, Bertha (also known as Jessie to avoid confusion), George, June, Martha, Norma, and Roscoe. The second Bertha (Jessie) was born in 1904, shortly after the first Bertha's death. His sister married Chatto, and they named their daughter Maud Chatto. Martine was also cousin to one of the warriors with Geronimo in 1886, Yahnosha (Yanosha, Yahnozha). Like Ka-teah, Martine became a prisoner of war and eventually moved to Fort Sill, Oklahoma. He and his family lived in the same village as Ka-teah. After 1900, Martin headed the village, which also became known as "Martine's village." Griswold, "Apaches," 13, 94; Ball, *Indeh*, 109; Thrapp, *Frontier Biography*, 4:344–45.

42. Miles's Safe Conduct Pass (July 9, 1886), Gatewood Collection, letter 17.

43. Gatewood to Miles (October 15, 1886), Gatewood Collection.

44. George Medhurst Wratten (January 31, 1865–June 23, 1912) first came in contact with Apaches shortly after his family moved from California to Arizona when he was fourteen. Close contact with the Apaches gave him the opportunity to learn the various Apache dialects. As good Apache interpreters were a rarity, Wratten soon found employment as both an interpreter and scout. Albert E. Wratten, "George Wratten, Friend of the Apaches," *Journal of Arizona History* 27, no. 1 (Spring 1986): 91–92. Sometime after the Apache prisoners of war moved to the Mount Vernon Barracks in Alabama in 1888, Wratten married Annie, a Chokonen and Chihenne Apache. At that time she was seventeen or eighteen (she died in 1913). They had two daughters: Amy (born in 1890) and Blossom (born in 1894). Wratten and Annie divorced before the Apaches left Alabama, probably in 1894. See Griswold, "Apaches," 49. Griswold erroneously typed Annie's birth date as 1817 (it was probably 1871), which would have made her seventy-one when she married the twenty-three-year-old Wratten.

45. Wratten, "Friend of the Apaches," 91–92.

46. This paragraph is from Gatewood, "Surrender," 11–12. However, in "Surrender 2," 10, Gatewood wrote: "It was made my duty, under the orders of General Miles, to accompany these two men with proper escort for protection [from] Mexicans or Indians, & to see to it that they should have a chance to deliver their message, & that they should deliver it." Although the completion of Gatewood's mission confirms that it was his assignment from its inception, these words could—depending upon the interpretation—lend a different light on Bay-chen-daysen's assignment.

47. Gatewood hired Whaley just before he dropped into Mexico at a salary of $100 per month. Gatewood to the AAAG in the Field, Fort Bowie (July 25, 1886), Gatewood Collection.

48. Gatewood to Miles (October 15, 1886), Gatewood Collection. Thrapp, *Conquest*, 353, mistakenly claims that Gatewood set out for Mexico on July 13.

This could not have happened, as he met Miles on the thirteenth and did not reach Bowie, where he outfitted, until the fifteenth.

49. The Sierra Madres are actually two mountain ranges in Mexico, both of which are over one hundred miles wide: the 775-mile-long Sierra Madre Occidental (the western range) and the 810-mile-long Sierra Madre Oriental (the eastern range). "In the north they are desert regions, sandy and dry, dotted with creosote bush, and mesquite, yucca and ocotillo and a host of other plants . . . Farther south, where the ranges increase in altitude, their peaks [some of which are over twelve thousand feet] and high draws are home to trees and wild flowers of the temperate zones." Gatewood's search for Geronimo would be confined to the Occidental, which "is more rugged, more austere," and "contains complex, steep-sided canyons called barrancas," which can be very deep. Donald Dale Jackson and Peter Wood, *The Sierra Madre* (Alexandria VA: Time-Life Books, 1975), 21–22.

50. Parker, "Service with Gatewood," 4. See also Kraft, *Gatewood & Geronimo*, 141.

51. See Gen. James Parker, "Old Army" (manuscript form), 19, Gatewood Collection, for Gatewood's statement and Parker's reply. Thrapp, *Conquest*, 354n14, erroneously discounts Parker. Apparently he did not know how sick Gatewood was at this time or later, or that Gatewood considered quitting a number of times before completing his assignment.

52. Gatewood to Miles (August 7, 1886) and Gatewood to Miles (October 15, 1886), both in Gatewood Collection; Brig. Gen. James Parker, "The Geronimo Campaign," in *The Papers of the Order of Indian Wars* (Fort Collins CO: Old Army Press, 1975), 97 . Parker wrote, "He [Gatewood] pleaded he was sick and was not in fit condition to travel."

53. Parker, "Geronimo Campaign," 98.

54. Just before Gatewood and Parker found Lawton, they met packer Henry Daly, who had packed for Gatewood in 1883. Daly gave them directions to find Lawton's camp. He later wrote, "I was feeling so badly that I did not recognize Lieutenant Charles B. Gatewood, Sixth Cavalry, who was with the party." A strange statement, but one that cannot be ignored: Gatewood's condition had continued to deteriorate during the entire hunt for Geronimo. By this time he must have been an emaciated shadow of his normal slender self. Henry W. Daly, "The Capture of Geronimo," *American Legion Monthly* 8, no. 6 (June 1930): 31. See Wood, *Chasing Geronimo*, August 3, 1886, 88, for Gatewood's inflamed bladder.

55. Wood, *Chasing Geronimo*, August 3, 1886, 88.

56. Gatewood mistakenly refers to Parker as a captain. He was only a lieutenant at this time. Wilds Preston Richardson (March 20, 1861–May 20, 1929) joined the Eighth U.S. Infantry after he graduated from the Military Academy

in 1884 (twenty-second of thirty-seven). His company (H) was transferred from California to Arizona Territory at the end of December 1885, and he arrived at Fort Bowie in February 1886, allowing him to see extensive duty in the field that summer when he served under James Parker, who commanded a troop of Fourth U.S. Cavalry in Mexico. After seeing duty in the Southwest, he saw extensive duty in Alaska beginning in 1897. Richardson became a first lieutenant in 1889, captain in 1898, major in 1904 (Ninth U.S. Infantry), lieutenant colonel in 1911 (he had transferred to the Thirteenth U.S. Infantry in 1908), colonel in 1914, and brigadier general in 1917 (National Army) serving in France as part of the Thirty-ninth Division. Returning to the United States in 1919, he reverted to his regular army rank of colonel (March 15, 1920) and retired six and a half months later (October 31, 1920). A year after his death, Congress posthumously promoted him to brigadier general (June 21, 1930). Altshuler, *Cavalry Yellow*, 279–80; Thrapp, *Frontier Biography*, 4:439–40.

57. Gatewood miscounted; Parker's command consisted of sixty-two men. In addition to the troop of cavalry and detachment of infantry, Parker also had fifteen Yaqui Indian scouts and a pack train. See Parker, "Service with Gatewood," 3; Richardson to Gatewood Jr. (February 10, 1926), Gatewood Collection, letter 201. Richardson did not think much of Parker's Yaqui scouts, whom he called Mexicans.

58. This sentence is from Gatewood, "Surrender 2," 11, and has been used here as it is a better lead-in to this section. In it, Gatewood referred to Lawton as "colonel," using instead the captain's rank at the time of the writing of the draft. In "Surrender," 15, Gatewood wrote: "In a few days, we arrived at the camp of Captain Lawton, who has since been promoted to a lieutenant-colonelcy in the Inspector General's Department." The "boundary line" Gatewood refers to is the United States–Mexico border.

59. When Gatewood found Lawton and decided to attach himself with the captain, he wrote: "I have the honor to report to you that my escort, the command of Lieutenant Parker, 4th Cavalry, is in such condition as to be unable to proceed further, and has accordingly returned to the United States. I therefore request to be allowed to accompany your command subject to your orders, until circumstances may favor carrying out the instructions of the Commander of the Department of Arizona." Gatewood to Lawton (August 6, 1886), Gatewood Collection microfilm, reel 7.

60. This and the next two paragraphs are only in Gatewood, "Surrender 2," 11–14½.

61. See Kraft, *Gatewood & Geronimo*, 145–48.

62. Thomas J. Clay to the post adjutant, Fort Huachuca (August 17, 1886), Gatewood Collection.

63. Leonard Wood, *Chasing Geronimo*, August 19, 1886, 98. For Wood's refusal

to grant a medical discharge, see Wood, *Chasing Geronimo*, 135n7; and Richardson to Gatewood Jr. (February 10, 1926), Gatewood Collection, letter 201.

Leonard Wood (October 9, 1860–August 7, 1927) received his medical degree from Harvard Medical School in 1884. After failing in private practice, he became an assistant surgeon in the Army Medical Corp (January 5, 1886), stationed at Fort Huachuca, Arizona. When Lawton's command moved into Mexico in May 1886, Wood accompanied it as medical officer. Wood's stamina proved exceptional, and he served with Lawton during the entire scout, seeing it through to Geronimo and Naiche's surrender to Miles in September, and in May 1898 he received the Medal of Honor for his conduct during the campaign. In 1887, he transferred to California to serve at Miles's headquarters, which would again place him in close proximity with Gatewood. Undoubtedly Gatewood's requests to return to the United States during the hunt for Geronimo for medical reasons and Wood's refusal to grant the requests, along with the proposed murder of Geronimo and the Apaches during the return trek, continued to act as a barrier in their personal and professional relationship. At the conclusion of the campaign, Wood joined Miles's inner circle whereas Gatewood forever hovered on the edge. Marrying Louise Condit Smith in 1890, Wood's career continued to flourish. He became a colonel in the Rough Riders (May 8, 1898) and saw action in Cuba, becoming a brigadier general of volunteers (July 8, 1898), major general of volunteers (December 7, 1898), and military governor of Cuba (1899). In 1901 he became a brigadier general in the regular army, and in 1904, after a swirl of controversy, a major general, and in 1916, chief of staff. After that time his career suffered a number of setbacks, including an unsuccessful bid for the Republican nomination for president in 1920. Altshuler, *Cavalry Yellow*, 376–77; Thrapp, *Frontier Biography*, 3:1590; Kraft, *Gatewood & Geronimo*, 146–47, 150, 184–85.

64. The number of men that accompanied Gatewood ranges from six to sixteen Indian scouts and from six to ten soldiers. See George A. Forsyth to William A. Thompson (August 21, 1886), Gatewood Collection; Wood, *Chasing Geronimo*, August 19, 1886, 98; Daly, "The Capture of Geronimo," 31. Daly mistakenly places Tom Horn with Gatewood at this time.

65. L. Arvizu to Governor of Sonora, Mexico (August 31, 1886), microfilm, Historic Archives of Sonora, reel 24 (Sonoran State Archives, roll 24), Arizona Historical Society, Tucson; Bill Hoy, *Spanish Terms of the Sonoran Desert Borderlands* (Calexico CA: Institute for Border Studies, San Diego State University, 1993), 23.

66. This paragraph is a merging of Gatewood, "Surrender 2," 14½; Gatewood, "Surrender," 16, and a loose page in "Surrender," new p. 20, that is part of a handful of loose and randomly numbered pages contained at the rear of "Surrender."

67. This figure is from Gatewood, "Surrender 2," 15. In Gatewood, "Surrender,"

16, Gatewood puts the mileage at seventy. Actually, here he is referring to the entire trip.

68. Wilber Elliott Wilder (August 16, 1856–January 30, 1952) first served in Indian Territory as a member of the Fourth U.S. Cavalry after graduation from the Military Academy in 1877 (thirty-second of seventy-six). After transferring to the Southwest, he won the Medal of Honor for his participation in the action at Horseshoe Cañon, New Mexico, on April 23, 1882. On January 16, 1884, he married Violet Blair Martin. Two and a half years later, he served in Mexico and was in Fronteras when Geronimo and Naiche sent two women there to obtain supplies from the prefect while supposedly negotiating a meeting. He met these women and supposedly sent word to the Apache leaders that they should deal with the Americans and not with the Mexicans. He became a captain in 1891, colonel in 1898 (Fourteenth New York Volunteer Infantry), lieutenant colonel in 1899 (Forty-third U.S. Volunteer Infantry), major in 1901 (Fourteenth U.S. Cavalry), lieutenant colonel in 1906 (Eleventh U.S. Cavalry), colonel in 1911 (Fifth U.S. Cavalry), and brigadier general in 1917 (National Army). He reverted to his regular army rank of colonel in 1919, only to be promoted to brigadier general seven years after he retired in 1920 (February 28, 1927). Altshuler, *Cavalry Yellow*, 368–69.

69. In Gatewood, "Surrender 2," 16, Gatewood's words have a different meaning; instead of massacring everyone: "the men would be killed & their women & children sold into slavery."

70. Kraft, *Gatewood & Geronimo*, 151–52.

71. Thomas Horn (November 21, 1860–November 20, 1903) served the army as packer, interpreter, and scout. He would later write-narrate a book about his life in the West wherein he embroidered the truth of his participation in what actually happened. Thrapp, who listed Horn as "scout, assassin," dismissed Horn's memoirs as "largely fictitious, and rarely dependable." Thrapp, *Frontier Biography*, 2:675.

72. Gatewood also still had his own "small outfit" of Wratten, Martine, Kateah, and Huston with him.

In 1885 Clay became ill with dysentery while stationed in New Mexico and returned to his home state of Kentucky to recover. By the summer of 1886, he had returned to the Southwest and volunteered to join Lawton's command, which was already in Mexico hunting the warring Apaches. After delivering supplies to Lawton, whom he joined south of Cuchuta Ranch in Sonora, he became Lawton's battalion adjutant. See Thomas J. Clay, "Some Unwritten Incidents of the Geronimo Campaign," in *The Papers of the Order of Indian Wars* (Fort Collins CO: Old Army Press, 1975), 114.

73. Ward was a pseudonym that American humorist Charles Farrar Browne (1834–67) used when he wrote a column for the *Cleveland Plain Dealer*. The

fictitious Ward, a traveling showman, became notorious for his poor grammar and spelling, which in turn made him immensely popular—so much so that Brown adopted the name. In 1859 he joined the staff of *Vanity Fair*, and with the success of a humorous lecture, "The Babes in the Wood" (1861), he became a professional lecturer. *Funk & Wagnalls New Encyclopedia*, 29 vols. (New York: Funk & Wagnalls, 1986), 27:148.

74. Although this section on the march has a good mix from both drafts, the finding of the pants is from Gatewood, "Surrender," 20. However, in Gatewood, "Surrender 2," 19, Gatewood describes the discovery totally differently, almost making one think that the pants could be a good omen: "We discovered what might be taken as a signal to us that we might proceed without harm, & that was a faded pair of canvass trousers hung up on a bush near the trail & at the entrance of a canyon that offered a fine chance of ambush. Whether to trust the apparent significance of the flag or not, was a serious question."

75. Gatewood named the day as August 23 (see Gatewood, "Surrender," 22), but he was off by a day. His error has led others to date the meeting with Geronimo incorrectly. See Gatewood to Miles (October 15, 1886), Gatewood Collection, for the correct date. Gatewood mistakenly called the Teres Mountains the "Torres" in "Surrender," 22.

76. Martine brought a gift with him. "Geronimo . . . had cooked some mescal and from this he took in his two hands enough of this mescal to make a lump about the size of a man's heart. This he squeezed together, wrapped it up and told [me] to take [it] to Lieut[enant] Gatewood. He said that [it] was a token of his surrender and that when the mescal had been sent there would be no reason for Gatewood to doubt his earnestness in planning to give up." Martine and Kayitah, "The Story of the Final Surrender of Geronimo," as told to O. M. Boggess, Superintendent of the Mescalero Indian Reservation (September 25, 1925), Gatewood Collection, 3. See also "Indian Scout Tells of Geronimo's Surrender; Two Captors Live on New Mexico Reservation," *San Diego Union*, May 24, 1927.

77. Most of this sentence is from Gatewood, "Surrender 2," 22. It is considerably longer than what Gatewood said in "Surrender," 23: "[Naiche] . . . sent word that we would be perfectly safe so long as we behaved ourselves."

78. In "Surrender," 23, Gatewood states that Brown had thirty Indian scouts. Robert Alexander Brown (November 7, 1859–September 30, 1937) graduated from the Military Academy in 1885 (eleventh in a class of thirty-nine) and joined the Fourth U.S. Cavalry just in time for the last Apache war. During the summer of 1886 he commanded Indian scouts in Mexico. Over the years Brown would rise in rank to first lieutenant in 1891 (Seventh U.S. Cavalry) and captain in 1899 (Eighth U.S. Cavalry). Twice during the late 1890s he became a major of volunteers (1G), and during the second tenure he served as aide to Gen.

Arthur MacArthur in the Philippines. He eventually became a colonel in 1916 and brigadier general of the National Army in 1917 during World War I, but this rank was reduced to colonel when he joined the First Division, Army of Occupation in 1919. Altshuler, *Cavalry Yellow*, 45.

79. Abiel Leonard Smith (July 14, 1857–April 24, 1946) graduated from the Military Academy a year after Gatewood (fortieth in a class of forty-three). However, at this time he outranked Gatewood due to the seniority rule, having become a first lieutenant on June 30, 1883. Gatewood did not become a first lieutenant until January 3, 1885. After graduation from the Military Academy, Smith was assigned to the Nineteenth U.S. Infantry but quickly transferred to the Fourth U.S. Cavalry, where he served in Texas, Kansas, and New Mexico, before serving in Arizona Territory. He received a brevet for his participation in the hunt for Geronimo in Mexico during the summer of 1886. Smith married Florence Compton in Walla Walla, Washington, on June 29, 1890. He became a captain in 1892, major in 1898, lieutenant colonel in 1901, colonel in 1905, brigadier general in 1916, and retired two years later. Altshuler, *Cavalry Yellow*, 306.

80. Lawton to Gatewood (August 24, 1886), Gatewood Collection.

81. S. M. Huddleson, "An Interview with Geronimo and His Guardian, Mr. G. M. Wratten," 2, in the Gatewood Collection; and Martine and Kayitah, "Surrender," 3–4.

82. Martine and Kayitah, "Surrender," 4. See Wratten Interview, 4, for the amount of time before the Apaches appeared at the location for the meeting.

83. While a prisoner, Ahnandia (1860–February 7, 1892), who later used the name Ralph Ahnandia, learned to speak English at Fort Pickens, Florida. Using his new skill, he worked with interpreter George Wratten translating his people's words. After the move to the Mount Vernon Barracks in Alabama, he returned to his first wife, Dahn (Chihenne Apache). He died of tuberculosis. Griswold, "Apaches," 1–2.

Tah-das-te (b. 1860) married Ahnandia just before he went on the warpath for the last time. She was also known as Dah-des-ih, Dah-des-ti, Dah-des-te, Tdah-das-te, and Tah-das-te. Her sister was one of Naiche's wives, Ilth-goz-ey. Griswold, "Apaches," 130.

84. Beshe (b. 1816) had many names, including Be-she, Bes-he, Bishi, Beche, Bishee, Bish-shee, and Old Bishop. Along with his wife, U-go-hun (b. 1828), a Chokonen Apache who was also known as No-goh-hin, U-go-hin, and W-go-hnn, Beshe was still living when the U.S. government moved the Apache prisoners to Fort Sill, Oklahoma. U-go-hun was not only Ha-o-zinne's mother but also Zhonne's mother by another husband whose name has been lost to time. Griswold, "Apaches," 7, 143.

Ha-o-zinne (b. 1862) also used the names Hau-zhinne, Hah-o-zinney, and

Hau-zinna, which mean "Standing Up Straight Like a Tree." She and Naiche had six children: Christian Jr., Jacob, Amelia, Hazel, Granville, and Roscoe Naiche. She lived to see the end of the Apaches' confinement as prisoners of war and moved to the Mescalero Reservation with Naiche. Griswold, "Apaches," 55.

85. Zhonne (b. 1865) lived to return to the Mescalero Reservation after the Apache exile ended. He was given the name Calvin and was sometimes known as Calvin Zlomme. He was born before his mother, U-go-hun, married Beshe, and his father's name is unknown. After the surrender in 1886, Zhonne entered the Carlisle school on July 8, 1888, at the age of thirty-five. After completing his education seven years later, he moved to Fort Sill, Oklahoma Territory, and married Lucy Loo-is-ah (Lozah), whom he most likely met at Carlisle when she was married to Tsisnah. They moved the Mescalero Reservation when presented the opportunity. Griswold, "Apaches," 89, 153.

86. Fun's (1866–92) Apache names were Yiy-zholl, Yiy-gholl, and Yiy-joll; he was also known as Larry Fun. His siblings included Tsisnah, (Benedict) Jozha and Jah-ken-ish-ishn (Black Girl). Although Ball, *Indeh*, 172n2, lists Perico and he as brothers, they were only half brothers, having the same father, Nas-tih-deh, "who died at San Carlos 'long ago,'" and different mothers. Ball, 8, also lists Fun as a half brother of Geronimo, but this seems inaccurate. After becoming a prisoner of war and making the prisoner move to the Mount Vernon Barracks in Alabama, Fun joined the Twelfth Infantry (Co. I) and became a corporal. He later became a sergeant in the Seventh Cavalry (Troop L). Griswold, "Apaches," 40, 118, 142.

Tsisnah (1864–1900), whose name is pronounced "Chis-nah," had the following Apache names: Tisnah, Chisnah, and Tesuah. In captivity, he was known as Burdette Tsisnah. His other siblings included (Benedict) Jozha and Jah-ken-ish-ishn (Black Girl). Perico and he had the same father, Nas-tih-deh. Unlike his brother Fun, he attended the Carlisle Indian School in Pennsylvania (April 30, 1887–November 10, 1890) with his wife, Lozah (b. 1868), a Chokonen Apache who was also known as Lucy Loo-is-ah. After they left Carlisle and returned to the Mount Vernon Barracks in Alabama, he enlisted in the Twelfth Infantry (Co. I) and eventually attained the rank of sergeant. After the move to Fort Sill, Oklahoma, Tsisnah divorced Lozah and married Big Belle, and Lozah married Zhonne. Neither marriage garnered any children for Tsisnah. Griswold, "Apaches," 89, 118, 142.

Perico (b. 1852) was also known as White Horse. His half brothers, who also surrendered in 1886, included Tsisnah, Fun, and Eyelash. His first cousin was Dakluge, who as a boy eventually surrendered with Mangus and later became Geronimo's interpreter when the old warrior dictated what eventually became his autobiography. Second cousin to Geronimo (and not his brother), Perico was also related to Betzinez (first cousin), Naiche's second wife (E-clah-heh), and Ahnandia (first cousin). When the Apaches made their last breakout from captivity in May 1885, his first wife, Hah-dun-key, accompanied him. She was captured on August 7, 1885, when Captain (not Major) Wirt Davis's Indian scouts attacked Geronimo's camp. In November 1885 Geronimo, he, and others raided Fort Apache. One of the women they captured was Bi-ya-neta Tse-dah-dilth-thlilth, a Bedonkohe and Chihenne Apache (b. 1858), who became Perico's second wife. They would eventually have five children. Griswold, "Apaches," 40, 118, 142; Ball, *Indeh*, 8, 174 and n. 2; Robinson, *Voices*, 112; and Kraft, *Gatewood & Geronimo*, 100, 103, 139.

87. Jasper Kanseah (1873–1959), at age thirteen, was Geronimo's youngest warrior at the time of the 1886 surrender. He entered the Carlisle Indian School on November 4, 1886, and spent the next nine years as a student, leaving on November 7, 1895. He eventually moved to the Mescalero Apache Reservation, where he died. Griswold, "Apaches," 75.

88. Chee-hash-kish, a Bedonkohe, married Geronimo after his first wife, Gee-esh-kizn (also known as Alope), was killed by Mexican troops in 1850. Mexicans captured her in 1882 at Casas Grandes, Chihuahua, Mexico, when Geronimo and other Apaches tried to negotiate a peace at that pueblo—their goal being to obtain mescal and aguardiente. On the first day of the negotiations, everything went well and the Apaches and Mexicans celebrated together. However, before dawn, the Mexicans attacked the Apaches. Many died, many were captured, and some, including Geronimo, escaped. Geronimo never saw Chee-hash-kish again. It has been rumored that she eventually married one of the warriors captured with her. Griswold, "Apaches," 18, 59; Kraft, *Gatewood & Geronimo*, 13–14, 223n20.

Chappo (1864–c. September 18, 1894) was also known as Chapo, Chapa, and Charpo. His full sister was Dohn-say (Lulu Geronimo, Lucy Dohn-say, Tozey), who married one of Geronimo's warriors, Dahkeya (Dahkuja, Mike Dah-ke-ya), who was a Nednhi Apache. After moving to the Mount Vernon Barracks, Alabama, the government shipped Chappo to the Carlisle Indian School in Pennsylvania (July 8, 1888). While there he became ill with tuberculosis and on August 7, 1894, he returned to the Mount Vernon Barracks. A little over a month later he was scheduled to rejoin his people, who had moved to Fort Sill, Oklahoma, but this transfer never happened, and he died at the Barracks. Griswold, "Apaches," 27, 43–44; H. Henrietta Stockel, *Survival of the Spirit: Chiricahua Apaches in Captivity* (Reno: University of Nevada Press, 1993), 135.

Noh-chlon (b. 1870), a Bedonkohe also known as Nahd-Clohnn, was truly a child bride because she was only sixteen at the time of the final surrender. Although her exact death date and that of her child with Chappo are unknown, their lives were not long, as both died in either Florida or Alabama. Griswold, "Apaches," 43, 100.

89. Siki Toclanni's (1866–1967) mother was Clee-hn by an unnamed husband

before becoming the third wife of Chihenne chieftain Loco. Also known as Juanita, her cousin was the Chihenne Apache James Kaywaykla, who told his story to Eve Ball (*In the Days of Victorio*). Siki had been at Tres Castillos, Chihuahua, Mexico, on October 15, 1880, when Victorio and seventy-seven other Apaches died. Captured along with sixty-seven others, she had been sold into slavery only to escape three years later. Stockel, *Apache Nation*, 36–37. On that night of horror, soldiers "dragged [Siki] from her horse and tied [her] to a scrubby tree." Ball, *Days of Victorio*, 169. See 170–74 for her ordeal in captivity and escape. She married Rogers Toclanni (or *Toclanny*), a scout, soon after her escape. Their marriage endured the years as prisoners of war: he worked with other Apache leaders to gain their freedom and eventually traveled to Washington DC, with other delegates, to discuss the end of their incarceration. Both survived the exile to return to the Southwest, living their final days at Whitetail on the Mescalero Apache Reservation. See H. Henrietta Stockel, *Chiricahua Apache Women and Children: Safekeepers of the Heritage* (College Station: Texas A&M University Press, 2000), 66, for her marriage and return to the reservation; Betzinez, *Geronimo*, 190; Ball, *Indeh*, 290, for Toclanni's efforts to end Apache imprisonment; Robinson, *Voices*, 29, 271, for her Mexican name and blood relations; and Jo Martín, "Women Warriors: Secret Weapon of the Apaches," *New Mexico* 75, no. 8 (August 1997): 94, for the date of her death.

   Lozen (d. June 17, 1889), Victorio's younger sister, supposedly never married. Little is known about her. Sherry Robinson called her "a female warrior and medicine woman, . . . a remarkable person in any time and [in] any culture." Robinson, *Voices*, 3. Robinson states, "Their [historians'] skepticism and cautions noted, I say this: Lozen was real. Along with comments about her in transcripts, I found two pieces of information [while going through Eve Ball's papers] that settled the question for me. One was James Kaywaykla's handwritten note describing Lozen, who was his aunt. The other was Eve's note to herself on a Kaywaykla transcript: 'Find out more about Lozen.' These are hardly the words of someone in the process of making up a character." Robinson quotes Eve Ball: "Lozen was no ordinary woman and the Warm Springs [Chihenne] regarded her . . . as a holy woman because of the Power she had of locating the enemy and of healing," and "Geronimo's people called her Woman Warrior. Her own Warm Springs Apaches called her Little Sister and revered her as a holy person" (4). Kaywaykla said, "She could ride, shoot, and fight like a man." Ball, *Days of Victorio*, 21. She died at the Mount Vernon Barracks of tuberculosis. Martín, "Women Warriors," 94. Griswold, "Apaches," 90, claims that Lozen's name was pronounced "Lu-zen." For additional information on Lozen, see Robinson, *Voices*, 3–15; Martín, "Women Warriors," 92, 94; Ball, *Days of Victorio*, 9–10, 14–15; Stockel, *Chiricahua Women*, 72–75; and Stockel, *Apache Nation*, 29–30, 43, 46.

   90. Yahnosha (1865–c. 1954), a Nednhi and Chokonen Apache, was also known

as Yanosha, Yahnozha, Yahnoza, Edwin Yahnosha, and Edward Yahnosha. His sister, She-gha, was Geronimo's fourth wife. Yahnosha was supposedly related to Naiche, and later when he married a Chihenne named Rachel Tsikahda, he became related to Loco and his family. Four of their children died in captivity at Fort Sill, Oklahoma. Another two lived to see the end of the Apache exile and moved to the Mescalero Reservation in New Mexico with their parents in 1913. Their last child was born shortly after they returned to New Mexico. Griswold, "Apaches," 148; and Debo, *Geronimo*, 91 (and n. 11).

Little is known of La-zi-yah (1840–96) and his brother Nah-bay (b. 1841), who were also known as Lie-sah and Lazaiyah and as Nah-ba, Nahi, and Nay-bay. Nah-bay's infant girl has been lost to the ages. Griswold, "Apaches," 86, 100; Stanley to AG, Washington DC (October 11, 1886), NA, M689, roll 186.

The Nednhi Apache Garditha (b. 1876) was a "[y]oung orphan boy with Geronimo's band at the final surrender." Also known as Gat-deet-cleh, Gat-delt-eh, and Kact-hah, he was either Charlotte's brother or cousin. Griswold, "Apaches," 40, 89.

Hunlona (1865–March 9, 1895) was also known as Hunloua, Lo-nah, Han-lun-eh, Hunlueh, Eli Hunlona, and Dutch. It is not known whether his wife, Do-lan (1850–1900), a Chokonen, surrendered with Geronimo and Naiche. Their daughter, Bessie Hunlona, eventually became Bessie Gooday. Hunlona became a student at Carlisle on July 8, 1888, and died there six and a half years later. Griswold, "Apaches," 31, 58.

Alchintoyeh (1877–c. 1919/20) was the son of E-jo-nah (1834–1900), a Nednhi and sister of Sam Kenoi's mother. Also called Althchintoyah, Alchintoyah, Al-chin-eh-to-yah, and Regis Alchintoyeh, he attended Carlisle from April 30, 1887, until November 7, 1895. After leaving school, he moved to Fort Sill, Oklahoma, and then to Apache, Oklahoma. He eventually married a Comanche woman, but her name is unknown. Griswold, "Apaches," 3, 34. His riding with the band at the September 1886 surrender raises questions: How did mother and son become separated? Did she return to the United States with the bulk of the band after surrendering to Crook at the end of March 1886? If so, why did Alchintoyeh not accompany her?

Charlotte (b. 1877), a Nednhi, has also been called Lo-sahnne, Lo Sahnne, Charlotte Leo Sahnne, Le Salinne, and Leo Sahumi. She was either the sister or cousin of Garditha, who also surrendered with Geronimo in 1886. In later years, she became Talbot Gooday's second wife (an unknown date sometime after 1890) but the marriage did not last, ending somewhere around 1893. If this dating is correct, she was a very young divorcée. She subsequently married Horace Yah-nah-ki (whom she later divorced) and Fred Godeley, and she ended her life at Mescalero. Griswold, "Apaches," 89.

91. Eyelash (1870–1950), also known as Lot, was the uncle of Annie, who later

married George Wratten. During 1882–83, he rode the war trail with Geronimo as an apprentice warrior and horse holder, and would later surrender with Geronimo and Naiche in 1886. His first wife, Edith Jones, lived long enough to see captivity at Fort Sill, Oklahoma; his second wife was Chatto's sister, Gotsi (d. 1905); and his last wife was Beatrice Kaihtel. Griswold, "Apaches," 36.

In *Geronimo*, 63 (and n. 11) Debo states that She-gha (c. 1851–September 28, 1887), a Nednhi and Chokonen Apache, who was Yahnosha's sister, became Geronimo's fourth wife sometime around 1861, but this does not seem possible, for she would have been a very young bride. Debo adds (*Geronimo*, 91) a possible second wedding year, 1871, and this seems much more reasonable. She would be with Geronimo at the surrender, only to be separated in Florida. By the time the government transferred her to Fort Pickens, Alabama, her health had deteriorated, most likely from pneumonia, and she died there. See also Stanley to AG, Washington DC (October 11, 1886), NA, M689, roll 186; Debo, *Geronimo*, 333–34; Griswold, "Apaches," 148.

92. In *Gatewood & Geronimo* I mistakenly said that Perico held Geronimo's son, Robert Geronimo, in this photo. This is an impossibility, as Robert was born August 2, 1889. See Debo, *Geronimo*, 342; Griswold, "Apaches," 44.

93. Panocha is raw or coarse sugar made in Mexico that is available in loaf form.

94. The sentence on the tobacco was pulled from an additional loose p. 25 that was grouped with the other loose edited pages at the back of Gatewood, "Surrender."

95. Gatewood is referring to Geronimo's brother-in-law Yahnosha; his sister was She-gha.

96. This paragraph is from Gatewood, "Surrender 2," 16–17, and is from earlier in the manuscript. It seemed out of place in the earlier location, as Gatewood had not yet found Geronimo.

97. Gatewood's entourage consisted of Martine, Wratten, Horn, perhaps Yestes, and a soldier who may have been named Koch. Martin Koch was either a member of Lawton's Troop B (Fourth U.S. Cavalry) or Troop G (Fourth U.S. Cavalry). See Wratten Interview, 5; Gatewood Jr. to Hermann Hagedorn (May 11, 1929), letter 368; Charles Maurer to Gatewood Jr. (June 4, 1926), letter 265; War Department, Adjutant General's Office, Memo, which includes muster rolls for Troop B for the months of June and August 1886 (May 3, 1926), letter 254. All are in the Gatewood Collection. Although Maurer states that Koch told him that he was with Gatewood, Koch does not appear on these rolls. See also Gatewood Jr., "Men with Father on Trip from Fronteras," Gatewood Collection microfilm, reel 4. Maurer also stated that Koch was a sergeant in Troop M, 3rd Cavalry, before joining the Fourth Cavalry. Unfortunately, the U.S. Army kept no records

of the soldiers with Gatewood after he left Fronteras. C. A. Bach to Gatewood Jr. (February 1, 1926), Gatewood Collection microfilm, reel 7.

98. The Southwestern land Geronimo refers to is the land that the Bedonkohes, Chokonens, and Chihennes claimed as their own prior to the U.S. invasion.

99. This paragraph and the next paragraph are only in Gatewood, "Surrender," 29–30.

100. The U.S. government did not round up these Apaches until August 30, 1886. Their journey east to Florida did not begin immediately, and the train that carried them into exile did not pass Albuquerque until the morning of September 14. See O. O. Howard to AG, Washington DC (August 30, 1886) and Howard to AG, Washington DC (September 14, 1886), Sen. Exec. Doc. 83, 51st Cong., 1st sess, 24–25, 28.

101. Naiche's second wife was E-clah-heh (1859–1909), a Bedonkohe Apache. His daughter was Dorothy (1876–1946), a Chokonen-Bedonkohe-Chihenne Apache, who eventually married James Kaywaykla. Her Apache name was Dehkluh-kizhee. Naiche's mother was Dos-teh-she, also known as Dos-tes-ey and Doh-teh-seh (b. 1838), which means "Something at the Campfire Already Cooked," was a Mimbreño Apache. Her father was Mangas Coloradas. Dos-teh-she, E-clah-hey, and Dorothy returned to the United States after the Apaches surrendered to Crook at Cañon de los Embudos, Sonora, Mexico, in March 1886. Griswold, "Apaches," 32, 34, 79, 106–7.

102. This paragraph is from Gatewood, "Surrender 2," 28–30.

103. In Gatewood, "Surrender 2," 31–32, this section appears at this location in the course of events. However, in Gatewood, "Surrender," 34–35, this section comes later, just before he is about to leave. As the placement in "Surrender 2" seems more logical, the corresponding section in "Surrender" has been moved forward and merged.

104. This merged paragraph regarding talking all night appears before Geronimo asking about Miles in Gatewood, "Surrender," 31, and after Geronimo asking about Miles in Gatewood, "Surrender 2," 34. It seems logical that this part of the conversation happened before the questions about Miles.

105. In this instance, "anzhoo" means "good."

106. This statement is from Gatewood, "Surrender," 33, and it is different from what Gatewood said in "Surrender 2," 34: "Geronimo then remarked that the President must be a good-hearted man to send such a commander to relieve the only one [meaning Crook] whom he himself had known, & it showed a like quality in his new general to send a messenger so far to make known his wishes."

107. Most of this paragraph is from Gatewood, "Surrender 2," 36–37. In Gatewood, "Surrender," 33, Gatewood lists his base camp as four miles distant.

108. Chappo, the "boy warrior son" of Geronimo, was twenty-two years old in 1886. Stockel, *Survival of the Spirit*, 135.

109. Lawton arrived at Gatewood's camp shortly before night. Wood, *Chasing Geronimo*, August 25, 1886, 101; Lawton to AG, Department of Arizona (September 9, 1886), Sen. Exec. Doc. 117, 49th Cong., 2d sess., 47.

110. This paragraph is only in Gatewood, "Surrender 2," 39–40. Gatewood erroneously overwrote "fifteen" and changed the number to "thirty" pounds of tobacco; earlier he stated that Lawton had sent him fifteen pounds of tobacco.

111. This paragraph is only in Gatewood, "Surrender," 38.

112. T. J. Clay to Gatewood Jr. (July 27, 1926), Gatewood Collection microfilm, reel 7.

113. Gatewood to Georgia (August 26, 1886), Gatewood Collection.

114. Gatewood's dating continues to be off. Wood, *Chasing Geronimo*, August 28, 1886, 104. In Gatewood, "Surrender 2," 41, Gatewood states: "On the 2nd day, we had had just halted to go into camp, when the disappointed Mexican commander . . . ," while in Gatewood, "Surrender," 39, he states: "We broke camp August 24th, & on the 26th, the disappointed Mexican commander . . ." In both instances, he is not close to getting the dates correct. As the years passed, others would also get this date wrong: for example, Cruse, in *Days*, 231, and Thrapp, in *Conquest*, 360, both named August 25 as the date of departure for the United States.

115. Lawton sent Wood and Smith to meet Aguirre. Wood immediately set out on his mule. Smith and Horn followed him. See Lawton to CO, District of Huachuca (August 28, 1886), Gatewood Collection; Wood, *Chasing Geronimo*, August 28, 1886, 105–6.

116. Wood, in *Chasing Geronimo*, August 28, 1886, 106, identifies himself as the courier.

117. This paragraph is only in Gatewood, "Surrender 2," 43.

118. Actually, Gatewood arrived with Geronimo, as did Naiche, Wratten, Lt. Robert Walsh, and three Apaches. See Wood, *Chasing Geronimo*, August 28, 1886, 106; R. D. Walsh to Gatewood Jr. (May 3, 1926), Gatewood Collection, letter 256; "Geronimo: Details of His Submission to the Inevitable," *Mississippi Republican*, November 22, 1886. Walsh stated that Geronimo and Aguirre only had two men with them (Naiche was one of Geronimo's seconds) and that they were mounted the entire time. "Inevitable" also had both sides mounted, including Gatewood. The American officers were off to the side. They were not mounted.

119. The direct quotes are only in Gatewood, "Surrender," 41–42, except for "nothing further," which is from Gatewood, "Surrender 2," 45.

120. This is from Gatewood, "Surrender," 42. In Gatewood, "Surrender 2," 45, he wrote: "We allowed them, however, to send several soldiers with us to carry back to them the news of the surrender when it should be finally accomplished." Note that there are two p. 45 in "Surrender 2." The text flows smoothly from

one page to the next. Apparently, Gatewood numbered the pages incorrectly and never realized it as no effort had been made to fix the error.

121. Martine and Kayitah, "Surrender," 4; Anton Mazzanovich, *Trailing Geronimo,* ed. E. A. Brininstool (Los Angeles: Gem, 1926), 252; Lawton to the CO, District of Huachuca (August 28, 1886), Gatewood Collection; Wratten Interview, 5.

122. Wood, *Chasing Geronimo,* August 29, 1886, 107.

123. Clay, "Incidents," 115.

124. Gatewood's statement is strange and contradicts itself. Most likely he had forgotten exactly how much time had passed before the Apaches traveled this distance. Since the Indians could easily travel this distance in a day, it logically follows that Gatewood refers to only one day, August 29. See Wood, *Chasing Geronimo,* August 29, 1886, 107, for a confirmation of the date and the distance traveled; eight of the twenty miles would come after the halt.

125. This is Perico's second wife, Bi-ya-neta Tse-dah-dilth-thlilth. Perico was not Geronimo's brother-in-law.

126. Eating with Perico's family is from Gatewood, "Surrender," 42–44. His version of the same meal in Gatewood, "Surrender 2," 45–47, was not merged and is presented here in its entirety. Notice that here, Gatewood also mentions a soldier. "Therefore, we had to do the best we could. There were Lieutenant Clay, Dr. Wood, myself, & one soldier. Our combined supply of rations consisted of one can of condensed milk that happened to be in my saddlebags. Night was coming on & the inner man had not yet been refreshed. Wandering around the camp, I noticed the squaw of Perico, brother-in-law of Geronimo, preparing the evening meal for the family. Perico was sitting there fondling one of his children, & I entered into conversation with him, & asked his squaw for a drink of water. Pieces of freshly killed venison were roasting on the coals, the coffee pot was exhaling a most appetizing flavor. The squaw was making tortillas, & tin plates & cups were laid out on the ground. He invited me to dine with them & I immediately accepted, saying that my two friends were also hungry as well as the soldier, & all we had was the can of milk which was donated to the mess. He directed the squaw to get out all their table service, a miscellaneous assortment of tin plates, cups, & iron forks, & motioning me to a seat on a stone, remarked that he was going to invite the others. He managed to give us a very palatable dinner, giving his own cup to Clay, & waiting on his himself. He did not need a fork for himself, for he would stick the end of a slice of meat in his mouth & cut it off with his hunting knife."

127. Wood, *Chasing Geronimo,* August 29, 1886, 107.

128. Clay, "Incidents," 115.

129. Wood, *Chasing Geronimo,* August 30, 1886, 107–8.

130. Frank C. Lockwood, *The Apache Indians.* (1938; repr., Lincoln: Univer-

sity of Nebraska Press, 1966), 306. Lockwood placed this statement at the San Bernardino Ranch; however, if the conversation between Smith and Lawton took place, it had to have been on the trail. Apparently, Gatewood Jr. approached Abiel Smith for information regarding Gatewood's actions in Mexico and received no response, which is not surprising. He pointed this out to Gatewood's friend, Matthias Day, who mistakenly thought that Smith guarded waterholes on the United States–Mexico border during the final days of the Apache war. See Day to Gatewood Jr. (August 9, 1926), Gatewood Collection microfilm, reel 7.

131. Wood, *Chasing Geronimo*, August 30–31, 1886, 108; Miles to Lawton (August 31, 1886), Gatewood Collection, letter 403. There are two dispatches dated the same day from Miles to Lawton urging the captain to make the Apaches real prisoners, and both are stored in the same grouping in the Gatewood Collection.

132. Beginning with the Apaches' fear upon arriving at Guadalupe Cañon through Lawton ordering Gatewood to remain with the command is only in Gatewood, "Surrender," 44–49. Gatewood's memory again failed him regarding the timing of events. On 44, he actually wrote: "A day or two afterward . . ." See Wood, *Chasing Geronimo*, August 30–31, 1886, 108. Both columns reached the cañon on August 31, 1886.

133. Actually more than a year's time had passed since the Apaches attacked the troops—the skirmish took place on June 8, 1885.

134. Wood wrote of the meeting between the officers: "We had quite a discussion about the matter, and it was arranged that in case of any ugly spirit breaking out during the conference or the Indians refusing to be reasonable[,] that each man should kill the Indian next to him." Hermann Hagedorn to Gatewood Jr. (April 18, 1929), Gatewood Collection, letter 349. At that time, Hagedorn was working on a biography on Wood.

135. Gatewood Jr. to Hagedorn (May 11, 1929), Gatewood Collection, letter 368. See also Wood, *Chasing Geronimo*, August 31, 1886, 108–9; Hagedorn to Gatewood Jr. (April 18, 1929), Gatewood Collection, letter 349; Clay, "Incidents," 115; and Gatewood Jr. to Hagedorn (April 2, 1929), Gatewood Collection, letter 362.

136. Clay, "Incidents," 115; Donald P. MacCarthy to Owen P. White (April 1, 1933), letter 420, and T. J. Clay to Mazzanovich (May 25, 1930), letter 391, Gatewood Collection.

137. It is interesting to note that Thomas Clay would later write: "I know of no difficulty your father had with Lawton during the campaign." T. J. Clay to Gatewood Jr. (July 27, 1926), Gatewood Collection microfilm, reel 7. In the same letter, he also wrote: "I never heard of any difficulty with Wood during this campaign[;] your father and he seemed quite friendly to this century."

138. Lawton to Miles (September 2, 1886), Gatewood Collection; Wratten Interview, 5; Wood, *Chasing Geronimo*, September 2, 1886, 109. Wood and Lawton both named the date of the arrival, which agrees with Wratten, who placed the

arrival on the fifth or sixth day of travel. Unfortunately a number of articles and books have incorrectly listed the arrival date, confusing modern readers.

139. Lee Coe, "Skeleton Canyon—Site of Historic Surrender," *Desert Magazine* 41, no. 2 (February 1978): 12, 14. That Skeleton Cañon is in New Mexico is fairly well established. However, in Charles Maurer to Gatewood Jr. (June 4, 1926), Gatewood Collection, letter 265, Maurer drew a map that clearly places the cañon well within Arizona, to the southwest of current-day Chiricahua at the southern end of the Chiricahua Mountains, in the Coronado National Forest. This map is incorrect. See also James W. Hurst, "Geronimo's Surrender—Skeleton Cañon, 1886," Southern New Mexico Online, *www.zianet.com/snm/geronimo.html*, accessed November 25, 2000. Hurst wrote: "On Route 80 south of Rodeo, New Mexico, near Apache, Arizona, stands a marker commemorating Geronimo's surrender. A short distance south of the marker is a road which leads east and then south-southeast to the actual surrender site. This is four wheel drive vehicle country, and heavy rains can render the road virtually impassible in spots. Once at the site, the ca[ñ]on road leads east and ends about two miles inside New Mexico. From there, travel is by foot following either the cañon floor (the creek bed) or a higher narrow trail." This is very true, as the author and his daughter almost got stuck in a hundred-yard mudhole on this dirt road while researching *Gatewood & Geronimo*.

140. R. A. Brown to E. A. Brininstool (April 5, 1921), Gatewood Collection, letter 89; Wratten Interview, 6; Wood, *Chasing Geronimo*, September 2, 1886, 109. Estimates placed Geronimo's camp somewhere between one and a half to three miles distance from the soldier camp.

141. Wood, *Chasing Geronimo*, September 3, 1886, 109. Wood also recorded Miles's arrival.

142. Gatewood, "Surrender 2," 48, ends with "I was sitting a little behind." It is an abrupt ending, leading one to believe there are missing pages. The rest of the text is from Gatewood, "Surrender."

143. Wood, *Chasing Geronimo*, September 3 and 8, 1886, 109, 111. He called the missing brother "a fairly well grown boy." Although I have not found any other references to Naiche's brother, this does not mean that Cochise did not sire any more sons. His older brother, Taza, had died on September 26, 1876. See also Clay, "Incidents," 115, who called the person Naiche grieved for a "relative."

144. Although Gatewood knew that Geronimo was not a chieftain, he still refers to him as such, most likely because the general public did not know, or care to know, the truth. In the population's eyes, Geronimo was the evil native who had waged war against two countries.

145. During the trip from Skeleton Canyon to Bowie Station, where the Apaches were loaded onto railroad cars for their trip eastward into captivity, Noh-chlon gave birth to her and Chappo's only child, a girl, on September 6.

Wood, *Chasing Geronimo*, September 7, 1886, 111; Kraft, *Gatewood & Geronimo*, 197. Griswold, in "Apaches," 100, mistakenly recorded that the birth occurred during the march to meet Miles at Skeleton Canyon.

146. O. O. Howard to AG, U.S. Army (September 7, 1886), NA, M689, roll 186. It is unclear how many prisoners rode to Fort Bowie with Miles. Miles to L. Q. C. Lamar Jr. (September 6, 1886), and Charles Farson to Gatewood Jr. (January 16, 1926), letter 177, both in Gatewood Collection, placed the number of Indians who traveled to Bowie with the general at five.

147. Clay, "Incidents," 115.

148. Field Orders no. 89, Department of Arizona (September 6, 1886), NA, M689, roll 186.

149. "Recapitulation," NA, M689, roll 186.

150. Stanley to AG, Washington DC (October 11, 1886), and a table that lists the captives by name (men and boys only), age, sex, and married state, NA, M689, roll 186.

151. Stockel, *Apache Nation*, 32.

152. Stanley to AG, Washington DC (October 11, 1886), NA, M689, roll 186.

153. Kraft, *Gatewood & Geronimo*, 198, 203–4.

Epilogue: Slow Fade to Oblivion

1. General Orders no. 24, NA, M1395. It was erroneously listed as General Orders no. 21 in Kraft, *Gatewood & Geronimo*, 202.

2. General Orders no. 37 (November 15, 1886), Department of Arizona, U.S. Army Department of Arizona General Orders and Circulars, 1870–86, microfilm roll 5 (1883–86), Arizona Historical Society.

3. See AG to Thomas McCulloh (December 4, 1886), NA, M1395, for information about the absence of an available position. McCulloh was Gatewood's father-in-law.

4. Henry W. Daly (July 12, 1850–September 18, 1931), an Irishman, migrated to the United States from Canada sometime around 1865. By the 1880s he had become a packer, and he first came in contact with Gatewood when he packed for the lieutenant during the return trip from Crook's Sierra Madre invasion in 1883. Thrapp, *Frontier Biography*, 1:372.

5. Daly to Gatewood Jr. (April 25, 1924), Gatewood Collection, letter 581. Daly wrote: "Some party in Prescott must have telephoned Miles your Father was in town and perhaps may have added he was talking. This of course Miles did not want known and he hastened to town in an ambulance."

6. Miles recommendation (December 28, 1886), Gatewood Collection. It can also be found in Papers and Recommendations Filed in Connection with the

Application of Charles Gatewood, NA, M1395, which contains recommendations from Gov. Edmund G. Ross of New Mexico, among others.

7. Lawton to AG, Department of Arizona (September 9, 1886), Sen. Exec. Doc. no. 117, 49th Cong., 2d sess., 48. Lawton wrote: "I desire to particularly invite the attention of the department commander to . . . ," and then he named Wood, Walsh, Finley, Brown, Benson, Smith, chief packer William Brown, and scouts W. M. Edwardy, Long, and Jack Wilson. Lawton described Wood as "the only officer who has been with me through the whole campaign. His courage, energy, and loyal support during the whole time; his encouraging example to the command, when work was the hardest and prospects darkest; his thorough confidence and belief in the final success of the expedition, and his untiring efforts to make it so, has placed me under obligations so great that I cannot even express them." Lawton commended Smith "for able support as second in command, and for volunteering for difficult and hard work in times of emergency."

8. W. P. Richardson to Gatewood Jr. (March 17, 1926), Gatewood Collection microfilm, reel 7. Richardson wrote: "The jealousies more or less in evidence at the time between different units and especially officers of different regiments is doubtless responsible for this situation." See "Sunburned Warriors," *San Francisco Chronicle*, October 20, 1886, and *Kalamazoo Telegraph*, October 27, 1886, for articles that claimed Gatewood deserved all the credit for the surrender.

9. Gatewood entries on rootsweb.com. Printouts in Kraft Papers.

10. Dr. Marcus E. Taylor to Gatewood (December 11, 1886), Gatewood Collection, letter 34.

11. Special Orders, no. 88 (February 15, 1887); Gatewood to AG, U.S. Army, Washington DC (February 7, 1887), NA, M1395.

12. John D. Weaver, *El Pueblo Grande: A Non-Fiction Book about Los Angeles* (Los Angeles: Ward Ritchie Press, 1973), 37; Hermann Hagedorn, *Leonard Wood, a Biography*, 2 vols. (New York: Harper & Brothers, 1931), 1:109.

13. Miles to AG of the Army, Washington DC (May 31, 1887), NA, M1395.

14. Charles Riepert to Gatewood Jr. (January 15, 1927), Gatewood Collection, letter 304. Riepert wrote: "I did not know [Gatewood] personally, but everybody [knew] that if it was not for Lt. Gatewood the campaign would [have] lasted much longer. . . . He was very popular amongst the men [as] we were sick and tired of the chase." See also Charles Farson to Gatewood Jr. (January 16, 1926), Gatewood Collection, letter 177. Writing about the surrender at Skeleton Cañon, Farson wrote: "I saw Lieut. Gatewood and spoke to the men of his detail. From what the men told me I thought Lieut. Gatewood should have had the credit for the surrender instead of Lawton." These are just two examples of the many letters Charles Gatewood Jr. collected from participants of the final campaign. Most follow this line of thought.

15. W. P. Richardson to Gatewood Jr. (March 17, 1926), Gatewood Collection microfilm, reel 7.

16. Georgia's anger at Miles and his officers remained her entire life. See Georgia Gatewood to Gatewood Jr. (April 4, 1909), Gatewood Collection, letter 79. Shortly after Geronimo died and the newspapers replayed the surrender once again, she wrote her son regarding his research on his father: "But I'll get something at any rate off my mind about that Geronimo affair, & I do assure you to mention, hear, or even think the name, has become to me a thing to wince at, and shrink from. When the papers first began to announce his death and to follow up with articles mentioning Lawton, Miles & that Wood man, or thing, I was stopped every where and I must say these people, all, said they knew it was your father did it all, alone, but none of the articles said so, except an editorial in a Cumberland paper, and I grew so enraged and sore and felt so helpless, that I wouldn't read any more articles and would not open a paper for fear of seeing some more to the same [e]ffect. . . . I realized your position in regard to Wood and I tell you, cautious as you may be, you will incur his enmity if you say a word without mentioning him, for he don't want the subject uncovered at all, & I seem to stand alone in my opinion of his unscrupulous vanity, & as he perjured himself for Miles, for his own advancement, so will Miles perjure himself now to uphold them both, & others will keep quiet." Britton Davis confirmed Georgia's belief that officers remained quiet, when he wrote: "Upon one thing, however, I have been always determined—that justice should some day be done your father in the matter of the so-called 'capture' of Geronimo. Wherever in private I have found interest in it, I have told the facts. And some two years ago reported them to the Historical Dept. of the Army in Wash[ington]. The death of Miles some four months ago released me from any feeling of delicacy I had in starting a controversy. His word now is not better, to say the le[a]st, than that of your father." Davis to Gatewood Jr. (September 3, 1926), Gatewood Collection microfilm, reel 7. For an example of how newspapers reported Geronimo's death, see "Old Apache Chief Geronimo Is Dead," *New York Times*, February 18, 1909, 7, which reported the following in a column-long article: "The old chief was captured many times, but always got away again, until his final capture, in 1886, by a small command of infantry scouts under Capt. H. W. Lawton, who, as major general, was killed at the head of his command in the Philippines, and Assistant Surgeon Leonard Wood, to-day in command of the Department of the East, with headquarters at Governors Island. The capture was made in the Summer, after a long and very trying campaign of many months, in which Lawton and Wood gained a reputation which will be long remembered in the annals of the army." Gatewood is not mentioned in the article.

17. Georgia Gatewood to Gatewood Jr. (May 5, 1909), Gatewood Collection, letter 82; Georgia Gatewood to Gatewood Jr. (date unknown, letter incomplete),

Gatewood Collection, letter 58; Hagedorn, *Wood*, 1:111; and Nelson A. Miles, *Personal Recollections and Observations of General Nelson A. Miles* (Chicago: Werner, 1896), 532. See also Daly to Gatewood Jr. (May 15, 1925), Gatewood Collection, letter 583. Henry Daly surmised that Miles refused to allow Gatewood to attend the ceremony because he wanted to keep him silent.

18. The other household belonged to Amos Kimball. Georgia wrote: "It was common gossip at Hdqrs that Amos Kimball had made much money at Govt. expense with Miles['s] connivance—notably on a contract for stoves for the Army—and that Miles had an old man of the mountain on his back in Kimbal[l] & had to take him everywhere he went." Georgia Gatewood to Gatewood Jr., letter 58.

19. Davis, *Geronimo*, 223.

20. Georgia Gatewood to Gatewood Jr., letter 58. Georgia claimed that Miles abused the power of his position and did not want it scrutinized.

21. Efficiency reports (1890), NA, M1395.

22. Crook to Gatewood (August 26, 1889), NA, M1395. See also Morrow to Gatewood (August 14, 1889); Willcox to AG, U.S. Army (August 16, 1889); Miles to AG, U.S. Army (December 28, 1886), all in NA, M1395.

23. Gatewood to AAG, Division of the Pacific (June 2, 1890); Headquarters, Division of the Pacific, Special Orders, no. 41 (June 2, 1890), both in NA, M1395.

24. Emily Natalie Gatewood (July 28, 1890–January 29, 1974) was the Gatewoods' last child. After attending the Mt. deSales Girls School and the Hannah More Academy in Maryland, she taught school. But apparently her education continued, for eventually she chose nursing as a profession and was employed in New York City. Sometime after 1920, Georgia moved to California to be near Charlie Jr., and Emily must have followed her mother west, for when an announcement stated she married Cecil Sinclair (c. early January 1931), she was a resident of California. The marriage produced one child, Terry Joyce Sinclair, but did not last, and Sinclair dropped from sight. Emily retired as a nurse and is buried in the El Cajon Cemetery in California. Dixie Smith to author (February 3, 2003) in Kraft Papers. See also Gatewood entries on rootsweb.com.

25. Note received, AG's Office (August 26, 1890), S.O. 215 Par. 8 (September 13, 1890); Headquarters of the Army, Washington DC, Special Orders, no. 215 (September 13, 1890); AAG, Headquarters of the Army, to Gatewood (September 15, 1890); and Gatewood to AG, U.S. Army (September 18, 1890), all in NA, M1395.

26. Robert Brown, Abiel Smith, and Marion Maus all retired as brigadier generals; Wilds Richardson, a brigadier general of the National Army, was posthumously retired a brigadier general; and Robert Parker, a major general in the National Army, was advanced to major general, retired. Others also retired with a high rank: Leonard Wood became a major general in 1901 and eventually rose to chief of staff; Wilbur Wilder retired as a brigadier general of volunteers; and

Robert Walsh retired as a brigadier general of the National Army. Henry Lawton was a major general of volunteers when he was killed in 1898.

27. Statement of the Military Service of Charles B. Gatewood, 38373 AGO, AG's Office (June 5, 1896), NA, M1395.

28. Gatewood to Post Adjutant (February 16, 1891) and medical certificate. Both are in NA, M1395.

29. General Orders no. 39, Headquarters of the Army, Washington (April 9, 1891), Gatewood Collection microfilm, reel 7. Obviously the location for Gatewood's feat was wrong. Nevertheless, it had to have felt good to receive the recognition. John Schofield was the major general commanding at this time.

30. Gatewood's efficiency report (1895), NA, M1395.

31. See Lt. Col. W. H. Carter, *From Yorktown to Santiago with the Sixth U.S. Cavalry* (Baltimore: Lord Baltimore Press, 1900), 265; Gatewood Statement of Military Service (June 5, 1896), NA, M1395. I have found no references of Gatewood being present when the army saved the hired gunmen from annihilation.

32. Captain and Assistant Surgeon Bushnell statement (September 3, 1892), NA, M1395. Bushnell also sheds light on the fire at Fort McKinney.

33. Carr, Miles, and Van Horn summaries of Gatewood all in Gatewood efficiency report, NA, M1395.

34. James Judson Van Horn (February 6, 1835–August 30, 1898) graduated from the Military Academy at West Point in 1858 (fourteenth in a class of twenty-seven) and after the Civil War (in which he was captured in Texas and later exchanged) saw extensive duty that ranged from the Southwest to Dakota Territory. During the Cibecue troubles during 1881, he reinforced Fort Apache with four companies from Fort Wingate in New Mexico Territory. It could have been at this time that he became acquainted with Gatewood, or if not, then certainly in 1892 when both were stationed at Fort McKinney, Wyoming. Altshuler, *Cavalry Yellow*, 340–41; Thrapp, *Frontier Biography*, 3:1471. Thrapp listed his birth date as "c. 1834."

35. Examination for Promotion, Case no. 481 (October 3, 1892), NA, M1395. See also Carter, *Yorktown*, 268–69; and certificate in the case of C. B. Gatewood, 6th Cavalry, appendix A, NA, M1395.

36. Headquarters of the Army Special Orders, no. 258 (November 3, 1892); Gatewood to the AG, U.S. Army (November 22, 1892), both in NA, M1395.

37. See Gatewood, "Campaigning against Victorio," 102. Dan Thrapp, in *Victorio*, 364n24, took exception to Gatewood's description of Victorio. Citing other contemporary descriptions of the chieftain for his reasoning, Thrapp flatly states that Gatewood never met the chieftain, or if he did, he confused him with Nana. He makes a lot of sense with his conclusions here, and correctly states that Gatewood often made mistakes with his dating in the article. This problem was not a one-time occurrence with Gatewood, as dating errors are also present in his

manuscript. Thrapp concludes that Gatewood "may have confused Victorio with Nana, already an old man, though still vigorous." Logically, I agree with Thrapp. However, Gatewood himself throws a wrench at the above with his statement regarding being assigned the duty of returning Victorio to the reservation in New Mexico—a fact the lieutenant took pride in. Sonnichsen in *Mescalero Apaches*, 188–89, blatantly misquotes Gatewood. He uses the same quote as used in this citation, but instead states that Gatewood described Nana. This is totally untrue and is not worth commenting upon, other than to point it out so that it is not repeated in the future.

38. M. F. Bowers, Sheriff, El Paso County, Colorado, request for Gatewood's services (June 4, 1894); AG's Office, Washington DC, 1st Endorsement, to H. M. Teller, U.S. Senator (June 13, 1894), both in NA, M1395.

39. Gatewood to AG, U.S. Army (October 10, 1894). See also C. W. Hine to AG, U.S. Army, Washington DC (September 10, 1894); Gatewood to AG, U.S. Army, Washington DC (September 28, 1894); AAG, Headquarters of the Army, to Charles W. Hine (October 28, 1894); Lobban & Hine General Merchandise statement (December 18, 1894). All in NA, M1395.

40. Capt. A. P. Blocksom to Regimental Adjutant, Sixth Cavalry (May 2, 1895); 1st Endorsement by Col. D. B. Gordon (May 3, 1895); 2nd Endorsement by Miles (May 29, 1895); Joseph B. Doe, Acting Secretary of War, 6th (and final) Endorsement (June 24, 1895); Medal of Honor, Case of Lt. Charles B. Gatewood (20635 AGO). All in NA, M1395.

41. Surgeon Edward B. Mosley to Miles (May 21, 1896); Surgeon Mosley to AG, U.S. Army (May 21, 1896); AG's Office statement (May 21, 1896); Gilmore, AAG, to CO, Fort Myer (May 22, 1896); Record of Death and Interment. All in NA, M1395. For Gatewood's seniority, see Altshuler, *Cavalry Yellow*, 139; and Arlington National Cemetery (arlingtoncemetery.com). In an interesting aside, Gatewood's brother DeWitt Clinton Gatewood (May 18, 1859–April 1937) married Minnie May Nelson on January 25, 1889, in Upshur County, West Virginia. He named his youngest son Charles Bare Gatewood (b. May 10, 1897) in honor of Bay-chen-daysen. International Genealogical Index. Like entries on the Web, some of the information found on the IGI is questionable.

42. Allegany Co. MD Frostburg Elect. Dist. 32 Census (ED53 SHT2 LN61), 280; Gatewood entries on rootsweb.com; Record of Death and Interment, NA, M1395.

43. See Kraft, *Gatewood & Geronimo*, for a complete rundown of Gatewood's medical problems.

44. Dan L. Thrapp, ed., *Dateline Fort Bowie: Charles Fletcher Lummis Reports on an Apache War* (Norman: University of Oklahoma Press, 1979), 102n5, writing about Gatewood's participation in the Geronimo war, stated that "his services were extensive and, in fact, indispensable. To Gatewood belongs the credit for finally bringing in the last of the hostiles, although he received none of the four

Medals of Honor given during the campaign and was otherwise professionally slighted. . . . That he was never in his lifetime given the recognition which was his due is to the discredit of his country."

45. Daly to Gatewood Jr. (May 28, 1924), Gatewood Collection, letter 584.

46. Thrapp, *Dateline*, 102n5.

47. Many Apaches living on the White Mountain Indian Reservation today have the surname of "Gatewood." More than likely the high esteem their ancestors held for the White Eye they knew as Bay-chen-daysen resulted in them choosing "Gatewood" as their name.

Appendix A: Old Black Joe's Devil

1. The Black Range has also been called Sierra de los Miembres and the Mimbres Range. Julyan, *Place Names*, 41.

2. Gatewood to Georgia Gatewood (June 30, 1885), Gatewood Collection, letter 7. The letter was postmarked from Fort Bayard, New Mexico, on July 11, 1885.

3. Charles B. Gatewood, "Old Black Joe's Devil," Gatewood Collection. The original of "Old Black Joe's Devil" in Gatewood's handwriting does not seem to exist any longer. What follows is a draft that was edited and typed by Gatewood Jr. To my knowledge it has never been published. Apparently Gatewood Jr. allowed historian E. A. Brininstool to read the manuscript, which includes an introduction that not only does not sound as if it were written by Gatewood but has nothing to do with Gatewood's scout. Brininstool suggested that the introduction be dropped as it insulted the reader's intelligence. I agree, and it has been dropped. See " 'Criticism' of 'Old Black Joe's Devil,' " which is thought to have been written by Brininstool, Gatewood Collection. See also Brininstool to Gatewood Jr. (June 8, 1925), letter 477, and Brininstool to Gatewood Jr. (July 10, 1946), letter 560, Gatewood Collection. The historian exchanged correspondence with Gatewood Jr., and his letters refer to him reading the latter's manuscripts.

4. This marked the end of Gatewood's active participation in the war until Miles summoned him to find Geronimo in July 1886.

5. Georgia Gatewood to Gatewood Jr. (June 9, 1927), Gatewood Collection, letter 595. Although she began the letter on the ninth, she added to it on June 16.

6. Undated handwritten note by Gatewood Jr., Gatewood Collection. In the same note, he added: "Mother has said that the Indians had 'dogs' which were crossed with bear-wolf and bear or cur and bear."

7. Bill Hilton Jr. to author (December 1, 2002), Kraft Papers. Hilton confirmed that the only marsupial native to North America is the Virginia opossum.

8. George Olin, *Mammals of the Southwest Deserts* (1982; repr., Southwest Parks and Monuments Association, 1988), 42. See 41–43 for a full description of the coatimundi.

Bibliography

Unpublished Sources

Arizona Historical Society, Tucson

Charles Bare Gatewood Collection

Davis, Britton. "A Short Account of the Chiricahua Tribe of Apache Indians and the Causes Leading to the Outbreak of May, 1885."

Gatewood, Charles B. "Gatewood on Experiences among the Apaches." Two manuscripts with the same title.

——. "Gatewood on the Apache Indians, Government Relations, Reservations, Courts, and Scouts."

——. "Gatewood on the Control and Management of the Indians (including the Outbreak of May 1885)."

——. "Gatewood on the Surrender of Geronimo."

——. "How the Judge Was Arrested & Tried."

——. "The Judge's Trial."

——. "Old Black Joe's Devil," ed. Charles B. Gatewood Jr.

——. "The Surrender of Geronimo." 1895.

——. "The Trial Chapter."

Gatewood, Charles B., Jr. "Britton Davis, Class of 1881." Undated type-written manuscript.

Huddleson, S. M. "An Interview with Geronimo and His Guardian, Mr. G. M. Wratten."

Martine and Kayitah. "The Story of the Final Surrender of Geronimo," as told to O. M. Boggess, superintendent of the Mescalero Indian Reservation, September 25, 1925.

Parker, Gen. James, Retired. "Service with Lieutenant Charles B. Gatewood, 6th U.S. Cavalry."

——. "The Old Army."

Historic Archives of Sonora, reel 24 (Sonoran State Archives, roll 24)

Petersen, James. "Joseph C. and Margaret A. W. Kay." Joseph C. Kay biographical file.

Rice, M. M. "Judge Sumner Howard." Reminiscences of M. M. Rice, MS 684.

U.S. Army Department of Arizona General Orders and Circulars, 1870–86, microfilm roll 5 (1883–86).

Arizona State Archives, Department of Library, Archives, and Public Records, Archives Division, Phoenix. Record Group 1, Office of the Governor, SG8, Bisbee–Naco Water Company: Indictment for False Imprisonment of Thomas M. Zuck by Charles B. Gatewood (#49), Indictment for False Imprisonment of Thomas F. Jones by Charles B. Gatewood (#50), Indictment for False Imprisonment of Joseph C. Kay by Charles B. Gatewood (#51); all were filed in the District Court of the United States for the Territory of Arizona, Third Judicial District, on February 10, 1885.

Church of Jesus Christ of Latter-day Saints Library, Salt Lake City UT. Gillett Griswold, comp., "The Fort Sill Apaches: Their Vital Statistics, Tribal Origins, Antecedents," 1970 (date of microfilm: May 26, 1976). Catalogue # XLIB 7–102 (order no. 0928251).

Fray Angélico Chávez History Library, Palace of the Governors, Santa Fe NM. Louis Kraft Papers.

International Genealogical Index

National Archives, Washington DC

> Letters Received by the Commissioner of Indian Affairs, 1882–86: letters 20507 and 21916.
> Record Group 94, Microfiche 1395 (five fiche), Letters Received by the Appointment, Commission, and Personal Branch, Adjutant General's Office, 1871–94.
> Record Group 94, Microfilm 689, Letters Received by the Office of the Adjutant General (Main Series), 1881–89: 1066 AGO 1883, rolls 174, 179, 180, 184. Papers relating to the war between the U.S. government and Apache Indians, 1883–86.
> Record Group 393, Records of U.S. Army Continental Commands, 1821–1920, Department of Arizona, 1870–93, Letters Received, Letters Sent, Miscellaneous Records; Microcopy M1072, roll 7, Letters Sent, Ninth Military Department, Department of New Mexico and District of New Mexico, 1849–90.

National Archives Collection of Census

1850 Shenandoah County VA 58th Dist. Census
1860 Allegany County MD Frostburg Dist. Census
1860 Shenandoah County VA Woodstock Census

1870 Allegany County MD Frostburg P.O. Census, roll 566
1870 Rockingham County VA, Harrisburg Twp Census, roll 1676
1880 Allegany County MD East Frostburg Census, roll 493
1880 Shenandoah County VA Stonewall Census, roll 1390
1900 Norfolk County VA Western Branch Dist., ED44, SHT12, LN15
1920 Allegany County MD Frostburg Elect. Dist. 32, ED53, SHT2, LN61

National Archives–Pacific Southwest Region, Laguna Niguel CA Record Group 21: Records of the District Court of the United States for the Territory of Arizona, Third Judicial District, 1869–1910, Criminal Cases A-83–5 to A-85–19, box no. 4, #52 (F. M. Zuck, T. F. Jones, and J. C. Kay Trial).

Preston County WV, **Public Records.** Will for Thomas McCulloh of Allegany County MD (probated December 11, 1896)

Rutherford B. Hayes Memorial Library, Fremont OH. George Crook Collection. Annual reports, official correspondence, and other papers concerning Crook's Arizona service.

Published Sources

Altshuler, Constance Wynn. *Cavalry Yellow and Infantry Blue: Army Officers in Arizona between 1851 and 1886.* Tucson AZ: Arizona Historical Society, 1991.

Ball, Eve, with Nora Henn and Lynda Sanchez. *Indeh: An Apache Odyssey.* Provo UT: Brigham Young University Press, 1980.

Ball, Eve, and James Kaywaykla. *In the Days of Victorio: Recollections of a Warm Springs Apache.* Tucson: University of Arizona Press, 1970.

Ball, Larry D. *The United States Marshals of New Mexico and Arizona Territories, 1846–1912.* Albuquerque: University of New Mexico Press, 1978.

Basso, Keith H. "Western Apache." In *Handbook of North American Indians: Southwest,* vol. 10, ed. Alfonso Ortiz, 462–88. Washington DC: Smithsonian Institution, 1983.

————, ed. *Western Apache Raiding and Warfare: From the Notes of Grenville Goodwin.* 1971. Reprint, Tucson: University of Arizona Press, 1993.

Betzinez, Jason, with W. S. Nye. *I Fought with Geronimo.* Harrisburg PA: Stackpole, 1959.

Bourke, John G. *On the Border with Crook.* 1891. Reprint, Lincoln: University of Nebraska Press, 1971.

Carter, Lt. Col. W. H. *From Yorktown to Santiago with the Sixth U.S. Cavalry.* Baltimore: Lord Baltimore Press, 1900.

Clay, Lt. Thomas J. "Some Unwritten Incidents of the Geronimo Campaign." In *The Papers of the Order of Indian Wars*, ed. John M. Carroll, 114–15. Fort Collins CO: Old Army Press, 1975.

Clum, Woodworth. *Apache Agent: The Story of John P. Clum*. Boston: Houghton Mifflin, 1936.

Cobos, Rubén. *A Dictionary of New Mexico & Southern Colorado Spanish*. 2nd ed. Santa Fe: Museum of New Mexico Press, 2003.

Coe, Lee. "Skeleton Canyon—Site of Historic Surrender." *Desert Magazine* 41, no. 2 (February 1978): 12–15.

Collins, Charles. *Apache Nightmare: The Battle of Cibecue Creek*. Norman: University of Oklahoma Press, 1999.

Cook, James H. *Fifty Years on the Old Frontier as Cowboy, Hunter, Guide, Scout, and Ranchman*. 1923. Reprint, with a foreword by J. Frank Dobie, introduction by Charles King, and a foreword to the paperback edition by Joseph C. Porter. Norman: University of Oklahoma Press, 1980.

Cozzens, Peter, ed. *Eyewitnesses to the Indian Wars, 1865–1890: The Struggle for Apacheria*. Mechanicsburg PA: Stackpole Books, 2001.

Crook, Brig. Gen. George. *Resumé of Operations against Apache Indians, 1882 to 1886*. 1886. Reprint, with notes and introduction by Barry C. Johnson. London: Johnson-Taunton Military Press, 1971.

Cruse, Thomas. *Apache Days and After*. 1941. Reprint, Lincoln: University of Nebraska Press, 1987.

Cullum, Bvt. Maj. Gen. George W. *Biographical Register of the Officers and Graduates of the U.S. Military Academy at West Point, New York, since Its Establishment in 1802, Supplement, Volume IV, 1890–1900*. Edited by Edward S. Holden. Cambridge: Riverside Press, 1901.

Daly, Henry W. "The Capture of Geronimo." *American Legion Monthly* 8, no. 6 (June 1930): 30–31.

Davis, Britton. *The Truth about Geronimo*. Edited by M. M. Quaife. 1929. Reprint, with a foreword by Robert M. Utley. New Haven: Yale University Press, 1963.

Davisson, Lori. "Fort Apache, Arizona Territory, 1870–1922." *Smoke Signal* 33 (Spring 1977): 62–80.

Debo, Angie. *Geronimo: The Man, His Time, His Place*. Norman: University of Oklahoma Press, 1976.

Faulk, Odie B. *The Geronimo Campaign*. New York: Oxford University Press, 1969.

Finerty, John F. "On Campaign after Cibicue Creek." In *Eyewitnesses to the Indian Wars, 1865–1890: The Struggle for Apacheria*, ed. Peter Cozzens, 236–61. Mechanicsburg PA: Stackpole Books, 2001.

Gatewood, Lt. C. B. "Campaigning against Victorio in 1879." *Great Divide* 11 (April 1894): 102–4.

Geronimo. *Geronimo: His Own Story.* Edited by S. M. Barrett; newly edited by Frederick W. Turner III. New York: E. P. Dutton, 1970.

Goff, John S. *Arizona Territorial Officials,* vol. 1: *The Supreme Court Justices, 1863–1912.* Cave Creek AZ: Black Mountain Press, 1975.

Goodwin, Grenville. *The Social Organization of the Western Apache.* Chicago: University of Chicago Press, 1942.

Granger, Byrd H. *Arizona Place Names.* 1960. Reprint, Tucson: University of Arizona Press, 1982.

Hafford, William. "Chat[t]o the Betrayed." *Arizona Highways* 69, no. 2 (February 1993): 14–17.

Hagedorn, Hermann. *Leonard Wood, a Biography.* 2 vols. New York: Harper, 1931.

Hatfield, Shelley Bowen. *Chasing Shadows: Indians along the United States–Mexico Border, 1876–1911.* Albuquerque: University of New Mexico Press, 1998.

Hodge, Frederick Webb, ed. *Handbook of American Indians North of Mexico.* Smithsonian Institution Bureau of American Ethnology, Bulletin 30. 2 vols. Washington: Government Printing Office, 1912.

Howard, Maj. Gen. O. O. *My Life and Experiences among Our Hostile Indians.* Hartford CT: A. D. Worthington, 1907.

Hoy, Bill. *Spanish Terms of the Sonoran Desert Borderlands.* Calexico CA: Institute for Border Studies, San Diego State University, 1993.

Huddleston, George, comp. *Huddleston Family Tables.* 1933. Reprint, Concord NH: Rumford Press, 1973.

Jackson, Donald Dale, and Peter Wood. *The Sierra Madre.* Alexandria VA: Time-Life Books, 1975.

Julyan, Robert. *The Place Names of New Mexico.* Albuquerque: University of New Mexico Press, 1996.

Kinevan, Marcos E. *Frontier Cavalryman: Lieutenant John Bigelow with the Buffalo Soldiers in Texas.* El Paso: Texas Western Press, 1998.

Knight, Oliver. *Following the Indian Wars.* Norman: University of Oklahoma Press, 1960.

Kraft, Louis. "Assignment: Geronimo." *Wild West* 12, no. 3 (October 1999): 36–41.

———. *Gatewood & Geronimo.* Albuquerque: University of New Mexico Press, 2000.

Lockwood, Frank C. *The Apache Indians.* 1938. Reprint, Lincoln: University of Nebraska Press, 1987.

Lummis, Charles F. *General Crook and the Apache Wars*. Edited by Turbesé Lummis Fiske. Flagstaff AZ: Northland Press, 1966.

Mails, Thomas E. *The People Called Apache*. 1974. Reprint, New York: BDD Illustrated Books, 1993.

Martín, Jo. "Women Warriors: Secret Weapon of the Apaches." *New Mexico* 75, no. 8 (August 1997): 90–96.

Mazzanovich, Anton. *Trailing Geronimo*. Edited by E. A. Brininstool. Los Angeles: Gem, 1926.

McClintock, James H., Arizona State Historian. *Mormon Settlement in Arizona: A Record of Peaceful Conquest*. Phoenix: n.p., 1921.

Mettler, Charles G. "Charles Baehr Gatewood." *Assembly,* April 1954, 1001–2.

Miles, Nelson A. *Personal Recollections and Observations of General Nelson A. Miles*. Chicago: Werner, 1896.

————. *Serving the Republic: Memoirs of the Civil War and Military Life of Nelson A. Miles*. New York: Harper, 1911.

Newton, John, ed. *The Buffalo Hunters*. Alexandria VA: Time-Life Books, 1993.

Ogle, Ralph Hedrick. *Federal Control of the Western Apaches, 1848–1886*. Albuquerque: University of New Mexico Press, 1970.

Olin, George. *Mammals of the Southwest Deserts*. 1982. Reprint, Globe AZ: Southwest Parks and Monuments Association, 1988.

Opler, Morris Edward. *An Apache Life-way: The Economic, Social, and Religious Institutions of the Chiricahua Indians*. 1941. Reprint, New York: Cooper Square, 1965.

————. "The Apachean Culture Pattern and Its Origins." In *Handbook of North American Indians: Southwest*, vol. 10, ed. Alfonso Ortiz, 368–92. Washington DC: Smithsonian Institution, 1983.

————. "Chiricahua Apaches." In *Handbook of North American Indians: Southwest*, vol. 10, ed. Alfonso Ortiz, 401–18. Washington DC: Smithsonian Institution, 1983.

Ortiz, Alfonso, ed. *Handbook of North American Indians: Southwest*, vol. 10. Washington DC: Smithsonian Institution, 1983.

Parker, Brig. Gen. James. "The Geronimo Campaign." In *The Papers of the Order of Indian Wars*, ed. John M. Carroll, 95–102. Fort Collins CO: Old Army Press, 1975.

————. *The Old Army: Memories, 1872–1918*. Philadelphia: Dorrance, 1929.

Parsons, George Whitwell. *The Concluding Arizona Years, 1882–87*. Vol. 2 of *The Devil Has Foreclosed: The Private Journal of George Whitwell Parsons*. Edited by Lynn R. Bailey. Tucson AZ: Westernlore Press, 1997.

Perry, Richard J. *Apache Reservation: Indigenous Peoples and the American State*. Austin: University of Texas Press, 1993.

————. *Western Apache Heritage: People of the Mountain Corridor*. Austin: University of Texas Press, 1991.

Portrait and Biographical Record of Arizona. Chicago: Chapman, 1901.

Prucha, Francis Paul. *The Great Father: The United States Government and the American Indians*. 2 vols. 1984. Reprint, Lincoln: University of Nebraska Press, 1986.

Robinson, Sherry. *Apache Voices: Their Stories of Survival, as Told to Eve Ball*. Albuquerque: University of New Mexico Press, 2000.

Schaafsma, Curtis F. *Apaches de Navajo: Seventeenth-Century Navajos in the Chama Valley of New Mexico*. Salt Lake City: University of Utah Press, 2002.

Senate Executive Document no. 117, 49th Cong., 2nd sess.

Senate Executive Document no. 35, 51st Cong., 1st sess.

Senate Executive Document no. 83, 51st Cong., 1st sess.

Senate Executive Document no. 88, 51st Cong., 1st sess.

Simmons, Marc. *Massacre on the Lordsburg Road: A Tragedy of the Apache Wars*. College Station: Texas A&M University Press, 1997.

Sonnichsen, C. L. *The Mescalero Apaches*. Norman: University of Oklahoma Press, 1958.

————, ed. *Geronimo and the End of the Apache Wars*. 1986. Reprint, Lincoln: University of Nebraska Press, 1990.

Stewart, Kenneth M. "Yumans: Introduction." In *Handbook of North American Indians: Southwest*, vol. 10, ed. Alfonso Ortiz, 1–3. Washington DC: Smithsonian Institution, 1983.

Stockel, H. Henrietta. *Women of the Apache Nation: Voices of Truth*. Reno: University of Nevada Press, 1991.

————. *Survival of the Spirit: Chiricahua Apaches in Captivity*. Reno: University of Nevada Press, 1993.

————. *Chiricahua Apache Women and Children: Safekeepers of the Heritage*. College Station: Texas A&M University Press, 2000.

Sweeney, Edwin R. *Cochise: Chiricahua Apache Chief*. Norman: University of Oklahoma Press, 1991, 1995.

————. *Mangas Coloradas, Chief of the Chiricahua Apaches*. Norman: University of Oklahoma Press, 1998.

————, ed. *Making Peace with Cochise: The 1872 Journal of Captain Joseph Alton Sladen*. Norman: University of Oklahoma Press, 1997.

Terrell, John Upton. *Apache Chronicle*. New York: World, 1972.

Thrapp, Dan L. *The Conquest of Apacheria*. Norman: University of Oklahoma Press, 1967.

————. *Victorio and the Mimbres Apaches*. Norman: University of Oklahoma Press, 1974.

————. *Encyclopedia of Frontier Biography.* 3 vols. Glendale CA: Arthur H. Clark, 1988.

————. *Encyclopedia of Frontier Biography.* Vol. 4. Spokane WA: Arthur H. Clark, 1994.

————, ed. *Dateline Fort Bowie: Charles Fletcher Lummis Reports on an Apache War.* Norman: University of Oklahoma Press, 1979.

Tichenor, Bryan W. "Correspondence." *Prescott Morning Courier,* March 31, 1886.

Toole, James H. "Agent Tiffany Torn to Tatters." *Arizona Star* (Tucson), October 24, 1882. In *Eyewitnesses to the Indian Wars, 1865–1890: The Struggle for Apacheria,* ed. Peter Cozzens, 318–20. Mechanicsburg PA: Stackpole Books, 2001.

Utley, Robert M. *A Clash of Cultures: Fort Bowie and the Chiricahua Apaches.* Washington DC: National Park Service, 1977.

Weaver, John D. *El Pueblo Grande: A Non-Fiction Book about Los Angeles.* Los Angeles: Ward Ritchie Press, 1973.

Wharfield, Col. H. B. *Apache Indian Scouts.* El Cajon CA: privately printed, 1964.

Wood, Leonard. *Chasing Geronimo: The Journal of Leonard Wood, May–September, 1886.* Edited by Jack C. Lane. Albuquerque: University of New Mexico Press, 1970.

Wratten, Albert E. "George Wratten, Friend of the Apaches." *Journal of Arizona History* 27, no. 1 (Spring 1986): 91–124.

Web Sites

"Geronimo's Surrender—Skeleton Canyon, 1886," by James W. Hurst, www.southernnewmexico.com/Articles/People/Geronimossurrender-skelet.html, accessed January 1, 2005.

"Gill Family of Baltimore County, Maryland, and Canada." www.rootsweb.com, accessed January 13, 2001. Entries for Charles Bare Gatewood, Georgia Gatewood, and Charles Bare Gatewood Jr.

"Arlington National Cemetery." www.arlingtoncemetery.com, entry for Charles B. Gatewood.

Index

24, 126; —, strategy of, 119, 121, 198n31; —, safe conduct in, 122; —, Apache removal during, 140; —, at Skeleton Cañon, 152–53, 254n145; —, career on line during, 157; and Wood, 207n2, 240n63

Mimbreño Apache Indians, xvii, xxix, 219n65. *See also* Chihenne Apache Indians

Mogollon Mountains NM, 64, 66, 186n38
Mojave Indians, 15, 34, 36, 38, 40, 190n65
Molzos (La-zi-yah's wife), 154
Montoya, José María, 154
Moore, Charlie, 202n43
Mormon Church, 97, 108, 226n43
Mormons, 86, 87–88, 90–92, 189n63, 226n43; Mormon agents, 93; and selling of whiskey, 222n11
Morrow, Albert P., xviii–xx, 162, 185n26
Mountain Meadows Massacre (1857), 226n43
Mount Vernon Barracks AL, 13, 201n40, 237n44, 243n83, 244n86, 245n88, 246n89
Murray, Cunliffe H., 1, 3

Nacosari, Sonora, 128
Nah-bay (La-zi-yah's brother), 135, 154; background of, 247n90
Nah-dos-te (Geronimo's sister), 192n80
Nahi, 154. *See also* Nah-bay
Nah-ke-de-sah (Mangus's sister), 200n40
Naiche (Chokonen chieftain), xxix, *xxx*, xxxvi, 24, 63, 84, 100, *117*, 121, 123, 147, 154, 157, 170, 194n4, 201n40, 202n43, 215n42, 215n44, 232n13, 234n22, 236n41, 241n68, 247n90, 253n143; Aguirre incident and, 250n118; background of, 191n76; at Cañon de los Embudos, 113–14, 116; drunkenness of, 116; and Gatewood, 153, 167, 242n77; and Geronimo, 153; leaves reservation, 64, 173; mother of, 140; at Mount Vernon Barracks, 13; raids of, 34, 68; reasons for killing, 119; outbreak of 1885, 118;

—, and Gatewood, 133, 134, 138, 139, 140, 151; —, at Skeleton Canyon, 152, 153, 154; surrenders, 116; wives and children of, 135, 140, 243n83, 244n84
Naiche, Jane (Naiche's daughter), 232n13
Nana (Chokonen chieftain), xviii, xxii, 116, 194n4, 217n50; mistaken for Geronimo, 258n37
nantan, xxxv, 40, 46, 193n86
Nantan Enchaw, 40
Nas-tih-deh (Perico and Fun's father), 244n86
Natanes Mountains AZ, 35
Navajo Indian Reservation, 227n51
Navajo Indians, 13, 17–18; other names for, 13, 198n28; split from Apaches, 20
Navajo scouts, xvi; Gatewood on, 105, 120
Nednhi Apache Indians, xxviii, xxix, 13, 18, 192n80; and Americans, 145; and Bedonkohes, 219n61; and reservation, 173, 194n4, 203n48
Nelson, Minnie May (DeWitt C. Gatewood's wife), 259n41
New Mexico, 68; and citizens' fear of Apaches, 73
Noh-chlon (Chappo's wife), 135, 154; background of, 245n88; child's birth, 253–54n145
Nock-ay-det-klinne (Cibecue medicine man), xxv–xxvi
Noo-tah-hah (early Apache name), 14, 15, 20, 38
Norris, Basil, xxv

Ojo Caliente NM, xvii, xxi, 29, 184n21
Old Black Joe. *See* Black, Joe
Opler, Morris E., xxxiv, 169
Opoto, Sonora, 215n44
Order of the Indian Wars, 207n2
Outbreak (1881), 191n73
Outbreak (1885), 8, 73, 101, 173; reasons for, 7–8, 63, 101, 113, 123

CPSIA information can be obtained
at www.ICGtesting.com
Printed in the USA
LVOW01s0518230217
525133LV00001B/1/P